Living, Working & Doing Business in

CHINA

● A Survival Handbook ●

Leo Lacey

Cover photograph: Shanghai © feivuezhangjie (🖳 shutterstock.com)
Maps © Jim Watson
Cover design: Di Bruce-Kidman

Survival Books Limited
Office 169, 3 Edgar Buildings, George St, Bath, BA1 2FJ, United Kingdom
☎ +44 (0)1935-700060, ✉ info@survivalbooks.net
🖳 www.survivalbooks.net

British Library Cataloguing in Publication Data
A CIP record for this book is available
from the British Library.
ISBN: 978-1-907339-42-4

Printed in China by IP Softcom

Acknowledgements

I would like to thank my many friends, family members and colleagues who provided information and contributed to the successful publication of this first edition of *Living, Working & Doing Business in China*. In particular, my thanks go to my wife, Guo Zhao Li, for her patience and assistance, and to my sons for their encouragement. My heartfelt thanks also go to Su Su Gao, President of the Inject School of English, Professor Han Fule of North China University of Water Resources and Electric Power, Yin Dewen and his team from Yellow River Engineering, and to the helpful Ms Zhong at the Zhengzhou Public Security Bureau for their assistance, as well as to Brian Merifield and David Leffman.

Thanks are also due to Robbi Forrester Atilgan for editing, Lilac Johnston for proofreading, Peter Read for final editing and proofing, Di Bruce-Kidman for desktop publishing, photo selection and the cover design, and Jim Watson for the maps. Finally, a special thank-you to the many photographers (see page 316) – the unsung heroes – whose beautiful images add colour and bring China to life.

REVIEWS

Swiss News

"Rarely has a 'survival guide' contained such useful advice – This book dispels doubts for first time travellers, yet is also useful for seasoned globetrotters – In a word, if you're planning to move to the US or go there for a long term stay, then buy this book both for general reading and as a ready reference."

Living France Magazine

"If I were to move to France, I would like David Hampshire to be with me, holding my hand every step of the way. This being impractical, I would have to settle for second best and take his books with me instead!"

Reader (Amazon)

"I read most of the books available on this subject before migrating to Australia, so I feel confident enough to say that although this guide is sometimes exhausting... if you pick out the information which is relevant to you the information is golden."

The Riviera Reporter

"Let's say it at once. David Hampshire's Living and Working in France is the best handbook ever produced for visitors and foreign residents in this country; indeed, my discussion with locals showed that it has much to teach even those born and bred in l'Hexagone. It is Hampshire's meticulous detail which lifts his work way beyond the range of other books with similar titles. This book is absolutely indispensable."

ICI (Switzerland) AG

"We would like to congratulate you on this work: it is really super! We hand it out to our expatriates and they read it with great interest and pleasure."

Reader (Amazon)

"I have been travelling to Spain for more than seven years and thought I knew everything - David has done his homework well - Excellent book and very informative! Buy it!"

American Citizens Abroad

"It's everything you always wanted to ask but didn't for fear of the contemptuous put down – The best English language guide – Its pages are stuffed with practical information on everyday subjects and are designed to complement the traditional guidebook."

Reader (Amazon)

"A must for all future expats. I invested in several books but this is the only one you need. Every issue and concern is covered, every daft question you have but are frightened to ask is answered honestly without pulling any punches. Highly recommended."

France in Print

"Covers every conceivable question that might be asked concerning everyday life – I know of no other book that could take the place of this one."

Reader (Amazon)

"This book is highly recommended to serious people who are look for Immigrating to Canada. This book is very useful since you will know exactly what all u must do and what all u must not do when you are in Canada. It gives u an OUTLINE of Jobs and many other things which u must know when you want to settle in Canada. A MUST TO READ FOR IMMIGRANTS"

(We want to thank this reader for their enthusiasm!)

REVIEWS

Important Note

China is a vast country with many faces, a variety of ethnic groups, religions and customs, as well as continuously changing rules, regulations and prices. We cannot recommend too strongly that you check with an official and reliable source (not always the same) before making any major decisions or taking an irreversible course of action. However, don't believe everything you're told or read – even, dare we say it, herein!

Useful addresses and references to other sources of information have been included in all chapters and in Appendices A to C to help you obtain further information and verify details with official sources. Important points have been emphasised, in bold print or boxes, some of which it would be expensive, or even dangerous, to disregard. Ignore them at your peril or cost!

NOTE

Unless specifically stated, the reference to any company, organisation or product in this book doesn't constitute an endorsement or recommendation. None of the businesses, products or individuals listed have paid to be mentioned.

Contents

13. INSURANCE {#13-insurance} 175

14. FINANCE 183

15. LEISURE 199

16. SPORTS 217

17. SHOPPING 229

18. ODDS & ENDS 245

19. THE CHINESE 261

20. MOVING HOUSE OR LEAVING CHINA 267

APPENDICES 273

INDEX 305

Author's Notes

♦ Times are shown with the suffix am (ante meridiem) for before noon and pm (post meridiem) for after noon (see also **Time Difference** on page 258).

♦ Prices quoted should be taken as a guide only, although they were mostly correct at the time of publication, and unless otherwise stated usually all taxes. To convert from other currencies to *renminbi* (RMB) or vice versa, see 🖥 xe.com.

♦ His/he/him also means her/she/her (please forgive us ladies). This is done to make life easier for both the reader and the editor, and isn't intended to be sexist.

♦ The Chinese translation of many key words and phrases is shown in brackets in *italics*.

♦ All spelling is (or should be) British and not American English.

♦ Warnings and important points are printed in **bold** type.

♦ The following symbols are used in this book: ☎ (telephone), 🖥 (internet) and ✉ (email).

♦ Lists of **Useful Addresses**, **Further Reading** and **Useful Websites** are contained in **Appendices A**, **B** and **C** respectively.

♦ For those unfamiliar with the metric system of **Weights & Measures**, conversion tables are included in **Appendix D**.

♦ A physical map of China is shown inside the front cover and a map showing the provinces in **Appendix E**.

♦ A list of useful Chinese words and phrases is included in **Appendix F**.

FORTUNE COOKIE

Wudang Shan mountain, Hubei

Introduction

Whether you're planning to live or work in China or thinking about doing business there – this is **THE** book for you. Forget about all those glossy guide books, excellent as they are for tourists; this book was written exclusively with you in mind and is worth its weight in dumplings. It's been exhaustively researched, compiled and written by a long-term resident of China to meet the needs of anyone wishing to know the essentials of Chinese life – however long you're planning to stay, you'll find it invaluable.

General information about China isn't difficult to find and many books are published about this beguiling country (including our sister publication *Culture Wise China*). However, reliable and up-to-date information in English specifically intended for foreigners living, working and doing business in China isn't so easy to find, least of all in one volume. This book is intended to fill this void and provide the comprehensive practical information necessary to ease you into life in China. This country is still a mystery to many Westerners, although its emergence as a major power makes it increasingly attractive, particularly to adventurers, would-be entrepreneurs, and employees of businesses and organisations trading with China. Adjusting to a different environment and culture and making a home in any foreign country can be a traumatic and stressful experience – and this is certainly true of China.

Adapting to life in a new country is a continuous process, especially a country so utterly different as China, and although this book will help you through the 'beginner's phase' and minimise frustrations. It doesn't contain all the answers, but what it will do is help you make informed decisions and calculated judgements, instead of uneducated guesses and embarrassing mistakes. **Most importantly, it will help save you time, trouble, money and 'face', and repay your investment many times over.**

You may find some of the information in this book a bit daunting, but don't be discouraged – most problems occur only once and fade into insignificance after a short while (as you face the next half a dozen!). China is unusual, unpredictable and quite unlike Western countries; it's also addictive and a land of great opportunity, provided you're hard working and adaptable. Most expatriates agree that the longer you spend in this extraordinary country, the longer you want to stay. Certainly, a period of time spent in China is a wonderful way to enrich your life, broaden your horizons and, with luck (and hard work), make your fortune. We trust that this book will help you avoid the pitfalls of living in China and smooth your way to a happy and rewarding future in your new Chinese home.

Hao yun! (Good luck!)

Leo Lacey

January 2013

1.

FINDING A JOB
& DOING BUSINESS

Very few people from Western countries migrate to China hoping to find a job, although this may change in the future if the Chinese economy continues to boom. The vast majority of migrant job seekers are from neighbouring Asian countries or developing countries in Africa and most of these are illegal immigrants. Most foreigners who end up working in China either move there to work for an organisation based in their home country, or are living – or travelling long-term – in the country and work to supplement their income. A great many of the latter group teach English.

Western workers in China can be divided into three main groups. There are the employees who've been seconded from a government department or business at home to work at an office, branch or subsidiary in China; some are recruited while living in China but most are relocated by their employer. Then there are people, often retirees, who are attracted to the opportunity of doing something different and seek out teaching work within China's education system. Thirdly there are the travellers, often young people on backpacking holidays, who look for a temporary job in order to stay on in China for a while.

In addition, China attracts an increasing number of hopeful entrepreneurs who want to set up businesses.

▲ Caution

No foreigner is allowed to work in China, for an employer or for themselves, unless they have a Z type work visa, and these aren't always easy to acquire. For more information, see **Chapter 3**.

Many foreigners find the Chinese job market is restricted. Although the economy is accelerating at a rapid pace, so is its population – around 1.35bn in 2012 – and the Chinese are first in line when it comes to work. There has long been a demand for so-called 'foreign experts' in fields such as finance, engineering, telecommunications and information technology (IT), as well as those which require English language skills, such as teaching. However, foreigners now face increasing competition from Chinese students with degrees obtained in the UK and US, and even the 'experts' are finding their expertise challenged.

China has no 'migrant quota' as such. It doesn't need to attract overseas workers, skilled or otherwise, and doesn't encourage immigration. At the same time, the Chinese accept that foreigners can bring certain skills and knowledge to their society, thus they accept the presence of foreign staff at senior or confidential levels in branch offices established by overseas companies, but they expect companies to replace foreign staff with Chinese personnel as soon as possible. In short, foreign companies are welcome to exploit the benefits of trading in China provided China benefits from their presence, not only in the creation of jobs but also from the knowledge and skills that they bring to China.

ECONOMY

China has the fastest-growing economy is the world, second only to that of the US. Its nominal gross domestic product (GDP) was US$7.3 trillion in 2012 , putting it ahead of its old rival Japan, and many experts expect it to overtake America in the next decade. Yet the size of its population means that its per capita GDP is much lower – similar to that of Ecuador or Iran – and many of its people have yet to benefit from the economic boom. Nevertheless, China now has over 100 US$billionaires and tens of thousands of US$millionaires and its urban population is becoming increasingly affluent, eating more meat and investing in consumer durables from televisions to cars. However, there's still a great deal of poverty in rural China where many families subsist on as little as two dollars a day.

Industry accounts for the largest slice of GDP (almost 47 per cent), closely followed by services (44 per cent), with agriculture a distinct third (9 per cent) despite the fact that farming employs almost 40 per cent of the population. The major industries include mining and the processing of commodities such as coal, ore, iron and steel, petroleum and chemicals, and manufacturing (cars and other transportation, textiles, food and electronic goods). China leads the world in exports, shipping out over US$1,900bn in goods in 2012, well up on the previous year, with the US its largest customer. Its trading rivals have accused it of manipulating the value of its currency in order to increase its export power – flooding the West with cheap goods – although this hasn't dented its trading powers.

The downside to this economic explosion is perhaps an overheated economy, but inflation is currently low and stagnant: in late 2012 it was just 1.7 per cent and although there have been rising food prices – a factor which further divides the rich and poor – the incipient property boom seems to be (for now at least) under control. Average house prices increased by only 1.8 per cent in the year to June 2012, with the government having taken a number of measures to reduce property speculation.

What is amazing about China's economic growth is that – unlike its main competitors the US and Germany – it has a planned economy. The communist government has left little to chance. However, national planning is no longer

as all-embracing as it was in the early days of the People's Republic of China and, these days, under a system of 'socialism with Chinese characteristics', to quote former leader Deng Xiaoping, it's a far more free-wheeling society than even ten years ago.

Today, after 30 years of massive change, China is still evolving; this time from a country that grew out of the development of a massive overseas export trade to a country that is expanding by meeting increased domestic demand. The credit crunch, which has affected the global economy since 2007, severely influenced even China's export-oriented output and caused a major government re-think. More and more funds are being pumped into improving the country's infrastructure and to opening up the central and western provinces rather than into the already heavily populated and prosperous east and south.

At the same time, the emphasis has shifted from quantity to quality as China seeks to add value to its goods by producing more technologically advanced products and to improve quality to at least the equal of that achieved in developed countries.

It's an incredibly exciting time to be living in China. New roads, railways, airports, factories, offices and homes are springing up everywhere and the pace of change is staggering. Nowadays, China is building more expressway (motorways) each year than the UK has built in total since World War Two. However, such rapid progress comes at a price. The boom in construction has led to overcapacity in some major industries such as cement and steel making, and a rationalisation and closing of some recently-built facilities has been necessary, but this isn't easy to implement as every province is quick to emphasise that their facilities are essential.

No one appears willing or able to admit that even China itself sometimes struggles to keep up with the pace of its progress, and a foreigner entering this maelstrom of productivity is in for a strident wake up call.

UNEMPLOYMENT

In the days of the Cultural Revolution, unemployment was unheard of as everyone worked for the common good of the country, even if they earned little for their efforts. This attitude lingered on until the end of the 20th century, with many people in state-run enterprises enjoying job security, plus a regular income and benefits – a concept which was known as the 'iron rice bowl'. However, as China began to look more towards the West, privatisation began and labour laws

were introduced, many employers have been unwilling to commit to long-term contracts and the new employment legislation was – and still is – often ignored. The result is a fluid and erratic jobs market where demand dictates supply.

It's difficult to gain a full picture of unemployment in China, as jobless figures are normally only measured within urban areas and exclude migrant workers – those Chinese who move to more prosperous parts of the country to find work. On this basis, in June 2012 the official unemployment rate was recorded as 4.1 per cent, but estimates suggested that if migrant workers were included it would increase to around 9 per cent. Neither figure takes any account of rural areas, where there's considerable unemployment and under-employment.

Migrant workers, who make up the bulk of the 800m strong labour force, regularly move between the city and country, taking jobs in factories and on construction sites when available, and then moving back to an agricultural lifestyle when the contract finishes and the workers are laid off. As such, they're never technically unemployed, although they have no job security and no social assistance to fall back on. In China there's very little social security and unemployment benefit is limited to the lucky few whose boss has made sufficient contributions, therefore many jobless people are dependent on family support.

EMPLOYMENT PROSPECTS

As a foreigner you need to have certain specific skills to succeed in China. There's no requirement for blue-collar workers – over 70 per cent of the population is unskilled – and even the trades are well supplied. If you're a skilled tradesman, such as a plumber, and plan to set up your trade in China, think again. There are plenty of plumbers, electricians, mechanics and hairdressers already and, while you could possibly find work, the salary would be nowhere near the level you could earn in your home country. You would find it virtually impossible to live on around 1,000 *renminbi* (RMB or *yuan*) or £100/US$150 a month.

But there's work in China for expatriates, especially for those with some ability to speak and understand the local language. The main areas in which to look for employment are listed below.

Government Organisations

Foreign embassies and consulates employ their own nationals in senior positions, although most junior roles are filled by local (Chinese) people. In between, there are a few posts where confidentiality is an important factor – for example, certain administration posts, and less senior roles in immigration departments such as entry clearance officers – and these jobs may go to locally-based expatriates, often the wives or daughters of diplomats and other foreign executives who already possess the necessary Z visa (see **Chapter 3**). Such jobs are frequently advertised on embassy websites. If you have some knowledge of *Putonghua*, or Mandarin as it's called in the West, then your chances of being taken on are greatly increased.

It's worth noting that embassy staff are sometimes treated as if they were working in their home country and this may have a bearing on your tax situation. For example, if you work for a UK embassy or consulate in China, you may be liable to pay UK income tax as your workplace is regarded by the UK tax authorities as being on British soil.

The British Council, which promotes Britain and its interests, offers employment to teachers of English and other subjects and to examiners for the International English Language Teaching System exams (⌨ britishcouncil.org/china.htm).

> The addresses and phone numbers of foreign embassies in China, as well as major countries' chambers of commerce, are listed in Appendix A.

Non-Government Organisations (NGOs) & International Businesses

Major positions are normally filled by personnel from the organisation's home country – who are flown in on a generous relocation package – and most of the jobs available to local foreigners are low level ones. However, sometimes an appointee filling one of the more senior positions becomes sick or has to return to his home country for personal reasons and, in such cases, organisations sometimes look to the market in China for a replacement. To identify such opportunities, check the websites of the relevant chambers of commerce, which publicise vacancies, some of which are surprisingly senior and well-paid.

Vacancies are also sometimes advertised in the various free 'expat' magazines, e.g. *City Weekend*, *China Expat* and *The Beijinger*, which are distributed around the major cities in places where expats gather, such as bars. There are also a number of employment agencies for expats operating in the major cities, although most of these deal, almost exclusively, in recruiting people to teach English.

If you have skills in a particular field that would be useful to a specific organisation, e.g. knowledge of computer-aided design which may be required by an international firm of architects, there's nothing to stop you approaching them directly and asking for an interview. Make sure that you're appropriately dressed and have a copy of your CV (résumé), plus a copy of any qualifications and the names of referees. You need to be realistic and only apply for jobs that you're able to do and where you won't face too much local competition. If you've worked as a clerk in a UK or US bank, you're unlikely to find a similar job in China where the banking system is very different and you'd have to compete with a mile-long queue of Chinese graduates applying for the same job.

As everywhere, your job-hunting success depends on correctly identifying what you can offer to an employer which other candidates may lack. As a Westerner you have the advantage of being a native speaker of English, the default second language in China, and possibly you have experience of relevant businesses practices in your home country – both abilities which a Chinese applicant cannot match. However, to your disadvantage, you probably have little if any ability to speak *Putonghua* and that could be important to your prospective employer. Whatever your skills, you must sell yourself hard, emphasising your good points, while trying to avoid revealing your failings.

☑ **SURVIVAL TIP**

Don't forget the *Yellow Pages*. China has no telephone directories for individuals or residential addresses, but it has a directory of businesses and other organisations called *Yellow Pages China*. They can usually be found in the rooms in larger hotels and can tell you if there's an office of the 'XYZ Corporation' in that city and provide its address and phone number. This resource is also available online (🖥 yp.net.cn/english). Other useful business directories include Alibaba (🖥 alibaba.com) and Made in China (🖥 made-in-china.com).

Schools & Universities

Since the '90s China has included the study of English in its school curricula, initially in secondary education and later in primary schools. Nowadays it's even taught in kindergartens. There's a tremendous demand for the English language and it's become the de facto second language of the country. However, in the majority of cases, lessons only cover reading and writing. Oral English – speaking and listening/comprehending – is rarely taught by Chinese teachers.

As a result, there's a huge demand for native English speakers to teach oral English at every level of education and, if you're aged over 21 and under 65 and possess a bachelor's degree in almost any subject from a reputable university, there are jobs galore. No previous teaching experience is necessary, although it's welcomed.

If you wish to act as an examiner for either International English Language Teaching System (IELTS) or Test of English as a Foreign Language (TOEFL) tests in China, you must have both a degree and three years' experience of teaching adults. These jobs may also require you to have a TEFL (Teaching English as a Foreign Language) or TESOL (Teaching English to Speakers of Other Languages) qualification from an accredited school, such as Trinity or Cambridge – these qualifications are useful for any would-be English teacher.

The Chinese have quite a rigid view of what constitutes 'a native speaker of English': someone with white skin, fair hair and blue eyes, and preferably from Australia, Canada, New Zealand, the UK or the US. This 'definition' isn't written into any job specification, but applicants who don't fit a Chinese interviewer's image of a native English speaker may find that the vacancy they applied for has suddenly been filled.

If you want to have a job lined up before you arrive in China, there are several possible approaches:

◆ UK residents can apply through the British Council.

◆ Contact an employment agency in China via the internet, but be careful. Don't pursue the matter further if they ask you for a fee and check that the employment conditions offered are approximately similar to those described in **Chapter 2**. There have been instances of some agencies committing applicants to working excessive hours.

◆ Decide where you want to live, then use the internet to identify universities and schools in that city. Most have a website advertising English teaching posts.

To work at a kindergarten or school, rather than a university, the first two options are the only ways to go, other than contacting a specific 'international school' in China. The latter provide a more sheltered introduction to the Chinese education system, although they usually demand some sort of teaching qualification.

If you don't comply with the above criteria, don't give up. Once you're in China, you'll discover that 'rules' aren't always strictly interpreted and it isn't unusual to find 'native English speakers' who come from distinctly non-English-speaking countries such as Russia or Italy. If a school or university wants to employ you, they can tell the provincial Foreign Affairs Department that you're the only suitable candidate for the job and request permission to employ you, which is usually granted.

If you're already in China, the best way to find a teaching job is to check out the expatriate magazines (which often advertise openings), apply to agencies and network among expat acquaintances.

Chinese Government Organisations & Chinese-owned Businesses

The opportunities for a foreigner to work within a Chinese-managed organisation are very limited, not just because of the language barrier but also because expatriates have different expectations of salaries and working practices. The two sectors where foreigners can gain a foothold in China are professional sport (particularly basketball and soccer) and law. All the large law firms from the US, the UK, Australia and Canada have offices in either mainland China or Hong Kong, and there's a constant demand for lawyers and other legally-trained staff to join partnerships in mainland China.

The only other regular full-time jobs within Chinese organisations commonly available to expatriates are within the media. *China Daily*, the only national daily English language newspaper, regularly employs a number of expatriates. There are also positions available with China Central Television (CCTV), particularly the English-language channel CCTV News, as news readers, weather announcers or presenters for travel or documentary programmes. If you're fluent in French, Russian, Arabic or Spanish, CCTV may also employ you to present programmes in these languages. Local TV and radio stations are becoming similarly open minded towards the employment of expatriates. Such jobs are rarely advertised overseas and you must track them down once you're in the country.

If the idea appeals, CCTV and local TV stations also need expatriates to play bit parts in their innumerable 'soaps'. There's no requirement to

join the Chinese equivalent of Equity – not that there is one – and while the pay isn't brilliant, the experience is priceless. Or you could provide the voice over on promotional films for manufacturers focusing on the overseas market. A clear voice and good enunciation are all you need.

If you're prepared to put your conscience in your pocket and your tongue in your cheek, there's another type of 'acting' job. Some Chinese-owned businesses like to hire foreigners on a freelance basis to impress the competition; bringing along a 'foreign advisor' or 'foreign manager' to a meeting, especially with clients in less sophisticated parts of the country, makes a big impression. As a result, there are opportunities, often advertised by employment agencies, for well-dressed, mature-looking Caucasians to pretend to be members of the bidder's group. Age is an advantage. If you're aged 40 or older – or look older than your years – you could earn anything between 1,000 and 2,000 RMB for attending a single meeting and pretending to be 'our boss from Germany'. All you have to do is nod at appropriate times and say 'xie, xie' (thank you) at the end. Be warned that the meeting often terminates with a lengthy banquet at which the client will do his best to drink you under the table.

Such is the importance of English in China that banks and insurance companies often hold competitions among their staff to find the best English speaker. For this they need judges and are delighted if they can find a native English speaker with a good voice and sufficient gravitas. It may be a one-off occasion, but if word gets around you could find yourself carving out a career as the Simon Cowell of English-speaking contests.

WORK ATTITUDES

The Chinese are diligent workers, although their number one loyalty is to themselves. Most youngsters study throughout their early years to gain the vital qualifications which will open the doors to a profession, as opposed to a job, that provides more security. Those who cannot make the grade as lawyers, doctors or engineers look to the state-run organisations where they may still achieve a job for life – although there's no longer a guarantee of this – and have the opportunity of gaining some extra benefits on the side. The state employs a large proportion of the workforce, while the remainder work for private businesses or, if they're lucky, for themselves.

Whatever job they manage to obtain, Chinese workers take it seriously. They do as they're asked and rarely question their boss's instructions or think 'outside the box'. If they cannot manage a task they may simply not attempt it for fear of losing face, and hope that their inactivity isn't noticed. This can be a dilemma for foreign supervisors who may need to ensure that a task is within their employees' capabilities before delegating it.

A Chinese office can be a curiously old-fashioned place, with junior staff standing up to welcome their boss and calling him Mr (*Xiansheng*). The Western practice of using first names and inviting input from workers has yet to take hold in China.

However, don't be deceived by the humble and low-key attitude of Chinese workers. Under the surface lurks the soul of an entrepreneur and most are looking for any opportunity which may provide a stepping stone to becoming a boss themselves. Self-employment is the end goal for many Chinese, whether it's running a small shop or 'borrowing' an idea from their employer, improving on it and then setting up

a rival business with a better product and more competitive prices. At the very least they'll be studying the jobs market and poised to move on if another employer offers them a better position.

One of the most unique aspects of the Chinese workforce is its reliance on 'migrant' labour – workers from the countryside who perform the majority of unskilled work in factories and on construction sites. There are some 200m migrant workers providing a source of labour that can be turned on or off as required. If they're no longer required, either permanently or temporarily, they can be dismissed and, in the absence of alternative work, must return to their farms in the countryside and eke out a living on the land.

City residents regard migrant workers as a necessary resource but treat them somewhat unfairly. Migrants almost invariably work under worse conditions than the locals. The *hukou* system of registration makes it difficult to transfer residency from one area to another, so many migrants are permanent outsiders and have city residents' rights denied to them such as schooling for their children or compensation in the event of an accident.

Despite this treatment, their contribution to China's economic success is immeasurable. China now aims to produce goods that achieve international quality standards and, well supervised, the migrant workforce is quite capable of doing this. So much so that many world-renowned companies are basing all their production in China and things that you buy because they're American, German or Japanese, such as Olympus cameras, Sanyo televisions and even VW Polo cars, are manufactured in China by subsidiaries of the original company, and assembled by farmers from the western provinces. And they're none the worse for that.

WORKING WOMEN

One of the major things that the Communist Party achieved in 1949 was the liberation of women. Mao Zedong famously said that 'women hold up half of the sky', meaning that they could do anything that men could do, and they've not looked back since. Far more than in the West, women in China are treated as equals by men. The majority of women of working age have jobs and women make up over 45 per cent of the workforce, receiving exactly the same remuneration as men doing the same job.

Many women work in more traditional female roles such as nursing, but many others do 'men's jobs', such as car mechanics, bus drivers and construction workers – there are even female miners. Further up the ladder, there are plenty of women engineers, pharmacists, accountants and so on, while female cadres can be found at many levels within government departments. The one area where women are underrepresented is politics, although this may be due to a lack of interest rather than exclusion.

The 'glass ceiling' is much thinner for women seeking promotion in China than in many developed countries and women can be found at every level of society, business and industry. Some have become famous for their achievements in establishing major businesses and achieving great wealth through their endeavours. In 2012, the Hurun Report (hurun. net) revealed that the three richest women in China were all multi-billionaires led by Wu Yajun, owner of a property development company, with a cool $6.5 billion.

In this way, many women are freer than their sisters in the West. They can go to work and seek promotion, knowing that their children are safe at home looked after by grandma (and sometimes grandpa). A close family connection means they don't have to juggle their responsibilities as many Western women do. However, at the same time, many women, particularly migrant workers, work at the expense of their personal life. It isn't unusual for a husband and wife to have jobs at opposite ends of the country and only meet a few times a year.

INDUSTRIAL RELATIONS

Although trade unions exist in China, their role is less clear cut than that of unions in the West. They largely act as a buffer between employer and employees and aim for an ideal where bosses and workers work in harmony to achieve optimum production. However, most union representatives are directly employed and paid by employers and therefore often feel duly bound to take the employers' side in a dispute.

Despite or perhaps because of this, the government is keen for workers to have union representation and has successfully put pressure on all foreign joint ventures to allow the establishment of unions; even multinational companies such as US retail giant Wal-Mart, which has resisted unionisation in other countries, has been persuaded to comply.

Strikes and lockouts were a rare and unusual event until recently, but in recent years there's been growing discontent among workers who feel that the softly, softly approach of unions wasn't doing enough to support them. This resulted in some major upheavals at well-known international companies during 2010, including a strike at a Honda plant in Guangdong province which led to wage increases at a number of industrial plants.

Although it's unlikely that as a foreign worker you'll be asked or expected to join a Chinese union, you might benefit from union support, not just in negotiating better salaries but on issues such as enforcing labour laws, supporting workers with industrial diseases such as pneumoconiosis (black lung) and silicosis (which is rampant in the mining industry), helping workers obtain compensation for work-related injuries, and clamping down on bosses who withhold pay illegally.

> About a quarter of the Chinese workforce belongs to a union. The largest is the All-China Federation of Trade Unions (acftu.org.cn), an umbrella organisation representing a number of smaller unions with over 190m members. Not surprisingly, the ACFTU has close links to the Chinese government.

QUALIFICATIONS

Apart from a degree from a major university, which can open many doors in China, many Western qualifications aren't relevant or helpful in China. An NVQ2 in hairdressing or social care won't help you find work in these fields as there are just too many Chinese willing to do these jobs and for a much lower wage. There's no system for recognising other countries' diplomas or certificates unless they have international prestige, such as qualifications in medicine or law.

That said, a dossier of neatly filed certificates looks impressive, and prospective employers will be more likely to give you their time if you show evidence that you've invested in your education, even if it isn't particularly relevant to the job.

If you're seeking employment as an English teacher at a school or university it's **essential** to have a copy of the certificate certifying your degree. This need not be a degree in English but does need to be a bachelor's degree (or higher) in a mainstream subject and awarded by a reputable university. It's worthwhile taking a few copies of this and any other qualifications with you to China. A TEFL/TESOL certificate (see page 20) is also impressive and may be a requirement for some positions.

If you're employed by an overseas organisation, you must satisfy their recruitment criteria regarding the necessary qualifications. However, for some jobs in China, particularly the more off-the-wall ones, a clear speaking voice may be enough to get your through the door.

The ability to speak and understand Chinese isn't, in most cases, necessary if you're working for a foreign-based organisation or a school or university. You can get by without it, and at educational establishments there's always someone who can speak sufficient English. It's a bonus if you can understand even rudimentary Chinese, but it isn't essential (see **Language** on page 37).

☑ SURVIVAL TIP

If you plan to work in China, your employer may insist upon an annual medical (the employer pays). If you're found to have HIV/AIDS or another serious STD you're liable to be summarily dismissed and deported.

GOVERNMENT EMPLOYMENT SERVICE

Although foreigners in China comprise less than one in 2,000 of the population, there's a government-sponsored recruitment agency aimed at expatriates called China Job (💻 chinajob. com), which is where prospective employers can post openings for foreigners. Historically, the vast majority of its jobs have been for English language teachers and lecturers, illustrating the importance that the government places on this role, but there are other positions available. In late 2012 it had postings for sales managers, analysts and engineers within the growing industrial sector, an English editor for an expatriate website, and even sales staff to promote foreign wines throughout China.

China Job holds regular job fairs in major cities such as Beijing, Guangzhou and Shanghai which are specifically aimed at expatriates, and are a good place to obtain information about work opportunities if you're already in China. Check out the website for upcoming dates.

PRIVATE EMPLOYMENT AGENCIES

There are a number of private employment agencies run by and for the Chinese, but in addition some of the larger overseas employment agencies, such as Manpower (💻 manpower.

com.cn), Kelly Services (💻 kellyservices.cn) and Adecco (💻 china.adecco.com), have branch offices in China and advertise jobs which are open to foreign applicants. Chinese employers do use agencies to find key staff, therefore it's worthwhile checking their job vacancy postings, although you're likely to be competing with well-qualified Chinese candidates.

For top flight executive positions, there are a number of recruitment and headhunting firms operating in China, such as Bo Le Associates (💻 bo-le.com), Korn/Ferry International (💻 kornferry.com) and Stanton Chase (💻 stantonchase.com). There are also many smaller agencies, sometimes run by expatriates, that tend to focus on locating and recruiting people to teach English (see below). Agencies for temporary staff usually specialise in providing Chinese workers such as cooks and tradesmen to foreign companies, rather than finding temporary positions for foreigners.

Online Agencies

The rapid development of the internet has led to a huge increase in the number of online recruitment agencies and 'job search' sites (just Google 'jobs in China'). As with employment agencies, a great many of the jobs are for teachers. Some sites charge a subscription fee to access their vacancy lists, but many permit job seekers to view and respond to vacancies free of charge. It's also possible to post your CV online (again, usually free), but it's wise to consider the security implications of this move; by posting your home address or phone number in public view, you

---

Leading Chinese Job Websites

chinasemester.com

craigslist.com

englishfirst.com/trt/teaching-english-in-china.html

esljobs4teachers.com

expatjobschina.com

job168.com/english

jobchina.net

monster.com.hk

shanghai.baixing.com

sinoculture.com

teachabroadchina.com

tefl.com

english.zhaopin.com

could be laying yourself open to nuisance phone calls or worse.

Note that some Chinese websites don't usually include an English-language version unless a major or international organisation is involved. However, you can obtain a rough-and-ready translation using the (free) Babel Fish translator provided by the search engine company Alta Vista. Type 'http:babelfish.yahoo.com' in your browser, then enter the address of the website that you wish to have translated in the Babel Fish dialogue box that appears; you'll then be presented with an instant translation of the web page in question – although you shouldn't expect it to be idiomatic or even very accurate! Google offers a similar translation tool.

JOB TYPES

Contract Jobs

There are no permanent jobs in China, unless you work for a large state-run organisation and are Chinese, or are being seconded to China by your overseas employer. Almost all jobs in the private sector are offered on a contract basis and last for a specific time period. The same goes for teaching where you may be taken on for one or two terms. Teaching contracts for more than one year are unusual, with renewal contracts being issued, one year at a time, as required. There's no guarantee or, indeed, legislation whereby a foreigner's job becomes permanent if a temporary contract is renewed more than twice, although this does apply to Chinese employees.

Working to a contract isn't such a disadvantage as it seems. It means that your employer must keep you on for the duration of the term and allows you to have a firm plan for the (fairly immediate) future but remain flexible in the long term. It's likely that there will be more job opportunities and you may well want to move on. In the meantime you can use your time to make as many useful contacts as possible, which is a key to finding the best positions.

Part-time, Temporary & Casual Jobs

There are a surprising number of opportunities for casual work in China with a variety of employers. Many an expat has been asked if they would be willing to model some clothes for use in an advertisement. These are often 'one-off' jobs but they pay quite well; at the very least you should get some free clothes.

Many businesses and organisations need native English speakers to assist them in a variety of ways, from providing voice-overs to judging contests or even appearing as a 'foreign associate' at important meetings. Again, such jobs may prove to be a one-time opportunity but they can pay well – a fee of 500 or 1,000 RMB isn't unusual, although you shouldn't demand payment but rather let them offer it – and you may be treated to a nice meal with the company brass afterwards.

If you're employed, your contract may contain an 'anti-moonlighting' clause stating that you cannot take a second job or that you must ask your employer's permission first. However, many teachers find that they have some spare time and, provided their employer agrees, take on extra part-time teaching work.

A number of organisations run trainee and work exchange programmes for students and recent graduates. For most programmes you must be aged under 30. Programmes include the following:

◆ Technical and commercial students wishing to gain experience by working in China during their holidays can apply to the International Association for the Exchange of Students for Technical Experience (IAESTE) in over 60 countries (🖳 iaeste.org). Applicants must be enrolled at an educational institution as a full-time student of engineering, science, agriculture, architecture or a related field of study, or be undergraduates in their penultimate year of study aged between 19 and 30.

In the UK, applicants should apply to IAESTE UK, c/o Education Section, British Council, 10 Spring Gardens, London SW1A 2BN, UK (☎ 020-7389 4114, 🖳 iaeste.org.uk).

◆ For students and those within a term of graduation, the Council on International Educational Exchange (CIEE) provides the opportunity to teach English in China on a short-term five or ten-month contract. Some placements are with families in developing areas and provide a crash course in Chinese culture. Contact the CIEE, 300 Fore Street, Portland, ME 04101, USA (☎ 207-553-4000, 🖳 ciee.org) for information.

◆ AIESEC is a student-run, non-profit organisation that provides paid internships in business and technical fields in over 87 countries and territories, including China. You can contact the AIESEC chapter at your university for details of qualifications and application procedures. In the UK, contact AIESEC UK, 29-31 Cowper Street, 2nd Floor, London, EC2A 4AT, UK (☎ 020-7549 1800, 🖳 aiesec.co.uk).

◆ *Transitions Abroad* magazine, aimed at Americans, is a good source of information about educational and exchange programmes. Its website (🖳 transitionsabroad.com) contains listings of programmes for studying, working and volunteering.

JOB HUNTING

People seconded to a role in China are more likely to be selected for a job by their employer than to have chosen it themselves; but as China grows more foreign professionals are actively seeking employment there. In addition, recent retirees or students on a 'gap' year may want to look for work in China. There are a number of resources which can help, Including the following:

◆ **Internet**: even if you're already in China, the easiest way to access jobs information is online. Virtually every employer and agency has a website, as do universities and schools. The various chambers of commerce and overseas business organisations (listed in **Appendix A**) have websites, and these frequently have details of vacancies among their member companies. You should also look on embassy websites to see what jobs are available.

Online job agencies (see page 24) usually have a search facility allowing you to specify different types of job and even locations. You should frequently check the websites of recruitment agencies (see page 24), as new jobs are posted regularly. If there's an organisation or school which appeals to you, keep tabs on its website as new positions are often posted there; some companies prefer not to use expensive recruitment agencies and use their own resources to find employees.

◆ **Newspapers & magazines**: there are a great many free publications aimed at expatriates in China which are circulated in the major cities, in bars, clubs and other places expats hang out – try *City Weekend* (🖳 cityweekend. com.cn), *Time Out Shanghai* (🖳 timeoutcn. com/tosh) and *The Beijinger* (🖳 thebeijinger. com). Most carry job advertisements, although many of these are for teachers and not all will be genuine. Occasionally there may also be advertisements in national publications such as *China Daily* (🖳 chinadaily.com.cn).

Many Chinese newspapers carry job advertisements and it's possible to access online editions (see 🖳 onlinenewspapers.com/ china.htm), but these are only useful if you can read Chinese characters and most jobs are for Chinese or, at the very least, those with Chinese language skills.

International newspapers and magazines sometimes contain advertisements for positions in China, including the *Financial Times* and the *Wall Street Journal* (for business managers), the *Economist* (economic research and university teaching and administrative positions), the *International Herald Tribune*, and occasionally the broadsheet English Sunday newspapers.

◆ **Employment agencies**: it's worth signing up with international recruitment agencies with a presence in China, as well as Chinese-based or expat-run agencies. One of the most useful is China Job (🖳 chinajob.com) which is sponsored by the government and lists a range of jobs, particularly in teaching English. It also runs regular job fairs.

◆ **Your current employer**: if you work for an international company with interests in China, ask the human resources team if there are any openings which would suit you. It can be much easier for a company to transfer a current member of staff than go through the process of recruiting someone new.

◆ **Unsolicited applications**: don't be afraid to turn up on the doorstep of an employer and

ask about employment. The Chinese admire proactive behaviour and provided you're polite and well-dressed, and take a copy of your CV and qualifications, staff will usually ensure they're passed on to the appropriate person. It isn't unknown for foreigners to secure a job in this way. If you have legal training, it may be worth approaching one of the international law firms with offices in China, such as Allen and Overy LLP, Baker & McKenzie, Freshfields Bruckhaus Deringer LLP, Herbert Smith or Slaughter & May. A useful website is 🖳 hg.org/firms-china which lists international law firms operating in China.

When sending unsolicited enquiries by mail or email, be sure to state the type of work you're looking for, e.g. administration or teaching, when you're available to start and relevant skills such as your knowledge of Chinese.

♦ **Your contacts**: in China, who you know is every bit as important as what you know, and you should cultivate contacts assiduously which may open the door to a job. You're far more likely to get an interview if you know someone who works at an organisation.

CURRICULUM VITAE

Your CV – or résumé as the Chinese call it – is an essential job-hunting tool, and you should ensure that any prospective employer receives a copy. It should be brief and to the point, rather than listing every accomplishment, and include personal details such as your nationality, date of birth, marital status, language skills and qualifications. It should also detail your work experience (including job titles) chronologically, starting with the most recent, and highlighting the experience and qualities that make you suitable for the position for which you're applying. Mention any experience you have of travelling in China and be sure to paint it in a positive light. Photos aren't obligatory but if you have one that makes you look good it

isn't a bad idea to attach it to the top right-hand corner of the first page. As well as your CV, include photocopies of your degree and any other qualifications that are relevant to the job.

Address your application to the manager of the personnel or human resources department (it's frequently called HR in China) and include a covering letter, stating why you're interested in the job/organisation and when you could start work. This is particularly important if you're applying from abroad.

INTERVIEWS

If you're invited to an interview, dress neatly but not extravagantly. Answer any questions truthfully but keep the emphasis on why you're suitable for the job. It doesn't hurt to mention that you enjoy living in China and any criticism of China should be avoided.

Chinese employers don't (yet) go in for tricky psychometric testing – many don't even ask for references – although international organisations may set a range of tasks and even a series of interviews to whittle down candidates. However, even if your interview is no more than a brief chat, the etiquette can be quite formal, therefore address the interviewer as Mr/Mrs (*Xiansheng*), don't sit down until invited to do so, and shake hands on arriving and leaving.

SALARY

Until quite recently, China was deemed a 'hardship' posting for expatriates, and candidates were offered a range of incentives to persuade them to apply. The enormous strides the country has taken over recent years means that this no longer applies in most of the major cities, although rural areas can still be a test for foreigners.

Living deep in the countryside of central or northwest China is very different from the cosmopolitan lifestyle in the major east or south-coast cities, and the lack of even basic amenities in these areas can make life difficult for expats. If the salary sounds too good to be true, open an atlas and check where the job is!

These days, staff transferred from their home country to a branch in China generally receive the same salary, together with a relatively small living allowance paid in local currency. However, they also receive a number of perks (see below) including free accommodation. These arrangements are fairly typical of postings to positions within government, NGOs or major business organisations.

Where such positions are filled by applicants already living in China, a somewhat lower salary/benefits package may be offered. Basic salaries vary enormously according to the size and status of the organisation, but as a rough guide, an engineer recruited locally could expect to earn around 14,000 RMB a month, while a sales manager at an average-sized company might earn 10,000 RMB a month.

Working for a Chinese state-run organisation is a different matter again. Salaries for expatriate teachers are considerably higher than those paid to Chinese teachers who frequently receive as little as 1,000-1,500 RMB a month, but they're still very low compared with Western salaries. The norm in both state schools and universities is 3,500-4,000 RMB a month, paid for ten months of the year (September to June) to teachers with a bachelor's or master's degree, and 5,000 RMB a month for those with a doctorate. In certain cases, such as at a prestigious university in Beijing or Shanghai, they may be a little higher.

It's important to bear in mind that this salary is only a part of the total benefits provided to teachers at Chinese state schools and universities and, for most, it's sufficient. You may have the opportunity to boost your wages from other sources. There's a huge demand for part-time teachers to teach at 'crammers' – private schools that open after school hours, at weekends and on public holidays. At these, expatriates can earn 80 to 150 RMB an hour, with 100 RMB the average hourly rate. Many teachers work for a state school and then top up their salary with hours at a crammer, but check your contract or ask your employer to be sure

that you're permitted to do so. Salaries at private schools and universities run by foreign joint ventures tend to be higher. Teachers seconded from Dulwich College in the UK to their branch campuses in China could receive as much as they would in the UK.

If you manage to land a job with the Chinese media, the salary can be quite good. A weather announcer on CCTV earns around 10,000 RMB a month, but the hours are a drawback as your services are required in the early morning, at lunchtime and again in the evening, with long gaps in between. As an actor in a bit part in a TV 'soap' for a television production company you could earn around 800 RMB or as much as 1,000 RMB for an eight-hour day, even if you aren't needed for the full eight hours.

Of course, such salaries are beyond the dreams of many ordinary Chinese whose wages are dramatically lower. A Chinese engineer or office manager may earn 2,250 RMB a month, a nurse 1,650 RMB and a car mechanic just 1,100 RMB. Wages also depend on the city or region, with higher wages paid in the more industrialised centres in the east and south. There's no national minimum wage, which is set on a variable scale by the provinces and ranges from 11 RMB an hour in Beijing to just 4.5 RMB an hour in Guangxi province. The Wage Indicator website provides a fairly comprehensive guide to salaries in China (🖥 wageindicator.org/main/minimum-wages/china).

Benefits

For expatriate employees of overseas governments, NGOs and joint ventures, the principal fringe benefits are as follows:

◆ **Home leave & paid holidays**: this is usually a three-week break every six months for single workers, while those who have their family with them get a six-week break once a year. It's assumed that you'll use your break to fly home and economy class airline tickets are provided.
    Most schools and universities pay for a one-way economy class ticket for foreigners signing a six month (one term/semester) contract or a return ticket for those signing for a year (two terms). In addition, expat teachers are usually paid their full salary during the mid-winter holiday period that divides the two semesters, provided they sign a one-year contract.

◆ **Accommodation**: if you're employed by a foreign government, NGO or business joint venture, it's likely that your employer will provide furnished rent-free accommodation for expatriate employees. Both foreign and

Chinese teachers are provided with furnished accommodation on campus.

♦ **Medical costs**: if you work for a government agency, NGO or joint venture, you should be covered by a health insurance policy for all medical expenses which will require you to use specific international hospitals for diagnosis and treatment. Such policies don't always cover dental or optical treatment costs. Some employers maintain in-house doctors and/or nurses to provide medical assistance for minor conditions, and it's sometimes a requirement that you consult them before visiting the designated hospital.

Most schools and all universities have on-campus clinics which can be used free of charge by expatriate teachers. In addition, employers usually reimburse medical expenses (at a local Chinese hospital) up to a relatively small sum. However, local hospitals aren't usually expensive (see **Chapter 12**). If you're too ill to attend classes, it's essential to get the on-campus clinic to authorise your absence, otherwise you won't be paid.

♦ **Food**: foreign teachers at universities can eat at the various canteens/restaurants on campus very cheaply indeed, while expatriate employees engaged on construction or mining projects may have an on-site canteen where all meals are provided free. Most office-based businesses expect you to pay for your own meals from your overseas living allowance.

♦ **Domestic travel**: it isn't uncommon for expatriates teaching at universities to be paid an annual sum to cover the cost of domestic travel – effectively 'sight-seeing' money – amounting to between 2,000 and 5,000 RMB a year.

Pension

When expatriates are transferred to China by their home employer, it's customary for the employer to continue to pay into their superannuation or pension fund; and if the employee contributes, then appropriate deductions from his salary will continue.

See **Chapter 2** for more detail about the terms of employment in China.

Income Tax

Provided you earn no more than 57,600 RMB in a year, as a foreigner you won't be liable to pay income tax. If you earn more than this, Chinese income tax will be levied on everything above

4,800 RMB a month on a fairly rapidly increasing scale up to a maximum of 45 per cent.

If you've been seconded from abroad and your salary is paid into an account in your home country, the Chinese tax authorities will deem you to be a non-resident for tax purposes and there'll be no obligation for you to declare this part of your income until you've worked in China for more than three years. For information, see **Chapter 14**.

SELF-EMPLOYMENT & DOING BUSINESS

If your business plan involves, for example, a straightforward purchase of specific materials or the outsourcing of manufacturing, then China is a relatively simple place to conduct business, apart from the inevitable difficulties that can arise from language problems. However, working in China as a self-employed person setting up a new business is much more complicated.

The majority of 'foreign' investors in China come not from Europe or the US, but from Hong Kong and Taiwan (autonomous Chinese regions), although the number of Europeans is growing, particularly from Britain and Germany. The most popular sectors for foreign investors are manufacturing and export.

The cultural differences, bureaucracy and language problems in China mean that establishing a business isn't an easy process. The line between business and friendship is often blurred, with the Chinese choosing to work with relatives and close friends rather than with strangers, even if they aren't always the best choice. Westerners may view this as nepotism but for the Chinese it's a matter of trust. In order to do business with the Chinese, whether as a partner or client, you first need to establish a friendly relationship and gain their respect and trust. The lure of money alone isn't enough.

Certain aspects of business may frustrate you. While the Chinese are at the forefront of new technology, their design ability lags behind many other countries and they lack an understanding of what appeals to foreigners. These are areas where your know-how can be invaluable.

In order to start a business or work for yourself you must possess a Z visa, which it's possible to obtain on the basis of being self-employed, but it isn't easy. You must be able to demonstrate that your business will generate sufficient income to support yourself and that you have enough funds to live on until it does. Having a potential Chinese partner with *guanxi* (connections) to support your application helps, as does a working knowledge of Chinese and previous experience in China.

If your business is a one-man operation that you can run from home, there's nothing to prevent you from doing so in China, where many small businesses are operated from home. However, you mustn't create problems for your neighbours and you'll still require a Z visa.

⚠ Caution

Bear in mind that there are over 1.35bn people in China and they all need to make a living, therefore competition for a new business is intense.

One of the major problems of working with the Chinese is their magpie mentality. Introduce a new idea and you risk having it copied – by your partner or a member of staff, who won't hesitate to leave and set up a rival business, or by an outsider. Copyright protection in China is porous, to put it mildly.

Furthermore, you cannot rely on a written contract to protect you in the same way it would in the West. The Chinese may put many hours into negotiating an agreement, but that doesn't mean they'll stick to it, and many revert to their 'old' way of doing things irrespective of what's been agreed in writing. The courts aren't much help either, as they tend to base their decisions on what they think is 'reasonable', rather than what's been agreed or the views of either party, and the only way to resolve differences is by direct and friendly negotiations.

Despite all of the problems, an increasing number of expatriates succeed in establishing businesses in China – some manage it on their own, although the majority create a partnership with a Chinese spouse. Most businesses are in the leisure and tourism sector, such as running bars, restaurants and hotels, although foreigners have succeeded in many fields, including advertising, architecture, design, education and public relations.

In such a fast-moving country the possibilities are endless, although you need to be cautious. In most cases it's the Chinese who are making the fortunes, and even some major Western corporations have been spectacularly caught out due to their failure to fully understand how business is conducted in China. The marketplace is already crowded and there are an incredible number of small businesses. Research shows that most have a lifespan of 12 years and for every one that opens, another one fails.

Setting up a business in China takes time (see **Bureaucracy** opposite) and you should use this period to make as many useful contacts as possible. Arm yourself with plenty of business cards with your company details on one side in English and on the other side in Chinese, including your email address and mobile phone number. You'll be handing them out like confetti, so get a little box to carry them in (as the Chinese do). When receiving a card from someone, treat it with respect: read it, thank the person and store it somewhere safe.

Don't rely on help in setting up your business from your country's embassy or consulate. While they can warn you about problems in particular areas and should be able to provide contacts for lawyers and other professionals, most career public servants have never worked in business and many don't understand it. You're better off contacting your home country's chamber of commerce and the various overseas business organisations (see **Appendix A**).

Location

China is such a huge country that where you set up in business can be as important as what you decide to do. The two largest cities, Beijing and Shanghai, are as different as Washington, DC and New York or London and Manchester. Beijing is the seat of government with a great sense of history, while Shanghai has a much more modern outlook and is China's financial hub. The south coast cities of Guangzhou and Shenzhen are also major trading and business centres, but don't ignore less well-known cities, particularly as the local authorities may offer incentives to business start-ups.

The pros and cons of the main locations are as follows:

♦ **Beijing**: China's capital is a Mecca for tourists due to its palaces and historic places, so if you plan to work in the hospitality or tourist industry there's probably no better place to be. It's a well-organised city with good facilities, and the major embassies and consulates are located there. However, Beijingers can be rather self-important and may not offer such a warm welcome as people in some other cities.

♦ **Shanghai**: This huge metropolis is even larger than Beijing and can be difficult to navigate, but its waterfront location with numerous wharfs and warehouses makes it a major centre for import and export business. Many useful business associations and consulates are also located there. Shanghai is a dynamic city and its people are clever, both with their hands and their minds. For some businesses, such as import/export or hospitality, there are

few better places than Shanghai to commence operations, but it isn't cheap.

♦ **Guangzhou**: This southern port was the first city in mainland China to accept a European presence and it has a long history of trade. Its people are astute and are influenced by the close proximity of Hong Kong. If you're in the textiles or clothing business, then Guangzhou is the place to be, as there are countless factories in Guangdong province.

♦ **Shenzhen**: close to Guangzhou but completely different, Shenzhen has grown from a small village in just 30 years to become a production powerhouse, supplying cheap labour to neighbouring Hong Kong. Many of its people are migrants, drawn by the opportunity to work and make money, but as manufacturing moves from cheap and cheerful to more technologically advanced products, the city faces a shortage of skilled workers. Skilled foreigners could find that their knowledge and abilities are in demand.

Away from the 'big four', there are at least another 100 lesser-known cities with populations exceeding 1m and plenty of scope for starting a business. Most are far cheaper to live in than the larger conurbations; labour is also cheaper, as are the rental costs for factories and offices. In addition, there are often substantial incentives from local governments and there's also less competition (at least for now). Places such as Dalian, Qingdao or Xiamen are pleasant places to live and are on the coast, with a less frantic pace of life and built to a more human scale than mega cities such as Shanghai. The only negative is that their location may mean extra travel and transportation costs.

Take time to look around and do your research before deciding where to base yourself. As Deng Xiaoping said, 'It doesn't matter whether a cat is black or white, so long as it catches mice'. Provided you're successful and make money, it doesn't matter where you do it.

Wherever you decide to locate, resist the temptation to use the name of the city in your company name as this has serious financial implications. When you register your company name, you must deposit more funds as 'working capital' if you include the host city's name. The sum increases even more if you include the name of the province, and the words 'China' or 'Chinese' will cost you dear.

Bureaucracy

There are two options available to foreigners starting a business in China: either a joint venture with a Chinese partner, which is much preferred by the authorities, or a wholly-owned foreign enterprise.

The process of registration can be long and drawn out and you should allow four to six months to complete it, although a good Chinese partner with reasonable contacts can do it in half this time or less. Much depends on the size of the proposed business and the sector or industry in which you decide to operate. In 2011, the World Bank ranked China 79th out of 183 countries for ease of doing business but a lowly 151st for starting a business.

There's a fairly rigid set of requirements which must be followed in a fixed sequence:

♦ Register with the Ministry of Commerce through the local Industry and Commerce Bureau.

♦ Register with the tax authorities on a national and provincial level.

♦ Register your company seal with the Foreign Administration department of the Public Security Bureau. Every company in China must have a unique seal and all official documents must be stamped with this in red ink.

♦ Open a Chinese/foreign currency bank account and deposit your operating capital (see below).

♦ Register at the local Foreign Exchange Administration Bureau and obtain a Foreign Currency Certificate.

♦ Register expatriate staff and their families with the Public Security Bureau (PSB). The PSB will want to know their place of residence and must be informed if any leave your employment or relocate.

♦ Register with the local Customs office.

The cost of doing all the above is relatively inexpensive – between 1,000 and 2,000 RMB – but the amount of cash or security you must deposit at your Chinese bank as operating capital is a much more serious sum. It varies according to the nature of the proposed business. A wholesale business or manufacturing company is required to deposit at least 500,000 RMB, a retailer around 300,000 RMB and a consultancy or foreign language centre around 100,000 RMB. If you plan to operate nationally rather than locally, costs are considerably higher. Your bank will know the precise sum required for this depending on your business plan.

Business Licences & Permits

This is a complex area and, ideally, you need a Chinese partner or business advisor to assist you. Numerous permits and licences are required and the situation changes frequently. Unfortunately, if the local government wants to find fault, they can usually interpret the law to show that you were doing something without the necessary licence, even unknowingly, so beware.

If there's an accident or other unfortunate event, the authorities are quick to point the finger of blame. In one widely-reported, recent incident, when misguided excavations caused a part-built block of apartments in Shanghai to collapse (killing a worker), the two most senior managers deemed to be responsible for the building were charged with not having the appropriate licences and authorisations, and sentenced to long prison sentences.

Employment Laws

Since 2008, China has had fairly comprehensive laws covering employment (described in more detail in **Chapter 2**), particularly with regard to the employment of foreigners. However, the main reason these laws were initially promulgated was the discontent caused by the flagrant abuses of migrant Chinese workers, and employment laws are principally aimed at these lower paid workers and their effect on foreigners is incidental.

Thus for factory workers the maximum working week is 44 hours, with all hours worked in excess of 44 paid at overtime rates. Office workers, however, usually work a 40-hour week. All employees are entitled to a written employment contract detailing the salient points of their position. Labour laws also cover holiday entitlements, maternity leave, unfair dismissal, the withholding of wages, payment of social security insurance contributions, safety at work, plus issues such as probationary periods and the

rights of full-time employees. Note that part-time employees aren't usually covered by these laws.

The law requires that all employees receive a written contract, and failure to provide one for 12 months can give an employee the right to his employment being treated as permanent. All employment contracts must contain the following information:

◆ the employer's name and address;

◆ the employee's name and address;

◆ the nature of the job (but not necessarily the job title);

◆ the start date of the employment;

◆ the duration of the employment;

◆ details of any provisions for extending a contract;

◆ terms of notice for dismissal or resignation;

◆ rules for disciplinary action or dispute resolution (normally via the local Dispute Arbitration Committee).

Details of salary, any benefits, leave, sickness provisions and other matters don't need to be included in the contract, but can be if an employer wishes. Should an employer issue two successive contracts to an employee (including probationary contracts) a third successive contract must be an open-ended or permanent contract. Note, however, that on dismissal of a permanent employee, the compensation that an employer is obliged to pay (under most circumstances) is limited to a month's pay for each year or part year of service, and at a rate no more than three times the average wage in the city where the employee worked. Should an employee be dismissed for disciplinary reasons, the employer should retain a permanent record of the reason for termination, as he could be at risk of a claim for compensation at some time in the future.

Hourly or monthly rates for probationary employees are required to be not less than 80 per cent of the wages for an equivalent permanent employee. For Chinese employees there are set hourly overtime rates: 150 per cent of the standard hourly rate for hours worked in excess of normal working hours on weekdays, 200 per cent for overtime worked on Saturdays or Sundays, and 300 per cent for hours worked on statutory public holidays. Time off in lieu may be given by the employer for working on a Saturday or a Sunday, but cannot be given in lieu of a public holiday.

Legal Representation

To say that someone is representing his company in negotiations doesn't have serious implications in most countries, as all parties taking part in such negotiations appreciate that they have strictly limited powers. They usually only represent their company up to clearly defined limits and if something more serious arises they must refer back to their superiors. The powers given in cases like this are seen simply as a delegation of responsibility – up to a limit.

However, in China things are different and all foreign companies and foreign-Chinese joint ventures are required by law to have a named 'legal representative'. He or she must be a highly placed individual with broad powers and with potentially unlimited personal liability for the entire company's actions, performance and finance, in so much as they may affect China and its people.

The person chosen is usually an expatriate with a senior position, such as the chairman or chief executive or, with joint ventures, possibly the general manager. Whoever holds this position and is accepted by the Chinese authorities – and it could be a Chinese partner – must be fully aware of his responsibilities and liabilities, and should have an appropriate personal liability insurance policy provided by the company. Furthermore, the company itself must be insured against liability from the actions of the appointed legal representative, who must have clearly defined powers and responsibilities.

This is a complex area of Chinese company law and for anyone considering starting a company in China it's essential to obtain legal advice on this issue (although it's unlikely to be a complicated problem for a one-man business).

Decision Making

This can be a long-winded business in China. Don't anticipate instant decisions – patience is essential. Most Chinese people like to ascertain both sides of every question and to assess the merits and disadvantages of each at length – and then discuss it with their colleagues – before making a decision. They like to follow the mainstream view and prefer not to take an independent line, which means that decisions tend to take much longer than Westerners expect.

Business Contracts & Agreements

These should follow standard wordings wherever possible and, despite concerns about how or whether the other party will adhere to them in practice, should be agreed in good faith. If problems arise, then the Chinese courts are there if necessary. However, the courts have a certain disadvantage for a foreign company in that the proceedings are conducted in Chinese and foreign lawyers are barred. As an alternative, arbitration – covered in most standard forms of contract – could be considered.

Several arbitration organisations can provide a service in China (see box below) that takes these disadvantages into account and, subject to both parties agreement, allows proceedings to be conducted in a foreign language and permits the use of foreign lawyers. With goodwill on both sides this can provide an alternative avenue for resolution of difficult disputes, although almost certainly the best route to resolution remains direct negotiation between the parties without the intervention of either a court or arbitrator.

Arbitration Centres in Mainland China:

- Beijing Arbitration Commission
- China International Economic and Trade Commission
- Chinese European Arbitration Centre
- Shanghai Arbitration Commission

Intellectual Property

It's absolutely vital that a company has a clear plan to ensure the protection and retention of sole ownership of any intellectual property, trade secrets or processes that it possesses and relies upon. There's nothing too large or too small that it cannot be copied, as some of the world's major corporations have discovered to their cost in East Asia. Access to confidential information must be kept to the essential minimum and any staff involved need to sign all-embracing and binding non-competing and confidentiality agreements. **It cannot be emphasised enough that Intellectual property in every form needs to be fully protected.**

Recruitment & Retention of Staff

Whether you're recruiting one person to help you in a one-man business or a number to set up a production line, it's important to ensure that you offer not less than the minimum wages and conditions required under local employment laws. **These must be the absolute minimum that you offer.** The Chinese love nothing more than to be able to put a glaring headline in the papers telling the world that you, a foreign company, are under-paying your staff, and the memory of this will rumble on for years.

If you have a local rival, try to find out what they pay and make sure that you at least match it. By all means use local agencies to recruit people, although in China it pays to offer existing staff a bonus for each recruit that they bring to the company. This technique is often used in the West but is almost unknown in China. Such a bonus needn't be large, say two or three thousand RMB for each recruit taken on and retained for at least six months.

Bear in mind that finding employees is less of a problem than retaining them. In private industry there tends to be a rapid turnover in personnel and it's essential to keep a wary eye on working conditions and employee satisfaction, and ensuring that things such as toilets, tea ladies or the employee canteen are as good as possible. Don't give employees a reason to become dissatisfied. This includes making sure that you don't treat foreign staff too obviously different from Chinese staff and letting employees see that there are opportunities for advancement within the company, perhaps by promoting a good worker from the production line to a supervisory or staff position quite early in the start-up of a company. You'll never entirely stop the loss of employees to other companies, but you can reduce it by looking after employees and respecting them and their problems.

Loans, Grants & Incentives

There are no grants available from the national government to foreigners wishing to start a business in China, but this doesn't mean that there's no financial help. There may be funding available from an organisation in your home country; for example, British citizens should check out UK Trade & Investment (🖥 ukti.gov.uk) and visit the UK government's Business Link website (🖥 businesslink.gov.uk) for the latest information.

A more likely source of assistance is the various incentives that are available from provinces or cities outside the 'big four' of Beijing, Guangzhou, Shanghai and Shenzhen. The Chinese are keen to spread the influence of foreign money to areas where industry is more limited, and many 'Inner China' cities and provinces offer considerable inducements, ranging from exemption from local taxation for a period to cheap labour and other benefits.

Loans are usually only obtainable from registered banks. There are a surprising number of unofficial sources of funds from private investors, but these are regularly closed down by the authorities for being illegal. There are no building societies or long-established investment banks in China. Most banks require security for any loan they make, usually a lien on land or a building, although in exceptional circumstances another asset might be considered.

Premises

Every city has office space to let and many have ready-built factory buildings available. Those in areas away from the 'big four' cities are considerably cheaper to lease or rent, and may even include an initial rent-free period if they're owned by the local government. Offices can be rented either empty or fully equipped and serviced. Many cities have office blocks known as business centres where, for a fixed fee, you can rent an office complete with telephone, broadband and even a receptionist. Additional items such as office machinery are available to rent or may be located in a central office for use by everyone in the building.

☑ SURVIVAL TIP

Don't try to save money by renting sub-standard office space. The Chinese appreciate 'front' and they won't respect you if your office doesn't look like that of a prosperous concern.

Working from home is possible, and there's nothing to stop you using the services of a nearby business centre (often in a hotel) for faxing and printing, but no matter how small your business, it must be registered and you must have a 'Z' visa in order to work in China.

Professional Advice

No matter what type of business you propose setting up, you'll need professional advice, whether it's straightforward help with interpreting or translation, an accountant to help sort out taxation, a lawyer to review contracts, or an architect or town planner to advise on any problems associated with establishing an office or factory. If you have a Chinese partner, you should seek his advice regarding professional advisors and also contact the nearest Chamber of Commerce associated with your home country. Doing business in China is likely to be very different from your homeland and the more contacts you have the better.

Marketing & Advertising

The extent of your marketing depends on your proposed customer base. If your customer base will consist solely of other expatriates, then the local free expat magazines are the best places to advertise your business. However, if you want to attract the Chinese you must promote yourself through the Chinese media, such as newspapers, radio and television. SMS (text) advertising and flyers distributed by hand or via local newspapers are also popular. Bear in mind that spreading your (hopefully excellent) reputation by word-of-mouth is one of the best marketing tools in China, and that an event such as a banquet to entertain business associates will be appreciated much more than an expensive TV promotion.

BUSINESS ETHICS

Loss of Face

The Chinese aren't remotely as sensitive on this issue as the Japanese but, none the less, to make a Chinese feel a loss of face (i.e. loss of dignity or reputation, humiliation) is a serious error and should be avoided at all costs. You can also give someone face, for example by supporting their suggestion or praising something that they say or do, which is just as important as avoiding openly disagreeing with someone. You should never make someone feel small, especially in front of others and avoid teasing as it's too easily misunderstood.

Losing your temper or forgetting your manners is even worse, as not only does the person on the

receiving end of your outburst lose face, but you will also in the eyes of any Chinese witnesses. If you feel that it's necessary to speak negatively or correct a member of your staff, you should ensure that you're alone with him when you do so and that no one can overhear or witness your conversation.

Formality

The Chinese like to follow a set and known procedure, whether it's the way in which a conference is conducted or even the way that people address each other at work. Thus for conferences you'll find that they're rarely held one-to-one, but are usually major meetings to which everyone remotely involved is invited. They're usually set around a large table, possibly with flowers in the middle, with each place indicated by a fresh note pad, a sharpened pencil and a teacup. The two opposing negotiating teams sit opposite one another, with the leaders seated centrally

The first item on the agenda is the inevitable exchange of business cards, which has its own customs and formality. You should always hand your card, Chinese face (and right way) up, to each person on the other team. It should be held with both hands (papers handed to others should also be handed with two hands) and presented as if it was an important document – which it is to the Chinese! When you're handed someone's card, you should read it and then lay it on the table in front of you, which is repeated with everyone's card; don't ignore any and don't immediately stuff them into you back trouser pocket and sit on them! At the end of the meeting, gather them together and store them carefully in your briefcase. People will smoke during the meeting and some will answer their mobile phones, but treating a business card with disrespect is something to be avoided if you're to be respected.

The two leaders will make introductory speeches for their side but thereafter the team members will do all the talking. Tea will be served throughout, but it's unlikely that any serious decisions will be made during the meeting, the purpose of which is to put forward each sides viewpoint and build relationships between the parties.

The Chinese expect meetings to be conducted in a manner that would be approved by Confucius. i.e. with the avoidance of open conflict, the maintenance of appropriate behaviour and the preservation of face. Trying to speed up a meeting or being too direct is not what's called for at most meetings. You must be patient and respectful.

At these meetings you'll almost certainly need to bring along an interpreter – your opposite number will have done the same. Using an interpreter is a skill and isn't easy, and should be practised and prepared for before a meeting. You must speak in short self-contained sentences and wait for the interpreter to translate each time. It's a lengthy and laborious business and it's advisable after the meeting has closed to have a review of what's been said with your interpreter, in order to ensure that he has correctly related what you said.

Over the days following the meeting ideas may get floated between the parties on an informal basis and the Chinese may well suggest a compromise, whereby rather that accept either party's position, it might be possible to find a middle way. After ideas have been exchanged in this informal way then, and then only, the principals of both parties may meet alone and quietly reach an agreement.

For business lunches or dinners (called banquets by the Chinese) the seating should also be arranged formally, although it's unlikely that much serious business will take place during the meal. Such banquets are often looked upon more as a reward for ploughing through a meeting rather than as an opportunity to continue work-related discussions. The principal guest should be seated at the head of the table facing the door into the dining room. The host should sit beside him and the guest and host teams should then be paired with their equals around the table, with the more senior people closest to the head of the table. Be prepared for round after round of toasts.

Guanxi

One of the first words of Chinese that you're liable to come across in the course of doing business in China is *guanxi* and the need for it, yet it's one of the words most misunderstood by Westerners, many of whom mistakenly think that it means bribery. It doesn't and translates literally as 'relationships' or 'connections'. Wikipedia correctly describes it as 'a personal connection between two people in which one is able to prevail upon another to perform a favour or service, or to be prevailed upon. The two people need not be of equal social status'. Therefore a business partner with a wide circle of contacts, some in positions that might be important to you, is someone with a lot of *guanxi* and would be a useful person to have as a partner.

Guanxi is very much a part of everyday life in China and many people there work to build up a wide network of friendly relationships with members of their extended family, school friends, people from university, workmates and others who share their interests (such as golf or tennis club contacts) in the knowledge that, at some time in the future, there could be an occasion when their help may be of assistance. Of course, this works both ways and it crosses all social boundaries. Money doesn't come into it. Someone is asked for help to influence a third party because of their relationship with them, not by giving them money or extravagant gifts – that would be bribery and not *guanxi*.

Gifts

Since the days of the earliest Chinese emperors, the giving of gifts to people who might be of importance to you has been a common practice, and it still occurs today. However, it's a practice that must be used, if it's to be used at all, with care. And, of course, it works both ways – people

may try to press gifts onto you with the aim of influencing you.

If you feel that it would help to create a friendly relationship by giving a gift, you should make sure that it's something thoughtful, preferably something from and typical of your home country, or perhaps a not too expensive pen with your company's name on it or a bottle of wine. It doesn't need to be a Montblanc pen or a vintage bottle of claret, but something that you would appreciate receiving (so don't be stingy either). It should be wrapped – preferably in red paper (avoid either black or white) – and if possible let others see you give it. This will give the receiver face and also ensure that it's open and above board and won't be misconstrued as a bribe. (Don't be surprised if later you receive a gift in return.) For this reason, many companies have a policy of declaring and pooling all gifts received by employees at every level, although employees should be able to keep a small personal gift given in good faith. Keeping things out in the open also helps to avoid accusations arising of any untoward influence.

WORKING ILLEGALLY

China is still a cash-based economy – many employees are paid in cash and don't have bank accounts – but this is changing, and as a foreigner you may be under closer scrutiny. As soon as you're earning over 4,800 RMB a month or 57,600 RMB a year, you're required to declare your income and pay income tax.

While there are opportunities to work 'under the radar', maybe doing a little modelling for a clothes manufacturer or posing as a foreign businessman to help colleagues impress their competitors, if the authorities get a whiff that you're working without the correct visa they'll come down on you hard. The majority of illegal workers are from other Asian countries, labouring away in sweatshops and on building sites, and if caught they're deported. However, just because

you're a Westerner, don't imagine that the same won't happen to you.

LANGUAGE

The majority of expatriates who move to China cannot speak Chinese. Most never master the complexities of Chinese characters, but many learn how to read pinyin and you should make this a priority. Pinyin is the direct transliteration of Chinese characters into a Roman or Latin script, i.e. the same alphabet used in the English language. It provides a relatively simple way of pronouncing Chinese as the Chinese speak it.

Pinyin is a phonetic transliteration in that letters are pronounced exactly the same, and this follows the English pronunciation with a few exceptions (see box). There are no words with irregular pronunciation to trip you up, such as 'cough' or 'dough' in English. Note that it's designed to help foreigners and most Chinese don't understand it, so there's no point in leaving a note for your cleaner in pinyin because she won't be able to read it.

Pronouncing Pinyin	
Letters you need to be aware of are:	
Letter	Sound
C	like 'ts' in hats
Q	like 'ch' in cheese
R	like the 'r' in *bourgeois*
X	like 'sh' in shine
Z	like 'ds' in buds
Zh	pronounced like the letter J

The only irregularity is the letter 'I', which sounds like the 'ee' in bee unless it follows c, ch, r, s, sh, z or zh, in which case it's pronounced like the 'er' in mutter.

Chinese is expressed in pinyin in situations where foreigners may need it, such as road signs. You can practise your pronunciation by reading them out loud. You may need to break the words down into syllables – thus Wangfujingnandajie, the main shopping street in Beijing, is pronounced wang-fu-jing-nan-da-ji-er – but keep practising and you'll quickly master the basics of speaking Chinese, even if you never learn to read it. A good dictionary is essential and you should buy one which includes pinyin. The *Times Essential English Chinese Dictionary* is excellent, but you'll probably need to buy a copy before you arrive as good dictionaries that include pinyin are difficult to find in China.

Mastering pinyin is the key to learning 'survival' Chinese and this should be enough, as most expats don't need to be fluent. You can get by at first with a small vocabulary, but this will increase as you learn more about the country and its people, and your ears tune in to the different dialects.

Although there are many different languages in China, including Wu which is spoken in some of the east coast cities and Cantonese (*Yue*) which is spoken in the south (and Hong Kong), the official national language is *Putonghua*, known in the West as Mandarin, which is understood throughout most of the country. Pinyin is based on *Putonghua*. Very few foreigners learn to read and write *Putonghua*, which is a test even for the Chinese as it consists of some 50,000 characters. Even educated people may know only between 3,500 and 5,000 characters, and this number is sufficient for most everyday purposes.

As you become more accustomed to seeing Chinese script, you'll start to recognise certain characters, such as those for 'Men' and 'Women' on toilet doors and the signs for 'Entrance' and 'Exit'.

Numbers are much easier. They're usually written in figures, as they are in the West. One exception to this is the doors in school classrooms, which are numbered in Chinese characters in an effort to teach children the right way to write them.

For more information about learning Chinese, see **Learning Chinese** on page 120.

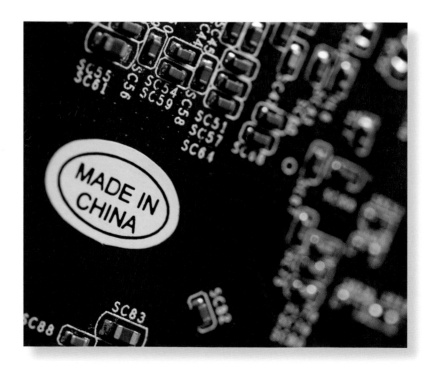

2.

EMPLOYMENT CONDITIONS

E mployment law is still in its infancy in China, but there's legal protection for employees, both Chinese and foreign, and it's as well to know what it covers. The Labour Contract Law was introduced in January 2008 to ensure better protection for workers and to tackle a growing number of labour disputes which were threatening the country's economic growth. The law was brought in not only to regulate Chinese employers but also overseas companies, some of which had located in China to take advantage of a large and eager workforce which could be easily hired and fired. Large organisations cannot ignore it – indeed, some have now moved their operations to other Asian countries with fewer regulations – but smaller employers may still try to bend the rules to their advantage.

The labour law includes provisions to limit the working week, ensure holiday entitlements, protect employees against unfair dismissal or the withholding of wages – a common problem in China – provide arbitration in disputes, ensure social security contributions are made and improve safety in the workplace.

How much you're covered by Chinese law depends on who you're working for. If you're seconded by an overseas organisation, the laws of your home country may apply. The Chinese government has no specific conditions of employment which apply purely to foreign employees other than those foreign expatriates working as teachers in State schools and universities. If you're working for any other Chinese employer, you should be covered – at the very least – by the basic Chinese employment law outlined in this chapter.

EMPLOYMENT CONTRACTS

The backbone of the labour law is the employment contract. This may be a collective contract negotiated with a union and covering all employees, or an individual contract between an employer and employee. It sets out the responsibilities, rights and duties of both employer and employee.

Contracts differ according to the job – a teaching contract will be different from one for an engineer employed in the construction industry – but all must include the following details:

♦ the employer's name and address;

♦ the employee's name and address;

♦ the nature of the job (but not a job title);

♦ the commencement date of employment;

♦ the duration of employment;

♦ any provisions for extending the contract, if applicable;

♦ terms for dismissal or resignation;

♦ rules regarding disciplinary action or dispute resolution.

Standard individual contracts don't have to cover such areas as your salary, benefits, holiday or other leave, sickness or notice periods, so there are no legal guarantees that you'll receive these benefits and you'll have little recourse to a fair resolution if you don't. Don't expect employers to be generous in China (or anywhere else for that matter). Even if you've been with them for years, they'll try to employ you as cheaply as possible and with as few extra benefits as they can. Employers don't see this as unfair; it's simply good business.

Employees of a foreign invested enterprise (FIE) should have better protection as they're obliged to keep records for their employees – Chinese and foreign – stating such provisions as salary, leave entitlement, and probationary and notice periods.

Note that in China, contracts are invariably for full-time jobs. Part-time and temporary work exists, but workers who are paid hourly have little or no legal protection. Should you find yourself working part-time alongside your main job – and your employer allows it – it's unlikely you would sign a contract to do so. Modelling clothes or teaching in your spare time at a crammer is likely to be for a few hours, cash in hand, and no redress if you're no longer required.

The main types of contract you're likely to sign in China are as follows:

♦ **Overseas-based employer or joint venture with a Chinese partner**: contracts are usually for one year. Each company or organisation will have its own unique employment contract which may include additional benefits, such as the provision of accommodation, utilities, holiday flights and a relocation package (see below).

♦ **Chinese employer**: organisations such as the *China Daily* newspaper or one of the radio or television companies would probably offer a contract that mirrors those of their Chinese employees, e.g. a trial period of two months followed by a temporary contract for six months.

♦ **Chinese schools & universities**: most use a standard form of contract published by the State Administration of Foreign Experts Affairs (SAFEA). Contracts are usually for one or two semesters or terms (Chinese schools have two semesters a year).

Even if you have a contract in black and white, your employer may try to wriggle out of it or take advantage of any conditions that aren't clearly stated. Sadly, this is more likely if you're employed by a Chinese organisation or teaching establishment. Some teachers have arrived at their school to find their wages are lower than stated, their accommodation is a gloomy dormitory, and their employer is unwilling to refund their air fare or even assist with obtaining a work visa. The best way to ensure that a school honours its promises is to contact other teachers. Forums such as the one on Dave's

ESL Café (⌨ eslcafe.com) are a good place to do this.

> ## ☑ SURVIVAL TIP
>
> Check your contract carefully to ensure it includes the details you agreed with your employer, e.g. the dates and time you'll be employed for, and that the name of the employer is correct. If you think you work for Joe Bloggs Ltd. and the contract states your employer as Joe Bloggs (China) Ltd, take care, as this could seriously affect your employment rights and your pension.

TERMS OF EMPLOYMENT

The following sections cover the main terms of employment which may or may not be covered in your employment contract.

Relocation & Travel Expenses

Most foreign workers travel to China with a job already arranged. Major overseas employers usually offer a generous relocation package, and even schools and universities provide funding towards your airfare if they recruit you from abroad.

Overseas organisations generally make your travel arrangements for you, providing tickets to and from China for you and your family; if you're very senior, these may be business class. They should also pay for your visas. Time you spend travelling to your new work location in China and home again should be paid as working time at your basic salary, less any overseas and local allowances (see below), and employers usually cover the cost of public transport to and from airports. On arrival they should send a car to collect you. If you already live in China, your employer may offer to pay your domestic relocation costs by plane or train, but you probably need to ask first.

Less generous employers may require you to pay for your flight and provide an interest-free loan. This should be written off over the first year of the contract unless your employment is terminated early, e.g. at your request or due to a misdemeanour, in which case you're liable to pay for the remaining portion of the fare.

Most schools and universities fund an economy single ticket from your home country to China if you're signing up for a single semester – it's your responsibility to find another job or get yourself home – or a return economy ticket if you're signing up for two semesters, i.e. a year. Even if you're taken on while already in China, you may be able to negotiate assistance with air fares.

Accommodation

If you're moving to China to work for an overseas employer, accommodation will almost certainly be part of the deal. This is usually an apartment – only top executives warrant a villa – in a modern block within reasonable distance of your workplace. Apartments are usually fully furnished and equipped, so it's highly unlikely your new boss with pay for you to ship in your three-piece suite or washing machine from home, although most should fund a reasonable amount of excess baggage. You're expected to maintain your apartment in good condition, e.g. not rip up the carpets or paint it bright orange. As a bonus, your employer normally pays for utilities, e.g. electricity, water and gas, and also pays your telephone (excluding overseas calls) and broadband bills.

If you're already living in China then you're unlikely to be offered a free furnished apartment, although you may be able to negotiate a contribution towards your rent if you're moving to a location where rental costs are much higher, e.g. from Xi'an to Beijing. This will depend on how keen an employer is to hire you.

Almost all universities and many schools provide accommodation for teachers within their campus grounds, where teachers are expected to live (both foreign and Chinese). Many Chinese teachers are allowed to retain their apartment after they retire and continue living there until they die. Some teachers' apartments are old and scruffy while others are modern and smart. All are fully furnished and have cooking facilities, a fridge, even a TV and computer with internet access – which you'll need when planning your lessons – plus heating and/or air-conditioning. Like overseas employers, schools cover the cost of your utility

bills and even your internet connection (but not overseas phone calls). You can also make use of on-campus facilities such as tennis courts or croquet 'greens' (usually sand!) in your spare time.

Local Transport

Most employers expect you to travel to the office at your own expense, particularly if your remuneration includes a local living allowance, and company cars are rare. Some of the larger organisations have them, but they're usually fleet cars with Chinese drivers and can only be used for company business. There are advantages to this: you don't have to learn to cope with the Chinese style of driving on Chinese roads – unless you want to – and it saves you the hassle of trying to find somewhere to park, which can be a nightmare in cities such as Beijing.

Many schools and universities located outside city or town centres have a school mini bus that provides transport to the main shopping areas at weekends. Expat teachers often buy a cheap bicycle for getting around the campus and local area.

Salaries & Benefits

Most full-time workers in China are paid monthly, just after the end of the month. In many organisations your salary is paid directly into your Chinese bank account. However, China is very much a cash society and a surprising number of employers prefer to pay their staff in cash. If you work for a Chinese employer, you may have to visit the cash office to collect your salary and don't be surprised if it's counted out, note by note, in front of your co-workers. This is embarrassing if you're paid more than they are and receive a much thicker bundle of notes, as often happens in China.

If your earnings render you liable for Chinese income tax – in 2012 income tax was levied on income of over 4,800 RMB a month or 57,600 RMB a year – tax will be deducted by your employer before you're paid. You should receive details of this on a pay slip. Currently there are no deductions for Chinese social security, which doesn't apply to foreigners, although this may change in the future (see **Chapter 13**).

Overseas Organisations

If you work for a foreign company or joint venture, you may receive your salary in three separate payments:

◆ **Basic salary**: this will be paid to your bank account. If you've been seconded from home, it may be paid in your home country's currency and into your home bank account.

♦ **An overseas (or hardship) allowance**: this is to compensate you for the 'traumas' of living away from home. It will quite likely only be paid if you've been seconded from home, i.e. not if you were taken on while already living in China, and may also be paid directly into your home bank account. You won't receive this extra payment when you're on home leave.

♦ **A local living allowance**: this covers incidental living expenses and is usually paid in Chinese currency as a monthly cash payment. Again, it isn't paid when you're on home leave.

Schools & Universities

Expatriate teachers are usually paid in cash each month, like their Chinese colleagues, although they usually earn quite a bit more. Wages are paid for the ten months that you work, so if you earn 4,000 RMB a month it works out at 40,000 RMB a year, and you need to set some aside for holiday periods.

Holiday Money

University teachers are frequently offered a local 'travel allowance' in addition to their salary – anything from 2,000 to 5,000 RMB – paid in two instalments, one at the end of each semester. The organisation expects you to use it to fund a sightseeing tour of China and better familiarise yourself with the country's culture and heritage, but you can blow it on beer if you wish. Some schools offer a similar perk.

Working Hours & Overtime

The Western concept of the working week is now the norm. Most people work from Monday to Friday and have a two-day weekend. Chinese labour laws set the official maximum working hours at 44 a week and many Chinese employees officially work a 40-hour week, although many put in considerable overtime, often unpaid, for the good of the company and to ensure that they keep their jobs. This industrious attitude is a major reason why China's economy has taken off with such energy. Generally foreigners are also expected to work overtime, if necessary, often without payment.

Your working hours will depend largely on the sector in which you're employed, as shown below for selected industries.

Retail & Construction

In these sectors, there's often a requirement to work at weekends and during holidays. Shops are always open during holiday periods to take advantage of the increased trade, while construction projects almost never cease, particularly during the summer. Chinese manual workers and shop assistants are paid higher rates for overtime or working during public holidays, but not many foreigners do unless it's stated in their job contract, in which case you may be paid for overtime or, more usually, get time off in lieu.

In industries where overtime and weekend working is standard, your contract will probably specify a normal total number of hours per week – on construction sites this could be as many as 60 hours – and an appropriate way of compensating the employee for working in excess of these. Foreign construction staff are expected to work the same hours as Chinese manual workers.

Office Staff

Most office workers put in 40 hours a week, working eight hours a day from Monday to Friday between the hours of 8.30am and 6.30pm. Flexi-time is rare, although in 2010 the Beijing authorities, in an effort to reduce (or spread) the rush hours, ordained that all government personnel would start and finish half an hour later. Lunch breaks at overseas organisations are usually an hour, but some Chinese companies take much longer breaks, up to three hours – from midday until 2.30 or 3pm isn't uncommon – and make up their hours earlier or later in the day. Many workplaces have an in-house canteen, but it's more common for staff to eat at a nearby small restaurant; sandwich bars are almost non-existent.

Teachers

The school year comprises two semesters (terms), the first one from September to late January, the second from March to June. Both schools and universities hold their classes principally on weekdays, with expatriate teachers teaching 14 to 16 hours of classes each week, usually between 8am and midday and again between 3 and 6pm. There may occasionally also be classes later in the evening, perhaps until 9pm.

Classes are usually of one or two hours' duration and start promptly on the hour, although the actual teaching time is 50 minutes as there's a ten-minute break at the end of the hour to allow students (and teachers) to move from classroom to classroom, use the toilet or grab a drink.

A 16-hour working week doesn't sound much but there's a lot more work to do outside the classroom. Teachers are expected to prepare their lessons to designated curricula using 'teachers' versions' of the specified books provided by the school, to design and set any tests required, and to mark these in their 'spare' time. A conscientious teacher will spend a total of 25 to 30 hours a week on school-related work. Apart from lessons, teachers may find themselves asked to help, or join in, at impromptu basketball sessions or other exercise activities during meal breaks or spare periods.

Holidays & Leave

This section covers annual and public holidays, and also time off for other reasons, e.g. illness.

Public Holidays

China has seven national public holidays (listed in the table below), although there are a surprising number of other holidays that are celebrated in specific regions or only by certain sections of the community. Whether or not you get the day off depends on your job sector.

Employees of overseas governments, such as embassy staff, are fortunate in that they can take time off on their home country's national holidays as well as most Chinese public holidays – they take several days off during Chinese New Year or Spring Festival, but not the full 15. Employees of Chinese organisations get time off for public holidays, while those working for foreign non-government organisations (NGOs) and businesses may even be required to work on these days in return for substitute days off (some foreign joint ventures in the retail, construction or mining industries are open 365 days a year).

Teachers don't work on Chinese public holidays, although they may be required to work at weekends to minimise loss of teaching time if a holiday falls midweek. They also get time off on Teachers' Day (*Zhaoshi Jie*, 15th September). Some expatriate teachers get an extra one or two days' holiday at Christmas and/or Thanksgiving, but only if it's specified in their contract; otherwise these days are treated as normal working days.

If a public holiday falls on a weekend, it isn't the custom for Chinese to take an extra day off in the week. In fact they often work during weekends before and after public holidays to make up for the lost time!

Some public holidays in China are on a fixed calendar date, e.g. New Year's Day, but others depend on the lunar calendar and fall on a different day each year. For a full list of public holidays, see the table below

Chinese National Public Holidays	
Date	**Holiday**
1st January	New Year's Day (*Yuan Dan*)
Late January/February	*Chinese New Year and Spring Festival (*Chun Jie*)
5th April	Tomb Sweeping Day (*Qing Ming Jie*). Families visit their ancestors' graves and tidy them, leaving 'gifts' for the departed and setting off firecrackers
1st May	Labour Day (*Wu yi guoji lao dong jie*) – a three-day holiday
June/July	*Dragon Boat Festival (*Duanwu Jie*) – a three-day holiday
September/October	*Mid-Autumn Festival (*Zhongqiu Jie*). Celebrated with moon cakes with the family but not usually with time off work.
1st October	National Day (*Guoqing Jie*). Celebrates the founding of the People's Republic of China and extended to a full week's holiday in 2012.

* The actual date of the holiday depends on the lunar calendar.

If you work in certain provinces, you may also get time off on local holidays, e.g. Water Splashing Day which takes place in mid-April in Yunnan province (prepare to get very wet!) or Confucius' birthday on April 28th which has special significance in Shandong province.

The Chinese are beginning to adopt some Western holidays, such as Valentine's Day and even Christmas Day which is an excuse to hang coloured lanterns and for people to buy gifts for the family from shop staff wearing Santa hats. That said, 99 per cent of the population works on Christmas Day as well as Boxing Day, and Easter is only celebrated by Chinese Christians.

By far the most important festival is Chinese New Year/Spring Festival. This 15-day holiday is the highlight of the year and, for migrant workers, is sometimes the only holiday they get each year and their one chance to see their families. As a result, roads are chaotic and public transport is absolutely choked at the start and end of this break, a time known as *Chunyun*. Unless you're Chinese, it's advisable to spend this time at home.

Annual Leave

Although the Chinese get about ten days of public holidays (not including weekends) a year, the amount of annual leave is comparatively limited and often depends on how long they've worked for their employer. Some Chinese government departments give no annual holiday at all to staff until they have worked for five years, after which they get five days holiday a year, increasing by an extra day each subsequent year. Thus a foreigner working for a Chinese organisation will have to negotiate hard with their employer to secure any leave entitlement and is unlikely to get much leave other than public holidays.

Foreign employees of overseas governments, NGOs or business organisations are usually employed on a one-year contract with a block of annual leave. Single people are offered three

weeks after completing 23 weeks of work, while those who've brought their families to China get a six-week break after 46 weeks of work. It's assumed they'll return home and flight tickets are usually provided. Employers usually ask for a month's notice of any planned home leave. No local allowance or 'hardship' payments are paid during this time.

Teachers who sign up for just a single semester get no paid leave, other than public holidays, but those who sign up for two semesters are paid for the long winter vacation, which runs from late January to the beginning of March.

Sick Leave

Although employees' benefits are limited, there's a Chinese system of sick pay for employees who've served sufficient time with their employer. However, this generally only applies to employees who are covered by a collective contract; individual contracts don't have to specify your sickness entitlement. If you're working for a large foreign organisation, some sort of medical insurance should be included in your package, and you should ensure that your entitlement to certain types of leave, in particular sick leave, is fully detailed in your contract so that you receive payment, as well as medical care, if you fall ill.

Teachers can attend a campus clinic and you should always report to the doctor or nurse if you're too unwell to attend lessons. If you have a valid reason then (hopefully) your boss won't dock your wages for not teaching while ill.

Other Leave

Chinese labour law has a provision for maternity leave (but not paternity leave) although this only applies if you're Chinese and within the country's social insurance system. There's no such thing as parental leave – the grandparents are on hand to do any child-minding – or compassionate leave.

Insurance & Pensions

Anyone relocating to China with a large organisation should have a good health insurance policy included in their package, although it's advisable to check exactly what you're covered for, if there's any excess, and whether you must pay for treatment and reclaim the cost later. Many policies insist you use expensive international hospitals and clinics. Such cover is unlikely with a Chinese employer and you should invest in your own health insurance policy – see **Chapter 13** – or put your trust in the Chinese health system. At the very least, you should have a travel policy which covers repatriation in a medical emergency.

If you're injured or killed at work your employer may be obliged to pay out compensation to you/your family, but it will be nowhere near the huge sums paid out in the West.

Teachers, too, must look after themselves. Many schools and universities carry no health or work accident insurance for foreign staff. Indeed, their contracts may require you to take out a personal accident insurance policy (they won't check) and if an accident occurs they'll do their level best to avoid being held liable.

Pensions are a tricky area. Foreigners don't, as yet, pay Chinese social security contributions so you won't be able to pay into a Chinese pension fund. And China doesn't have social security agreements with other countries such as the UK or US. So your only option is to start or maintain payments to a private pension fund or your home country's state pension fund. If the company you work for in China is a special company, set up solely to oversee operations in China, it may not be able to provide continuity for your existing company pension arrangements. You should consult an independent financial advisor to ensure that you don't lose out. Chinese employers, including schools, don't offer foreign staff any pension benefits and expect you to take care of this yourself.

Probationary Periods, Notice & Contract Termination

Probationary periods are generally set by regional governments and can be as short as two weeks or as long as six months, depending on the length of your job contract. Officially, it's necessary to give 30 days' notice to terminate a contract, although this can also be by mutual consent. An employee can be dismissed for any number of reasons, e.g. discipline, incompetence, unauthorised absence or because the employer faces bankruptcy, and dismissed employees should receive a month's severance pay. However, these areas are rarely covered by a basic individual contract and you'll have to negotiate them yourself.

Education & Training

A number of overseas governments, NGOs and business organisations offer free or discounted Chinese lessons to new employees, as do some schools and universities. These are worth taking advantage of as they offer a chance to master the basics of *Putonghua* (Mandarin) at your employer's expense.

Unions

Although there's quite a lot of trade union representation in China, membership isn't open to foreigners. For more information about unions, see page 33.

Other Terms

There are a few terms which are often included in Chinese work contracts that you may not have encountered before, some of which are outlined below.

Religion & Politics

Most foreigners' contracts contain clauses specifically forbidding interference in religious or political affairs in China and requiring expatriate staff to show respect for Chinese morals and customs.

Medical Examinations

The Chinese are keen that foreign staff are in good health and, especially, that they don't have any major sexually-transmitted diseases – this is a sensitive subject in China. Thus it's a requirement for all state-owned businesses or facilities such as schools or universities to ensure that foreign passport holders have an annual (or bi-annual) check-up at a medical centre designated by the Public Security Bureau (PSB). This may even be a condition of issuing your work (Z) visa. Your employer will arrange this and receive a copy of the medical report (you won't see it). Medical examinations are thorough – expect to spend at least an hour with the doctor – and include a chest x-ray and blood tests.

⚠ Caution

If medical tests reveal you to have a serious sexually-transmitted disease, such as syphilis or HIV/AIDs, your employer is obliged to report this to the local PSB. You're likely to be taken under police escort to the nearest international airport and deported!

Restrictions on Second Jobs

Most employers forbid you to work for anyone else in your spare time. This doesn't mean you cannot act as a referee at an amateur football game at the weekend, but it would be wise to mention it to management. The same applies to any voluntary work. Many teachers' contracts leave this possibility open and you may be able to teach extra lessons, either privately or at a crammer, provided it doesn't interfere with your main teaching work and that you obtain permission first.

Discrimination

Although there are no laws preventing discrimination on the grounds of age or gender, discrimination isn't a major problem in China, where foreigners are usually judged on their abilities rather than their age or appearance – although some recruiters expect all English teachers to be blond and blue eyed. However, jobs are often advertised in a discriminatory manner, e.g. 'married man aged between 30 and 45 sought as manager' or 'attractive young lady required as personal assistant to CEO'. This is entirely legal and, to the Chinese, logical. A middle-aged family man is less likely to leave his position after a few months, while the boss will appreciate having a good-looking secretary. However, in a country where age is respected and women have genuine equality with men, being female or older isn't a disadvantage and there are lots of English teachers working in Chinese schools and universities while drawing an old age pension in their home country.

WORKING CONDITIONS

These can be similar to – or very different from – abroad. At a foreign government, NGO or business organisation you may find yourself in a smart new office, well designed and equipped with the latest technology. In the main cities your office surroundings may be no different from those in a Western city. Only in the less developed locations will you really notice a difference.

Teachers, however, are in for some culture shock. Chinese class sizes are large – generally not less than 45 students. Primary and middle school classes may have 70 or even 90 pupils, although the number drops to around 45 in high schools as some students leave to start work. Classes at universities usually number around 35 students. Despite the large class sizes, students are rarely disruptive; the vast majority want to learn and most students are respectful to teachers.

Classrooms and desks can be pretty basic; the worst-equipped schools are in rural areas. Universities usually have more modern rooms and often a computer monitor and keyboard on every desk. However, no matter how good the classrooms are, the toilets will be far from pleasant (see page 259).

It's unlikely that your work will be supervised to ensure that you're doing a good job; other teachers may join your classes but only out of curiosity. However, department heads will ask your students whether you're a good teacher so, in effect, you have the whole class monitoring your progress.

CHECKLISTS

When considering taking up employment in China the following checklists may prove useful.

Salary

♦ How much is my total salary and how is it made up, i.e. what allowances, if any are included?

♦ How much of the salary will be paid in my country's currency directly into my home bank account?

♦ What salary will I be paid during periods of home leave?

♦ Will I receive a 'travel allowance' at the end of the teaching year?

Relocation Expenses

♦ Will my flights be paid for?

♦ Are travel expenses between my home and the airport recoverable?

♦ Are days spent travelling to and from China paid as working days?

♦ If I resign before the end of my contract, will I have to pay back some of my air fare?

♦ Will the employer pay for excess baggage and if so how much can I bring?

Accommodation

♦ What accommodation is provided and how is it furnished/equipped?

♦ Who pays for utilities?

♦ Is my accommodation far from the workplace and, if so, what transport is available?

Working Hours

♦ What are the weekly working hours?

♦ Will I receive overtime payments or time off in lieu?

Holidays & Leave

♦ What is the annual leave entitlement?

♦ What are the paid public holidays?

◆ Is your airfare to travel home on holiday paid by your employer and, if applicable, does it include your family members?

Insurance

◆ What health insurance is included and what does it cover me for?

◆ Do I have to take out an insurance policy and if so, what will it cost?

◆ For how long will I be paid if I'm ill or incapacitated?

Pension

◆ Can I continue to contribute to my current company or private pension?

◆ Will my employer make contributions to a company pension?

◆ Should I set up a personal pension while in China?

Other Terms

◆ Does the employer offer free or subsidised lessons in Chinese?

◆ Is a company car provided? And is there free parking at my workplace?

◆ Are there any fringe benefits, such as free meals in a company or campus restaurant?

◆ Will I receive a list of my duties and responsibilities and a copy of the employment contract?

◆ In the case of a dispute, under which country's law will it be settled?

Employer

◆ Is the employer a foreign company operating in China, a Chinese private organisation or a government-run organisation?

◆ Is it a sound, i.e. long-established and profitable, organisation with a good reputation?

3.
PERMITS & VISAS

Citizens of almost every country require a valid passport and an appropriate visa in order to enter the People's Republic of China. The only exceptions are citizens of Hong Kong or Macau who can travel to and from mainland China using a Mainland Travel Permit (issued for a period of up to ten years), and citizens of Brunei, Japan, Singapore and San Marino who are allowed a visa-free stay of up to 15 days. All other nationals, including Americans, Australians, British and those from European Union (EU) member countries, must apply for a visa in advance.

▲ Caution

Don't attempt to visit China without a visa or in the hope of obtaining one on arrival. You'll be refused entry and sent home on the next available flight, which you'll have to pay for.

China is a remarkably homogeneous society – over 90 per cent of its population are Han Chinese – although it's still home to 56 ethnic minorities. However, there are comparatively few foreigners, and outside the major cities you can go months or even years without seeing another Western face.

For years, estimating the number of foreigners in China was difficult. However, the government claimed it included foreigners in its 2010 census and some more reliable figures have since emerged. A report in the *China Daily* based on the 2010 census revealed that the number of expatriates living in China for three months or more stood at 593,852, an insignificant number when compared with the country's 1.35bn plus population. Many were from neighbouring countries such as Japan, Korea and Myanmar, with Koreans providing the largest number of expats (120,750) in *China Daily*'s 'top ten' foreign populations. A surprising finding was that second place went to the Americans (71,493), although the numbers of other Western expats were much lower: 19,990 Canadians, 15,087 French, 14,446 Germans and 13,286 Australians (no figure was given for Britons).

The vast majority of expatriates live in one of the four major cities. The 2010 census revealed that Beijing was home to 91,128 expatriates in November 2010. Earlier reports had estimated the foreign population of Shanghai to be around 150,000 and that of Guangzhou just under 58,000. It's surprising that there hasn't been an earlier effort to calculate the overall foreign population. Since foreigners first started visiting China, the authorities have kept tabs on them through the Public Security Bureau (PSB) which operates a system of registration for foreign residents, and visas have been pretty much universal.

The visa system is fairly simple if strict, but there's no reason why most foreigners shouldn't be granted a visa to visit or – provided they have valid employment or sufficient funds – to work in China.

The information in this chapter is intended as a guide only, as the rules and regulations regarding visas are subject to change. It's important to check the latest regulations with a Chinese mission or visa agent before applying. A list of embassies and consulates is included in **Appendix A**.

Chinese citizens face equally stringent visa requirements when travelling to other parts of the world, including the EU and US. Unless they live in Guangdong province, they even need a visa to visit Hong Kong or Macau, even though these destinations are Special Administrative Regions of China.

IMMIGRATION ISSUES

Until the latter part of the 20th century, China was effectively closed to outsiders, so the issue of immigration is a fairly recent one. The country hasn't been seen as an enticing destination for economic migrants, and the Chinese have been more concerned by the problems of internal migration as country dwellers move to the cities in search of work, putting increasing strain on the wealthier eastern provinces. However, its recent economic growth is changing this, and China is now drafting immigration laws to cope with an increasing influx of foreigners. Some foreigners are economic migrants – Guangzhou has an emerging African community – but many more are Westerners keen to get involved in and profit from the Chinese boom.

For the majority of Chinese, immigration into China by people of other nationalities is a non-subject. It doesn't even occur to most that anyone from the West would want to immigrate to China. They have, after all, been emigrating abroad since the 19th century, to Australasia, the Americas and, later, Europe, in search of a better life. However, some foreign nationals, such as Vietnamese and Africans, do view China as a desirable destination, although they find visas difficult to come by and many enter illegally, only to be deported once discovered.

China has a huge pool of unskilled labour that will snap up any job, no matter how unpleasant or boring. This attitude is only just beginning to change as the repercussions of the one-child policy begin to bite and the population grows older, but for the present there's no pressing need for immigrants and the only non-Chinese who are welcomed are those who bring skills and talents that benefit the country.

The Chinese don't look upon expatriates from the West as competition for jobs that they might otherwise have; they think of them as a race apart, neither more nor less clever, but different, and able to do things that the Chinese cannot

do – yet (just give them time!). They respect most Westerners for the particular knowledge and skills they can learn from them, but they don't kow-tow to them or regard them as in any way superior.

VISAS

With few exceptions, every foreigner who wants to visit China must first obtain a visa before arriving in the country. The type of visa depends on the reason for your visit, whether a holiday or business trip or a period of residence. There are some general points to consider:

♦ There are five main types of visa: visitor/tourist, short-term business/study, long-term study, work and permanent residence. See the box below for the full range of visas.

♦ Visas can be issued for 30, 60 or 90 days or for six months, a year or, occasionally, two years. They may be single, double or multiple entry. Tourist visas are normally issued for 30 days with provision for a single entry but you can request a longer stay and should be able to get your visa extended or even changed at an office of the PSB.

♦ All visas require you to enter the country within three months of the issue. Delay and you must re-apply.

♦ Visas are subject to fees and these differ according to your nationality. See page 55 for more information on fees.

♦ Processing times are around four working days (i.e. not including weekends or holidays) or three if you pay extra. It's also possible to speed up the process by visiting certain

Visa Types	
Type	Applies to
C	Crew members of aircraft, trains and ships temporarily in china.
D	People wishing to take up permanent residence.
F	Business, lectures, cultural/scientific exchanges and short-term study of less than six months.
G	People transiting china on a stopover lasting more than 24 hours. If the stopover is less than 24 hours and you don't leave the airport, you don't need a transit visa.
J1	Foreign correspondents on long-term assignments.
J2	Foreign correspondents for a specific short-term event or a one-off news story.
	Tourists and people on family visits.
X	Students wishing to study for longer than six months.
Z	Anyone planning to work in china, and their family. You must usually have a firm offer of employment in China to obtain a Z visa.

embassies and consulates, in particular the Ministry of Foreign Affairs of the PRC in Wanchai, Hong Kong (💻 fmcoprc.gov.hk/eng). If you're applying by post, you need to allow extra time for postage. For security, it's best to use a registered or 'signed for' postal service.

Visas consist of a pale green form glued into and occupying a full page of your passport. The type, e.g. L, is indicated at the top of the form with details of the period of validity, which starts from the date of entry into China and not from the date of issue of the visa.

Applications

Visas can be obtained from embassies and consulates of the People's Republic of China or through an agent. Many agents offer this service, including Chinese Visa Direct (💻 chinesevisadirect.co.uk) and Rapid Visas (💻 rapid-visas.co.uk), but it's easy enough (and cheaper) to apply yourself.

First you need an application form. This is a simple document, which you can obtain from a Chinese mission or download from a mission website. It asks the usual questions, such as name, marital status and date/place of birth, as well as your occupation.

The form is used for all visa applications and there's a section which asks for the purpose of your visit, e.g. tourism, visiting friends, study or employment. Note that when providing details of your intended trip, it's advisable to avoid mentioning either Tibet or Xinjiang, even if you plan to go there, as these provinces are sensitive and reference to them could result in a delay in the issue of a visa or even its refusal. If you wish to visit Tibet, you'll need a special permit and must arrange this once you're in China.

If you're applying to work or study in China you must complete an additional form giving details of your employer/school, education and qualifications. This form is also required if you're making an application outside your home country, e.g. applying at the Chinese embassy in Bangkok during a tour of Southeast Asia.

Once you've completed all the forms – in block capitals – deliver or mail them to the nearest embassy or consulate. In some countries, such as the UK, applications are handled by an outside agency and you can apply by post, in which case you must print out and complete a declaration and a payment authorisation form so that your fee can be deducted from a debit or credit card. In other countries you must apply in person and may need to pay in cash.

As well as the forms, you must provide any other relevant documentation (see below), a colour, passport sized (30 x 40mm) photograph taken against a white background, and your passport. Your passport must be valid for a minimum of six months beyond the expiry date of the visa.

It may be necessary to have certain supporting documents translated into Chinese by an official interpreter, particularly if they're unusual or aren't in English. Your nearest Chinese mission should offer an interpretation and certification service.

If you work in the media and plan to do anything media-related in China, you must apply for a J1 or J2 visa. It isn't permitted to work without one, even on a casual basis. If you're just visiting or plan to teach but have a media background, it's better not to admit this in the occupation box. The Chinese authorities often suspect the intentions of foreign media and may think you're trying to sneak into the country to write an exposé. Just describe yourself as something else, such as 'company employee'.

Tourist/Visit Visas (L)

If you're a tourist you're required to provide the addresses and phone numbers of the hotels where you'll be staying – or at least those where you have a reservation – and if staying with friends, give details of your host and who's funding your trip. The form also asks for your current employer/school and details of any insurance and illnesses.

It's important to note that you aren't permitted to work or study while holding an 'L' type visa. However, it's possible to change it to a work (Z) or study (X) visa, provided you fit the relative criteria, by visiting an office of the Public Security Bureau (PSB).

Short-term Business/Study Visas (F)

In the case of an F visa for a business trip or a short period of study, you must provide a letter of invitation from the organisation that you'll be visiting or a letter of admission to an educational establishment. Many foreigners claim that it's much easier to secure an F visa if you apply through an agency in Hong Kong.

Student Visas (X)

Students planning to study for more than six months must provide a letter of admission and a student application form, available from the school or from the Ministry of Education. You may also need a medical certificate. Note that you aren't permitted to work or do business with an X visa.

Work Visas (Z)

Employees must provide a letter of invitation from their employer or, even better, a copy of their contract of employment. If they're bringing their spouse and children or other dependents, they must also provide documents proving the relationship, such as marriage/birth certificates.

Permanent Residence Visa (D)

The key to obtaining this elusive visa is a letter of approval of your permanent residence in China, issued by the PSB office in the region where you plan to live. However, approval is usually only given to close relatives of Chinese citizens or to people who've made a large financial investment, or other major contribution, in China. Generally, applicants should have lived in China for at least five years and not left the country for more than 90 days a year. Possession of a 'D' visa is a stepping stone towards obtaining a permanent residence card (see page 56).

A useful contact for information about Chinese visas is the Chinese Visa Service Application Centre, e.g. 🖥 visaforchina.org.uk in the UK, which handles all UK applications at its centres in London and Manchester. It's possible to make an appointment online and to track your application via the website. The service's website also has downloadable forms and up to date information about visas and how to apply for them.

Multiple Entry Visas

A multiple entry visa is useful if you're planning a tour in Asia or have business to attend to in more than one country, but it doesn't necessarily mean that you can stay as long as you like. Some multiple entry visas have a clause which allows you to spend only 30 days in China at a time – fine if you're an area manager making flying visits to your Chinese base but no good if you're planning to spend six months or a year in the country. Most people with this type of visa simply fly down to Hong Kong (which still counts as leaving the country) for a day once a month. It's possible to obtain a multiple-entry visa without this qualification, which gives you more flexibility and saves the cost of popping in and out of China, so it's worth asking for this when you apply.

It's essential you don't overstay your visa period by even a day, as this will result in a large fine – 500 RMB (about £50 or US$80) for each day or part of the day that you're illegally in the country – and your visa will be cancelled, meaning you have go through the application process all over again – from outside China.

Visas for Hong Kong or Macau

Although both these ex-colonies are now Special Administrative Regions (SARs) of China, citizens of most Western countries including the UK and US can visit them without a visa – although this isn't an option for the mainland Chinese! Foreigners may also cross the border to the nearest city in mainland China – either Shenzhen from Hong Kong or Zhuhai from Macau – and stay for up to six days without a Chinese visa. However, they cannot otherwise enter mainland China without a visa, or apply for one while in Shenzhen/Zhuhai.

Hong Kong is also one of the easiest places to apply for a Chinese visa. The process is remarkably simple and quick. Most travel agents in Hong Kong can issue 30-day Tourist (L) visas, as can a number of the more upmarket hotels, but if you need a visa with a longer validity or a work or study visa, then the cheapest and best place to apply is usually the visa office at the Ministry of Foreign Affairs of the PRC, on the fifth floor of the Low Block at the China Resources Building, 26 Harbour Road, Wanchai. This office is open from 9am to 12.30pm and 2pm until 5pm on weekdays and until 12.30pm on Saturdays.

EXTENDING OR RENEWING YOUR VISA

Most visas can be extended or renewed in China at the local office of the Public Security Bureau (PSB). Tourist visas can usually be extended by a further 30 days and sometimes more than once. As a general rule, extending your visa in a city other than the big four of Beijing, Guangzhou, Shanghai or Shenzhen is less hassle. However, in all cases, you'll need to complete an application form and provide all the documentation once again, i.e. your passport, a photo (which can sometimes be taken at the PSB), proof that you're free from HIV/AIDS (if your renewal will extend your stay in China to more than six months) and current proof of your place of residence in China. Renewal at a PSB office usually takes a full working week and you must pay the current visa fee.

If you arrive in China with a tourist visa and want to work, it's usually possible to change your L visa for a Z visa. To do this, take your passport to the PSB together with all the necessary supporting documentation that you need to apply for a work visa (see page 54), plus a photo, medical evidence that you aren't HIV positive and proof of your registration of residence. In other words, you must apply again and pay for a new visa, but at least you don't have to leave China and apply from your home country. If all your paperwork is in order, your new visa will take around one working week to be issued.

Don't be tempted to work, even in a casual role, without first obtaining a Z visa. People may claim you can get away with not doing so, but the PSB do keep an eye on foreigners and you're likely to get caught. If so, you'll be deported and your passport stamped accordingly, effectively preventing you from returning for a long time.

The Chinese take the validity of visas very seriously. Overstaying a visa renders the holder liable to a fine of 500 RMB for each day and this rule is strictly applied. Being caught working without the correct visa can lead to deportation and considerable loss of face, and you'll have problems obtaining a visa in the future.

VISA FEES

The fees for visas vary and aren't based on the visa's type but on its duration and flexibility, the method of processing and your nationality. For example, in 2011 a UK citizen paid from £30 for a single entry tourist visa up to £180 for a one-year multiple entry student visa, whereas an American paid £70 for any type or length of visa. An extra £15 was payable for 'express' processing, i.e. one

Visa Fees			
Fee Category		**Amount**	
	UK Citizen	**US Citizen**	**Other Countries***
Visa Fees			
Single entry	£30	£70	£20
Double entry	£45	£70	£30
Multiple entry (6 months)	£90	£70	£40
Multiple entry (1 year)	£180	£70	£60
Application Fee (fees apply to all nationalities)			
Regular (within 4 working days)		£36	
Express (within 3 working days)		£48	
Postal applications		£54	

day quicker. These charges appear quite illogical but they reflect the sum charged by the applicant's country if a Chinese citizen needs a visa (called reciprocity). In addition, there's an application fee which varies depending on whether you collect the visa in person or want it forwarded to you. In 2011, this ranged from £36 to £54. Note that fees aren't refunded if your application is unsuccessful.

The fees (which are revised periodically) shown in the above table apply to the UK only and are from the UK Chinese embassy's website (see 💻 chinese-embassy.org.uk/eng/visa/fees/t649903. htm). For fees in other countries, contact your local Chinese mission.

RESIDENCE

Foreign residents are quite a new phenomenon in China which only began to accept an influx of foreign tourists in the '80s. The majority of foreigners who visit China stay for a limited period of time – provided their tourist or business visa remains valid – but those coming to work or study for six months or more, i.e. with an X or Z visa, must visit the PSB and obtain a residence permit. The main types of permit are:

♦ **Foreigners' Residence Permit**: valid for up to a year (sometimes two) and issued to employees and longer-term students. This is the most commonly held permit type among foreigners working in China.

♦ **Foreigners' Permanent Residence Card**: this allows the holder to stay in China on a permanent basis and is renewed every ten years. These are only rarely issued to certain qualifying people.

You or your employer must apply for your residence permit at the PRC within 30 days of your arrival.

Foreigners' Residence Permit

This is sometimes known as a 'green card', like those issued in the US, and should be given to you by your employer to use as your ID in China; many expats carry this booklet with them rather than their passport. It isn't a card but a small green booklet containing your photo, your name in both English and Chinese (the closest appropriate characters), your address, date of birth, the date of the permit's issue and its validity – all stamped with the seal of the PSB. It must be renewed annually.

Foreigners' Permanent Residence Card

Since 2005 a limited number of foreigners have been granted permission to stay long term in

China on a Foreigners' Permanent Residence Card. These cards allow you to work without having to show proof of employment or register your place of residence. Obtain one of these and you no longer need a 'green card' or work permit, although the PSB will check up on you at least once a year. It also means that you have no Chinese visa stamps in your passport and on arrival each time in China you can go through the gates marked 'Chinese Only' and save yourself a long queue with the other foreigners.

However, obtaining a Foreigners' Permanent Residence Card is a true test of your resolve and determination. It involves obtaining numerous documents from your home country, your employer and the Chinese authorities, as well as countless visits to government departments and a Chinese notary. It's probably no exaggeration to say that it can take at least two years to reach the end of the paper trail and that you should factor in several flights home to get all your documents in order. Any that don't originate in China must be certified by both your own country's authorities and the Chinese embassy or consulate in that country.

If approved, the card is issued by the PSB at the final discretion of the Ministry of Foreign Affairs in Beijing. The cost of all this is about 1,200 RMB, plus taxi fares, hotel bills and airline tickets.

There are a number of key requirements that applicants must fulfil. You must be of good health, proven by a health certificate issued by the Health Quarantine Department in China or from a

medical institution in your home country. You must be law abiding and have no criminal convictions in China or abroad, which means obtaining a police report from your home country. You must also fit into one of the seven categories described below.

Investors (Category 1)

Someone who has made a large direct cash investment in China, either in a foreign invested enterprise (FIE) or a joint venture with a Chinese investor in prospecting for and exploiting petroleum. Investing in stocks or property isn't sufficient. The investment should amount to at least US$500,000 and could be as much as US$2m, depending on the location and type of business, and the investor must have a clean Chinese tax record for at least three years. All company documentation and tax records are required to support the application.

Incumbents (Category 2)

Someone who has held a prominent position in a company or organisation for at least four years, e.g. as a manager, director or professor, and lived in China for at least three years. He must be employed by a government department or state enterprise, a key college/university or an FIE, preferably in an important industry such as new technology. Applicants must have proof of their own credentials and, if necessary, those of their employer.

Special Personnel (Category 3)

Someone who has made an outstanding contribution to China. They might be a well-known scholar, entrepreneur, artist or even a sportsman, provided they've had a notable impact on the economic development or social advancement of China or are of significant value to the Chinese. Applicants are usually recommended by a government ministry and must verify their qualifications and achievements.

Spouses & Children of Category 1, 2 or 3 Applicants (Category 4)

Children must be aged under 18 and unmarried. Certificates proving the relationship(s), e.g. marriage/birth certificates, are required. This category also includes other dependent family members.

Spouses of Chinese Citizens or Established Foreign Residents (Category 5)

Spouses can apply for a Permanent Residence Card provided the marriage has lasted at least

five years and the applicant has been resident in China during that time. The couple must be living together and able to support themselves.

> China doesn't recognise civil partnerships or same-sex unions. To apply for permanent residency as a spouse, you must be in a heterosexual relationship and married.

Children of Category 5 Applicants (Category 6)

Children can also apply, provided they're aged under 18 and under the care of their parents. This also applies to adopted children and stepchildren.

Older Dependents (Category 7)

Older people who have relatives in China can apply, provided they're aged 60 or over, have lived in China for at least five years and have no closer relations overseas who could better support them. Applicants are required to prove that they and their family have a means of support and adequate accommodation.

◆ Full information about the above categories and the supporting documents required can be obtained from your nearest PSB.

◆ If you're successful in obtaining a Foreigners' Permanent Residence Card, don't be surprised if Chinese officials still ask to see your visa, or hotel receptionists refuse to accept it in lieu of your passport. Many Chinese have never seen such a card and they're still a comparative rarity, particularly outside Beijing and Shanghai, and are issued infrequently. In mid-2011, only some 1,500 visas had been issued to date, so holders are in a rare and fortunate minority.

Shanghai Five-Year Residence Permit

In 2010, the Shanghai authorities introduced a five-year residence permit to encourage scientific researchers, top managers and investors to bring their skills to this east-coast business hub. It's similar to the Foreigners' Permanent Residence Card albeit with less restricted eligibility. The catch is that you can only apply for it in Shanghai.

The permit may be applied for by foreigners living full-time in Shanghai and by foreigners with F-type multiple entry business visas who visit the city on a regular basis but don't actually live there. Confusingly, they're available for both three- and five-year terms and cost between 500 and 600

RMB if you make a personal application to the PSB.

Those eligible for the Shanghai permit include:

♦ Foreigners who've received some sort of 'honorary citizen' award such as the Magnolia awards, which are named after Shanghai's official flower and recognise major contributions to Shanghai or China. They're the highest awards which a city's government can bestow on a foreigner. About eight are presented each year.

♦ Foreigners with special or unique talents which are rare among the Chinese population, including some foreign celebrities.

♦ High-level employees of state-run scientific research institutions, colleges and universities.

♦ Foreign legal representatives, general managers, vice presidents and chief financial officers of certain high-level foreign-invested technology or export enterprises.

♦ Legal representatives, high-level management personnel and researchers working for multinational corporations with their regional headquarters in Shanghai.

♦ Senior staff of foreign invested enterprises which have a registered capital investment of US$3m or more.

Like the Foreigners' Permanent Residence Card, the Shanghai Residence permit is only issued in exceptional circumstances and there were only around 500 in circulation in 2011.

Take at least ten passport size and ten thumbnail size photographs (36x25mm/1.5x1in and frequently used in China) with you. They're required for almost every application. Colour photos with a white background are preferred.

WORK PERMIT

If you're offered a job in China, your employer must apply for most of the requisite documents and permits on your behalf. The most important are the Foreigners' Resident Permit (see page 56), the Foreign Expert's Certificate, which is effectively your work permit, and the Employment Licence for a Foreigner. Your employer must obtain these documents within the first month following your arrival.

Foreign Expert's Certificate

This small pale grey booklet is normally retained by your employer and, should you change jobs, is passed on to your new boss. Like the Foreigners'

Resident Permit, it's valid for one year and must be renewed by your employer at the PSB each year. Effectively, this booklet is your work permit.

> Don't let being called a Foreign Expert go to your head. Every expat who works in China is called a 'foreign expert', although it doesn't mean that you're actually an expert in anything!

Employment Licence for Foreigners

This document allows your boss to employ you. It's a single sheet of A4-sized paper printed in English on one side and Chinese on the other, in green print with a bright red seal on it. This is a genuinely beautiful document that looks like an old-style share certificate and is usually retained by the employer. If you're leaving China, it's worth asking if you can keep it, as it makes an unusual memento of your time in the Middle Kingdom.

Forbidden city, Ming Dynasty painting

4.
ARRIVAL

The vast majority of people arriving in mainland China enter the country by plane at one of the three major gateway airports; Beijing's Capital, Guangzhou's Baiyun or Shanghai's Pudong. Many other cities have international airports, such as Chengdu, Guilin and Shenzhen, and some flights arrive at Shanghai's second airport, Hongqiao, but most Westerners arrive at one of the big three gateway hubs.

On arrival, your first task is to negotiate immigration and customs, and this should present no problems – provided you have a valid visa. With a few exceptions, everyone entering China requires a visa (see **Chapter 3**) and if you arrive without one, you'll find yourself on the first available flight home. Chinese customs and immigration officials are usually courteous, but most speak little or no English, so you cannot negotiate with them.

There are a number of tasks that you must complete on or shortly after your arrival, which are described in this chapter.

IMMIGRATION

Immigration procedures begin on the plane, when foreigners are given immigration and customs declaration cards to complete prior to landing. If you arrive at a time when there are specific health concerns, such as the H1N1 (bird) flu scare in 2009, you may also be required to complete a health card. The immigration entry card requests personal details, such as your name, passport number, your address in China and the reasons for your visit. The customs card requires you to make a declaration if you're importing certain prohibited or restricted items (see page 62) and whether you've exceeded the duty-free allowances (see page 243).

There are separate immigration queues: one for Chinese citizens and one for foreigners. Immigration is controlled by uniformed police, members of the Foreign Affairs Department of the Public Security Bureau (PSB), who check your visa, stamp your passport and clear you into the country. This should take no more than

a minute per person and it's rare for them to ask questions. The immigration police tend to treat most foreigners equally, unless they're exceptionally scruffy or otherwise look 'different' from the herd (non-white people can sometimes have problems). However, while you're unlikely to be greeted with a beaming smile and a 'Welcome to China', it's equally unlikely that you'll have to produce sheaves of documents or proof that you have sufficient money for your visit.

▲ Caution

Take note of the entry date on your passport stamp. Even if you've a multiple entry visa, you may only be allowed a 30-day stay on each occasion – this will be stated in the conditions of the visa. If you overstay you risk a fine of 500 RMB per day and may have to forfeit your visa.

If you're given a health card to complete, it contains a number of health-related questions, such as whether you've had contact with birds, with people suffering from bird flu or have any suspicious symptoms, ranging from 'snivel' to 'AIDS/HIV' – be careful how you answer. Once completed, it must be handed over at the health desk.

CUSTOMS

After clearing immigration you can collect your bags from the baggage claim area – trolleys are usually free (no coins required) – and proceed to customs where you hand in your customs declaration form. You may be stopped just short of the customs area and asked to show your baggage receipt. This will be verified against your bags to ensure you haven't picked up the wrong bags by mistake.

Customs is divided into red and green channels. Red means you have something to declare and green means you have nothing to declare, i.e. no more than the duty- or tax-free allowances, no goods to sell, and no prohibited or restricted goods. If you're sure that you have nothing to declare, go through the 'green channel'; otherwise go through the red channel (it's best to check the latest information on duty-free allowances and restricted goods so you can avoid the 'red channel' where possible).

Customs officers can stop travellers randomly in either channel, but it's quite common for there to be no one on duty and foreigners are rarely stopped and searched. You're more likely to arouse suspicion if you're young and oddly or untidily dressed, or you have a vast amount of baggage or no baggage at all.

If you're caught with prohibited or restricted goods, you may have them confiscated, or you could risk a fine or even be deported from the country. There's a list of officially prohibited items below, but other items can sometimes cause problems. Customs officers are often interested in electronic goods and may want to check out your laptop or iPhone. There have been stories of people being charged 'duty' on iPads and other hi-tech equipment. Officially, you're only allowed to import one camera but it's unlikely you'll be stopped for carrying a couple of digital cameras or a small camcorder. A huge video camera that you perch on your shoulder is another thing altogether as it could mark you out as a member of the foreign media and hence a potential undesirable.

Foreigners planning to stay in China as a temporary or permanent resident can import a reasonable amount of belongings tax free, provided they're for your personal use, i.e. you don't plan to sell them and have owned and used them for at least 12 months. There's more information on shipping your belongings in **Chapter 5**.

There are no limits on the amount of money you can import, although if you're carrying over US$5,000 or 20,000 RMB in cash or its equivalent, you're required to declare it on your customs form.

Restricted & Prohibited Items

There are a number of items which you may not bring into China or which you must declare on arrival. These include:

♦ Weapons (including imitations), ammunition or explosives.

♦ Radio transmitters and receivers.

♦ Poisons or addictive drugs, such as heroin, morphine or marijuana. China still imposes the death penalty for those found guilty of trafficking hard drugs, and there several dozen foreigners languishing in Chinese prisons for importing even minor amounts of ecstasy, so be warned. If you're bringing in prescription drugs, it's as well to carry them in their original packaging and have a copy of the prescription with you.

♦ Certain animal and plant products which may carry diseases. For information about importing pets, see page 254.

♦ Any manuscripts, printed matter, films, photographs, tapes or discs which may be deemed detrimental to the political, economic, cultural or moral interests of China. This is a grey area. It includes pornography (which is largely unobtainable in China) and also encompasses top-shelf magazines such as *Playboy* or *Penthouse* (which are regarded as pornography).

But publications can be banned for no obvious reason or at the discretion of customs officials. In 2009, some foreigners entering China overland had their copies of the *Lonely Planet* guide to China confiscated, allegedly due to the fact that a map in the book showed Taiwan in a different colour from China, suggesting that it was not a part of China. This was despite the fact that you could buy the book at the Foreign Language Bookstore

in Beijing. Books and other material with a religious theme can cause problems, so use your common sense. You can bring in a copy of the Bible for your personal use but bringing in a dozen wouldn't be allowed; you might be an undercover missionary aiming to convert the population to Christianity!

There are a few other exclusions. For example, you may not bring in any exposed film, although you can bring in plenty of unexposed film. Officially you're meant to declare any gold or silver, e.g. jewellery, weighing over 50g (2oz), as well as cameras, watches and other valuables, but most people don't bother and are rarely stopped. As long as your possessions are for your own use, and pose no threat to China, you should sail through customs with ease.

▲ Caution

Every suitcase and piece of hand baggage goes through an x-ray machine on arrival in China, therefore you cannot just slip in banned or restricted items and hope that customs won't notice.

For more information, contact the Chinese Customs Administration (010-6519 4114, 💻 customs.gov.cn, with a limited section in English).

ARRIVALS

Chinese airports are much like those in the West, and the arrivals area should look fairly familiar (apart from the sea of Chinese faces). Although few airport employees speak English, signs are written in both Chinese and English and you shouldn't have any trouble finding your way around.

If someone is meeting you, they'll usually stand in the arrivals area holding a board with your name on it – quite possibly misspelt. If not, make your way to the official taxi queue. Don't be surprised if you're stopped by a 'taxi driver' as you exit the terminal. There are often pirate taxis touting for business, but they usually charge more than official taxis. The queue may look dauntingly long but usually moves quickly, and there's an official on hand to ensure the driver knows where you're going. Make sure that you have some Chinese *renminbi* (RMB) as few taxi drivers will accept foreign currency. There are money

exchange counters in arrivals where you can change cash or traveller's cheques into RMB.

Don't tip Chinese taxi drivers. Tipping has been officially illegal in China since 1949 and it isn't expected. If you do round up the fare it's quite likely that the driver will give you change, thinking that you've made a mistake.

REGISTERING WITH THE PSB

Foreigners must register their address with the Public Security Bureau (PSB) within one month of moving to China. This is normally done at the local PSB office nearest to your new address. If you move address you must notify the nearest PSB office to your new residence within a month of moving and obtain a new registration document.

The registration document is a single A6 page which, once completed, must be taken to the main PSB office for your area, i.e. the one which handles visa renewals and residence permits. Note that the document doesn't contain your photograph, but the PSB requires a thumbnail size photo when your name is entered into the ledger, therefore it's advisable to carry a supply of photos with you.

If you're coming to China to work, e.g. as a teacher, your employer will handle the registration process for you. If you aren't employed, but rather on business or taking a lengthy break to visit family or tour the country, you must do this yourself.

REGISTERING WITH YOUR EMBASSY

Nationals of some countries are required to register with their local embassy or consulate as soon as possible after their arrival in China. Even if registration isn't compulsory, most embassies like to keep a record of their nationals resident in China, and it may help to expedite passport renewal or replacement, or notification in the event of an emergency.

FINDING HELP

There are no citizen's advice bureaus or similar organisations in China to help newly-arrived foreigners settle in. That said, few arrive without some sort of support network, be it friends, family or, in most cases, their employer. If you're seconded to China by your employer, you will, to an extent, be insulated from the real China. Most relocation packages include accommodation, services, healthcare, and even a car and driver if you're lucky, and there are people on hand, both colleagues and human resources staff, to help you find your feet. Even teachers have the comfort of living on campus, and can turn to fellow teachers and management for advice.

In the (unlikely) event that you arrive in China on your own, there's a network of expat clubs and places where foreigners gather – often bars. Your embassy should be able to provide some contacts, and you can also try the various chambers of commerce or even a branch of the China International Tourist Service (CITS, ⌨ cits.net), where you should at least find some English-speaking staff. There are also a number of websites for expats with online communities and forums, such as Allo Expat Beijing (⌨ beijing.alloexpat.com) and Shanghai Expat (⌨ shanghaiexpat.com) – see **Appendix C** for more contacts. Bear in mind that advice from fellow expats, whether you meet them online or in a bar, isn't always completely correct or unbiased.

By far the largest barrier for most foreigners is language. While the Chinese don't do things so very differently from anyone else and are invariably helpful towards strangers, requesting and understanding information is a headache, since relatively few Chinese speak or comprehend English. Gaining even a basic grasp of *Putonghua* (Mandarin Chinese) before you arrive will be enormously helpful.

CHECKLISTS

Before Arrival

The following checklist contains a summary of the tasks that should (if possible) be completed before your arrival in China:

◆ Obtain a visa, if necessary, for you and all your family members (see **Chapter 3**). Obviously this **must** be done before your arrival in China.

◆ If possible, visit China to compare communities and schools, and arrange schooling for your children (see **Chapter 9**).

◆ Find temporary or permanent accommodation (see **Chapter 5**) and arrange to buy or rent a car if you'll need one. If you purchase a car in China, you must register it and arrange insurance (see **Chapter 11**).

◆ Arrange the shipment of your personal effects (see **Chapter 5**) to China.

◆ Arrange health insurance (see **Chapter 13**) for yourself and your family.

◆ Obtain an international driving permit, if necessary.

◆ Open a bank account in China and transfer funds (see **Chapter 14**) – you can open an account with some Chinese banks from abroad. It's best to obtain some *renminbi* before your arrival, which will save you having to change money immediately on arrival.

◆ Collect and update your personal records, including medical, dental, schools, insurance (e.g. car insurance), professional and employment (including job and bank references).

◆ Obtain an international credit or charge card, which will prove useful in China.

Don't forget to bring all your family's official documents, including birth certificates, driving licences, marriage certificate, divorce papers or death certificate (if a widow or widower), educational diplomas and professional certificates, employment references, school records and student identity cards, medical and dental records, bank account and credit card details, insurance policies and receipts for any valuables.

You'll also need the documents necessary to obtain a residence or work permit (if applicable) plus certified copies, official translations and numerous passport-size photographs (students should take at least a dozen).

After Arrival

The following checklist contains a summary of tasks to be completed after arrival in China (if not done before arrival):

◆ On arrival at a Chinese airport, port or land border, have your visa cancelled and passport stamped, as applicable.

◆ Depending on your destination, you may wish to hire a car (possibly with a driver) for a week or two, or even buy one. Note that it's difficult to get around in rural areas without a car.

◆ Register with the local Public Security Bureau within one month of your arrival.

◆ Register with your local embassy or consulate (see page 63).

◆ Open a bank account and give the details to your employer.

◆ Arrange schooling for your children (see **Chapter 9**).

◆ Arrange whatever insurance is necessary (see **Chapter 13**).

5.

ACCOMMODATION

C **hina is a vast country, roughly the size of the United States and, like the US, its population is divided between sophisticated conurbations and a vast rural heartland; half the population still lives in the countryside. Most city-dwellers live in apartments and detached houses, called villas, are rare, while private gardens are virtually unknown.**

Chinese statistics are so huge that they're difficult to grasp at first. Nearly a fifth of the world's population – some 1.35bn people – lives in mainland China. Four times as many people live there as in the US, and there are over 100 cities with over 1m inhabitants. The east and south central regions are the busiest and most crowded – this is where most foreigners live – in complete contrast to the peaceful and often beautiful interior where agriculture dominates and life appears to have changed little in the last century. Yet even in the most remote provinces there are busy and populous cities: Urumqi, the capital of the Xinjiang autonomous region, presents an unexpected panorama of skyscrapers in the middle of an arid desert plain and is home to some 2.5m people.

Since the end of the Cultural Revolution in 1976, China has been progressively reinventing itself and the pace of change has moved at lightning speed, although much of the country's long and colourful history has been erased. Entire districts have been razed to the ground and replaced with new apartments. Beijing's *hutongs* (a maze of alleyways) and Shanghai's French Concession are being enveloped in a sea of modern construction. Even housing developments built just after 1976 are being pulled down and replaced. Almost every building in China is less than 40 years old.

The pace of change has been matched by the relentless rise in property prices. In Shanghai they rose by a massive 150 per cent between 2003 and 2010, and even the worldwide credit crunch has done little to curb property inflation. While the rest of the world was enduring a property slump, Chinese property prices rose an average of over 10 per cent countrywide between November 2009 and April 2010. The government has introduced a series of measures to curb the enthusiasm of speculators, but many investors still view property as a better route to riches than bank interest rates or a languishing stock market (and many buyers pay cash with 'grey' money).

It isn't just a thirst for profit which has contributed to so much new construction, but also a change in cultural attitudes. Until the '80s, virtually every city dweller lived in an apartment provided by their employer – usually poorly designed, badly built and lacking modern conveniences. As China pulled itself towards the 21st century, people increasingly want a modern home. The work unit has given way to a more capitalist way of doing things, and owners of new factories no longer want to be tied to their workforces by providing housing; they'd rather pay higher wages and leave them to find their own accommodation. Thus more people now have their own home, either rented or owned.

> ### ▲ Caution
>
> Home ownership is a little different in China, where you own the property but not the land it's built on – all land belongs to the state, which can claim it back after 70 years. The only exceptions are houses built before the founding of the People's Republic of China in 1949, which are treated as being freehold.

The vast majority of Chinese prefer to own rather than rent their home, although for young couples in expensive cities renting may be the only option. Statistics are difficult to come by, but according to international consultants Gerson Lehrman Group, some 80 per cent of city-dwellers own their own homes. This is a high percentage compared with many Western countries such as the US (69 per cent) and Germany (41 per cent).

Foreign investors have been able to buy residential property in China since 2002, although they must live in the country for a year before they can make a purchase. Many have made excellent investments, while others have been badly burned. In some areas it may only be foreigners and wealthy Chinese who can afford to buy. While outside the main cities, a new-build shell sells for around 7,000 RMB per square metre, in desirable parts of Beijing or Shanghai you can pay ten times as much. These high purchase prices are reflected in the rents, which range from 8,000 to Over 100,000 RMB a month in central Shanghai, but could be as low as 800 RMB a month for a good one-bedroom ($37m^2$/$398ft^2$) apartment in one of the third-tier Chinese cities.

The property market may be of little concern to many Westerners arriving in China. Few emigrate there intending to stay for the rest of their lives. For most it's a temporary move; a couple of terms teaching in a Chinese university or a work secondment for a few years. It's only if they fall in love with the country – or with a Chinese person – that they consider putting down long-term roots.

Most foreigners who visit China for a few months to a year are provided with accommodation by their employer, but some may need to find rental accommodation and a few may decide to become investors. This chapter explains the different options when looking for somewhere to live in the Middle Kingdom.

DECIDING WHERE TO LIVE

If you take a job in China, you'll have no choice over where to settle and will probably end up in or near one of the big four conurbations. However, if your work plans are more flexible, e.g. you're trying to decide between teaching posts in different parts of the country, you may have to make a choice about where to base yourself.

Very few foreigners live in China's western provinces, except for a few teachers in far-flung universities. The vast majority settle in major cities in the more developed eastern part of the country, often in one of the cities listed below – although rarely in Chongqing, Shenyang or Wuhan, all heavily-polluted industrial centres that (not surprisingly) expatriates prefer to avoid.

The cities listed below have a sizeable expat population, a reasonable transport infrastructure and access to some home comforts, such as imported Western foods in the supermarkets and an expat social scene. This section explains the main advantages and disadvantages to living in each city.

The Big Four

Beijing, Shanghai, Guangzhou and Shenzhen are often referred to as the big four. They're the leading cities in terms of economic development: the first-tier cities. Both Beijing and Shanghai are major municipalities, while the other two are in Guangdong province and close to Hong Kong.

Beijing (pop. 19.6m)

China's capital city and seat of government has good employment opportunities for expats. All countries have their embassies in Beijing and it's the base for many international companies, with a wide choice of (expensive) accommodation – only Shanghai has higher rents – and international schools. Its history makes it an interesting place to live – it feels much more Chinese than Shanghai – and there's no shortage of entertainment, from theatre to sport, plus numerous 'foreign' restaurants.

The major drawback in Beijing is pollution, which is exacerbated by its distance from the coast and the regular dust storms that blow in from Mongolia. On some days visibility can be down to not much over 100m (328ft) and local expats claim that living in Beijing can have the same negative effects on your health as smoking 20 cigarettes a day. Fortunately, the much cleaner countryside is a relatively easy drive away in every direction, aided by the excellent system of ring roads and expressways.

Shanghai (pop. 23m)

Shanghai is a city buzzing with energy, a city that never sleeps. It's the Chinese equivalent of New York or London and probably the only place where you can sometimes forget you're in the People's Republic of China. The largest port in the country and home to more expats than any other city on the mainland, it offers excellent job opportunities and an exhausting social life – at a price. At its thoroughly modern heart, Shanghai is all about money and full of Chinese Gordon Gekkos in new BMWs and Mercedes cars, on the road to getting rich quick.

The major drawback, apart from the eye-wateringly high rents, is that Shanghai has no obvious centre, but is more a series of sprawling suburbs which never seem to end. Getting out of the city is no easy feat and you can drive for an hour or more before glimpsing open fields.

☑ SURVIVAL TIP

It's possible to enjoy some of the benefits, and less of the downsides, of Shanghai by locating in one of its neighbouring cities such as Hangzhou (see below) or Suzhou. They're close enough for occasional visits, although maybe not for a daily commute.

Guangzhou (pop. 10m plus)

Built at the head of the Pearl River Delta, one of the three economic hotspots in China, Guangzhou has been trading with Westerners for some 600 years. Back then it exported silk and spices; now it's a textiles hub, dispatching socks and T-shirts across the world. The capital of Guangdong province, it's a long way from Beijing and often appears more influenced by nearby Hong Kong than by the capital's rulebook. The result is a freewheeling boom town where business is brisk and you need to keep your wits about you.

There are fewer consulates, more limited entertainment options and far fewer top-class international restaurants than in Beijing or Shanghai – although it's the best place to sample Cantonese cuisine – but it's an attractive and sometimes scenic city. Shamian Island, home of early foreign concessions and close to the centre, is a charming spot and is home to probably the nicest hotel in the whole of China: the White Swan. Another bonus is the warm, if damp, weather. Guangzhou is close to the Tropic of Cancer and rarely sees snow.

Shenzhen (pop. 9m plus)

Shenzhen is the newest megacity in China, dating back a little over 30 years. Just across the border from Hong Kong, it was a tiny fishing village in 1979 when Deng Xiaoping announced it as the first SEZ (Special Economic Zone) in the newly opened China, and it proved such a draw that barbed wire fences had to be erected to keep would-be workers out! Shenzhen has since proved irresistible to entrepreneurs and has a reputation as a city where you can get things done fast, if not always well.

There's a thriving expat population, attracted by good weather, reasonable rents and lots of business opportunities – as well as easy access to Hong Kong. There's excellent shopping and a lively social scene, and less congestion (and pollution) than in the other big four cities. The downside is that Shenzhen is a city of transients, both foreign and Chinese, and as a result it can be rather unwelcoming and soulless.

Alternative Cities

The following seven cities all have a growing expat population and are easier – and much cheaper – places to live than the big four. All, barring Nanjing and Xi'an, are on or near the eastern coast.

Dalian (pop. 3.5m)

This seaside city in Liaoning province is a clean, green and pleasant place with one of the largest expat communities in northeast China. Major industries are shipbuilding and information technology (IT) and there's plenty to see and do, from golf to fishing, plus some lovely coastal scenery. Once known as Port Arthur, Dalian has been occupied by the British, Japanese and Russians, and is now home to many Japanese and Koreans. Property prices are reasonable, although its growing popularity is starting to push up the cost of living.

Hangzhou (pop. 6.3m)

Many Chinese rate this city in Zhejiang province as the most beautiful in China. Life revolves around West Lake, a vast stretch of water at the city's heart, complete with cafés, boats and glorious views. A wealth of temples and pagodas, a great night market and the city's famous *Long Jin* (Dragon Well) tea make it a magnet for tourists, but it's also a thriving business centre and only two hours' drive from Shanghai. However, paradise doesn't come cheap. Rents are geared to the wealth of the populace and prices reflect the tourist dollar.

Nanjing (pop. almost 8m)

The capital of Jiangsu province, Nanjing sits beside the Yangtze River and is a peaceful place with a turbulent past. One of the four ancient capital cities of China, its population was infamously massacred by Japanese troops during the '30s. Although it lacks the sophistication of Shanghai, there's a sizeable expat population and prices are much lower than on the coast. There are plenty of parks and access to mountains and woodland, and a good social scene.

The main disadvantage is the climate which can be insufferably hot in summer. It's justifiably known as one of the 'three furnaces' along with Chongqing and Wuhan, but while Nanjing is a major industrial city – it's the current home of MG cars – it doesn't suffer from the stifling pollution which blights its fellow 'furnaces'.

Qingdao (pop. 7m)

Surrounded by mountains and sea, Qingdao in Shandong province was voted China's most 'liveable' city in 2009. Its name translates as 'green' or 'lush' and its temperate climate makes it a comfortable place to live. Though it's a large port and industrial centre, there are some great beaches along its extensive coastline – it was the base for the yachting events at the Beijing Olympics – and it has the laidback atmosphere of a seaside city. Qingdao is famous for being the home of Tsingtao beer; the locals learned the art of brewing from the Germans when the city was a German concession. There are few disadvantages to joining Qingdao's friendly expat community, although it isn't a destination for lovers of high culture.

Tianjin (pop. 12m plus)

Tianjin is one of China's four giant municipalities and is spread over a huge area on the northeast coast. Tianjin City is its cultural centre, and its architecture reflects the several foreign concessions that were based here in the 19th century, including a French cathedral and ornate Italian villas. An important industrial and economic city, it's attracted many major companies from

Nestlé to Airbus and work opportunities are excellent. However, many businesses are located in one of the major economic development areas, such as the Tanggu port area, which are a lengthy commute away from the city centre. Though a modern city, Tianjin has managed to remain resolutely Chinese and makes a good alternative to Beijing – without the dust storms or pollution – which is only 30 minutes away by high-speed rail.

Xiamen (pop. 2.5m)

Once known as Amoy, Xiamen in Fujian province is on the southeast coast and only 100km (62mi) from Taiwan and popular with Taiwanese retirees. The heart of the city is Xiamen Island, once a stronghold of pirates, and the sea still influences the city's industries which include shipbuilding and fishing – locally caught fish is excellent – as well as manufacturing and financial services. Xiamen is relaxed and reasonable priced, and popular with expats and tourists. Among its many attractions is Gulangyu Island, where there's a wealth of old colonial architecture and no vehicles whatsoever, making it a wonderful antidote to the seething traffic of mainland China.

Xi'an (pop. 8m)

When Marco Polo made his way to Xi'an at the end of the Silk Road 600 years ago, it was one of the most important cities in the world. Even now, Xi'an has its own unique character. The relics of its past greatness have not been eradicated, while its architects have created some of the most pleasing modern buildings in China. It may be located far west in inland China (Shaanxi province), but Xi'an has a lot to offer expats besides a peek at the incredible Terracotta Army, from its excellent Muslim-influenced food to a roaring nightlife fuelled by a large student population. It's also a leading centre for technological fields, including aviation, telecommunications and computer software, and many businesses have relocated there. Despite its heavy traffic, pollution and the tendency of some locals to treat every foreigner like a tourist, the pleasingly low cost of living is a major point in its favour.

MOVING HOUSE

For the majority of foreigners, China is a temporary home. Most don't relocate there as they would to Australia or the US, taking all their worldly goods with them in a shipping container. More often they put them into storage and rent out the family home, or sell it and invest the proceeds so they can buy again on their return. Those who are staying for less than a year might leave their home and contents in the care of friends for the duration.

> ### ☑ SURVIVAL TIP
>
> If you put your belongings into storage while you're in China, make sure they're fully insured. It isn't unknown for storage warehouses to burn down or be flooded.

But what if you're in the minority and want to ship your whole life, lock, stock and barrel, to China? The best advice would be, think again! Aside from the expense of hiring, packing, insuring and transporting the contents of your home to China, which can amount to many thousands of pounds, there's the headache of getting them through Chinese customs once they arrive. And you'll face the same process in reverse when you return home. It takes at least four to six weeks for a shipment to travel from the UK to China, or up to three months from the US. Air freight is much quicker, but prohibitively expensive for all but the most essential items.

Most foreigners move into furnished accommodation provided by their employer, so there's little chance your new boss will be willing to pay your shipping costs. Even if you're moving to somewhere unfurnished, it's much cheaper to furnish it locally. Furniture and electrical goods are inexpensive in China, and there's also the option of buying secondhand from expats who are leaving the country and selling them when you leave. Some electrical goods may be incompatible with Chinese voltage, and if you're moving from a three-bedroom semi in Doncaster to a high-rise apartment in Dalian, your worldly goods may be too large for your new home. The Chinese manage with far less space and storage than most Westerners.

If all this hasn't put you off, then choose your removal company wisely: go for one which is a member of an organisation such as the International Federation of Furniture Removers (FIDI) or the Overseas Moving Network International (OMNI) so that you have a guarantee that another member will get your goods there if your company cannot fulfil its obligations. Obtain several quotes, and find out what they include, e.g. insurance, customs clearance, storage (while your goods are waiting to be cleared by customs) and delivery to your Chinese address. Most international removers offer a door to door service, but there are some which deliver your belongings to a port and then leave you to hire a local agent to clear them through customs.

It's essential to use a company that works closely with a Chinese partner, as only the Chinese have the knowledge to navigate their complex customs system. Expect to complete many forms and ensure that all the details are correct, as without the correct documentation, customs may impound your belongings for weeks or months and/or impose hefty fines. You should still expect them to slap arbitrary import duty onto at least some of your personal effects, and your removals company should be able to advise you on the necessary paperwork and taxes.

Always ensure that your consignment is fully insured, not necessarily by the removal company which may not provide the best cover. You need an all-risks marine insurance policy from domicile to domicile, underwritten by an established insurance company. As well as an inventory, you should take photographs or videos of any valuables for insurance purposes. And be sure to read the small print, so that you know what's required in the unlikely event that your ship sinks in the South China Sea and you have to make a claim.

There are some must-have items which you cannot obtain in China and which it may be worth taking with you – see page 242 for examples. It's worth checking your airline's excess baggage charges so that you can compare this with the cost of airfreight. If friends plan to visit, persuade them to bring some items in an extra suitcase. It's much easier to slip your belongings past customs in a bag than through customs in a container!

Relocation Companies

If money's no object, a relocation company can remove a lot of the hassle from moving abroad. From arranging visas and finding schools for your children, to helping you to get to grips with the culture and find your way around after your arrival, they offer a wide range of services – at a price! They usually handle corporate moves for companies relocating high-flying executives, but there's nothing to stop you hiring one independently. You can find one through the International Relocation Associates (TIRA, 🖳 tiranetwork.org) or check the local *Yellow Pages* under 'Relocators'. Orientations is a TIRA member with offices in Shanghai (Suite 801 ASA Building,188 Jiangning Lu, Shanghai 200040, ☎ 021-3252 0790, 🖳 orientations.asia/index.php).

CHINESE HOMES

One of the first things that will strike you on arriving in China is the incredible number of high-rise buildings under construction. Most aren't offices, but residential blocks being built to accommodate the increasingly large and affluent population.

In China, most city-dwellers live in an apartment, in a city block or complex or, more usually, within an 'estate'. Most estates consist of between ten and 20 blocks, each ranging from six to 12 storeys. The estate is walled with a gated entrance and may be landscaped with grass, flower beds and a few trees. As well as apartments, there are parking facilities, a management office and a shop or two, and there may also be exercise facilities such as an outdoor gym and even a small clinic. Some complexes in major commercial districts incorporate shopping centres and subway stations.

These estates are, in effect, the modern version of China's old villages transported into the hi-tech age, although they lack the communal atmosphere of a rural village. The Chinese don't throw their doors open to all and sundry, and you may live there for some time before getting to know your neighbours, if at all. Your main contact will be with staff from the management company which handles repairs and security for the residents. A few estates are primarily inhabited by foreigners, e.g. embassy staff or employees of a large organisation, and these are usually more sociable.

Feng Shui

Man Chinese are less concerned about the decor and facilities in an apartment than they are about its layout and the direction it faces. *Feng shui*, which translates as 'wind-water', is a set of aesthetic values which can boost positive energy – or block negative vibes – and modern buildings are designed with its principles in mind.

High rise is not a bad thing in China, where the higher the floor, the higher the rent. Height buys you more security and privacy and gets you above the smog line, and provided the block is over seven storeys high, there'll be a lift. Any less, and you'll get fit walking up and down the stairs!

There are few alternatives to estate living, as these urban villages have swallowed up much of old China. On the outer fringes of most cities, some older two or three-storey buildings still exist, although they're poised to disappear to make room for more estates. Some architecturally important buildings remain, such as the old brick courtyard houses in central Beijing (*siheyuan),* the long, low terraced homes (*li nong*) which line the narrow lanes in old Shanghai, and the European villas in cities where foreign concessions once held power. A few brave and wealthy people take these on. Unlike the British, most Chinese cannot see the appeal of old houses: too many ancestors and too much work!

Even the very wealthy live on estates, although their compounds are far more luxurious, complete with tennis courts, health clubs, swimming pools and restaurants, and they live in penthouse apartments or, more often, villas: large detached houses with three or more bedrooms, gardens and multi-car garages, in designs which wouldn't look out of place in Beverly Hills. There's even more of a premium on these houses since the construction of new villas was officially banned in 2006 because they take up too much valuable land space. That said, the building of villas continues in a limited number of places, albeit illegally.

Away from the cities, most people live a rural life in basic one or two-storey dwellings of brick or stone. Many lack facilities such as central heating or even modern plumbing, but most have one benefit that their city cousins cannot aspire to: a private garden or land for growing food.

TEMPORARY ACCOMMODATION

For a foreigner moving to China, 'temporary' can mean from a few weeks to two or three years. The destination is unique in that the majority of new arrivals have accommodation provided for them for the duration of their stay, and only a few expatriates employed by Chinese organisations, or those who decide to stay on after a job, period of study or teaching assignment has finished, must make their own living arrangements.

Students

As a first-year student in China, you may opt to live on campus, where accommodation usually consists of dormitory blocks made up of single rooms. At some universities these are large enough to take two beds, and you may be expected to share, or pay an additional fee to have a room to yourself.

Rooms are simply furnished with a bed, small desk and chair, plus a soft chair for relaxing. They have a power point and a telephone point for your laptop, plus heating or air-conditioning depending on the region, but don't expect a television or computer or any means of cooking – students eat at the campus canteen. Bedrooms may contain a wash basin but toilets and showers are often communal. The toilets are almost always of the squat variety and you'll have to provide your own toilet paper. Some washing areas have sinks for washing clothes, but washing machines are rare.

If you think that's basic, bear in mind that Chinese graduates sleep four to a room, while undergraduates live in six-bedded dormitories!

It's worth looking at the website of study establishments to see what you could be letting yourself in for. Many include photos or videos of the buildings, facilities and accommodation available.

Teachers

Most schools and universities accommodate their foreign teachers in apartments on campus. These are similar to those provided to Chinese staff, and the main variable is the age of the building. Accommodation is comfortable though rarely luxurious. Expect a bedroom, living area, small kitchen and shower room with a sit down toilet (a real treat in China!), all furnished, though not to show-home standards. A computer is almost always included, however, and your utility bills are paid by the school.

Employees of Government Organisations, NGOs & Foreign Companies

The vast majority of employees of government organisation, NGOs and foreign companies are housed in a furnished apartment – rarely a villa – which is rented or owned by their employer. The size and specification depend on how high up the corporate ladder you are and whether you have your family with you, but most are nicely furnished and well equipped, with a fully fitted kitchen, en-suite bathrooms, an internet connection and, if you're lucky, a small balcony. Some are equipped right down to tooth mugs and teaspoons. The apartment will

almost certainly be in a block in an estate and be situated close to your workplace or convenient for public transport, such as a subway station. If you work for an embassy you may be housed in a compound with other embassy staff.

Staff working on construction projects are invariably housed near to the worksite, in barracks, apartments or even small houses. On larger construction projects there are usually canteens and facilities for sport and entertainment

Short-term Accommodation

Hotels

When you first arrive in China, you may need to spend a few days in a hotel while your apartment is prepared, or a few weeks while you look for somewhere to rent. Chinese hotels span the whole range, from five-star luxury down to basic lodging houses (which are normally only accessible to Chinese citizens).

Five-star hotels are genuinely five-star, with every imaginable facility, and are usually located in a prime spot. But they aren't cheap. You can expect to pay 1,500 to 3,000 RMB a night or even more in the largest cities. However, most expatriates find that a three- or even a two-star hotel provides all that they need other than a Western-style breakfast, which is only served in four- or five-star hotels. Negotiate a good discount and you should pay between 250 and 380 RMB a night, possibly with a Chinese breakfast of congee (rice porridge), fried bread sticks and hard-boiled eggs included.

Never pay the official rate if you can avoid it – the Chinese don't. Check out the room rates displayed on the wall and ask the receptionist for their lowest rate. He or she won't blink an eye,

Tang Paradise hotel, Xi'an

and will probably offer you a considerably lower rate than the one posted.

A good way to obtain a discount is to make use of one of the hotel booklets handed out at Chinese airports. Over 100 Beijing hotels take part in these schemes, with discounts ranging from 50 to 70 per cent, and similar discounts are available in all large cities. To take advantage of the discount scheme, phone the agency which issues the booklet and it will reserve your room. On arrival, all you need do is quote your booking reference. The only snag is that not many discount agents can speak English, therefore you may need to ask a Chinese friend to make the call.

An alternative is to use a budget hotel. Many have been built over the last five years. The largest budget hotel chains are Jin Jiang Hotels (☎ 800-819, 5677, 🖥 jinjianghotels.com/portal/en/index.asp), with over 200 hotels, followed by Motel 168 (☎ 800-820 7168, 🖥 motel168.com – in Chinese), so named because rooms cost from 168 RMB, and Home Inns (☎ 800-820 3333, 🖥 homeinns.com/index/index.aspx – in Chinese). The China Hotels website (🖥 chinahotels.org/index.html) offers a good search facility for budget hotels. Most provide clean, simple accommodation, complete with TV and en-suite bathroom, for between 150 and 220 RMB a night with Chinese breakfast for a small extra cost. They're basic but totally acceptable.

Long-Term Hotel Stays

This isn't yet a common practice in China, and the discount you're offered may be little better than the rate that you obtain by using hotel discount booklets (above). However, a long stay has many of the advantages of a serviced apartment at a fraction of the cost, and you have all the hotel's facilities included. The main disadvantage is the small space – usually just one en-suite room, but it can be a sensible arrangement if you're single.

RENTED ACCOMMODATION

Renting is always a wise option, even if you intend to buy in the long term, as it allows you to get to know the country and area before deciding whether you want to live there permanently. It's more flexible than buying, and frees you up to move on to another part of the country – or the world. It also avoids the expense and the dangers of buying a property which can sometimes be a risky business in China.

It's now possible for a foreigner to rent an apartment in almost any building in China; long gone are the days when all expats were gathered together into estates known as 'foreign compounds'. There's no shortage of places to rent in major cities, where the buy-to-let business is booming. By far the largest choice is in apartments. These range from basic one-room walk ups with cheap flooring, no kitchen appliances, a squat toilet and hardly enough room to swing a cat, to luxury penthouses fitted out with marble, gold taps and all mod cons, plus fabulous views across the skyscraper skyline. Most are somewhere in between these extremes.

The majority of apartments have two or three bedrooms; one-bedroom and studio flats are rare, as are four-bedroom properties. Central heating is only installed in properties in the northern half of the country.

Furnished or Unfurnished

The majority of standard rental apartments are unfurnished. Furnished apartments are available but are often small, e.g. one bedroom, and are usually only available as short-term lets – for a week or even a day – although they may not cost any more than an unfurnished flat. Renting larger furnished properties is more difficult, although if you take over a property occupied by an expat they can often be persuaded to leave much of their furniture behind, particularly if they're leaving the country. In areas where there's a glut of rental property, some landlords are furnishing apartments to make them easier to let.

In the big four cities, serviced apartments are available. Many are located within large hotels, and offer the lessees access to hotel facilities such as business centres, gyms and the English-speaking concierge service. Most are in upmarket blocks such as the Kerry Centres in Beijing and

Shanghai, and are aimed at the well-heeled executive and his family, but they're worth investigating as an alternative to a hotel room for a short-to-medium term stay. In Shanghai, for example, less luxurious serviced properties are appearing on the market, offering more limited facilities but lower rents.

Finding a Property to Rent

This can be a simple or difficult affair depending on a number of factors, such as the location (and its impact on your commute), the size of the apartment and how much you want to pay. Non-stop construction and the number of Chinese investor-landlords means that there are usually plenty of places to choose from, but rents are high in major cities although they fall quite dramatically the further you are from the main commercial or business centres.

Before starting your search, it pays to put in some time researching possible locations. Obtain a city map from a newspaper kiosk or from outside the railway station, mark on it the location of your office or school, and other important places such as your children's school, major supermarkets and subway stations, and use it to pinpoint convenient areas.

☑ SURVIVAL TIP

Make sure you can read a map before buying it. Most are in Chinese characters and difficult for foreigners to use, so check that street names are also written in pinyin.

There are a number of ways to find a rental property, including the following:

♦ Ask friends, colleagues and even your boss if they know anywhere to rent or if they can recommend a reliable agent. Some employers need to accommodate staff and may be able to help you obtain a discount on an agent's fees.

♦ Look at the free weekly and monthly expatriate magazines – and their websites. Many have extensive classified sections where you'll find many advertisements for apartments to rent. *City Weekend* (🖳 cityweekend.com.cn) and *The Beijinger* (🖳 thebeijinger.com) are good places to start. China Daily was also carrying advertisements for high quality apartments within Beijing's central areas in late 2012.

♦ Dip into the Chinese real estate magazines. These are provided free to read at Chinese coffee bar chains such as Dio and New Island Coffee, and include details of nearby estates, plus rental and purchase prices. Though published in Chinese, they're clearly laid out and aren't difficult to understand.

♦ Check out property portals. Some, such as Beijing Ascot Realty (🖳 beijingascotrealty.com) and Beijing Real Estates (🖳 beijingrealestates.com) target the expat market. Others are only in Chinese, so you'll need some help in deciphering them, but at least you'll know the prices are aimed at Chinese tenants rather than 'wealthy' foreigners.

♦ Visit any blocks and estates that you like the look of. Management companies usually know which apartments are empty, and can put you in touch with the landlord.

♦ Use an agent. Although estate agency is quite a new phenomenon in China, there are plenty of property agents targeting foreigners; most advertise in expat publications. The advantages of using an agent are that they can arrange multiple viewings and negotiate with landlords on your behalf, as well as drawing up contracts. The disadvantage is that they charge a fee; usually a month's rent, but as much as two months' rent in some cases. And many only market expensive, upmarket properties.

The US company, Century 21, has made inroads into China, and has franchises in over 30 cities, i.e. not just Beijing and Shanghai (🖳 century21cn.com – mainly in Chinese). They have a reputation for being helpful and professional, so may be a good place to start.

It's advisable to ask a Chinese friend to assist in your property search or even to negotiate for you. Landlords are more obliging and less liable to push up the rent when face to face with a Chinese applicant.

Costs & Payment

Rental fees for apartments and villas vary widely around the country, with rents in Beijing, Shanghai and Shenzhen the highest. The relentless rise in property prices since 2000 has had a knock on effect on rental values, which have increased in direct proportion. The factors which most influence rents are location, facilities and size, plus the floor (the higher you are and the better the view, the more expensive an apartment will be), how new the block is, and the proximity to smart shopping and business areas.

China's cities are arranged in levels or tiers, with the big four cities comprising the first tier.

Tier two includes around 20 cities, e.g. the major municipalities of Chongqing, Tianjin, important provincial capitals such as Chengdu and Nanjing, and those which have attracted a lot of foreign interest and investment such as Dalian and Qingdao. Tier three includes important but less populous cities such as Wuxi and Yichang.

A luxury two-bedroom apartment that rents for 10,000 RMB in Beijing could be had for 5,000 RMB in a tier-two city or even 2,000 RMB in a tier-three city. However, even in Beijing or Shanghai, if you're prepared to commute for an hour to get to work or live in a smaller apartment in an older building, you can halve your monthly rental outgoings.

There's no form of rental control in China, and landlords can set their own rent and increase it each time the contract is renewed; many cannot resist asking for more in areas which are preferred by foreigners. If the rent is quoted in dollars rather than in RMB, then you're almost certainly paying over the odds. Don't hesitate to negotiate hard with a potential landlord, just as you would when buying a pair of jeans or a kilo of fish at the market. Many apartments look unoccupied; indeed some are unfinished, the owner having bought it as a shell without the funds to complete it. Around 50 per cent of all property in China is bought as an investment rather than a home.

Investors who complete the internal fixtures and fittings are keen to let their property to pay off the costs, and may agree a below-market rent if it secures them a tenant more quickly. Because expatriate assignments are usually for three years or less, the Beijing apartment costs (shown above and below) are for properties ready for occupation and complete with basic furniture, although most apartments in smaller cities are rented finished but unfurnished.

If you're doing your own thing – and paying your own rent – you can save money, even in Beijing, by renting in the outer suburbs. However, if you feel that being in the centre of things is essential then the table below shows what you'll get for your money in central Beijing (complete with basic furniture) for 15,000 RMB a month or less in mid-2012.

Property Sizes & Typical Rents in Beijing in mid-2012

Property	Size in Square Metres (m²)			Monthly Rental		
	Smallest	Largest	Average	Cheapest	Dearest	Average
Studio	60	76	72	8,500	12,000	10,250
1-bed apt.	75	132	91	10,000	28,000	13,300
2-bed apt.	97	247	150	11,000	55,000	19,200
3-bed apt.	132	500	217	12,000	100,000	29,000
4-bed apt.	175	450	269	23,000	70,000	35,200
5-bed apt.	420	590	505	39,000	150,000	83,000
3-5 bed villa	270	642	402	25,000	75,000	37,000
2-4 bed cyd*	120	300	195	22,000	60,000	35,200

* cyd = a courtyard home

Note that rents vary depending on the exact location, quality, size, what's included in the rent (such as utilities, parking, fees, etc.) and the management company, and can vary by up to 50 per cent.

Beijing Apartments up to 15RMB per Month mid-2012

	Area (in m²)			rice in RMB/month			Percentage
	min.	max.	Av.	Lowest	Highest	Av.	of Rentals
Studio	60	90	74	8,500	12,000	10,400	90%
1-bed apt.	70	115	93	10,000	15,000	13,300	78%
2-bed apt.	97	171	130	11,000	15,000	13,600	35%
3-bed apt.	132	163	147	12,000	14,000	13,300	3%

Rental payments include VAT at 5 per cent. Some landlords may discount the rent if you don't insist on an official receipt (*fa piao*) for each payment. However, you should ensure that you have some record of payments made, even if it's just the landlord's signature in a home-made rent book. It's best to pay your rent into his bank account if possible.

Illegal sub-letting to foreign tenants is rare – an expat in a low-cost housing estate reserved for the Chinese would stick out like a sore thumb – but there's nothing to stop you asking to see a potential landlord's ownership certificate which proves that he owns the property.

Contracts & Deposits

Rental contracts are signed by both parties. They should state the name of the landlord and tenant, what the rent is, when it's due and how long the contract is for. They also set out both parties' rights and responsibilities, such as ensuring that everything is in full working order (landlord) and paying the management fees (tenant). Agents can be useful at the contract stage, as they can explain the details and ensure that both sides are happy with the contract. Never sign a contract that you don't fully understand.

Contracts are usually for 12 months' duration. Most landlords are unwilling to let their property for less than six months, and some may prefer to sign you up for two years or more. Signing the contract commits you to paying the rent until the end of the lease period, even if you have to move out early due to relocation, although you may be able to negotiate your way out of this in an area where rental properties are in high demand.

Rent is always paid monthly in advance, and landlords may ask for two or three months' rent in advance. They also require a security deposit, usually equal to a further two months' rent. In all you should budget to pay a sum equal to six months' rent at the outset, particularly if you're renting through an agent who will want at least a month's rent as his fee.

How much of this you'll eventually receive back depends on the honesty of your landlord. Inventories are rarely used, and it might pay to take date-stamped photographs to prove the condition of the apartment on moving in. However, if your landlord decides to hang on to your money in order to redecorate the entire apartment after you move out – even if there's no damage

whatsoever – then there's little you can do, short of withholding the last few months' rent. A foreign tenant who takes a Chinese landlord to court almost never wins.

It can take as long as six weeks to sort out a contract and move in to your apartment. Don't forget that you must let the Public Security Bureau know your new address within 30 days of moving in.

Additional Fees

In addition to rent, tenants (not landlords) are required to pay a fee to the management company which looks after the estate or block (see page 82). There may also be a charge for parking your car. For a guide to the cost of utilities, see page 82.

BUYING A HOME

The current state of the Chinese property market can at best be described as buoyant, but no longer frantic. There remains a steady demand for new property, not just because the Chinese need somewhere to live but also because so many investors have few alternative places to invest. The result of the recent heavy over investment has pushed prices up by 10-15 per cent a year, far in excess of any savings bond, which has served to encourage investors to pour even more money into property, which in turn has pushed up prices further. The result has brought about a state of super-inflation of property, particularly in the big four cities, where the average property in Beijing is now worth 27 times the average household income (in London the ratio is closer to five). The market has quietened considerably under new restrictions on property ownership imposed by the government, but there was little sign of any fall in property prices at the end of 2012.

Property speculation is by no means limited to the Chinese. Many expatriates have bought

property in Beijing, Shenzhen and, particularly, Shanghai and profited handsomely when selling on. It isn't usually worth buying, as opposed to renting, unless you intend to spend several years in a country, but China is a case apart. Even now, many financial experts believe that buying an apartment for your family's use during your stay in China could be looked upon as a good investment, particularly if, as anticipated, China re-values the RMB upwards. However, others predict that it may not be long before the bubble bursts.

If you decide to invest in Chinese property, you must be prepared for some rough and tumble as you'll be up against stiff competition. No matter that new blocks are going up by the day, any new apartments offered for sale are sold quickly, sometimes before the construction even begins, and you need to be quick to catch a bargain.

There's a difference between buying an investment and buying a home, and if your goal is a nice place to live, then you might be better off looking at pre-owned (secondhand) homes which are usually cheaper.

Whatever you do, don't expect buying property in China to be the same as at home. For example, the Chinese rarely engage a lawyer to deal with conveyancing – the process is quite different from the UK property transaction, and quicker, and there are no obligatory inspections. However, fewer regulations mean more risks, and there are plenty of people ready to cheat you by selling you a property that's worth far less than the quoted value, or even one which they don't actually own; while stories abound of developers who never complete their blocks, or who cut corners by using substandard materials. The old saying 'caveat emptor' (buyer beware) is particularly apt in modern China.

Restrictions

As a foreigner you're only allowed to buy one property, and you cannot do so until you've lived in China continuously for over a year. You cannot legally buy a second residential property for any purpose – even as a second home – unless you establish a locally registered investment company for this purpose. To do this requires government approval, which can be difficult to obtain.

You're free to put in a bid on any apartment in any area – there are no geographical restrictions. However, in a move to enable ordinary Chinese to buy a home, the government has implemented a requirement for new developments to include a minimum proportion of small and affordable apartments within their estates. These apartments, which are frequently subsidised by the local government, aren't usually available for foreigners to purchase. In any event, they're snapped up instantly, often by wealthy buyers pretending to be poor; a recent case in Shenzhen revealed one such 'poor buyer' to be a government official whose son was being educated in France!

⚠ Caution

There's virtually no freehold property in China, where all land belongs to the state. What you buy is the right to use to land for a period of time, currently 70 years. At the end of the 70 years, the state can reclaim it and there's no provision for compensation. In the meantime, if the state, in the guise of the local government, decides that your property is on land that's required for a new road – or even land that a developer is willing to pay a premium for – it can force the occupants to leave their homes. In this case compensation is paid, at a rate calculated by the local government, although it's possible to appeal against the valuation.

Cost

Like everywhere else in the world, the price of property in China mainly depends on three things, namely location, location and location. However, it also depends upon a fourth factor: timing. Prices are on a rollercoaster, and while they're generally on an upward trajectory, on occasion they can also come down.

Asking prices (based on the size in square metres) are almost never based on the costs involved in purchasing the land and constructing the building; rather the developer asks for the maximum he thinks he can get for a property. A good example is a group of properties in Shenzhen that were priced at 7,000 RMB/m² in

2007. The asking price increased to 14,000 RMB/m^2 in 2008 and then dropped to 8,500 RMB/m^2 in 2009 before ending at 12,000 RMB/m2. These changes reflect the market and what the developer thinks he can get, not their actual value.

Property costs the most in Beijing, Shanghai and Shenzhen. A survey published in *China Daily* early in 2010 indicated the following average prices per m^2:

Average Property Prices	
City	Average Cost per m² (RMB)
Beijing	25,010
Shanghai	20,819
Guangzhou	11,577
Dalian	10,134
Qingdao	9,800

Note that these were average prices and for property in locations well away from city centres – location is the number one factor influencing prices – and timing (when you buy). They effectively mean that you cannot buy a new two-bedroom apartment which is closer than 30km (18mi) from the centre of Beijing or Shanghai for anything less than 1m RMB. A more centrally located development of apartments in Beijing was put on the market in early 2011 at almost 44,000 RMB/m^2 and over 70,000 RMB/m^2 was being asked for some swish apartments in the city centre. There was even one estate in central Shanghai where the price per m^2 was a whopping 150,000 RMB – or just over £15,000/US$24,000!

One effect of this has been to push buyers further and further out of town. Anyone hoping to buy a more affordable home, say around 10,000 RMB/m^2, must look at areas which are a long commute from the city centre: at least 30km (18mi) in Beijing or Shanghai, 20km (12mi) in Dalian or Guangzhou and 15km (9mi) in Qingdao. Other cities are catching up fast. Average prices in third-tier cities were around 7,000 RMB/m^2 in 2011; but even in these areas, developers were asking for around 17,000 RMB/m^2 for top of the market properties.

Of course, it's possible to spend a lot less – or a lot more. If you don't mind buying a pre-owned, slightly scruffy and small apartment in an undesirable corner of Beijing, you could pay as little as 3,000 RMB/m^2, although you would be in fierce competition with those Chinese who are actually trying to buy a home. If money's no

object, 70,000 RMB/m^2 could buy you a 680m^2 (7,320ft^2) six-bedroom penthouse. Villas are even dearer: a 450m^2 (4,844ft^2) villa in Beijing could cost over 12m RMB, while a Hollywood style mansion covering 900m^2 (9,699ft^2) would set you back over 25m RMB. Restored courtyard buildings in the *hutongs* are even more expensive.

Chinese apartments are designed with families in mind, and most have three bedrooms. For every one-bedroom apartment for sale in Beijing, there are around eight two-bedroom units, 12 three-bedroom units and two four-bedroom units.

Prices are negotiable – but only to an extent. The asking price for a property is normally the very least that the vendor is willing to accept, and buyers often have to bid more than the asking price to secure it.

Fees & Additional Costs

Your budget should allow for an additional 4 to 8 per cent of the purchase price to cover associated costs. The main costs are the deeds tax and stamp duty which amounts to between 3 and 5 per cent of a property's value, and a one-off contribution to the city maintenance fund which goes to the local government and equals around 2 per cent. If you decide to use a lawyer, you must budget for his fees, and there'll be an arrangement fee if you're taking out a mortgage. One extra fee which applies only to foreigners is that of having your Chinese name notarised, which isn't expensive.

There's no requirement to use an estate agent, and many buyers deal direct with developers. There's also no requirement to hire a lawyer to handle the purchase process. The Chinese don't bother with them and neither do most foreigners. If you decide you'd feel more secure with some legal help, then ask around for recommendations. The British Embassy's website includes a list of English-speaking lawyers (⌨ ukinchina.fco.gov.uk/en/help-for-british-nationals/when-things-go-wrong/if-you-need-lawyers).

One extra cost which may come as a shock is the expense of finishing your new apartment. Many are sold as an empty shell (see page 80), and the cost of completing it to your own specification is likely to add at least 20 per cent to the final cost.

Don't forget to budget for removal costs, as well as general running costs which may include estate management company's fees, building and contents insurance (see page 180) and property taxes (see page 194).

Estate Agents

Estate agents (realtors) are far less important in China than in countries such as the UK and the US. With so much focus on new properties, developers are the first point of contact for many buyers. You may only need an agent if you're looking for a pre-owned home or one outside a city. If you do use an agent, you shouldn't be asked to pay a fee as their charges, which are usually between 1 and 2 per cent, are paid by the vendor. Note that the industry isn't regulated in China, and the quality of service varies greatly.

Buying Off Plan & Shells

Developers frequently sell every single apartment in a new development 'off plan', before they've even begun to excavate the foundations. At the cheaper end of the market, people will queue, sometimes for days, for the chance to put a deposit on a new apartment, only to find the best ones are already reserved, either for the developer or his 'friends' in local government, or to be sold later at a higher price.

Your only guide to the finished block may be a model of the development on show at the on-site office. These are usually detailed, and include larger-scale models cut away to reveal the layout of rooms and suggestions for finishing and furnishing them. Lavish brochures are available, often featuring pictures of idyllic countryside (which have nothing to do with the property on offer – they're selling a dream), as well as scale drawings of the units to be built.

What you won't have is an actual apartment to walk around. Although some show homes are available in smaller cities, developments in in-demand areas are frequently sold before there's time to erect one.

☑ **SURVIVAL TIP**

If you want to buy a new property off plan, look carefully at the model of the estate and check how much landscaping the developer has included. Some estates are so barren they look like the Gobi Desert. Trees bring shade and seasonal colour, and can make an otherwise average block of apartments look attractive.

It's important to know that when you buy from a developer, you rarely end up with a habitable apartment. In most cases, you buy it unfinished, known in the trade as a shell. These are secured with double glazed windows and exterior doors; plumbing pipe-work is installed as far as kitchens and bathrooms, and electricity installed as far as the fuse box. However, the walls aren't plastered,

the floors are rough concrete; there are no internal doors, no skirting, cornicing or other trimmings, no light fittings or power points, no sanitary ware or kitchen cupboards, and no central heating or air-conditioning.

Finishing the property is up to you. Most buyers instruct a 'decoration company' to do this – the Chinese aren't into DIY – and you should select one carefully and be very clear about how you want the apartment to look. Some companies quote an impossibly cheap price, hoping to make a profit by charging you for changes and extras. However, if you give them clear instructions and don't change your mind, you'll get the work done at a bargain price and as quickly as promised.

The advantage of buying a shell is that you can have it exactly as you want it; moving or adding lighting and power points, positioning TV and telephone points, selecting your ideal kitchen and bathroom(s), and choosing your tiling and your colour scheme. You can ensure that you have an oven – rare in China, where most people cook on a two-ring hotplate – and Western style toilets.

The disadvantages are the time and expense. It can take between six and 16 weeks to complete your shell, depending on the size of your property and the enthusiasm of your decorator. The cost amounts to around 20 per cent of the initial purchase price, although the sky's the limit if you choose marble tiles, Jacuzzi baths and a high-grade kitchen.

Ready & Pre-owned Property

In the big four cities, some developments are sold fully completed and ready to move into, even with curtains and blinds installed, but these are generally top of the range properties. Cheaper apartments and those in second- and third-tier cities are almost always sold as shells.

If you don't want the hassle of finishing off your new purchase, you can buy a pre-owned property. Second-hand homes, as they're known, are frequently cheaper because they aren't so popular with the Chinese, most of whom insist on living in a new property where no one has set foot before; there's a general aversion to the idea of living somewhere where someone may have died.

As with any pre-owned home, not every element will be to your taste and you may have to spend money on décor, bathrooms and other elements. Check also that the property is structurally sound. Some older developments were 'thrown up' at an incredible pace and the standard of workmanship and quality of materials leaves a lot to be desired, and there's no system of structural surveys to highlight faults and potential problems. Bear in mind also that there

may be considerably less than 70 years to run on the lease, at the end of which the government could reclaim the land the property is built on.

CONVEYANCE

The first step is to ensure that a property is legal. All properties in China have a title document, known as an ownership certificate, which contains details of the property and the owner. Always ensure that the vendor is the person named on the certificate. It's unlikely anyone will scam you if you buy through a reputable estate agent or from a well-known developer, but it's as well to know what to look out for.

Once you have your offer accepted, the purchase process begins. The first stage is a government-approved contract which both purchaser and vendor sign. **Don't sign anything until you've read it thoroughly and understand it.** If necessary, obtain an independent translation. Shortly after signing, you'll be asked to pay a deposit which could be as much as 40 per cent of the agreed price. If you pull out of the deal, you may forfeit some of your deposit to compensate the developer for any costs incurred, although he won't get to keep it all! If you're buying a pre-owned property, you can insert a clause stipulating which fixtures and fittings are included in the sale, although this isn't usual. Those Chinese buyers who acquire a secondhand house usually rip it apart and start afresh rather than live with the previous owner's décor and appliances.

If you're buying off plan, you may be required to make stage payments during the build, with a final payment on completion. The contract should stipulate a completion date, and if the developer fails to hand over the property on that date you can claim on them for compensation. Most projects are completed on time.

When you're ready to buy, you apply to register a transfer of title deed at the estate transaction office. Approval can take up to 15 days. Once approval is obtained, the final monies are paid, along with any taxes and fees (see page 79), and the title deed is transferred.

As a non-Chinese buyer, you're required by law to have a Chinese name: this is usually comprised of the characters which best match the syllables of your Western name, and has no specific meaning. However, the validity of this name must be notarised – a process that takes two or three days and costs 100-200 RMB. It's used on all documents relating to the property. If you're likely to be out of the country when documents need to be signed, you may give someone power of attorney to sign on your behalf, which must also be notarised, either in China at a notary public office or at the Chinese embassy or consulate in your home country.

Around three months after the purchase of a new property, the developer should provide you with a green A5 size booklet confirming that the full price has been received and all taxes paid.

After a lengthy wait – possibly a year or longer – you'll receive your ownership certificate, confirming you as the holder of the title deeds. This is a red, padded booklet containing details of the property, including a floor plan of the finished property; this may differ slightly from what was shown in the brochure. This is your copy of the deeds to the property; the actual deeds are held by the estates transaction office. It isn't unknown for the Public Security Bureau, which is involved in the issue of this certificate, to decide that the number of your property as stated by the developer is incorrect, so you may find that you have a slightly different address.

⚠ Caution

The information is this chapter was correct at the time of writing, but China's fast-moving property market is subject to constant and unpredictable changes. New laws are brought in, fees are increased and processes become more complex. It's recommended that you seek up to date advice from a legal expert before embarking on the purchase process.

Inventory

When you move into a property that you've purchased, check that the vendor hasn't removed any items that were included in the price (and the contract), such as fitted cupboards, kitchen appliances or even light fittings. It's also worth taking readings from the water and electricity meters on the day you move in so that you don't end up paying for the vendor's usage.

UTILITIES

This is the collective name for electricity, gas and water supplies. In China, both gas and electricity are used for heating and cooking; some properties have gas-fired boilers and radiators, while others rely on electrically-powered under-floor heating. Electricity also powers air-conditioning in the southern provinces. In many older and rural properties, people still rely on coal-fired boilers which contribute to the clouds of pollution over many cities, although China is under pressure to reduce its carbon emissions and cleaner fuels are installed in modern homes.

Electricity is supplied by the state though a number of regional companies. The State Grid Corporation of China (💻 sgcc.com.cn/ywlm/index.shtml) is the body which oversees suppliers. Electricity isn't particularly expensive at present – most residential properties are charged at between 0.5 and 0.7 RMB/Kwh – but as demand grows, so prices are likely to increase. The voltage is 220 (50 Hz), so most European appliances work in China, although American ones may need a transformer. Chinese plugs have two round pins, two flat pins or three flat pins (see 💻 electricaloutlet.org for a guide) but there are many types of multi-plug adapters sold so that you shouldn't need to change plugs on foreign appliances. All light bulbs have screw rather than bayonet fittings.

Natural gas is available throughout the country, although not all properties have a gas connection and many use bottled gas. In 2011, the cost was between 2 and 6 RMB per cubic metre. Many people pay for their gas using a card which is inserted into the meter and can be topped up with credits at the gas company. A similar system is sometimes available for electricity usage.

Water and sewage are handled by the local government and usage is metered. Charges are levied at around 15 RMB per cubic metre.

Your home will already be connected to the local water, sewage, electricity and, possibly, gas supply. It may also have telephone, internet and television connections. If your accommodation has been provided by your employer, then they may also cover the cost of your bills, but private tenants normally have to pay their own bills. Utility bills are sent out monthly and can be paid at the supplier's office or at your bank, where you can set up direct debits. Some landlords and management companies pay utility bills and then pass the charges on to you; the only problem with this is the risk of being overcharged, as it's unlikely you'll get to see the original bills!

Central Heating

Central heating is rarely found in homes south of the Yangtze River, but is essential in the northern provinces. It's still often installed and controlled by the local government which turns it on each autumn on 15th November and off again on 15th March, irrespective of the weather at the time.

There's no Chinese equivalent of rates or council tax for residential properties in China, where local governments reap much of their income from the sale of land to developers, but this cannot last much longer. The government is looking at a form of 'Property tax' for the future and in 2012 began trialling a form of 'property tax' in two cities: Chongqing and Shanghai. At present this tax only applies to those purchasing second properties and is an annual fee of between 0.5 and 1.2 per cent in Chongqing and 0.4 and 0.6 per cent of the purchase price in Shanghai. Beijing appears likely to follow next.

Much of the maintenance undertaken by local councils in other countries is handled by the management company which looks after your block or estate. They remove and dispose of rubbish, keep public areas (including lifts, stairs, roads and gardens) clean and tidy, maintain street lighting and drainage, and deal with issues such as noisy neighbours. There's a monthly fee for these services which is paid by all residents, whether owners or tenants, and reflects the size of individual properties and the amount of work undertaken, although it's generally much less than service charges in the West. The management fee doesn't include insurance, which is up to individual owners to arrange. Very few Chinese bother with household insurance – or any other kind of insurance, for that matter.

The management fee is calculated at between 0.8 and 1 RMB per square metre per month, so a 100m^2 (1,076ft^2) apartment could cost you an extra 80 to 100 RMB a month. Charges are higher for villas – 3 to 6 RMB per m^2 per month – due to the extra work required to maintain the gardens. Bear in mind that you also pay for any sports and leisure facilities in a complex.

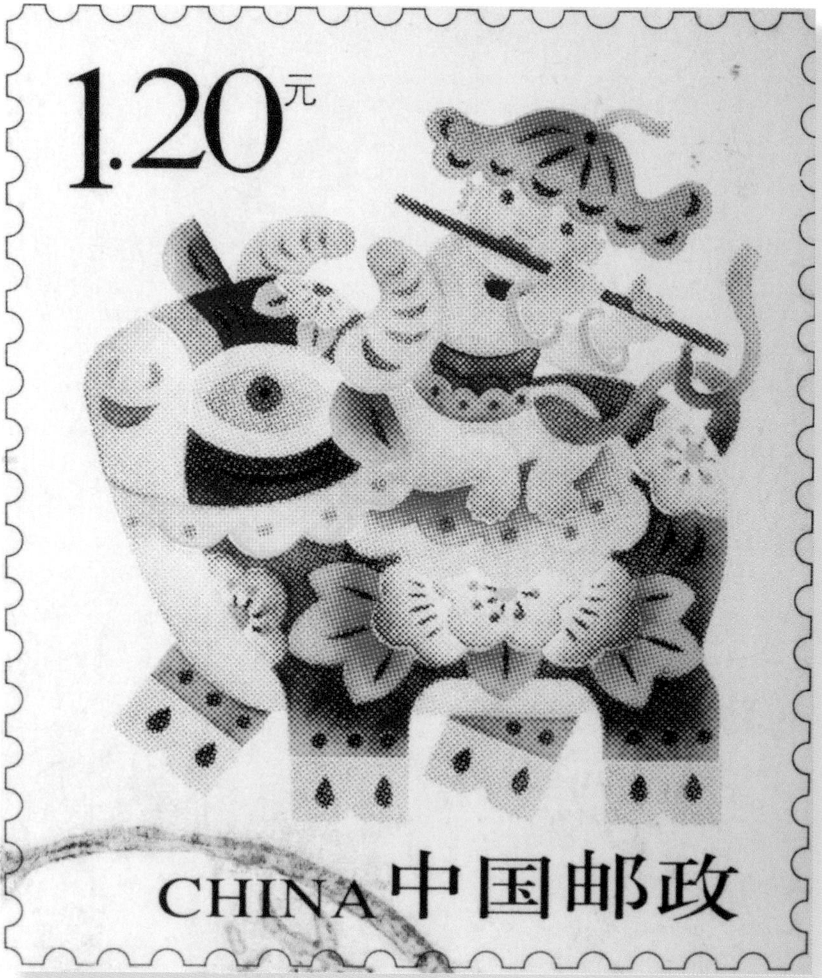
1.20元
CHINA 中国邮政

85

6.
POSTAL SERVICES

The state postal bureau, China Post, is one of the pillars of Chinese society. A job with China Post is considered a good career move and its employees are proud to work for the organisation. You see many postmen (and just as many postwomen) dressed in their smart dark green uniform and this colour, together with their distinctive yellow logo, is displayed on all post office buildings, post boxes and vehicles.

China has one of the oldest postal services in the world. Over 3,000 years ago, the Shang Dynasty devised a way of sending messages across its territory, not dissimilar to today's postal system. The current state service was established in 1949 and is one of the busiest in the world.

China Post now handles some 8.5bn letters and 86m parcels a year and recorded revenues in excess of 160bn RMB in 2010. In recent years its turnover has been steadily increasing, in notable contrast to many struggling postal systems in the West. It's efficient, reliable and inexpensive.

There are over 80,000 post offices in China. Every town has at least one, and in cities there's a main post office, plus numerous branch offices. The post office has a monopoly on stamps and you cannot buy them elsewhere. Packaging materials for sending parcels are also sold; in fact, you must wait until you're at the post office before sealing your parcels (see page 88).

China Post's main role is to provide an efficient postal service for letters and parcels. It has yet to follow the Western postal systems' diversification into retail and financial services, although larger post offices can arrange money transfers and there's a China Postal Savings Bank. This is a separate operation, and you cannot bank or withdraw money at a post office. Most post offices have a special counter for philatelists, and during the Mid-Autumn Festival they sell inexpensive parcels of moon cakes for people to mail out to relatives or friends. You can even ask the post office to deliver your morning paper.

Information about China Post is available online (chinapost.gov.cn – in Chinese only) or by phoning 11185 (Chinese only).

BUSINESS HOURS

Post office business hours in China are usually from 8am to 8pm seven days a week at main post offices, which often includes public holidays. Branch offices and post offices in small towns may be open for fewer hours, but never on less than six days a week, and they rarely close for lunch. A few major city branches provide a service 24 hours a day, seven days a week.

LETTER POST

Both domestic and overseas mail is generally reliable. You may encounter the occasional foreigner who claims his mail has been opened by the post office, but this is more paranoia than fact. China Post is too busy to examine expats' letters. If a letter is sent with insufficient postage, it will still be delivered. It may have a sticker on it showing the underpayment, but this is rarely requested from the addressee.

Post Boxes & Deliveries

Post boxes are mainly free standing, dark green steel boxes at waist height featuring the China

Post logo. They have two slots for letters; one for local mail and the other for long distance and international mail. They're usually emptied once a day around 6pm.

You may struggle to find one as there aren't many post boxes on the streets. Most people take their mail to the post office for dispatch, and you'll always find one there. Many of the major hotels also have a post box on their reception desk and you can post your mail into one of these; you don't need to be a hotel resident to use it.

Local mail is usually delivered the next day and long distance mail within two days. Postal staff have upgraded to delivering their letters by electric bicycles, while parcels and Express Mail Service (EMS) deliveries are transported by van. In the major cities there are two deliveries on weekdays, one on Saturdays and sometimes also one on Sundays. In smaller cities a single delivery, six days a week, is more usual.

Domestic Letters

For standard domestic mail within China, letters to local destinations cost just 0.80 RMB, provided they weigh no more than 20 grams. Each additional 20 grams or part of 20 grams costs 1.20 RMB, so a 50g letter costs 3.20 RMB to post, while a packet weighing 75g costs 4.40 RMB. Any size of envelope up to A4 is accepted for letter post. There are no classes of mail in China, although there's an express service (see below).

Domestic Letter Rates		
Item	**Rate in RMB**	
	Local	**Other Cities**
Postcard 0.80	0.80	
Letter up to 20g	0.80	1.20
Each extra 20g or part thereof	1.20	2.00

Note that local means within the same county, not within the same province.

Express Service

For a single extra payment you can use the 'express' service which claims to deliver your mail faster, although there are no guarantees. It costs an additional 40 RMB for any letter or package weighing up to 500g, or 70 RMB up to 1kg, irrespective of whether you're sending it to the next town or overseas. You receive a receipt and, for an extra 3 RMB, the post office will call

to advise you when the item has been delivered. This is quite an expensive service for domestic mail, therefore if you're sending a lightweight but urgent parcel such as documents within China, you may be better off using the alternative and more secure Express Mail Service (see page 89).

Chinese Addresses

The Chinese include the same information in their address as Westerners do, but in the reverse order, putting the country first and the addressee's name last, as shown below.

Country	*P R China*
Province/postcode	*Henan 450012*
City	*Zhengzhou*
Street/house number	*Ren Min Lu 22/7*
(Apartment 7, 22 Ren Min Road)	
Recipient (surname first)	*Wang Xiaoli*

Most envelopes have a printed box in the top left corner for you to write the postcode, while the stamps go on the top right corner.

All postcodes comprise six digits, with the first two denoting the province, region or major municipality, and the remainder pinpointing the city or town and delivery post office, e.g. all postcodes between 450000 and 479999 are reserved for Henan province and those starting with 45 indicate the provincial capital Zhengzhou. You can check postcodes by calling China Post on ☏ 11185.

It's normal to write the address for domestic mail using Chinese characters – bear in mind that most Chinese, including the postman, cannot read pinyin – there's usually someone at the post office who can write it out for you. If friends or family are writing to you in China, ask them to address their mail in English **and** in Chinese characters as this will better ensure that it reaches you. It's worth sending people some business cards, showing your contact details in Chinese, so they can stick one onto the envelope.

It isn't common practice to write your address on the back of the envelope, but it can be done – preferably in Chinese.

International Letters

You can buy airmail envelopes at post offices but there are no 'airmail stickers' available for regular envelopes; instead your mail is rubber-stamped with an airmail designation.

It's okay to address overseas mail in English, but you'll be asked which country you're mailing to as there are four different postage rates. Mail sent to Australasia, the US and most countries in

Europe, including the UK, are all included in one single rate (see below).

International Delivery Times

Service	Delivery time
EMS	2 to 4 days
Express letter	3 to 7 days
Airmail	5 to 15 days
Surface mail	1 month plus

Airmail

There are four different airmail charges based on four different world zones, with zone 1 the cheapest and zone 4 the most expensive:

Zone	Countries
1	Hong Kong, Macau and Taiwan, as well as neighbouring countries, including Japan, Korea, Mongolia, Vietnam and the Central Asian states.
2	Other Asian countries or regions.
3	Australasia, Canada, Europe and the US.
4	All other countries.

It costs 6 RMB to send a letter weighing up to 20g by airmail to zone 3 countries, e.g. the UK or US, plus 1.80 RMB for each additional 10g or part thereof. Thus a letter weighing 35g costs 9.60 RMB. A small package weighing up to 100g costs 18 RMB to the same destination, plus a further 15 RMB for each additional 100g or part thereof, thus

a 250g package would cost 48 RMB. For the full range of airmail charges, see the box below.

Express Post International

You can speed up your airmail (a little) by paying for the 'express' service, which claims to reduce the delivery time by one to three days and is cheaper than the Express Mail Service for overseas post. The cost is 40 RMB for items weighing up to 500g or 70 RMB if they weigh from 500g up to 1kg.

Other Services

♦ **PC Letter**: the Chinese have begun using internet technology to speed up the mail with a system called PC Letter. This allows the sender to email their letter to a designated post office which then prints it off and mails it to the recipient. It's a good way of contacting someone who doesn't have access to a computer and allegedly cuts the cost of sending a letter anywhere in the world to just 3.50 RMB. The system is new and is only available in the largest municipalities, e.g. Beijing, Shanghai, Tianjin and Chongqing, but if successful may be rolled out to the rest of the country. In order to use it you must pay a 50 RMB deposit to cover the cost of computer software and delivery charges.

♦ **Newspaper Delivery**: you can ask your postman to bring your daily paper along with the mail. There's no charge (e.g. for delivery) for this service, which is limited to national newspapers and magazines. To arrange a regular delivery, you must pay your postman cash in advance for, say, a year's supply of *China Daily* and it will arrive each morning with your post. Local newspapers are delivered by paper 'boys' or 'girls' – usually grown men or women – who also collect and recycle your old newspapers.

Airmail Fees

Item	Cost (RMB)			
	Zone 1	Zone 2	Zone 3	Zone 4
Letter up to 20g	5.00	5.50	6.00	7.00
Each additional 10g or part thereof	1.00	1.50	1.80	2.30
Postcard	4.50	4.50	4.50	4.50
Small package up to 100g	14	16	18	20
Each extra 100g or part thereof	9	12	15	18

> ### ⚠ Caution
>
> It isn't unusual for overseas magazine or newspaper subscriptions to go astray. This isn't necessarily the fault of China Post but of publishers who use the cheapest mailing route through various other countries. However, if the postman cannot deliver a magazine to an address because it won't fit through the letter box he may return it to his sorting depot, which then returns the magazine to the main sorting office in Beijing, and from there it either vanishes or turns up later several months out of date!

♦ **Post Restante**: available at main post offices, this service allows you to pick up your mail at the post office and is useful if you're moving around the country. There's a 3 RMB charge for each item of mail received (you must show ID such as your passport when making a collection). Mail is kept for up to 60 days before returning it to the sender.

Letters for *post restante* should be addressed to you at your chosen post office as follows:

> Your Name
>
> c/o *Post Restante*
>
> Main Post Office, e.g. Shenzhen GPO
>
> Street
>
> City
>
> Province/postcode
>
> P R China

♦ **Collector's Stamps & Postcards**: most large post offices maintain a separate desk where you can buy first day covers and other specialist stamps. Each year, China Post publishes a hard-bound book containing all the different stamps issued during the year, and these are also sold at this counter. The Chinese are great collectors, and many view stamps as an excellent investment: there are stories of people who have managed to buy houses from the proceeds of highly collectable stamps!

You can also buy postcards of major places of interest in the local area, although you may have to buy a complete set rather than, say, a single card or ten of a particular postcard that you'd like to send to all your friends.

PARCEL POST

Parcel post is calculated on weight and distance, with an initial charge covering up to 500g and then a further charge for each additional 500g or part thereof. The maximum weight is 35kg for both domestic and international parcels. Parcels are usually sent by Express Mail Service at no extra charge (see opposite). You can pay an additional fee to register or insure the contents (see below).

Sending parcels may test your patience as you cannot just turn up at a post office with your package sealed and ready. China Post requires customers to use an 'approved' cardboard box, which ranges in size from 125x75x85mm (5x3x3.5in) up to 530x290x370mm (21x12x15in) and your parcel will need to fit into one of these; although if it's smaller than the smallest box you may be able to get away with sending it as a package by letter post. Boxes cost from 2 RMB for the smallest up to 10 RMB for the largest.

The post office also insists on overseeing the packaging process, so ready-sealed parcels will simply be opened and packaged again. Take the item, together with any soft packaging such as bubble wrap, to the post office where staff will sell you a box and supervise the packing.

If you're sending an item overseas you must complete a customs declaration form, which involves taking the parcel, still unsealed, to a separate customs desk for inspection. It can then be sealed and taken to a third desk where you pay the postage costs and receive a receipt. Keep this just in case it goes missing. The entire process can easily take 30 minutes per parcel, so don't plan to send all your family's Christmas presents during your lunch hour.

Receiving a parcel isn't always a simple matter either. Parcels mailed to you in China are usually delivered by van, which is fine if you're at home or it fits through the letter box; if not, the postman

Parcel Post					
Item		**Cost (RMB)**			
	Domestic	**Zone 1**	**Zone 2**	**Zone 3**	**Zone 4**
Up to 500g	20	98	123	168	378
Additional 500g (or part thereof)	6	70	80	105	195

will leave a message for you to collect it. Parcels sent from overseas are treated as an unusual event, and you'll probably be contacted by phone and asked to collect your parcel at a certain place and time – it's advisable to ask your friends and family to include your phone number on any parcels they send. You must show proof of identity, e.g. your passport, when collecting mail.

Parcels are usually delivered within the same timescale as letters and EMS post.

Note that if people are mailing things to you from overseas, they should be aware that Chinese customs occasionally open parcels, therefore it would be unwise for anyone to send you anything which might fall under the category or restricted or prohibited goods (see page 62).

IMPORTANT DOCUMENTATION

China Post has three services which provide more security when sending important documents or valuables by mail:

Registered Post

This is available for letters and parcels and costs an extra 3 RMB. There are no special envelopes for registered post. You can use a normal envelope or an approved parcel box, and the post office will stamp it as registered and issue you with a receipt. If you pay an extra 3 RMB the post office will call you to tell you it's been delivered.

Insurance

You can insure the contents of letters and parcels, including those sent by EMS (see below) at a cost of 1 RMB for each 100 RMB of the item's value.

Express Mail Service (EMS)

Express Mail Service or EMS is a courier service offered by China Post. You can use it to send items weighing up to 500g, either within China or overseas, and many people use it to send important documents as it provides evidence of postage. There are special A4 sized cardboard envelopes for sending documents by EMS, but the service can also be used to send letters or small parcels.

EMS rates are the same as those for domestic and international parcel post, e.g. 20 RMB for a package weighing up to 500g within China or 168 RMB if you're mailing it to the UK (see page 87). It's faster than the so-called 'express' service but is considerably more expensive if you're sending items abroad. For more information about EMS, visit the dedicated website (🖳 ems.com.cn/english-main.jsp).

COURIER COMPANIES

Courier services such as DHL, Fed-Ex, UPS and TNT operate in China, but they struggle to thrive in the face of competition from cheaper Chinese courier companies and from China Post's EMS. The Chinese almost always prefer to use a Chinese service. Some expats believe that the major foreign courier services are faster and more reliable, but items sent by courier from overseas may be delayed when the company runs into the full force of Chinese bureaucracy at the customs desk.

MONEY TRANSFERS

All major post offices have a dedicated counter for money transfers, allowing you to send funds to a recipient anywhere in China; it's the Chinese equivalent of putting a cheque in the mail (Chinese banks don't issue chequebooks to individual customers). The process is simple: you complete a form, hand over the cash and receive a receipt. China Post then delivers the money within two days and calls the recipient when it's ready for collection. Charges depend on how much money you're sending but are usually 5-10 RMB.

This is a useful and reliable service, so much so that a number of embassies and consulates insist on using it for the transfer of visa fees.

CHANGE OF ADDRESS

If you're moving house, ask your postman for a change of address form, complete it and take it to your local post office – you may need to ask a Chinese speaker to help with this process. There's a charge of 100 RMB which is used as a deposit to cover the cost of redirecting your mail to the new address.

7.
TELECOMMUNICATIONS

C hina is now such a technologically advanced country, it's difficult to believe that only 25 years ago there were few private telephones. In those days many households and businesses had pagers, and if someone sent them a message they would search for a pay phone to access their messages and send a reply. Yet by 2012, there were over 1.3bn phone users in China; of these, almost 300m were fixed-line subscribers, while over 1bn had a mobile phone.

In just over 50 years, China has gone from being one of the most isolated to one of the most accessible countries in the world, with its finger firmly on the pulse of modern telecommunications. You can make a direct call to anywhere in the world from China, utilising some of the most up-to-date fibre optic technology; connections are fast and reception is excellent, and prices are a good deal cheaper than in the West. The internet is commonplace – there are at least 850m users – and young people 'talk' by text messaging and online chat services as much as they do face to face. And in every city and small town there's a proliferation of phone shops and telecoms businesses, and there are few places in China where you can escape the incessant ring tones of mobile phones.

Amazingly, this communications explosion is still controlled by the state, although even the Chinese government has found it difficult to manage. There have been attempts to censor the vast flow of information made possible by the advent of the internet – often referred to in the West as the Great Firewall of China – although censorship isn't as widespread or as strict as it's sometimes made out to be, and Chinese youth are adept at getting around it.

There's no telecommunications ombudsman in China, and customers must complain directly to the telecoms companies. The Ministry of Industry and Information Technology (🖥 miit.gov.cn) is responsible for the administration of the postal service, internet, broadcasting and communication – but not the content of programmes – as well as the production of electronic equipment and software. If you cannot get a satisfactory response from the phone companies, you can complain about your phone service by email to the ministry (🖥 chinatcc.gov.cn:8080/cmsadmin/shouli/shensu.jsp).

TELEPHONE COMPANIES

China Telecom (☎ 10000, 🖥 chinatelecom-h.com) is the largest telecoms operator in the country. A state-owned organisation, it maintains all fixed lines and also controls part of the mobile phone market. It's possible to route your call through other service providers, by using discount calling cards, but China Telecom is still your first port of call if you need a phone line installed or connected.

As in many developing countries, mobile phones are far more widely used than landlines, with over 1m new subscribers signing up each week. The largest mobile service provider is China Mobile, which has the largest network and customer base of any mobile phone company in the world, followed by China Unicom and China Telecom. Despite the state's domination of the sector, foreign telecoms companies are making inroads and Spain's Telefonica now owns 8 per cent of China Unicom.

INSTALLATION & REGISTRATION

Most foreigners who move to China to work have accommodation provided by their employer and a telephone line is usually part of the deal – many employers even cover the cost of domestic calls. However, if you arrive independently, you'll need to arrange your own phone connection. Virtually all homes, both new and pre-owned, have a telephone line and one or more telephone points already installed, and all you need to do is have the line connected and purchase a phone. If you need extra points, an electrician can do this cheaply.

The only way to get connected is to visit your nearest China Telecom office – you cannot arrange the connection online or by phone – and complete the registration procedure. It takes around 30 minutes and you must show some ID, e.g. your passport. The initial set up fee for a home landline is around 150 RMB and the monthly line rental 20 RMB. However, China Telecom requires you to pay a hefty deposit to cover the cost of calls – in effect, you pay for your calls in advance, as you do with a pre-paid mobile phone – and this may be as much as 500 RMB. The amount varies depending on where you live. The phone line should be connected almost immediately.

There are China Telecom offices in every town and in all major city districts.

If you have a problem with your telephone line, call China Telecom on ☎ 10000. Faults are usually attended to on the same day.

CHOOSING A TELEPHONE

China Telecom doesn't rent out telephones and you must buy one, either from one of their outlets or from an electrical goods or department store. Telephones are available in every shape, size and colour, from vintage '30s style handsets to phones concealed in a decorative porcelain ornament, and many come with a huge range of options, from hands free to caller ID, including cordless phones. Basic phones are cheap at around 30 RMB, so there's no point in bringing one from home (assuming it would work, anyway).

USING THE TELEPHONE

Using the phone in China is much the same as in any other country. The ring tone and engaged tones are similar to those used in the West. If you have problems getting through to a number, you can check it with directory enquiries (see page 97).

You need to be aware of the time differences when calling abroad to avoid calling in the middle of the night. Although China is spread across five time zones, officially it operates on a single time zone: Beijing time, which is eight hours ahead of GMT.

As a handy reckoner, Beijing time is:

♦ two or three hours behind Australia, depending on which state you're calling;

♦ eight hours ahead of UK time;

♦ between 16 and 19 hours ahead of the US, depending on which American time zone you're calling.

These times can vary according to the time of year; e.g. in summer time, when clocks are put forward one hour, Beijing is seven hours ahead of the UK. See **Time Difference** on page 258.

The Chinese often answer the phone with the word '*wei*'. This directly translates as 'hello', but is a word that's reserved for the phone. If you meet someone face to face, you say '*ni hao*'.

Codes & Numbers

All Chinese fixed line numbers have either 11 or 12 digits and begin with a 0. The first three or four digits are the area code, e.g. 021 for Shanghai, while the remainder are the subscriber's number. A list of area codes for major cities is given in the box opposite.

If you're calling someone in another city in China, you must include the full area code; e.g. to call someone in Shanghai from Chengdu, you would dial 021-1234 5678. However, if you're calling from within the Shanghai area, you only need to dial 1234-5678. For advice on making international calls, see below.

Mobile telephone numbers begin with 1 followed two digits for the service provider

Area Codes

The following codes are for the capital cities of China's metropolitan areas, provinces and autonomous regions.

Area	Code	Area	Code
Beijing	010	Changchun	0431
Changsha	0731	Chengdu	028
Chongqing	023	Fuzhou	0591
Guangzhou	020	Guiyang	0851
Haikou	0898	Hangzhou	0571
Harbin	0451	Hefei	0551
Hohhot	0471	Jinan	0531
Kunming	0871	Lanzhou	0931
Lhasa	0891	Nanchang	0791
Nanjing	025	Nanning	0771
Shanghai	021	Shenyang	024
Shijiazhuang	0311	Tianjin	022
Taiyuan	0351	Urumqi	0991
Wuhan	027	Xi'an	029
Xining	0971	Yichuan	0951
Zhengzhou	0371		

and then eight digits for the subscriber. The 86CallChina website has a useful function which allows you to identify the location where the phone is registered and avoid nuisance calls (🖳 86callchina.com/china-mobile-number-location-trace.htm).

International Calls

China's international telephone code is 86. If you're calling a number in China from abroad, you first dial the international entry code – in most countries this is 00, although in Australia, it's 0011 – and then 86, followed by the area code, omitting the 0, and then the subscriber's number. So to call someone in Shanghai (area code 021) from the UK, you would dial 0086-21-1234 5678. Making overseas calls from China is the same. First you must dial 00, followed by the country code, area code and number.

These calls are known as IDD (International Direct Dialling) and all domestic and (most) business phones can be used for IDD calls, although public telephones offering this service are rare. In hotels you frequently have to go via the operator to make overseas calls and whether you call from your hotel room or a hotel business centre, charges are very high. You'll be charged for a minimum call time of three minutes, even for shorter calls and sometimes even when the number is engaged.

Hong Kong, Macau & Taiwan

The two special administration regions (SARs), Hong Kong and Macau, are still treated as 'overseas' by mainland China and have their own international dialling codes: Hong Kong's is 852 and Macau's is 853. There are no area codes. If you want to phone someone in Hong Kong from the mainland you must dial 00 852 followed by the subscriber's number.

Taiwan is regarded as a province in China and has its own area code, 866, which is a combination of China's country code and a 6 for Taiwan, but it's still an international call. If you're calling Taiwan from China, you dial 00 866 and then the area code – Taipei's is 2 – followed by the number. This also applies if you're calling Taiwan from anywhere else in the world.

Free, Premium Rate & Reduced Rate Numbers

There are two types of toll-free or reduced rate numbers in China:

♦ **400 numbers**: these are ten digit numbers beginning with 400, which can be dialled throughout China as well as from mobile phones. Calls incur a small local access charge.

♦ **800 numbers**: these carry the prefix 800 followed by seven digits. These numbers are free from a landline, but there may be a charge if called from a mobile phone and not all 800 numbers are accessible from a mobile.

Toll-free numbers are usually provided by major organisations such as banks and airlines. Note that all calls to emergency services are free, even from a public phone.

As yet, there are no premium rate numbers (such as the 09 prefixes used in the UK) for chat lines, and all calls are charged at standard rates (see below).

Operator-assisted Calls

Other than in the most remote areas, where you may still have to call an operator to be connected to a number, the only times you'll speak to an operator are when calling directory enquiries (see page 97) or calling from a hotel room.

CALL RATES

Call charges vary from region to region, and also vary as a result of price wars between service operators. As a rough guide, local calls made using China Telecom cost up to 0.2 RMB per minute, while long distance calls cost between 0.4 and 0.5 RMB per minute. If you call overseas from your landline, routing your call through China Telecom, overseas call charges to Australia, Canada, European countries and the US are 8 RMB a minute.

You can cut the cost of calls further by using a discount card (see below) or by calling during off-peak times: if you phone abroad between midnight and 7am – a good time to catch people in the UK – China Telecom discounts calls by 40 per cent.

Calls from hotels or their business centres can be expensive, and you may be charged up to two or three times the normal rate.

Calling Cards

You can save money on phone calls by using a discount phone card, available from China Telecom and many other providers. These are pre-paid cards which you can buy almost anywhere, from post offices to street stalls, in values ranging from 50 to 500 RMB. Most can be used with any landline, some pay phones and even with your mobile if issued by the same service provider as your mobile phone. Many cards use internet protocol (IP) to transfer your

call along internet cables rather than the standard fixed telephone lines.

To use a calling card you must first input an access code – China Telecom's is 17900 – and select the language option, and then dial the card number, followed by a PIN number, before dialling the subscriber's number. The cost of the call is then debited from the balance on the card. This rather long-winded process can save you over 50 per cent on the cost of an international call.

The main disadvantage is that you must dial up to 30 digits to make a call – and it's easy to misdial and end up with a wrong number (although you can save the number and use speed dialling with many phones). Some mobile phone providers allow you to discount calls by inputting a simple five-digit code before the number.

Calling cards are often sold at discounted prices, enabling you to buy your call time in advance at a reduced rate; e.g. a card with 100 RMB of call time can be purchased for just 25 RMB. This should provide 1,000 minutes of local calls, about 660 minutes of long-distance calls or 12.5 minutes of overseas calls.

There are two types of cards available:

♦ **Internet Protocol (IP)**: these require you to dial a prefix number before the number you wish to call. They have the lowest rates, but reception can be variable and not all pay phones accept them.

♦ **Integrated Circuit (IC)**: these use the same technology as hotel door 'keys' and gas meter cards and are mainly used with public telephones. Your money is held in a small magnetic strip which you swipe through or insert into a slot in the phone. Charges for calls made using IC cards are slightly higher, but they're handy if you need to use public phones (see below).

☑ SURVIVAL TIP

The 85CallChina website (86callchina.com) provides lots of useful information about phone services and making calls in China, although its 'discounted' cards are available much more cheaply in China than via the website!

Most cards have a limited lifespan of up to six months, so make sure that you use your call time before they expire.

Note that the cheapest way to make calls, either domestic or international, is via your

which you duck into, while many are just standard phones on a wall. Many still accept coins, which can be problematical as most Chinese coins are very light and aren't always accepted, and for long distance calls you need a huge number of them. It isn't possible to make overseas calls from a pay phone using coins.

Many public phones accept cards (see **Calling Cards** above). Some work with an IP card, although most use the IC card system, particularly those in areas where there's no mobile signal, e.g. underground train stations. Charges are low if you use an IP card: local calls cost from 0.1 RMB a minute, long distance from 0.15 RMB a minute.

It's possible to make international calls with a card from some public phones, provided you have enough credit.

computer or an internet-linked mobile phone, using an internet telephony service such as Skype (see page 98).

TELEPHONE BILLS

Business users receive an itemised invoice each month, showing the charges for line rental, local calls, domestic long distance calls, itemised overseas calls and internet charges, but private subscribers frequently receive no invoice at all. The first you'll know that you've run out of credit on your account is when you cannot make outgoing calls, although incoming calls aren't affected. This means that the amount you deposited with China Telecom has almost run out and you must top it up.

To do this, either visit a China Telecom office or your bank. Bank staff are used to handling phone bills and will call the phone company, check how much you owe and transfer funds to cover any shortfall and provide a new deposit against future charges. So if you owe 50 RMB, you can instruct the bank to transfer 500 RMB to China Telecom which will restore your balance to 450 RMB. This is done instantly and your phone line is immediately unblocked. There's no fee for this service.

PUBLIC TELEPHONES

China has several types of public telephone, although they're becoming rarer as more people invest in mobile phones. In rural areas you may struggle to find one at all.

Some public phones resemble small red pagodas; others are like giant orange helmets

MOBILE TELEPHONES

China is one of the most mobile phone-addicted countries in the world and in 2012 over 1bn had a one, with their usage increasingly rapidly; it won't be long before the entire population has one! The major difference between mobile phones in China and the West is that the Chinese prefer pre paid (pay-as-you-go) phones. It's possible to get a phone on a contract, although the vast majority of users eschew this option. This may come as a relief to people from Western countries such as Australia and the UK, where the vast and sometimes misleading variety of schemes available makes choosing the most appropriate contract difficult.

Three companies dominate the mobile market. The largest by far is China Mobile (☎ 10086, 🖥 10086.cn), with some 590m subscribers, which has the widest coverage and uses the somewhat slow but reliable General Packet Radio Service (GPRS) system. Its main competitor is China Unicom (☎ 10010, 🖥 chinaunicom.com) which has about 170m subscribers and claims to cover roughly 350 cities. It operates via a wideband High Speed Code Division Multiple Access (HSCDMA) which can provide multi-media messaging and video streaming. China Unicom claims to be 10 per cent cheaper than China Mobile but reception can be a problem and high speed access isn't always as fast as you might wish. China Telecom has its own mobile phone service utilising the Evolution Data Optimised (EVDO) system. It's most popular with its landline service users, but has only a small slice of the market with around 94m subscribers. All three are largely state-owned, although some foreign telecommunications companies such as Telefonica and Vodafone hold minority stakes. Check the coverage and reception in your area before deciding which company to sign up with.

China's mobile phones operate on the GSM system (Global System for Mobile communications) on 900 MHz, thus most handsets imported from Europe can be used without problems; whereas handsets from the US or Canada, which operate on 850 MHz, cannot, and you'll need to buy a new phone (see below).

If your existing mobile phone works in China, getting connected is as simple as swapping your SIM card for a Chinese one. Some phones are locked to one service provider and cannot be used with another company's SIM, which you can check by calling your service provider or asking at a phone shop – many offer an unlocking service.

Chinese SIM cards can be purchased at any one of the countless outlets belonging to China Mobile, China Unicom or China Telecom. The first step is to register for an account, for which you'll need your passport. You then choose a number and receive your SIM. If you choose a prepaid option – China Mobile's Easyown is a popular one – it comes with a small credit which you top up as required. The last step is to activate your phone. Just wait a few minutes for it to ring and then dial the number that appears on the screen; your phone is then active and ready to use.

The cost of setting up your mobile phone is largely dependent on the phone number you choose (see box) and the amount of credit on your SIM card – this ranges from 30 RMB up to 300 RMB, and top ups are available in a similar range of values. You can top up your credit via the internet, at one of the many telephone shops, and even at small shops selling cigarettes and sweets. Credit is usually valid for up to six months, so if you're an occasional user you must remember to add credit periodically or your SIM card may expire.

You can get a phone on a contract – with a handset included – which is worthwhile if you need your phone for business and want to receive itemised monthly bills.

Mobile call charges are usually between 0.35 and 0.60 RMB per minute for local calls and about 1 RMB per minute for long distance calls, irrespective of whether you're calling another mobile or a landline. Calls overseas cost around 8 RMB a minute. Officially, there's a charge for both incoming and outgoing calls, but the intense competition between service suppliers means that incoming calls are rarely charged and you pay only for outgoing calls.

If you plan on making a lot of international calls from your mobile, China Mobile has special SIM cards, such as the Travel Plan50, which discount overseas calls by 50 per cent.

Chinese Phone Numbers

In China you 'buy' your mobile phone number and the amount you pay depends on the digits you choose. They typically cost between 30 and 300 RMB, with the more easily remembered numbers at the top end of the range. The Chinese are superstitious about numbers and prefer those which include the lucky number 8; the more 8s the more desirable the number, although most have been snapped up by China's millionaire businessmen. A totally random number, perhaps containing the number 4 – which in Chinese sounds the same as the word for 'death' – is the cheapest option.

Buying a Mobile Phone

Handsets are on sale everywhere: in supermarkets, department stores and the myriad telephone shops. Well known manufacturers such as Nokia, Motorola and Sony Ericsson produce phones in China, and control around half the market; the remainder belongs to Chinese brands such as Ningbo Bird.

An average handset costs about 600 RMB. You can pick up a cheap one for as little as 99 RMB, but it won't earn you much respect among your students or younger work colleagues; phones are a fashion statement among young people who pay a premium for the latest model, and will happily shell out up to 2,000 RMB for a handset that plays music, takes photos and connects to the internet.

One unusual type of mobile phone available in China is called a *Xiao Ling Tong*, which costs just 150 RMB but only works within a radius of 10km (6mi) from your home. This makes them ideal for children and (less fashion-conscious) teenagers who can use them to chat with friends but not to access the internet or call overseas.

DIRECTORIES

There are no residential telephone directories (*White Pages*) in China, either in book form or online. With so many Chinese sharing the same few surnames, compiling – or even using – such a directory would be an impossible task. For this reason, it's important to note down people's numbers or keep their business cards.

There are directories of business subscribers (*Yellow Pages*). Most hotels have them, as do Post Offices, and business subscribers can obtain copies from their telephone provider. You can also access Yellow Pages China online (🖳 yp.net.cn/english). Infobel (🖳 infobel.com) is a handy website which has links to several Chinese business directories.

Directory Enquiries

China has several telephone numbers which you can call for information:

◆ Local directory enquiries: ☎ 114

◆ Long distance directory enquiries: ☎ 113 or 173

◆ International directory enquiries: ☎ 115

◆ Time: ☎ 12117

◆ Weather: ☎ 12121

Bear in mind that only international directory enquiries are likely to have English-speaking operators.

EMERGENCY NUMBERS

There's no all-purpose emergency number in China. Rather, you must call different numbers for specific emergencies, as follows:

◆ Police: ☎ 110

◆ Traffic Police (in case of a traffic accident): ☎ 122

◆ Fire: ☎ 119

◆ Ambulance: ☎ 120.

In Beijing and Shanghai you can dial a private number (☎ 999) for all emergency services. In either of these cities, you can also call for an ambulance from United Family Hospitals. The numbers are ☎ 6433-2345 (Beijing) and ☎ 5133-1999 (Shanghai). The SOS Hospital in Beijing has its own emergency number (☎ 6462-9100).

It's advisable to keep these numbers by your home phone and programme them into your mobile.

INTERNET

China has taken to the internet like a duck to water and there are at least 850m users, with over half accessing the internet via their mobile phones. More and more people are hooking up via an ADSL (Asymmetrical Digital Subscriber Line) or broadband line. The service compares well with other countries: on average, China is about twice as slow as the UK when downloading information (3.91 Mb/s), e.g. receiving emails, but twice as fast when uploading (at 1.95 Mb/s), e.g. sending emails.

Most new buildings are wired for the internet, and hotel rooms have a connection for guests to use; in many places, wireless internet access (Wi-Fi) is available (see below). If you want an internet connection at home and your employer hasn't already provided it – and many do – broadband is available through China Telecom for a fixed charge of 100 RMB a month, allowing unlimited access to the internet 24 hours a day, seven days a week. This fee includes providing and installing a modem.

If you're a less frequent user, it's still possible to dial up to the internet as and when you need it, with calls charged at local rates. Access codes are as follows:

◆ ☎ 16300: log-in code 163, password 163

◆ ☎ 16900: log-in code 169, password 169

Wi-Fi is increasingly available in China, in hotels, cafés, hospitals and on university campuses, and many people use it to go online with their laptops or, more often, their mobile phones. All three mobile phone providers have 3G licences, so users can connect to the internet at broadband speeds provided they have an appropriate SIM card.

If you don't have an internet connection or a wireless device, you can still go online at one of China's numerous business centres or at an internet café. Business centres charge as much as 30 RMB an hour for you to use their computers, but provide a peaceful environment in which to work or check your email. Internet cafés are cheaper – between 3 and 5 RMB an hour – but can be rather noisy and smoky. Many are busy 24 hours a day, the clientele consisting of young men playing computer games such as *Warcraft*.

Internet cafés are viewed with a certain amount of suspicion by the authorities, and are regularly checked by the police and sometimes shut down. Under 18s are forbidden to use them, partly because of poor fire safety – this followed an incident when a fire in a Beijing internet café with an inadequate fire escape resulted in nine deaths – but also due to concerns about computer 'addiction'. The Chinese have set up 'boot camp' type organisations to wean youngsters off their dependence on the internet through physical hard work.

The Great Firewall of China

There are many tales of well-known websites being 'blocked' by the Chinese authorities but they should be taken with a pinch of salt. It's true that well-known websites such as Facebook, Hotmail and YouTube are sometimes rendered inaccessible, but rarely for long. And in spite of an on-going dispute over censorship between the Chinese state and Google, the search engine continues to provide a service to China, via Hong Kong, without interference from the mainland government, plus you can easily access one of its country-specific versions, such as Australian Google (🖥 google.com.au).

> If a media organisation broadcasts something which the government finds objectionable then it may be blocked, as is the case with the British Broadcasting Corporation (BBC). You cannot access the BBC's website in China unless you install a proxy browser or Virtual Private Network (VPN) such as Astrill (🖥 astrill .com) or Tor (🖥 torproject.org) on your laptop before arrival.

Most Chinese don't regard most website blocking as censorship but rather protection, and would be delighted if the government could find

a way to block some of the many pornographic websites which sneak into the country's web space.

Internet Telephony

You can enjoy cheap or even free phone calls using a Voice Over Internet Protocol (VOIP) system such as Skype (🖥 skype.com), VOIP (🖥 voip.com) or Vonage (🖥 vonage.co.uk). To use them, you just need a computer and internet connection, or an internet-enabled mobile phone with Wi-Fi access, plus a headset (earphones with a microphone) and the provider's free software – add a webcam if you want to make video calls. VOIP is usually free if you're calling someone who has the same set up, e.g. computer to computer, but it can also be used to make discounted calls to landlines and mobile phones.

Internet telephony is extremely popular in China, where the best-known provider is Skype. Although it has been occasionally blocked by the Chinese government, Skype is fully licensed to operate in China and is freely available in internet cafés and can be downloaded onto many mobile phones.

TELEGRAMS, TELEX & FAX

There's no longer a telegram service in mainland China – the internet has made it superfluous – but both telex and fax services are available. Any large hotel can send a fax for you from their business centre, but it isn't cheap. Expect to pay around 35 RMB for the first page and 5 RMB for each subsequent page.

If you plan to send and receive a lot of faxes, it's worth buying a fax machine; a wide range is available from supermarkets, department stores and electrical goods shops. Costs start at about 1,000 RMB for a basic model. Note that if you have a modem attached to your main telephone line and are using it to access broadband, you'll need a separate telephone line for the fax machine as the two cannot operate on the same line. Alternatively, you can buy a printer that allows you to scan documents and send the scanned documents as an email attachment.

8.
TELEVISION & RADIO

C hinese television is an acquired taste and of limited appeal if you don't speak the language. The state-controlled broadcaster, China Central Television (CCTV, 🖳 cntv.cn), dominates the airtime with a diet of news, game shows, Chinese opera and old movies, all interspersed with intrusive commercials. Overseas programming is limited – unless you can access it via the internet – and only one channel targets English-speaking viewers. Chinese radio mainly consists of music channels, although there's one station broadcasting in English and it's possible to listen to radio stations from abroad.

Programmes are listed in national and local newspapers or you can buy TV magazines: the best known is the state-owned *China Central Television* guide which covers CCTV's main 15 channels. All programmes are broadcast according to Beijing time.

TELEVISION

China Central Television broadcasts both nationwide and internationally, and its national channels are free to view. In addition there's a multitude of regional television companies. Almost every provincial government has its own TV station and, in many cases, there's a further station run by the provincial capital city. As a result, there are some 3,000 TV stations broadcasting throughout China, although the quality is generally poor.

All stations are commercial and cover their costs by broadcasting frequent advertisements; ads for medicines, alcohol and cars predominate. As a result, there's no television or radio licence in mainland China.

All Chinese channels broadcast in *Putonghua* (Mandarin) and there's a limited amount of foreign-language television, although it's possible to access some overseas channels at a cost. However, a new television provider entered the market in 2010 when Xinhua, the state-run news agency, launched its own 24-hour English-language news channel, CNC World (🖳 cncworld. tv), which it claims offers a 'global and objective' alternative to current news viewing. CNC World broadcasts documentaries and feature stories alongside straight news; a televisual version of the Xinhua news website (🖳 english.news.cn), it

provides foreigners with an alternative to the state broadcaster's CCTV News but is only accessible via cable subscription in China.

In most cities, you can receive between 40 and 60 TV channels free of charge. If you want more, you must subscribe to a cable service or invest in a satellite dish (which is officially illegal). The cable TV companies are government owned and have a monopoly on access to television programmes in a particular area.

The only places in China where there are television channels free from state control are the special administrative regions of Hong Kong and Macau. Some limited content from their commercial TV stations, such as ATV and TVB in Hong Kong and Macau's TDM, can be accessed in southern parts of the mainland, but most overseas channels are only available in upmarket hotels and the offices of organisations like the Public Security Bureau. Ordinary subscribers cannot afford them.

The Chinese fascination with all things technical means that current advances in TV viewing are being taken up fast. In 2011, China had just one high definition television (HDTV) station, CCTV 21, which shows highlights of the other channels in HD format, but was aiming to roll out the service to other channels. Meanwhile, digital television has arrived in the big four cities, where people now watch digital broadcasts via set-top boxes rather than relying on the old analogue signal. China plans to convert totally to digital TV by 2015.

Programmes

China Central Television is controlled by the State Administration of Radio, Film, and Television

(SARFT) and the Communist Party's Central Propaganda Department, both of which keep a strict eye on its content. The majority of viewing is family-friendly. Certainly, there's no danger of switching your set on in the late evening and witnessing soft porn, as you might in some European countries. There's a relentlessly upbeat nature to much of its programming – the word 'happy' appears in many programme titles – and a generally positive spin on news programmes, which are intended to show China in a good light to the rest of the world.

The most watched regular programme on terrestrial TV is *Xinwen Lianbo*, a rather straightforward news broadcast which goes out at 7.30pm each evening across several CCTV channels. Official statistics suggest that as many as 135m viewers regularly tune in. Compare this with America's *60 Minutes* which has drawn up to 25m viewers for its highest-rated broadcasts.

News is one of the mainstreams of TV programming, as are current affairs, and shows which expose the wrongdoings of officials (which are ratings winners). However, soaps and game shows make up a large slice of the schedule. Overall, the content is quite safe and undemanding; it isn't dissimilar to British TV in the early '80s, before the launch of Channel 4! Western programming has had some influence, and there's a Chinese version of Simon Cowell's talent show franchise, called *China's Got Talent*, but no indigenous versions of *Big Brother* or *Dancing with the Stars* (yet!).

Korean soap operas and stirring wartime dramas take up a lot of airtime, and Chinese television hasn't been able to follow the success

of the country's film industry in the West, e.g. *Crouching Tiger, Hidden Dragon;* and *Dream of the Red Chamber*, based on a classic Chinese novel and first shown in 1987, is probably the only Chinese TV series to be successfully sold abroad.

By far the most popular show of the year is the *New Year's Gala*, shown for two hours in the evening before the first day of Chinese New Year. This gathers together all the nation's most popular singers, musicians and 'cross talk' performers and is officially claimed to draw an 800m audience! Most Chinese wouldn't miss it.

China Central Television broadcasts over 20 different channels. The main ones, and their themes, are listed opposite.

Xinhua's new CNC World offers an alternative to CCTV News, although it's firmly focused on news, business and lifestyle rather than entertainment. The channel can be viewed via cable or over the internet on your laptop or mobile phone (🖵 cncworld.tv).

Local television includes a large number of provincial TV stations as well as city-based stations, e.g. Henan TV (provincial) with eight channels and Zhengzhou TV (Henan's capital city) with four more channels. Other than local news content, there's not much difference between them and many programmes are sourced directly from CCTV. Many local stations are free to air in the local area, and relayed to other parts of China via cable so, for example, migrants from Sichuan can keep up with their provincial news while working in Shanghai.

CCTV News

CCTV News (🖵 english.cntv.cn) is targeted specifically at English-speaking foreigners and competes directly with other global news channels such as BBC World, CNN and Sky News, with a claimed global audience of around 45m. It employs a number of international newsreaders and hosts including Mark Rowswell, a Canadian whose knowledge of China and its language has made him popular among the Chinese. You can watch the channel live online at 🖵 cctv.cntv.cn/englishnews.

Standards & Equipment

China broadcasts TV using the PAL-D system, similar to that used in Australasia. This means that TVs manufactured for use in North America (NTSC standard) and for the European PAL B/G or PAL-I systems may not function in China, although some foreign sets can be converted to operate under the PAL-D system. China plans to be completely digital by 2015, using the DTMB (Digital Terrestrial Multimedia Broadcast)

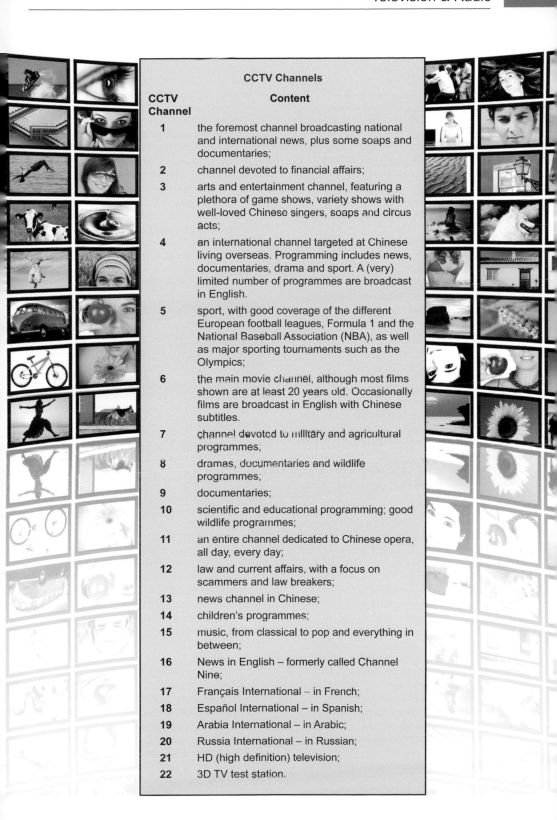

CCTV Channels

CCTV Channel	Content
1	the foremost channel broadcasting national and international news, plus some soaps and documentaries;
2	channel devoted to financial affairs;
3	arts and entertainment channel, featuring a plethora of game shows, variety shows with well-loved Chinese singers, soaps and circus acts;
4	an international channel targeted at Chinese living overseas. Programming includes news, documentaries, drama and sport. A (very) limited number of programmes are broadcast in English.
5	sport, with good coverage of the different European football leagues, Formula 1 and the National Baseball Association (NBA), as well as major sporting tournaments such as the Olympics;
6	the main movie channel, although most films shown are at least 20 years old. Occasionally films are broadcast in English with Chinese subtitles.
7	channel devoted to military and agricultural programmes;
8	dramas, documentaries and wildlife programmes;
9	documentaries;
10	scientific and educational programming; good wildlife programmes;
11	an entire channel dedicated to Chinese opera, all day, every day;
12	law and current affairs, with a focus on scammers and law breakers;
13	news channel in Chinese;
14	children's programmes;
15	music, from classical to pop and everything in between;
16	News in English – formerly called Channel Nine;
17	Français International – in French;
18	Español International – in Spanish;
19	Arabia International – in Arabic;
20	Russia International – in Russian;
21	HD (high definition) television;
22	3D TV test station.

standard. Not surprisingly, this is different from standards used elsewhere in the world, so it's likely that set-top boxes designed for use in the UK or US won't work in China.

There's little point in bringing television equipment from overseas to China as it's readily available and isn't expensive. Everything from small portables to huge flat-screen TVs are on sale at electrical goods shops, department stores and supermarkets; a 26in flat screen TV set costs between 1,600 and 2,000 RMB.

Most recently built apartments and villas are equipped with TV points and aerials to accommodate both terrestrial and cable television.

Free-to-air Stations

All of China Central Television's channels are free to air, with the exception of CCTV News and the other four foreign language channels, which are only available on cable in some areas. Local provincial and city stations are also free. In most places there are between 40 and 60 channels which can be viewed free of charge.

Commercial TV

There are no commercial channels in mainland China where all television output is state controlled. However, there are commercial channels broadcasting in Hong Kong and Macau. In Hong Kong, English-language programming is available on ATV World and TVB Pearl, but while some Chinese programming from TVB is shown in Guangdong province, it's subject to censorship by the Chinese authorities.

Cable & Satellite TV

If you want to watch anything other than CCTV or local television, you must subscribe to cable. This is widely available in China – many new apartments are wired for cable – and by 2011 over 88m viewers were tuning in. However, Chinese cable TV bears little resemblance to Sky or other Westerner broadcasters. Rather, it's another conduit for CCTV and the myriad provincial channels to reach your screen, along with other subscription-only stations such as Hong Kong's Phoenix Television. CCTV channels 15 to 20 can only be received in most places via cable subscription.

Most cable TV is offered in packages of 15 to 20 channels which cost from 450 to 1,000 RMB a year, including the decoder box, but it's as well to check which channels are provided as very few of them are in English. If you're lucky, you may find a package which includes National Geographic or the Discovery Channel, although they may be dubbed into Chinese, but it's unlikely you'll

receive HBO movies or sports channels such as ESPN, or even the CNN news channel. These are expensive and are usually only available to view in five-star hotels.

The only way to obtain television from around the world is to set up a satellite dish. These can be bought from around 60 RMB. There are companies offering satellite packages which they claim includes everything from HBO to the BBC, but they generally access systems outside China, e.g. in the Philippines, which is illegal. Just having a satellite dish in China is against the law. They were officially banned in the '90s and only major hotels are authorised to erect them – at considerable expense. If you must have one it's advisable to install it in a position where it cannot be seen; many people put them on a balcony or the middle of a flat roof. If someone in authority spots it, it will probably be confiscated.

> ☑ **SURVIVAL TIP**
>
> Satellite dishes won't work if the signal is blocked by trees or high buildings and the latter are omnipresent in Chinese cities.

Internet TV

One of the latest ways to watch television is via the internet. All you need is a broadband connection and a lead to connect your computer to your TV. Internet protocol television (IPTV) is popular in China, where a number of pirate websites upload the content of overseas channels on to their servers and broadcast them, with Chinese subtitles, sometimes within days of the episode being aired in its country of origin. This way they can watch programmes from overseas stations such as Australia's ABC, as well as HBO and the Asian Star network, and even the BBC. Of course, this isn't legal and pirate websites are regularly intercepted and closed down, only to pop up again at a different web address. University students usually know where to find them, so if you're a teacher it's worth asking your class for tips.

Most TV companies allow you to watch their programmes online, either as they're broadcast or for a period of time afterwards – this is sometimes known as 'TV on demand'. The catch is that you must usually be watching from an IP address within the country of broadcast, although you can get around this by subscribing to a virtual private network (VPN) provider which routes the signal through its own IP address before sending it on to you. British TV Anywhere (🖥 britishtvanywhere. com) offers this service anywhere in the world for less than £10/US$15 a month. A number of European TV channels are available online through the Beeline TV website (🖥 beelinetv. com).

You also have to find a way around China's internet 'nannies' which sometimes block the content of overseas websites, and you may need to install a proxy browser such as TOR (🖥 torproject.org) on your laptop or PC to get around this. Note, too, that the quality of transmissions may be affected by your download speed.

VIDEO & DVD

Video didn't last long in China where it was quickly superseded by VCDs (video compact discs). VCDs are still available in shops, supermarkets and market stalls, but have largely been replaced by DVDs and, more recently, Blu-ray Discs. VCD players can only play VCDs and music CDs, whereas DVD players can play CDs, VCDs and DVDs. Blu-ray players can play everything currently on sale.

Although counterfeit goods are officially illegal, the sale of pirated VCDs and DVDs is rife in China, with VCDs costing 5 RMB and DVDs from 0 to 10 RMB. Packaged boxes of entire TV series can be bought for just 200 RMB; not just Chinese series but also foreign ones such as *Desperate Housewives* and *The Sopranos*, often ripped from the screen and onto discs as soon as the series is over. Likewise, Oscar-winning movies are usually on sale within ten days of the awards ceremony. Most foreign films and TV series are in the original language with Chinese subtitles.

Beware of pirated VCDs or DVDs on sale in the street. Many are dubbed into Chinese, while others are of poor quality or even blank. Fortunately they're so cheap you can just throw the faulty disc away and buy another. However, there are plenty of shops where you can browse and select the discs you want. VCDs and DVDs on sale in state-run Xinhua bookshops are said to be genuine discs; they cost more than discs from street vendors but are still a great deal cheaper than in the West.

DVDs may be encoded with a region code, restricting the area of the world in which they can be played. The code for Western Europe is 2, while discs without any region coding are called all-region or region 0 discs. However, you can buy all-region DVD players and DVD players can be modified to be region-free, allowing the

playback of all discs (see : regionfreedvd.net and moneysavingexpert.com/shopping/dvd-unlock).

There are no DVD or video rental shops in China. With prices so low, everyone buys and no one wants to rent.

RADIO

Chinese radio is mainly music – either soft, tuneful ballads or Chinese versions of overseas pop music – interspersed with frequent frantic advertisements. News broadcasts and current affairs, weather and sports reports also feature heavily, and talk radio, where listeners phone in to air their views, is increasingly popular.

The state-run China National Radio (🖥 cnr. cn) broadcasts ten channels on both AM and FM. This is the station that once thundered propaganda out of loudspeakers in every village square, but now broadcasts a diet of news, music, culture and entertainment. There are special channels for popular music (Galaxy), Beijingers, ethnic minority interests and even one solely for elderly listeners. Although the

main language is Mandarin, there are broadcasts in Cantonese and various minority languages including Korean, Mongolian, Tibetan and Uygur. There is, however, nothing in English.

Another state-run enterprise, China Radio International (CRI), does broadcast in English, and in 57 other languages from Albanian to Vietnamese. China Radio International, once known as Radio Peking, is a huge operation, with 30 overseas bureaus, broadcasting news, current airs, economics, culture and entertainment. The English service (⌨ english.cri.cn/index.htm) which broadcasts on short wave, local AM/FM and online, is a blend of news, features and music (there's even a chart show with DJ Duggy Day!), as well as some interesting programmes on life in China from a foreigner's perspective and a regular slot on learning *Putonghua*. The main purpose of CRI is to introduce China to the rest of the world, but it's a useful resource if you're living in the country and want a different spin on news and current affairs.

As well as CNR and CRI, there are a great many local radio stations in every city; just turn the dial and see what you get. Unfortunately, broadcast quality is variable, and hisses and scratches are common interruptions on most transmissions.

If you want to listen to radio from home, you can now access most international stations via the internet – just download an online radio tuner such as Streema (⌨ streema.com) or go to your favourite station's website. China's censors rarely bother to jam radio transmissions or monitor online radio in the way that they sometimes do websites.

The hardy perennial global broadcasters BBC World Service and Voice of America can both be heard in China, either on short-wave radio or online. Radios are inexpensive in China but if you have a good short-wave radio you might want to bring it with you.

The BBC World Service (⌨ bbc.co.uk/worldservice) broadcasts worldwide, in English and over 30 other languages, and is the most respected international radio service in the world, with some 120m regular listeners. As well as news, current affairs and magazine shows, it also broadcasts sport, drama and entertainment – and is a comforting way for Britons to stay in touch with home. Voice of America (⌨ voanews.com) provides a similar service for Americans abroad.

Yungang Grottoes, Datong City (Shanxi)

9.

EDUCATION

The Chinese take education very seriously. Most see it as the principal, or even the only way in which individuals can secure their future in such a highly-populated nation. The introduction of the one-child policy in 1978 reinforced people's dependence on education. For many centuries, the Chinese relied on their offspring to support them in their old age and with a large family this was rarely a problem, but with only one child to pin their hopes on many will sacrifice almost anything to ensure that their child is educated to the highest standard and can prosper (and care for them) in later years.

The state also takes education seriously and has invested heavily in it, spending over US$100bn each year. Its programme of education reforms, which began in the '80s, has succeeded in raising the literacy rate to just under 96 per cent of the population, establishing some 600,000 schools and institutes of higher learning, and catching up with – and in some cases overtaking – Western countries. A straw poll of statistics suggests that in 2010, there were well over 200m Chinese students undertaking a course of study at any given time.

This is an amazing achievement in such a short period of time. In China's Imperial past, education was a privilege enjoyed only by the rich or favoured and even during the Cultural Revolution it was viewed as elitist. Education for all only became a reality in the mid-'80s under Deng Xiaoping who re-opened secondary schools and universities and introduced a standard nine years of compulsory education for all Chinese children.

Since 1986, children have been required to attend primary school from the age of seven to 12 and junior (middle) secondary school from 13 to 15. Within the cities and townships, school attendance is almost universal although, regrettably, in some country areas a proportion of students still fail to progress beyond primary education. Recent statistics show that just under 99 per cent of children attend primary school and 80 per cent attend secondary school, although the vast majority of the latter group (94 per cent) leave at 15 rather than progressing on to three more years' education at senior (middle high)

school. Students graduating from high school are considered to be very well educated.

There's no shortage of educational establishments in China. Statistics from the state news agency Xinhua reveal that in 2008 there were almost 400,000 state primary schools, some 62,000 junior or middle secondary schools and around 31,000 senior or high schools. According to China's Ministry of Education, in 2010 there were over 2,300 state universities or colleges and many other state learning institutions, such as vocational schools or schools for the physically disadvantaged. In addition to these government-run institutions, there are over 70,000 privately owned schools and some 1,300 private higher education facilities, e.g. universities and colleges. The number of private institutions could probably be trebled if you take into account the private kindergartens and 'crammers' that proliferate in every town.

The State Council assigns the Ministry of Education (🖥 moe.edu.cn) to oversee schooling, and schools are administered by provincial governments according to national guidelines. As well as certifying and appointing teachers, it also sets the curriculum which is increasingly geared towards science and technology rather than the arts. This, and the overall commitment to education, is one reason why China's global influence is increasing in leaps and bounds.

STATE SCHOOLS

The state school system in China is very different from that of the West. Well run, comprehensively funded and intensely competitive, state schools provide a hothouse environment for learning in which teachers are respected and motivated, students are diligent and there are almost none of the problems which plague many Western schools, such as truancy or disrespect for authority. Most Chinese schools run like clockwork, and the main reason some parents resort to the private sector is to augment their children's state-school learning and push them a little harder. All schools are co-educational and there are no single sex schools for boys or girls.

All schools funded by the state are officially free, although most charge parents fees to make up any shortfall in government funding; most parents pay something towards their child's education each semester, from state kindergartens to the end of high school and even on into higher education at a university or college. Fees vary from school to school and go directly towards the school's running costs. In some country areas they can take a large slice of the household budget, which is another reason why many rural children don't stay on at school, although there are no 'extras' to pay for such as textbooks which are provided by schools.

Public spending on education runs at 2.5 per cent of China's gross domestic product (GDP) and has been increasing by as much as 10 per cent year on year. Many schools in urban areas are well built and well equipped, although this is less true in the countryside (see below). In all cities, a few schools at both primary and secondary levels are singled out as 'key' schools, based on their academic record, and allocated the best teachers and equipment and the most

funds. Not surprisingly, competition for places at these schools is intense.

Rural Education

The emphasis on the importance of education doesn't extend to rural China, where half the population lives. Many country people have farms to run and don't hesitate to take their children out of school to labour in the fields as soon as they can legally do so; university is an unattainable dream for many rural Chinese. Even those children whose parents want them to learn have a far harder time in the countryside. There are fewer schools and children of different ages often end up being taught together in a single classroom. Things are improving but schools in rural areas generally lag far behind those in the cities and townships, and even those in the outlying suburbs of major cities are of a much lower standard than city-centre schools.

Parents & Teachers Associations

Parents have little input in state schools where the teachers and, ultimately, the state make the important decisions about students' education. Teachers do communicate with parents but this is usually only when a student appears to be failing to perform or regularly misbehaves. School reports are issued at the end of each semester, showing a student's progress in each subject but not his ranking within the class. Very few schools arrange parent-teacher days where parents can meet and talk to staff.

Curriculum & Homework

At primary school the curriculum is based around four core subjects: Chinese,

mathematics, science and English. Reading and writing in English is regarded as an essential skill in the new, Western-looking China, although children are rarely taught oral English (speaking and listening). When students move up to junior or middle school, the curriculum widens to encompass four more core subjects: physics, biology, history and geography.

The final three years of schooling at high middle school are optional and focus on future educational aspirations. Only three subjects are studied by all students – Chinese, English and maths – as classes are divided into arts and science fields. Arts' students study history, geography and political science, while science students study physics, chemistry and biology. After the first year, all efforts are concentrated on getting into university.

Examinations are a major part of Chinese children's lives. They're judged on their success in all-important tests rather than on their general school work, and much teaching focuses on getting them through exams rather than helping them to make their own discoveries or develop a creative mind. Teaching is often by rote, as students cram in as many facts as possible.

Homework occupies a large part of students' time. Primary school students have an hour an evening, increasing to up to two hours in middle school. High school students not only work until 10pm on six days a week but have an additional four hours of homework to fit in on Sundays, when many also attend crammers to brush up on their weaker subjects.

Choosing a School

Students normally attend the school nearest to their home but if a child does well at primary school, his parents may try to get him into a key school for the next stage of his education, even if it's a considerable distance from home and the fees are higher. Key schools are keen to attract the best students and maintain their high status, but not all attendees are academic high flyers. A few key schools keep some places open for less able students whose parents are willing to pay steep fees in order to gain a place. Fees can be 10,000 RMB or more per year.

Admissions

The academic year begins in September. Children are eligible to attend school once they're aged six, provided they reach the age of seven within the school year.

The choice of school is often quite limited at primary stage, and the local government's education department may allocate a place at the nearest school, which depends on where the family is registered as living (their *hukou*). At the end of primary school, pupils are assessed or may take an examination and, based on their results, the education department provides parents with an option of two or three middle schools which the child can attend. A similar process occurs at the end of middle school for students wishing to move on to high school.

In theory, there's nothing to prevent a foreigner sending their child to a state school, although some schools are unwilling to accept responsibility for foreign students. It depends on the individual school's policy. State schooling can be tough on a foreign child, particularly a Westerner, as all lessons are taught in Chinese.

School Hours & Terms

Rather than three terms, the Chinese school year is split into two semesters. The first semester starts in early September and continues until January, while the second begins in February or March and continues until July. The main holiday falls in winter, between January and March, and is dependent on the date of Chinese New Year and the Spring Festival, which fall at a slightly different time each year. There are also two mid-semester breaks: a week in October which coincides with the Mid-Autumn Festival and National Day, and a week in May around Labour Day.

Hong Kong Schools

Schools in Hong Kong follow the British pattern of three terms, with the school year starting in late August/early September and finishing in late June. They have one week mid-term breaks during the autumn and spring terms, two-week holidays at the end of the autumn and winter terms and a six-week break in summer.

School hours are long, even from the youngest age, with seven-year-olds putting in up to eight hours a day. Hours vary depending on the level of schooling and become progressively longer as a student's education intensifies. The main differences are as follows:

♦ **Primary school**: attendance is five days a week, Monday to Friday, from 7.15am to noon and then from 2.30 to 6pm, although younger children may finish at 4pm.

♦ **Middle school**: lessons start at 7.15am and continue until 12.15pm, when there's a break before the afternoon session from 1.30pm until 5.30pm. Lessons continue in the evening from 7.30 until 9pm, although the evening period may be set aside for homework. This regime is for five days a week.

♦ **High middle school**: morning sessions are from 7.15am to noon, afternoon lessons from 2.30 to 5pm, after which students are back at their desks between 6.40 and 10pm. It's a five day week during the first year, which extends to six days (including Saturdays) in years two and three, and students must also squeeze in homework on Sundays.

This high pressure learning environment leaves little if any time for extracurricular activities such as sports or science clubs. Most Chinese students are focused 100 per cent on study!

Despite the long school day, it's rare for state schools in cities to have canteens and most children go home for meals, eat at a nearby café or buy a snack from a roadside vendor.

Uniforms & Equipment

China has shrugged off decades of wearing near-identical clothing, and uniforms are now rare in state schools. One exception is the bright red scarf worn by Young Pioneers – a junior version of the Communist Party – on important days such as Chinese Communist Party Day on July 1st. Students must provide their own pens, pencils, notebooks and other paraphernalia, although textbooks are provided by the school.

Pre-school & Day Care

Nurseries and kindergartens are widespread and any parents who can afford it send their pre-school age child to one. Chinese kindergartens aren't just about play; they're also the first step on the long road to university, and the three to six year olds who attend them have short lessons in Chinese and basic arithmetic, as well as games and music. As a result of the current obsession with learning English, it isn't uncommon for the toddlers to take their first steps in learning the language at kindergarten.

Children attend on four or five days a week between 8.30am and 3.30pm. Some kindergartens open earlier and close later so that staff can look after children for extra hours to suit their parents' work patterns. Most also provide a hot lunch. It's an excellent system and so popular with parents that places at the best facilities are difficult to obtain. There are a few state kindergartens but the majority are private and some are bilingual, making them a good way of easing a foreign child into the Chinese education system. The drawback to private kindergartens is the cost: between 20,000 and 30,000 RMB a year, depending upon their location. If you can find a suitable state kindergarten, the charges are lower at between 12,000 and 18,000 RMB a year.

Day care, which offers a child-minding service, rather than pre-school education, is much less common. Most Chinese couples have a parent living nearby or even with them, and grandma looks after the day care of the little one. You often see groups of late middle-aged women in the park, sitting together chatting and knitting with toddlers playing close by.

Primary Education

Primary education lasts for five years, from seven to 12 years old. The emphasis is heavily on the 'three Rs' (reading, writing and arithmetic) and lessons in the core subjects of Chinese, mathematics and English take precedence. Both *Putonghua* (Mandarin Chinese) and pinyin are taught at this stage, and students begin the process of learning to read and write in English, which is deemed essential for later academic and work success. Other major subjects taught at this stage include music, art (e.g. drawing), computer basics, history, geography and physical education (PE). An important strand of the curriculum is moral behaviour – the equivalent of citizenship in a Western school – which focuses on the 'five loves': these are the love of the motherland, the people, socialism, labour and science. Before lessons commence, martial music is often played and sometimes there are a few exercises or a song.

Teachers stick with their subject so that one may teach only Chinese and another only maths but at several different levels, rather than having one teacher for each class who teaches all subjects. Classes are frequently large; 60

students are by no means rare and there could be as many as 100+ in areas where there are insufficient schools to cope with the growing population. Despite this, they're calm and studious places and Chinese teachers are rarely required to undertake crowd control.

Most schools are three-storey buildings, often arranged as an open square with concrete staircases at each corner and an open-fronted continuous corridor along each floor off which there are classrooms. There may be an asphalted area for play, perhaps with one or two basketball rings. Classrooms can be basic with tiled floors, old wooden desks, often in pairs, and a small dais for the teacher to stand on, with a large blackboard on the wall, although this would be bordering on luxury in some rural schools. Heating is only installed in areas where winters are cold, and then only operates between November and March.

Secondary Education

This is divided into two stages. The first stage, middle school, is attended by 12 to 15 year olds and is compulsory, while the second stage, high middle school, is optional for 16 to 18 year olds. Most parents want their children to stay at school until 18, but they can only do so if they pass an important set of exams.

On entering middle school, students take on new subjects, including geography, history and politics – all three put the emphasis on China's recent past, its policies and current global position. Maths and science subjects become more detailed and advanced, with biology and physics being added to the curriculum, while studies in Chinese and English remain important. Because around a fifth of children (mainly in rural areas) don't move on to secondary school, classes are somewhat smaller with 45 to 60 students fairly typical.

When students move on to high middle school, classes are much smaller – 35 to 45 students at most – but hours increase until students are working six days a week from early morning until late evening with breaks in between. After the first year, students are split into streams, with some focusing on the arts and others on sciences, although Chinese, maths and English remain core subjects. All students work towards an end of school qualification, the High Middle School Graduation Certificate, but the main challenge of the last three years of their education lies in preparing for the National College Entrance Examination (NCEE) at the end of their third year, and as June approaches, teaching gives way to intensive revision as each

concentrates solely on preparing for this all-important exam.

> ### Alternative Schools
>
> In additional to regular schools, China has around 1,500 state schools for the physically disabled, such as blind or deaf students. There are also special schools for students who aim for a career using foreign languages, e.g. as a translator, or in the People's Liberation Army, as sports professionals or even circus performers. Some of these start as early as primary level.

Examinations

Never underestimate the importance of examinations to Chinese schoolchildren. The pressure to gain good grades begins in primary school, as pupils' performance in the final year can have a direct effect on which middle school they attend. The better they do, the wider the choice of schools and there's even the possibility of making it into one of the key schools. The pressure continues through middle school as students work towards the Senior Secondary Education Entrance Examination (*Zhong Kao*). They must pass it to go on to the second level of secondary education, and places in the best high middle schools are reserved for those with the best grades. Students who fail this exam can move on to one of the many vocational colleges or go directly into the world of work.

It's possible for wealthy parents to 'buy' a place in the school of their choice if their child's exam results are poor, by paying higher fees. Fees of 8,000 to 12,000 RMB a year aren't uncommon in a top-level middle school, while entrance into a 'key' high middle school can cost as much as 30,000 RMB, assuming the school is willing to accept the student. Many aren't, as their key status depends on their students' academic honours.

The most anticipated (and feared) test is the National College Entrance Examination (NCEE), known in Chinese as *Gao Kao*. The parental frenzy that accompanies this test is astonishing. Many rent accommodation close to their child's school so he doesn't have to travel far and can enjoy home-cooked meals as he studies. On the big day, traffic around the examination hall is chaotic as anxious parents ferry their child there, and additional police are brought in to control the crowds. It's a major life event for the student and his parents, who believe that success in getting into university is absolutely imperative for their child's future happiness. Once the exam is over, newspapers are full of stories about students being caught cheating and teachers helping their charges to get an early peek at the exam papers.

The examination has a maximum score of 750, although the pass mark is usually in the low to middle 500s. This depends on the overall scores, and in a year when the majority of candidates do well, the bar is set much higher. It isn't until the results are posted on the internet that the candidates learn the score they needed to obtain entry to a university or college, and whether or not they've achieved it. Those who are successful can then apply to their chosen institute.

The pass mark changes each year, depending on the number of places available, the average scores achieved and the province or municipality in which the student has his *hukou*. Students resident in Beijing have an advantage, as more university places are reserved for Beijingers; those living in the most populous provinces such as Guangdong face the most competition with their peers.

If a student gets a score of even one point less than the pass mark, e.g. 529 when the mark is set at 530, their dreams are over and their parents are left to try to salvage something from the wreckage. They may try to arrange for their child to attend university in an overseas country – one reason why there are so many Chinese studying abroad – or enrol them at a private university in China, provided they can afford the steep fees. The third alternative is for the student to stay on at school for a further year and retake the examination, but many are unhappy to take this route because of the teasing they receive from the other students, therefore a number of schools have been established that provide specific teaching for those retaking the final examination. These are well attended but expensive.

Leaving

Students who complete nine years of education are allowed to leave school at the end of middle school. They can enrol on a course in a vocational or trade school or they may simply start work.

PRIVATE SCHOOLS

In all, there are some 70,000 private schools in China, catering to around 14m students, plus a further 1,300 private higher education establishments with some 1.8m students.

As the Chinese become wealthier and more aspirational, private education is catching on, although it's still for the privileged 'few' (in Chinese terms); either those who perceive it to be better than the state system – not necessarily the case – or those whose children aren't progressing well at a state school. Note that most private schools are designed for Chinese rather than foreign students, and may not follow international curricula or use English as their language of instruction. They aren't the same as international schools (see below).

Many private establishments focus on single subjects and act as a back up to the state system, while others offer a viable alternative for expatriate children. The main types which you might encounter are:

♦ **International schools**: mainly designed for the children of expatriates (see below). Some will only accept Chinese children if their parents hold a foreign passport.

♦ **Crammers**: these offer extra lessons in the evenings, at weekends and during school and public holidays, and provide additional teaching in specific subjects such as maths and, especially, English. Parents use them as 'back up' if their child is struggling in a subject required for the NCEE examination. A few also teach arts subjects, such as music.

♦ **Language schools**: these mainly focus on teaching English to adults. Many students are

working towards TOEFL (Test of English as a Foreign Language) or IELTS (International English Language Teaching System) tests as a requirement for emigration to Western countries. There are also specialist language courses such as Business English.

State School vs. International School

For expatriates, finding suitable schooling for their children is one of the major challenges when moving abroad. Some parents prefer to enrol them in a boarding school – or even a day school – in their home country, and fly them out for the long summer holidays, but this only works if there's a good family support network back home and you don't plan to stay in China for more than a few years. Another option is home schooling, although this puts a lot of pressure on the parent who takes on the teaching role.

Young children benefit greatly from attending a Chinese kindergarten. As well as making friends with local children, they pick up elements of the culture and learn a considerable amount of basic Chinese. However, once they reach seven, you must make the decision between state or private education.

State school may only be an option if they're adaptable and you plan to stay in China long term. The main benefit is that young children usually learn Chinese amazingly quickly and many act as interpreters for their parents. However, children aged ten or older can struggle in a Chinese school. It isn't just the language barrier but the fact that the schooling culture is much less relaxed than in the West. Many parents may feel it isn't fair to subject their child to a radically different method of schooling, particularly if they intend to move home or on to a different country in a few years' time.

Then there's the issue of finding a state school that's willing to educate a foreign child. Schools in Beijing tend to be more open towards accepting foreign students, but schools in less developed parts of the country may not want the responsibility.

An international school is the best option if your stay in China will be relatively short, or your children are at a crucial stage in their education. Teaching is generally in English and most follow a curriculum designed to blend seamlessly with those of other countries. Many have a connection with a specific country such as Canada, Germany, Japan, the UK or the US, and often tailor their lessons towards specific countries' university entrance examinations, e.g. British A-levels. Many offer the opportunity to take the International Baccalaureate, which is a

university-entrance qualification recognised in most countries around the world.

Another advantage of international schools is that they're fun and open-minded places in which to learn. Students from different countries study together and share each other's cultures and facilities, and the teaching staff are usually excellent. The major downside is the expense (see **Fees** below).

There are approximately 110 international schools (including kindergartens) in China. However, the majority only cater for children up to the age of 12 or 13 and only around 45 accept students up to the age of 18. The vast majority are situated in the big four cities, with the widest choice in Beijing and Shanghai. The capital (where most of the embassies are located) has American, Australian, Canadian, French, German, Japanese, Pakistani, Spanish and Swedish schools, while there are both American and German schools in Shanghai. However, there are also international schools in Chengdu, Hangzhou, Nanjing, Ningbo, Tianjin and Xi'an.

> ☑ **SURVIVAL TIP**
>
> If your child plans to go to university outside China, they must attend a school with a universally recognised accreditation, such as the Council of International Schools (CIS, ⌨ cois.org) or the European Council of International Schools (ECIS, ⌨ ecis.org).

International schools vary widely and you should be wary of taking the school's name at face value. Just because a school is called the Oxford International School, doesn't necessarily mean it has anything to do with Oxford University or even the city of Oxford. The Chinese are fond of using prestigious Western names to market less prestigious establishments, hoping perhaps that the good reputation will rub off on them. There are at least three schools which have a genuine connection with overseas establishments. These include the four branches of Dulwich College in Beijing, Shanghai, Suzhou and Zhuhai and the Harrow International School in Beijing. In addition, there are schools with connections to notable institutes in Australia, Canada, the US and other countries.

The best way to find a suitable international school – or state school, for that matter – is to talk to other expat parents. There's no substitute for independent recommendations.

For background information, there are a number of useful websites, including English Schools (💻 english-schools.org/china/index.htm) and Shambles (💻 shambles.net/indexoriginal.htm). Never take a school's claims at face value. Visit, look around, talk to the teachers and pupils and, if possible, the parents. Check the exam results and the percentage of students going on to higher education. And be sure to ask for your child's input as it's he (or she) who will be spending much of their time there.

If possible, you should start to investigate schools at least a year in advance of bringing your family to China, as the best ones fill up fast. Some have quite strict entrance criteria – or even an entrance exam – and most require prospective parents to pay a (large) deposit to keep a place for their child. This should be deducted from the first year's fees.

Children in China

Chinese children aren't 'wrapped in cotton wool'. They learn from an early age to look out for themselves. Health and safety is still a fairly abstract idea; safety barriers are often non-existent and just crossing the road is dangerous. Therefore growing up in China will instil in your children a much greater sense of independence and self-reliance. In many ways, China is safer than the West: people are more respectful and the almost total absence of a drug scene is a big plus if you have teenagers, although the ubiquitous use of cigarettes by young males, who seems to start smoking at around 12 or 13, rather counters this.

Fees

The worst aspect of educating your child at an international school is the often overwhelming expense. This puts them beyond the pocket of many parents, although if your employment package includes relocating your family, it should also include suitable schooling for your child.

In 2011, the annual fee for attending an international kindergarten was around 120,000 RMB. Fees at a reputable international school ranged from 160,000 to 220,000 RMB a year, depending on the age of the child; fees increase with the age of the student. Some schools charge a one-off application fee of around 2,000 RMB, and don't forget to budget for extras, such as uniforms, school trips, transport, lunches and so forth, which can easily add another 10,000 to 15,000 RMB per year.

Chinese private schools are much cheaper – some charge as little as 20,000 RMB a year – but they're geared towards Chinese students and they teach in Chinese. Many specialist schools have hourly rates: 60 to 100 RMB an hour to attend a crammer, 100 RMB an hour to learn a musical instrument, and up to 150 RMB an hour for English language tuition from an English native speaker – or up to 300 RMB in one of the big four cities – although teachers are only paid a fraction of these rates!

HIGHER EDUCATION

Third-level (tertiary) education falls into two categories in China. Further education refers to vocational schools and colleges (see page 119) while the term higher education refers to universities, sometimes called colleges or institutes.

Universities

In 2011, there were around 2,300 state-approved higher learning establishments in China, attended by some 28m students. In addition, there were over 1,300 private colleges, although they're seen as a poor substitute for the state universities. There's no entrance exam for private colleges but the qualifications awarded aren't as prestigious either.

Although China has poured money into its university system in recent years, with special emphasis on scientific and technical subjects, there aren't sufficient places to go around and there's intense competition among high school students to gain a place. According to the 2010 census, just under 9 per cent of Chinese had completed a university education, a much lower percentage than in many Western countries, although the number of graduates is growing annually and over 6m were forecast to graduate in 2010.

Just as there are key schools in China, so there were once key universities, although the description is no longer used. Those directly under the Ministry of Education's management, as opposed to provincial government control, are generally considered to be the best, and the top universities are in Beijing and Shanghai. Gaining a place at either Tsinghua or Beijing (Peking) University in Beijing or Fudan University in Shanghai is the ultimate reward for academic success, but there are also some good seats of learning in other Chinese cities, such as Nanjing University and Zhejiang University in Hangzhou. A list of state universities can be found on the China Today website (💻 chinatoday.com/edu/a00.htm).

Chinese universities are large; most have between 10,000 and 35,000 students. The majority teach a broad spectrum of subjects, but there are many that specialise in particular areas of study, such as medicine, engineering, agriculture or foreign languages. The language of instruction is Chinese, although a few institutes also have courses in English, e.g. Fudan University and Beihang University in Beijing.

The atmosphere at university is one of exhilaration and relief. New students find themselves suddenly free from the pressures of high school (and their parents' expectations) and are able to have fun as well as study. Nevertheless, they work hard and very few drop out or fail to obtain a degree.

The age of admission is usually 18, although on rare occasions an exceptional student may be accepted at a younger age; mature students are also unusual, although they're permitted to take undergraduate courses. The university year lasts from September to July, over two semesters, and most bachelor's degree courses take four years to complete. A master's degree takes a further two years, while a doctorate requires at least an additional two years.

As well as universities, China has a number of higher education establishments which train students for a career in specific organisations such as the Communist Party, the armed forces or the diplomatic service. The three main airlines also have their own colleges which train students to work as pilots and flight attendants.

Overseas Students

As well as Chinese students, China's higher education system also hosts around 200,000 foreign students each year. Most study Chinese, Traditional Chinese Medicine or martial arts, but it's possible to study academic subjects at a Chinese university or to take a master's degree or doctorate. Foreign students are actively encouraged and plans are in hand to increase the number to 500,000 by 2015.

For a guide to the universities which accept international students, see the Chinese Education and Research Network website (💻 edu.cn/english_1369/index.shtml) or the Chinese University and College Admissions System (CUCAS, 💻 cucas.edu.cn).

Fees & Expenses

Chinese students must pay to attend university, although the costs aren't high in comparison with other countries such as the UK or US. Families budget for this important expense and it's rare for a Chinese graduate to start his working life in debt. The main costs are:

♦ **Tuition fees**: 6,000 to 8,000 RMB a year.

♦ **Accommodation**: 1,600 to 2,000 RMB a year for a bed in a dormitory room (see below).

♦ **Meals**: around 4,000 RMB a year, eaten at the campus canteen.

If a student does particularly well, either in the NCEE exam or as an undergraduate, his university can nominate him for a 'scholarship' from the education authorities, meaning that some top students get their tuition fees largely paid for by their provincial government.

Classes are much smaller than in schools – usually 30 to 35 students – but hours can be long. They usually begin around 8am and don't end until 7 or even 9pm, although there's a three-hour lunch break between 12noon and 3pm. Undergraduates attend at least 14 two-hour classes a week in pursuit of a bachelor's degree. They also study a wider range of subjects as part of their course – perhaps three times as many as students in the West – and no matter what their major is, one of these subjects is English. This is one reason why there's such demand for native English-speaking teachers in China's third level of education.

A number of Chinese universities have links with overseas institutes, and it's possible for students to do two years of their course in China and a further two years at the affiliated overseas university – or the overseas university may send teachers to China during the students' final year. In both cases, the students are awarded a degree from China and a second degree from the overseas university.

Joint-venture universities include Xi'an Jiaotong-Liverpool University (🖳 xjtlu.edu.cn) located in Suzhou near Shanghai. As well as having over 60 international students, it also hosts around 750 students at the University of Liverpool in the UK. Britain's Nottingham University has gone one step further by opening a branch campus of its own in China at Ningbo (🖳 nottingham.edu.cn) and New York University has a branch campus in Shanghai (🖳 nyu.edu/global/shanghai).

Admissions

Admission to Chinese universities is based on exam results. Most students sit the NCEE in their last year of school and their final placement depends on their score. However, in 2010 an alternative admissions system was introduced, whereby some of the top universities could invite key schools to nominate exceptional pupils as prospective students; those students then sit the universities' own entrance exams rather than the NCEE. Despite concerns that the selection of 'exceptional' students could open up a new area for corruption, with wealthy parents offering bribes to schools to include their offspring in that category, the scheme gained government approval and now offers an alternative route into high education.

Foreign students can apply direct to universities, and their admission is dependent on their grades obtained in their home country's examinations.

Terms & Courses

The academic year is divided into two semesters. The first starts in September and finishes in January while the second starts in late February and finishes in July. The main holiday coincides with the Chinese New Year in late January/February.

The beginning of the first semester for first-year students is in total contrast to the party atmosphere in Western universities. Rather than dressing up for the fresher's ball, the new students – both men and women – don army uniform and undergo a three-week spell of compulsory military training, which includes living in barracks and even firing live ammunition. This short course of drill and discipline is in lieu of military service and foreign students aren't expected to participate!

Accommodation

All Chinese students are required to live on campus, which is rigidly applied. Parents pay for the accommodation and approve of the arrangement – they like to know that their child is secure. Student dormitories are a far cry from halls of residence in the West. Most consist of four or six bunks, plus desks and chairs. Showers, toilets and laundry amenities are shared. Canteens are provided (there are no cooking facilities in the rooms) but student lounges are rare. There are no student bars!

Living off campus in private rooms is forbidden until after graduation.

Degrees

Degrees are awarded at the end of the course in a formal ceremony on campus; most students wear a gown and mortar board for this momentous event and those who've done particularly well are singled out for praise.

After completing a bachelor's degree, there's the option to go on take a master's degree – subject to passing an exam – and then a doctorate. However, it's rare, if not impossible, for a student to move straight onto a post-graduate course immediately after obtaining their first degree. Most are under considerable pressure to find a job – few Chinese can afford to become 'professional students', accumulating qualifications rather than experience – and most post-graduate students have spent several years in employment before studying for a further degree.

By and large, Chinese degrees are recognised abroad, although those from the top universities such as Fudan, Tsinghua and Beijing University are more highly regarded and more likely to help secure a good job.

FURTHER EDUCATION

Students who don't progress beyond middle school or who fail the NCEE exam have the option of taking vocational training to prepare them for specific areas of work. In 2010, China had a total of almost 15,000 state-approved secondary vocational and technical colleges attended by some 20m students, while a further 9m students were studying in private secondary training institutions.

State Vocational Colleges

State vocational colleges run a variety of courses focusing on the professions, arts, practical skills and trades. The most common courses are:

♦ Four-year courses commencing at the end of middle school: these cover subjects such as commerce, legal work, fine arts and forestry.

♦ Three-year courses, commencing at the end of high middle school: these cover similar subjects (as above) and are often an option for students who fail to pass the university entrance examination.

♦ Courses in subjects such as cookery, tailoring, photography and agricultural services: these are aimed at middle school graduates and last from one to three years.

♦ Two-year courses in trades, such as carpentry or welding, which start after middle school. There are no formal apprenticeships in China and this is the only way for school-leavers to learn a trade. Much of the training consists of classroom work, although there's a small element of day release whereby students undergo practical training working in the trade.

> Students pay a fee to attend vocational colleges, although they're around half those charged by universities: between 3,000 and 4,000 RMB a year for tuition. Charges for accommodation and food are similar to those charged by universities.

Private Secondary Training Colleges

There are numerous private colleges providing training in specific occupations such as hotel management and the tourist industry. The quality of courses and fees payable vary greatly.

FOREIGN STUDENTS

As China's influence in the world becomes stronger, there's an increasing demand for knowledge of the Chinese way of life. In particular, both Westerners and other Asian nationals are interested in learning Chinese, and in discovering about Traditional Chinese Medicine (TCM) and martial arts. As a result, an increasing number of foreign adult students are studying in China.

Officially, in 2010 there were around 200,000 adult foreign students studying full-time in China, but this number didn't include the thousands of foreigners studying part-time or taking a short-term language course. Some 70 per cent of all overseas students in China come from Asian countries – Japanese and South Koreans account for almost half of all long-term foreign students in China – followed by 13 per cent from Europe, 11 per cent from the Americas, 3 per cent from Africa and 2 per cent from Australasia. In a poll of nationalities studying in China, the UK is a lowly 17th. The majority of students, almost 80 per cent, come to study Chinese; a further 10 per cent are focused on TCM, while the remainder choose from a range of subjects, particularly martial arts. For more information on studying TCM and martial arts, see pages 122 and 123.

Some 400 universities and colleges in China accept overseas students but most study in one of just nine cities: Beijing is the top choice, hosting 40 per cent of all long-term overseas students, followed by Shanghai with 12 per cent and Tianjin with 8 per cent. The top destination is Beijing University of Languages and Culture, which in 2010 had almost 6,000 overseas students, followed by Beijing University with 3,000 and Beijing Normal University with some 1,300; for those interested in TCM, the International Centre for Acupuncture in Beijing had around 500 overseas students. In Shanghai, Fudan University had just under 2,000 overseas students and the Shanghai University of Foreign Languages around 600. In all, 45 per cent of long-term foreign students were attending just 17 universities.

Long-term students have the option of taking a degree course – about a quarter do this – or a non-degree course, many of which are language courses. Most bachelor's degrees take four years to complete, although some degree courses in Traditional Chinese Medicine take five years. Non-degree courses can last for as little as a week – just to give you a taste of the subject – or as long as two years.

If you want to study in China, start by enquiring at your home country's Chinese embassy or consulate, which will provide a list of institutions offering courses in your chosen subject. Most have websites, so you can research their courses and facilities via the internet. There are also agencies that offer to help students find courses but, unlike foreign missions, many have a financial motive for recommending one institution over another.

If you plan to take a degree, rather than a short language course, it pays to visit China just before the start of a semester and investigate institutions in person. Some fail to live up to the promises made in their websites while others with less slick advertising can be a pleasant surprise. Ideally, try to talk to some expatriate students who are already studying there.

There are three exceptions to this strategy: the three main universities taking foreign students in Beijing. The Beijing Language and Culture University, Beijing University and Tsinghua University are all highly regarded – the Chinese equivalent of the Ivy League or Oxbridge – and it's unlikely you'd be disappointed by the facilities or tuition on offer, although you might prefer a more Chinese experience. All three attract a lot of expat students. These universities book up early and you should start making enquiries at least a year in advance of when you wish to start.

Courses aren't cheap – you can pay up to 34,000 RMB a year, not including accommodation, to study the Chinese language and culture at Beijing University, although the Chinese government awards scholarships to a surprisingly high 12 per cent of all foreign students. If you've gained a top degree in Chinese studies at a university in your home country, you stand a good chance of being accepted on a scholarship by a Chinese university to study for a master's, but for precise requirements you must study the individual universities' websites.

Once you've secured your study place, you'll need a student visa: an F visa for a study period of less than six months or an X visa for a longer course. The university can help with this. Some are prepared to enrol students at short notice, therefore it's possible to travel to China on a tourist (L) visa and then upgrade to an F or X visa in order to study.

LEARNING CHINESE

If you want to make the most of your time in China, it's well worth making the effort to learn some Chinese. The official language is *Putonghua* – the Chinese name for Mandarin Chinese – which is the language which is most often taught. It's also possible to learn Cantonese (*Guangdonghua*), although this is only really useful if you're living and working in Guangdong province or Hong Kong.

Putonghua/Mandarin isn't an easy language to learn. To master the intricacies of reading and writing its complex script takes years, even for Chinese students. However, there's a Westernised version called pinyin which transliterates all the characters into Latin (Roman) letters so that you can, with practice, learn to pronounce and understand conversation. This is as far as most foreigners ever get, but it's enough to allow you to shop, eat out, negotiate the transport system and the bureaucracy, and get to know the local Chinese. Without any knowledge of Chinese you'll risk remaining an outsider, only able to communicate with other expats and never really gaining a real insight into the Chinese or their culture.

The Chinese Proficiency Test

HSK stands for *Huang Shuiping Kaoshi* which translates literally as 'check your Chinese level test' although it's officially known as the Chinese Proficiency Test. It was designed and developed by the Beijing Language and Culture University and was first authorised to be used in 1992 to assess the proficiency of non-Chinese (i.e. non-Mandarin) speakers, such as foreigners, overseas Chinese and people from China's national minorities. Levels range from one to nine, and students require an HSK level of between three (intermediate level) and eight (even higher than advanced level with honours) before they can enrol in a degree course taught in Chinese at a Chinese university. Examinations are held annually on the mainland and in Hong Kong, Macau and Taiwan, as well as in several countries overseas.

It's advisable to start learning the language before you arrive. If you start putting in practice six or even three months beforehand, you'll arrive with enough basic knowledge to at least cope with exchanging greetings, asking for things in shops and counting up to ten. There are plenty of books, CDs and DVDs which can get you started (see **Appendix B**).

Many schools and colleges offer courses in basic Chinese or you can take an online course, some of which are free. Try to find one with an audio facility so you can hear how words should be pronounced. There are also 'virtual' classrooms which allow you to speak and interact with an online teacher, but for most people attending a 'real' course (combined with a book or website for back up) is the best solution.

Once in China, you can investigate local courses. Your employer may provide Chinese lessons as part of your job package or you could sign up for a course at a local university or school. Just practising your skills with Chinese people – most will be delighted that you're making the effort – is a great way to feel more comfortable with the language.

Very few foreigners study Chinese to degree level, so most courses are relatively short, from a few weeks to a year. You can take a degree in Chinese at a number of universities, but to do so you must usually already be able to speak Chinese up to HSK level six before you start (see box BELOW).

There's a wide choice of study venues, from small private language schools to state universities, but the overwhelmingly majority of language students head to Beijing, the home of *Putonghua*. If you want to learn Cantonese, you should head for Guangzhou or Hong Kong.

Many shorter courses are themed. Some are aimed at tourists and include visits to local attractions, while others focus on business Chinese and incorporate trips to factories. Some courses incorporate other subjects such as Chinese martial arts.

Most teaching establishments provide a package deal: a single fee covers your collection from the airport (but not your airfare), accommodation (not usually meals), tuition, insurance, social activities and visits to tourist sites, and your return trip to the airport. However, you can arrange a course independently, perhaps staying with a friend or in company accommodation.

University lodgings, particularly in Beijing, are expensive and many students try to find something cheaper off campus. 'Budget' accommodation usually consists of a single room with an en-suite shower room in a student dormitory block: clean and comfortable, with a fridge, air-conditioning, television, phone and internet access, but far from luxurious. It can add between 15,000 and 20,000 RMB to the cost of a four-week course – usually around 6,000 RMB for tuition alone – and works out at between 500 and 700 RMB a night. You can get a room in a three-star hotel for half the price.

Even students spending a full year at university are charged around 275 RMB a night for this grade of student accommodation. For the same sum, you could rent a student flat with a separate living room and kitchenette, which works out even cheaper if you share it with a fellow student. If your course lasts eight weeks or more, a third option is a two- or three-bedroom apartment with a proper kitchen (including such luxuries as a washing machine and microwave). If there's a group of students, this can be much a better deal as you can split the rental cost (around 320 RMB a night) between you.

It's also possible for a university to arrange for you to live in a hotel or to stay with a Chinese family. Home stay costs much the same as living in a student flat, but includes two meals a day and the main benefit is that you're immersed in the Chinese language all day, every day.

Courses can last for four, six, eight or 12 weeks, or for a semester (18 weeks) or two (36 weeks). A two-semester course with accommodation included costs between 110,000 and 120,000 RMB if you start in the spring, but you can save roughly 9,000 RMB by starting in the autumn, as you avoid the cost of paying for accommodation over the long summer vacation. If you can take the same course without accommodation, the fees drop to between 30,000 and 35,000 RMB.

In Beijing, the Beijing Language and Culture University (BLCU) is around 5,000 RMB cheaper for one or two semester courses than either Beijing University or Tsinghua University. For shorter courses, which Beijing University doesn't offer, there's little difference in cost between BLCU and Tsinghua.

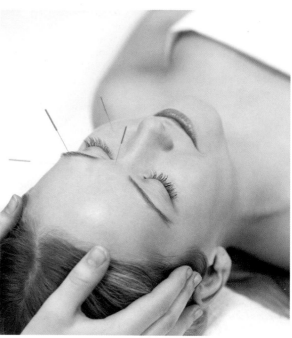

Some people take the view that because there are so many foreign students in Beijing – around 6,000 at BLCU alone – you spend all your time with foreigners and don't really immerse yourself in the language spoken by the native speakers. If this concerns you, there are plenty of excellent courses at universities throughout the country where you can study alongside Chinese students. If you want to study in a specific city, contact your nearest Chinese embassy or consulate for a list of schools or use the CUCAS website (🖥 cucas.edu.cn/listschool.php).

There are a number of foreign-owned language schools offering courses in Chinese. If you're already in China, you'll find them advertised in the free expat magazines or a quick search on the internet will throw up many names. Quality varies, as do the fees. However, for a real, in-depth course in a uniquely Chinese environment, you cannot beat the universities. Some useful contacts are provided in **Appendix C**.

OTHER COURSES

Traditional Chinese Medicine

The history of Traditional Chinese Medicine, or TCM as it's usually referred to, goes back over 2,000 years. The key difference between TCM and Western medicine lies in its approach to the cause and effect of illness. Western medicine concentrates on treating specific symptoms while TCM is holistic and treats the whole body in the belief that all parts of the body act together and illness occurs when this harmony is disturbed. Treating just the symptoms may result in a quicker cure but the condition may reoccur if you fail to treat its root cause by restoring the body's natural harmony.

Several techniques make up TCM, including physical treatments such as acupuncture, herbal medicine, massage and exercise. Although there's no clear scientific basis for their use, they clearly work, so much so that TCM has officially been recognised by the World Health Organisation (WHO), and is regularly used alongside Western medicine throughout the world. And, increasingly, Western doctors and other people with an interest in TCM are travelling to China to learn about it.

Within China there are some 90 universities teaching Western medicine, of which 22 also have departments teaching TCM. In addition there are 30 hospitals teaching just TCM. Most hospitals specialising in TCM offer courses, but some can only provide tuition by Chinese speakers, so to study with them you must be competent in Chinese up to HSK level five or six (see page 120).

Courses vary hugely in length. Some provide a brief introduction while others are in-depth courses leading to a qualification. The Beijing University of Chinese Medicine and Pharmacology (🖥 bucm.edu.ch) offers undergraduate programmes of four or five years, leading to a bachelor's degree in TCM. Tuition is in Chinese and costs 30,000 RMB a year. It also runs a number of short-term programmes that are taught in English. These vary in length from a week to five months and can be taken as a single course or several combined courses. Subjects covered include basic TCM theory, Chinese medical pharmacology, acupuncture, orthopaedics, *tuina* (massage) and *qigong* exercises, plus diet, weight reduction and anatomy (some short-term courses are also available in French, German and Spanish). Tuition fees are from 3,400 RMB for a week, 8,500 RMB for a month, up to 34,000 RMB for a five-month course.

Students staying for less than five months can rent a single room with private bathroom, TV, air-conditioning and phone for 76 RMB a day or a one-bedroom apartment for 156 RMB a day. A private room with a shared bathroom costs a little less and, if you want to stay for the full five months, rates are reduced by 16 RMB a day. The availability of these courses is subject to a minimum of five students; however, this is rarely a problem as most classes have around 25 students.

There are also excellent TCM universities in Guangzhou, Nanjing and Shanghai (addresses are provided in **Appendix A**). For more information about TCM, see opposite.

Chinese Martial Arts

When Westerners think of martial arts they usually think of kung fu (or *gong fu* as the Chinese call it) but there are many different forms of martial arts in China, dating back to the time of the warlords when the inhabitants of villages or temples had to learn to defend their homes. Nowadays the Chinese call all martial arts by the name *wushu* – *wu* means 'martial arts' and *shu* meaning 'skill in' – and focus on their health benefits rather than their use in self-defence. However, the popularity of film stars such as Jackie Chan has created a fascination with martial arts in the West and draws many foreigners to visit China – and, especially, the Shaolin temple in Henan province which is viewed as the birthplace of martial arts. Some come to sightsee but many also come to learn the skills of this ancient tradition.

Shaolin takes in some 50,000 students a year to learn the complexities of *gong fu*. Courses are open to anyone aged from 18 to 60, but most students are male and in the 20 to 25 age bracket. Many approach it as an additional skill to acquire after completing their academic studies, although some intend to make teaching it their career.

▲ Caution

If you're serious about learning martial arts, you need to be seriously fit before you arrive in China. Instructors will expect you to practice for a minimum of six to eight hours each day, except Sundays. After your first week, you'll have pains in every muscle, including those you didn't even know existed!

There are over 80 martial arts schools in and around Shaolin. Most have moved out of the grounds of Shaolin Temple and into newly built premises in the nearby town of Deng Feng. Many schools look impressive from the outside but are fairly primitive and aren't geared to accommodate foreigners. If you intend to study in Shaolin for a long period of time, it's best to book into a local hotel, check out some of the schools

and ask other foreigners for recommendations before committing yourself to a course. Fees vary between 1,140 RMB and 5,625 RMB per month – and you should haggle.

The largest school, Tagou, has some 7,000 students and is the place that most foreigners head for. It provides good rooms with a television, air-conditioning and a Western-style toilet, but costs 150 RMB a day or 4,560 RMB a month. Students are allocated their own private coach.

The regime at Tagou is tough. For six days a week, students are expected to get up at 5.30am and go for a group run. Breakfast is served at 7am, with formal training beginning at 8.30am and continuing until 11am. Lunch is followed by an afternoon siesta before training recommences at 4pm and continues until 7pm. There's more free training after dinner if you have the energy. If this sounds tough, consider that Chinese students usually study at Tagou for three years to achieve a satisfactory level of skill.

If you wish to get a taste of Shaolin *gong fu* but have only a few weeks to spare, the Song Shan Shao Lin Temple Xiao Long Gong Fu Training Centre in Deng Feng offers tuition, accommodation (in a shared room) and food for 2,850 RMB a month. It also has a four-week package, including flights to and from the US and assistance with visas, for a fee of between 9,200 and 11,000 RMB.

Some people find Shaolin too touristy, and there are alternative places to learn *wushu*. Wudang Shan in Hubei province has just 20 schools offering no-frills, serious training in small groups. However, the main school, Shang Feng, is very particular and expects participants to have reached a fairly advanced level. It was this facility that featured, with a cobra, in the 2010 Jackie Chan remake of *The Karate Kid*.

Shang Feng asserts that Wudang Shan is the birthplace of *taijiquan* (which Westerners often call, incorrectly, Tai Chi). However, the small village of Chen Jia Gou, outside Gong Yi in Henan province, makes the same claim, and there students can be counted in dozens rather than thousands and study nothing but *taijiquan*. However, if all you want to learn is a few of the basics, go to any park in China early in the morning and ask if you can join the people already exercising.

It isn't necessary to travel to a specific temple to learn martial arts. Virtually every city in China has a school or sports academy where you can learn. If you're at Beijing or Fudan University studying another course, you can sign up for a *wushu* course for any period from four weeks (22,000 RMB) to a year (118,000 RMB). Or, if you're travelling, there are good instructors in several styles in the backpacker haunts of Dali and Yangshuo. The most important thing to decide is how serious you are about it. The Chinese take *wushu* very seriously indeed, and learning it to perfection can be a lifetime's commitment.

For more information on Chinese martial arts, see page 224. Some useful contacts are also included in **Appendix A**.

Sanqing mountain, Jiangxi

Chinese high-speed trains

10.
PUBLIC TRANSPORT

C hina is a developing country and while it's developing incredibly fast, the luxury of private transport is beyond the means of most of the population, particularly those living in rural areas. Wealthy Chinese are addicted to their cars, the newer, larger and faster the better. However, away from the cities, public transport rules, together with the ubiquitous bicycle and basic agricultural machines such as tractors, which are often used to transport entire families as well as their crops and livestock.

In a country so vast and with such varied topography – China is as large and geographically varied as the US – creating a workable transport system has been a challenge to the technicians and engineers. However, they've risen to the task in recent decades and the country now has an comprehensive network of railways and roads. Rail travel is concentrated within the eastern half of the country but modern expressways increasingly connect the main centres of population as far as the westernmost cities.

However, the distances involved mean that long-distance travel can be a tiring and time-consuming exercise, and anyone who can afford it makes use of China's domestic airlines for longer journeys, although the masses still crowd onto the railways and long-distance buses, particularly at holiday times.

Within cities there are commuter buses and taxis and, in a number of the major centres, modern subway systems; many second- and third-tier cities are either already building or at least planning an underground or light rail system. These are becoming essential as the city centres become increasingly choked with cars. Despite the heavy traffic, you see thousands of cyclists calmly cycling along the congested highways, many looking as if they're peddling along a country lane. Should you be brave enough to join them, some cities have bicycles for hire or you can buy one cheaply.

CITY TRANSPORT SYSTEM

Most Chinese cities were never designed to cope with cars, and the massive increase in car ownership since 2000 has resulted in huge traffic jams and rush 'hours' that last all day. All cities have buses and taxis, some have trams and water buses, but the main way in which Chinese planners are tackling the gridlock is by building subway (underground rail) systems.

Beijing and Tianjin were the first to go underground, and Changchun, Chengdu, Chongqing, Dalian, Foshan, Guangzhou, Hong Kong, Nanjing, Shanghai, Shenyang, Shenzhen and Wuhan have all since followed, while the Beijing and Tianjin subways have been extended further into the suburbs. Virtually every major city is China now has a subway in planning or under construction.

All work in a similar way, offering clean, modern transportation at a very low cost: usually 2 to 5 RMB per journey. Tickets are available from ticket offices or machines. In some of the larger cities you can buy a smart card, similar to London's Oyster card, which allows you to load credit onto the card and use it to pay for journeys, sometimes at a discounted price. Stations are signed in pinyin as well as Chinese, and in some cities announcements are also made in English. The main drawback with most subways is the overcrowding at busy times, which makes it a battle to get on and off trains. It also makes them a great temptation for pickpockets and thieves, and there have been a number of cases in Beijing of men groping female passengers on subway trains during the rush hour. Disabled people will find the subways difficult to access, as very few have lifts.

The main public transport systems in the big four cities are as follows:

Beijing

The Beijing Subway (📇 bjsubway.com) is one of the oldest and largest in the world. It has 14 lines linking 172 stations and stretches from Nanshao in the north to Tiangongyuan in the south, taking in the main railway stations and the city's international airport. In addition, there's a suburban railway service which links to the subway and stretches as far as the Great Wall at Badaling. There's also an extensive bus service run by Beijing Public Transport Holdings (☎ 010-96166, 📇 bjbus.com).

The subway has a flat fare of 2 RMB while bus fares start from 1 RMB. The Beijing Transportation Smart Card or *Yikatong* is an integrated circuit (IC) contactless card which can be used to pay for journeys on the subway, buses and express trains to the airport. The card sells for 20 RMB, which is used as a deposit against journeys, and can be topped up in many places throughout the city. Card holders receive a large discount on bus fares.

Shanghai

With over 420km (260mi) of track, the Shanghai Metro (📇 shmetro.com) is one of the longest in the world, as well as being the busiest (in 2011 it served over 7.5m passengers a day). It covers all of urban Shanghai and many of its suburbs; one line links Pudong and Hongqiao airports. High speed rail provides transport to its more far-flung satellite cities such as Hangzhou. Shanghai also has a vast bus network with some 1,000 routes and the modern Zhangjiang tram. Metro fares are between 3 and 9 RMB, while bus fares are mostly 1 to 2 RMB. The Shanghai Public Transport Card (📇 sptcc.com) costs from 20 RMB and offers discounts on bus fares and the metro for frequent users, and can also be used to pay for parking, road tolls and even to buy gas/petrol.

Shanghai's Maglev Train

The Maglev (magnetic levitation) train running between Pudong airport and the Jinmao Tower station in downtown Shanghai is the only one of its kind in commercial use in the world. It's also the world's fastest passenger train, capable of speeds of up to 431kph (268mph) – faster even than a Formula 1 racing car. The Maglev, which opened in 2004, covers the 30km (18mi) route in under eight minutes and runs every 15 minutes from 6.45am to 9.40pm. The journey is expensive by Chinese standards – a one-way ticket is 50 RMB – but it's an astonishing experience and not to be missed. There are proposals to extend the line to Shanghai's second airport, Hongqiao, and on to Hangzhou in Zhejiang province.

Guangzhou

Guangzhou Metro has a network of eight lines covering the entire urban area, including one to the nearby city of Foshan (the only intercity underground line in China). Plans are underway to add a further seven lines and double the length of track to some 500km (310mi) by 2020. In addition there are some 450 bus routes, and in this subtropical city, most are air-conditioned. Guangzhou's location on the Pearl River means that water transport is also important and there's a water bus service linking important points along the river, as well as a fast ferry to nearby Hong Kong. Subway ticket prices range from 2 to 14 RMB, and the website (📇 gzmtr.com/en) has a handy fare calculator. You can buy a smart card which provides discounts of up to 40 per cent, but it can only be used on the metro.

Shenzhen

One of the newest subway systems in China, the Shenzhen Metro (📇 mtrsz.com.cn/eng) has just four lines and 49 stations, but is set for expansion. Shenzhen also has an extensive bus network with almost 500 routes. Metro tickets cost 2 to 7 RMB; buses between 1 and 5 RMB with the air-conditioned express buses charging the highest fares. The Shenzhen Tong smart card costs 25 RMB and can be used on the metro and most buses, and therefore plans to make it compatible with Hong Kong's Octopus Card in the near future.

TRAINS

The first railway to be built in China was constructed in 1876 by a private company, Jardine Matheson & Co (which still exists today). It was just 24km (15mi) long, linking Shanghai with Woosung, but it earned the displeasure of the Emperor and was closed within a year and later dismantled by the government. It was another two decades before railway construction resumed, but by 1935 there were around 20,000km (12,425mi) of operational track. However, the Japanese invasion in 1937 and the subsequent civil war damaged much of this, and when the People's Republic of China was founded in 1949, just half of the network was in working order. The new Communist government recognised the importance of the railways, and within 15 years had not only restored all the pre-1935 rail lines but had built a further 15,000km (9,320mi).

China now has the largest railway network in the world after Russia and the US. By the end of 2012 it had some 110,000km (68,350mi) of track and the country continues to extend and upgrade its system at a faster rate than anywhere else in the world.

China Railways has some 220,000 employees. It operates 5,700 railway stations and utilises 18,500 locomotives, 43,000 carriages and 600,000 wagons to run 3,000 passenger services and 33,300 freight services daily. Steam trains were still in use up to the mid-'80s, but all main line trains are now either electric or diesel, and over 30,000km (18,640mi) of track has been electrified.

In 2011, China Railways carried 1.86bn passengers and roughly 3.9bn tonnes of freight: mainly coal, iron ore, oil and steel. Some 60 per cent of all domestic goods are transported by rail, more than any other country in the world.

The two most important lines are the North-South line, running from Dongbei in the north, via Harbin in Heilongjiang province and passing through Beijing on its way to Hong Kong, and the East-West line which begins in Beijing and ends in Urumqi in Xinjiang province. These lines crisscross in Zhengzhou, Henan province which has the largest intersection, marshalling yard and junction in the entire system. Two of the three Trans-Siberian routes – the Trans-Mongolian and Trans-Manchurian lines – travel partly through China and terminate in Beijing.

▲ Caution

The Chinese rail system is concentrated in the east and south of the country. There are far fewer lines serving far western provinces, and if you're travelling there you may need to make some journeys by bus.

Throughout China, most of the track is standard gauge (1.435m/4ft 8in), in common with the rest of the world, although there are a few industrial, narrow gauge lines, and the mountainous line connecting Yunnan province with Vietnam is still only 1m (3ft 3in) gauge.

China has invested heavily in upgrading its rail track to allow the use of more high speed trains. By 2011, it had around 8,600km (5,345mi) of high speed routes handling speeds of up to 200kph (120mph), and 2,197km (1,365mi) of track on which trains can run at up to 350kph (220mph). It plans to have over 25,000km (16,000mi) of high speed track by the end of 2015.

As a result, journey times are decreasing all the time. Beijing to Tianjin used to take 80 minutes, but the introduction of trains capable of reaching speeds well in excess of 300kph (186mph) has cut the journey time to 30 minutes. In 2010, China unveiled the world's fastest train, the 380A (He Xie), which can cruise at 380kph (236mph) and (from summer 2011) speed passengers along the new Beijing-Shanghai High-Speed Railway, cutting the journey time by six hours (but see below).

China has a good safety record on its railways, and for journeys of less than 500km (310mi) or those between destinations served by a high speed link, it makes more sense to take the train than to fly. There's no time wasted at airport check in (or taking off and landing) and the train takes you right to the city centre rather than to an outlying airport. It's also considerably cheaper than flying, and it provides you with an unbeatable view of China's landscape as you thunder through the countryside. This still applies, however, in July 2011 an accident occurred at Wenzhou in which 32 passengers were killed. This was the country's first accident with their ultra-fast trains and China Rail immediately imposed a 50kph reduction on the maximum speed of their D and G class trains.

One of China's most scenic railway journeys is the Qinghai Tibet line that links southwest China with Lhasa in Tibet. Trains departing from Beijing, Chengdu, Chongqing, Guangzhou, Shanghai and Xi'an all travel along this stretch of track, the highest passenger railway line in the world. From Golmud in Qinghai province, it crosses the Tibetan plateau for 1,142km (710mi) rising to a maximum altitude of 5,072m (16,640ft) above sea level. Most of the journey is at over 4,000m (13,123ft) and every carriage carries canisters of oxygen to help passengers to combat altitude sickness. Over half of this section is built on permafrost and the views are spectacular. The train from Beijing takes 48 hours and fares are 389 RMB for a hard seat, 813 RMB for a hard sleeper or 1,262 RMB for a soft sleeper, plus the cost of a Tibet Travel Permit which you must have to enter Tibet. For more information about the route, see the China Tibet Train website (💻 chinatibettrain.com).

Train Classes

There are several classes of train, and ticket prices are based on both speed and facilities. All trains are identified by an alpha-numeric prefix: a letter distinguishing their class and a number for their route. The slowest and cheapest trains are the *putong che* which stop at every station and serve the more outlying corners of China; these provide a no-frills but fascinating way to see the country if you have no time constraints. Trains are identified by a number only, with no letter prefix.

The bulk of the rolling stock consists of regular express trains which connect the cities, travelling faster and stopping less frequently. These are graded as follows:

♦ K (*kuai* or quick): ordinary express trains travelling at up to 122kph (75mph).

♦ T (*ter* or special): a faster express reaching up to 142kph (88mph).

♦ Z (*zhi* or direct): an express with fewer stops, travelling at up to 162kph (100mph).

There are some trains prefixed Y (*you*) which are specifically for tourists and can travel at speeds of up to 200kph (124mph).

All current investment in rolling stock is concentrated on high speed trains. The earlier models are the D trains (*dong*). These sleek locomotives are similar to France's TGV and Japanese 'bullet' trains. The interior is like that of a plane, with all the seats facing forwards and a television screen over the doorway showing the speed at which you're travelling, which can be up to 252kph (156mph), although currently restricted to 200kph.

The latest high speed trains are the G class (*gaotie*) which came into service in 2011. They're taking over from the D trains on new tracks which can handle speeds of up to 350kph/217mph. Speeds are currently limited to 300kph (186mph) until the cause of the Wenzhou crash (see above) is identified and eradicated. These trains are ideal for businessmen as the first class seats can be turned to allow four to sit around a table, and hot drinks and airline style meals are available on board. The drawback to the added speed and comfort are the ticket prices. A seat on a G train costs around twice as much as one on a regular intercity express, but still much cheaper than travelling by air.

Accommodation

There are four different classes of tickets on most long-distance trains. These are hard seat (*yingzuo*), soft seat (*ruanzuo*), hard sleeper (*yingwo*) and soft sleeper (*ruanwo*). Additionally, on the new D and G class trains (see below), seats are classified as first class or second class, and on a limited number of prestige routes there are also deluxe soft sleepers.

Hard seat travel isn't as bad as it sounds. The seats used to be wooden, but are now the same as a typical commuter train in the West and for shorter journeys they're comfortable enough. However, for longer daytime trips, soft seats are preferable as they have a table between each two pairs of seats and good legroom.

The decision between a hard or soft sleeper has as much to do with privacy as with comfort. Hard sleepers comprise six bunks arranged in three tiers in a single compartment, each of which opens directly onto the train's corridor. Their mattresses are firm (like most mattresses in China) and you must climb a ladder to reach the upper bunks, but they're clean and spacious. However, there's nowhere to put your luggage so you must leave it on a luggage rack in the corridor. The highest berths are the cheapest but are closest to the overhead light, so are the best choice if you want to read.

Soft sleepers are more luxurious. There are only four beds per compartment, the mattresses are (slightly) softer, plus there's room for your luggage. You can shut a door onto the corridor making the berths feel more secure. However, a soft sleeper costs roughly 30 per cent more than a hard sleeper and many regular train travellers don't think they justify the extra expense.

A further class, the 'deluxe' soft sleeper, is the most comfortable option of all. Each compartment has just two berths plus its own private toilet and washbasin, so they're more like European sleeping cars. They're only available on a few selected routes: from Beijing to Hong Kong, Shanghai and Xi'an. Tickets cost twice as much as for a standard hard sleeper but it's still cheaper than flying and you can save the expense of a night in a hotel.

⚠ **Caution**

In all Chinese sleeper classes, there's no division of the sexes. Men, women and children all travel together in the same compartment.

Train & Station Facilities

The following is a summary of facilities available at Chinese stations and on trains:

Comfort & Refreshments

Stations are enormous but relatively bare. There are vast waiting rooms – including a special one for passengers with tickets for soft seats and sleepers, with huge sofas and a television – but little else. There are no restaurants and bars or shopping centres as you find in Western stations, although the concourse is surrounded by numerous small open-fronted stores selling fruit, snacks and drinks, and passengers stock up for the journey at one of these.

Once you're on the train, you can usually buy food from trolleys, such as fruit, chocolate and drinks, pre-packed meals and tubs of instant noodles – China's answer to the sandwich – as well as Chinese magazines and even socks. Virtually all trains and waiting rooms have a constant supply of hot water for making tea or reconstituting instant noodles, while some long-distance trains have a dining car (usually located next to the soft sleeper compartment).

Luggage

You can take as much luggage as you like provided you can carry it, although (surprisingly) bicycles are only allowed on certain trains. Once you're on a train there are luggage racks, but if you plan to leave your luggage for any length of time, e.g. overnight while you're in your hard sleeper berth, it's wise to secure it to the rack with a chain. All bags are x-rayed as you enter the station, so security is high and there have been no incidents to date of anyone trying to damage a train or harm its occupants. There are porters at stations, but it isn't easy to find one.

Smoking

There's officially a smoking ban on all trains except the slowest ones. However, smokers tend to ignore this and head for the toilets. The authorities are resigned to this, and even on the fastest luxury trains there are ashtrays in the toilets. Smoking is also restricted in stations, where there are special smoking rooms, although not every smoker uses them.

Telephones

Most stations have public telephones. On the trains themselves, there's no restriction (unfortunately) on the use of mobile phones, which can be a great irritant on long journeys.

Times

Most timetables are only available in Chinese, therefore it's difficult to find out which trains are running and when, unless you ask an agent. However, despite the language difficulties, it's quite difficult to miss your train. Its arrival is announced over a loudspeaker and shown on a screen in the waiting room and only then are you allowed on to the platform. Just follow the other passengers and walk alongside the train until you find the carriage number shown on your ticket. An inspector will check it and then allow you on to the train to find your numbered seat. Unlike in many Western countries, Chinese trains generally run on time.

Toilets

Most intercity and long-distance trains have toilets at both ends of each carriage, although these are usually of the Asian 'squat' variety and can be unpleasant to use. Never roll out of bed in a hard sleeper carriage and go to the toilet barefoot! On D and G class high speed trains and some soft sleepers, there are Western-style WCs, but even on the most luxurious trains you still need to carry a supply of toilet paper. There are free toilets in stations but, again, they can be pretty disgusting.

Tickets

The worst aspect of train travel in China is buying tickets. Although advance bookings are necessary for most long distance and overnight journeys, and particularly at holiday times (see box BELOW), it's impossible to buy tickets more than ten days in advance of travel.

China Railways is a victim both of its own success and of the ticket touts who prey on train travellers. There's little, if any, spare capacity

on most trains, and as soon as tickets go on sale, they're snapped up by touts (known as 'yellow cows') who sell them on to desperate passengers at double their face value. The police regularly crack down on these rogues, but they operate in every large railway station. It's quite usual for all sleeper tickets in both classes to be sold out two or three days before departure. You can usually turn up and hop on local services but if you're planning a long-distance journey by train, always check the availability of tickets at least a week before you travel or book through an agent.

This situation is further complicated by the lack of return tickets. As the ticket system becomes computerised, some booking offices can sell you separate tickets for your outbound and return journeys, but usually you can only buy a one-way ticket from the city you're departing from and must wait until you arrive at your destination in order to buy a return ticket. Thus you board your train unsure as to whether you'll be able to able to get back! It's advisable to buy your return ticket as soon as you arrive.

Tickets can be purchased at China Railways advance purchase offices in most city centres or even at the station itself, although it helps if you can speak Chinese. If not, it's easier to buy them through an agent (see opposite). You cannot, as yet, buy tickets from China Railways by phone or via the internet.

Tickets show the name of your destination, your carriage number, your seat number and the time of departure; the words are in Chinese but the numbers are recognisable. Note that all seats are reserved on Chinese trains except for the slow local trains. If you're travelling in a sleeper, the conductor comes round at dusk and collects your ticket and hands you a small metal token. He or she wakes you in the early morning and hands back your ticket, which you need in order to exit through the barrier at your destination.

Chunyun

This is the name for the period around the Chinese New Year when China's transport system descends into chaos. With every migrant worker heading across country to visit their family – often the only time they see them all year – the rail (and bus) services are hugely overcrowded. It's been estimated that there are more passengers travelling by rail in this two-week period than in an entire year on UK trains. This is a prime time for touts who swoop on tickets as soon as they go on sale, so reasonably priced tickets are as rare as hen's teeth. Those who are successful find themselves herded through stations and onto trains like cattle, only to repeat the same process on their return journey. Unless you absolutely must travel, it's best to avoid public transport during *Chunyun*.

Ticket Agents

The easiest way to buy a train (or plane) ticket is through a travel office in a large hotel. Larger hotels (three stars and above) have in-house agencies, and there are travel agents in city centres. Agencies charge a fee of around 20 RMB in addition to the ticket prices for their service, but compared with queuing and trying to make yourself understood at a station booking office, it's money well spent.

There are online ticket agencies in China but many charge grossly inflated prices. If pricing is in any currency other than RMB, then you're probably paying well over the odds. Online agencies come and go overnight, and while there are a few good ones, you're generally better off buying rail tickets through an agent in person.

Should you find that for some reason you're unable to use your tickets, it's possible to get a refund, but, in most cases, you only get around 60 per cent of your money back.

Discounts

Chinese rail tickets aren't particularly expensive and discounts are few and far between. Reduced price fares are sometimes available at less busy times of year, but there's no discount for senior citizens and children's fares are calculated on height rather than age: those who are less than 1.1m (3ft 7in) tall travel free, while children under 1.4m (4ft 7in) pay half fare. Discounts don't apply if they're occupying a sleeper berth.

The following table shows the range of ticket prices for a one-way (single) journey between Beijing and Shanghai.

Ticket Prices – Beijing-Shanghai		
Train	**Price**	**Journey time**
Slow commuter train	80 RMB	Up to 24 hours
Hard sleeper (T class)	350 RMB	10 hours
Soft sleeper (T class)	500 RMB	10 hours
Soft sleeper (D class)	730 RMB	7 hours
De-luxe soft sleeper (D class)	920 RMB	7 hours
Hard seat, 2nd class (D class)	327 RMB	7 hours

It takes around two hours to travel between Beijing and Shanghai by air, with a typical ticket costing between 650 RMB (with the maximum discount) and 1,130 RMB.

Further Information

A Railway Customer Service Center (☎ 010-12306, 🖳 12306.cn) was officially opened in 2011, although it's all in Chinese and cannot be used to book tickets. However, useful information about the Chinese Rail system is provided by Seat 61 (🖳 seat61.com/china.htm) and the China Train Guide (🖳 chinatrainguide.com). China Highlights allows you to search timetables using train numbers or destinations (🖳 chinahighlights.com/china-trains). For an excellent rail map of China, see 🖳 johomaps.com/as/china/chinarail.html.

BUSES & TROLLEYBUSES

Although buses are the poor relation of trains and subways, they still provide an important alternative whether you're taking a short local hop in the suburbs or crossing the country. In cities, buses cover those far-flung suburbs which subways haven't yet reached, and are a vital mode of transport in rural areas, particularly in the west of China.

Long-distance Buses

Although slower, less popular and cheaper than trains, long-distance buses can get you practically anywhere in China. The best are the clean modern cruisers, many of which are made by King Long or Yutong – both are joint ventures with overseas bus manufacturers, e.g. Germany's MAN – which are well equipped for longer trips with reclining seats, air-conditioning, toilets and even on-board movies, plus a place to stow your bags under the bus. The worst are the small 800cc minibuses (xiao mian bao che which means 'little bread loaf shaped bus') which are crammed beyond their capacity, although they're the only means of reaching the most remote villages. A

journey on one will take you to a China that few foreigners get to see.

Buses have a much less distinguished safety record than trains, and there have been a number of accidents, particularly involving crowded and poorly maintained minibuses in mountainous areas.

Most bus companies, large and small, belong to a local government organisation which sets the fares and maps out the routes. Some compete on the same routes, therefore it's advisable to shop around and see which offers the best service.

Don't underestimate the distances involved. It can take a day or two to travel from the east coast to a city in central China or to one of the southern cities – Xiamen in Fujian province to Shenzhen looks like a short hop on a map but is 580km (360mi) and takes eight hours. After many hours of potholes and sharp bends, even the most comfortable seat loses its appeal, while the standard of the toilets gets worse with each passing hour, leaving you longing for the next 'comfort stop' at a café or roadside diner.

Long-distance express buses (kuai che) are the best option on daytime journeys, and are fine for a four- or five-hour trip. If you're heading further, it may be better to travel overnight on a sleeper bus (wopu che). These are equipped with simple bunk beds. Even though the bunks are small – your feet will stick over the edge if you're over 5ft 7in (1.7m) tall – they allow you a more restful journey than trying to sleep in an upright position.

Bus tickets can be purchased in advance from bus stations, bus company offices and travel agents, although it's possible to turn up and travel on some routes – something that's usually impossible with the trains.

City Buses

Every city has a wide range of bus routes and services, most of which are run by the local government. Buses carry 40 to 60 people but become crowded in rush hour as many more try to squeeze on. This is unpleasant in summer, unless there's air-conditioning, and pickpockets sometimes target travellers. However, the Chinese are also polite and will often give up their seat to mothers with small babies and elderly travellers (this is also true on the subways).

The best buses are reserved for city centre routes, with the older jalopies condemned to seeing out their days in the suburbs. Generally there are two types of bus to choose from: ordinary and express buses, the latter indicated by a K prefix before its number. K buses are more comfortable, have air-conditioning and stop less frequently, although fares are twice as high as an ordinary bus (not that any bus fare in China is expensive). In some areas there are also tourist buses, often mini-buses that link the main attractions, which don't run to a timetable but simply depart once all the seats are full.

Routes & Timetables

The best way to learn the local bus routes is to hop on and see where you end up. You can always catch a taxi back. Although routes and timetables should be displayed at bus stops, they're usually only in Chinese, so it's difficult to figure out where they're headed. A city map – get one which includes place names in pinyin – often has bus numbers printed alongside main streets to help you work out which bus goes where.

Fares & Tickets

Fares in most cities are remarkably simple: 1 RMB for any journey on a standard bus or 2 RMB on K (express) buses. You enter a bus at the front and alight via a central door.

There are no tickets. On entering the bus, you drop your cash into a box by the driver (have the correct fare ready as most don't give change). Regular passengers, school children and pensioners can save on fares by buying a weekly or a monthly 'season ticket' allowing unlimited travel on that city's bus services. These are in the form of plastic cards which are swiped through a small box on boarding the bus.

Some major cities now allow passengers to use reloadable smart cards to pay for travel on subway systems, and possibly also on buses.

Trolleybuses & Trams

These were once a popular form of transport but have become less common due to the overcrowded streets, although the fact that they travel on a fixed route, and other traffic must get out of their way, may lead to their reintroduction. Shanghai phased out its trams in the '70s, but reintroduced a modern tramway (streetcar) between Zhangjiang Hi-Tech Park and Heqing Town in 2010. Tianjin has also established a new tram route, while other Chinese cities with trams include Changchun and Dalian.

FERRIES & WATER BUSES

In China, boats are used for recreation rather than transportation, for example, few people take the Three Gorges cruise just to get from Chongqing to Wuhan. They're also used to transport cargo, and the Yangtze in particular is a highway for barge loads of goods crossing the country. People are less likely to use boats for public transport, although they provide a quick route from the mainland to Hong Kong and Macau.

In cities situated on main rivers, such as Wuhan and Guangzhou, or those on the coast, such as Dalian, Shenzhen and Xiamen, water transport provides an alternative to the crowded streets. Most public water bus and ferry services belong to the local government, and in many cases vessels are old and facilities are basic or non-existent, but the fares are as low as on a city bus: just 1 or 2 RMB. People bring everything on board, from baskets of chickens to electric bicycles, and a trip on a ferry can be fascinating, but look out for pickpockets at peak hours.

Among the most useful ferries are those which traverse Shanghai's Huangpu River between Pudong and Puxi. Prices range from 1 to 3 RMB, depending on the age of the ferry and whether it has air-conditioning. For around 20 RMB you can take your car.

TAXIS

There are two main types of taxi in China: licensed taxis and pirate taxis. Although there's no specific colour to identify licensed taxis – the colour varies from city to city – they display a sign on the roof and have a coloured 'taxi' sign inside the windscreen, both of which are illuminated at night. They also have a meter to calculate the fare and, in many cases, to print a receipt. Fares should be displayed on the nearside rear window and there's usually a barrier between the driver and passengers.

Pirate cabs are often painted in the same colour as local licensed cabs to fool you, but the resemblance ends there. If you get in a cab and there's no meter or 'menu' of charges, chances are it isn't legal and you're better off getting straight out again. Some people believe that pirate taxis are cheaper, but an 'agreed' price for a trip often shoots up 'because of the traffic' and, as a general rule, using the licensed taxis involves less hassle. Pirate cabs are a particular menace around airports, where drivers prey on unsuspecting arrivals.

There's no point is risking a ride in an illegal cab, as genuine taxis aren't expensive and there are plenty to choose from. Beijing alone has over 200 legal cab firms. Fares vary from city to city, but all are based on an initial charge for the first couple of kilometres, e.g. 10 RMB and then a further 5 RMB for each additional kilometre. You pay more in the big four cities and considerably less in a tier-three city. You're also expected to pay any tolls. Tipping is neither required nor expected. In fact, it's officially illegal to tip in China and if you round up the fare, the majority of cabbies will insist on giving you change.

You can flag down taxis on the street. Just hold out your arm and it's likely that several will come screeching to a halt beside you. Most drivers are safe and sensible, but there's always the odd one who thinks he's China's answer to Michael Schumacher (without the skill). If you're really worried, ask him to stop, and get out.

Note that passengers are expected to sit in the back of taxis, although back seats often have no seatbelts. If you want to wear a seatbelt you must sit in the front, although this seat is traditionally reserved for women.

Communication can be an issue with Chinese taxi drivers, most of whom speak no English whatsoever. The best way around this is to carry a card with your address on it in Chinese characters, and obtain business cards for places you visit regularly. You can try pointing out your destination on a street map, but some Chinese taxi drivers are no better at reading maps than they are at driving.

Alternative Taxis

Not all Chinese 'taxis' have four wheels. Many cities have tuk tuks and pedicabs: three-wheeled auto rickshaws powered by motorbikes, electric bicycles and, rarely these days, bicycles. In Urumqi in Xinjiang province, there are even donkey carts. And for the brave (or foolish) there are motorcycle taxis which whisk you through the traffic, riding pillion. Drivers of tuk tuks and pedicabs can be tricky with foreigners, and sometimes try to overcharge by setting a fare in RMB and then demanding it in dollars. Whenever you use unmetered transport, always agree the price in advance and the currency in which it's to be paid.

AIRLINE SERVICES

China has one of the fastest growing markets for air travel in the world, second only to the US. In 2012, China had an airline fleet of over 1,500 aircraft, and it's predicted that, by 2029, this will almost treble to over 4,000. At the same time there were 180 civil airports in China, of which almost 100 were operating at full capacity; many are in the process of being enlarged. In Beijing, the new Terminal 3 which was built for the Beijing Olympics in 2008, is now the largest airport terminal in the world.

China has three major airlines, all state owned. These are the main national carrier Air China, China Eastern and China Southern, all of which serve both the domestic and overseas markets. Note that China Airlines is the Taiwanese national airline and shouldn't be confused with Air China, although it does fly to many destinations in mainland China.

Founded in 1988 and based at Beijing's Capital Airport, Air China (🖳 airchina.com) is a member of the Star Alliance grouping and one of the most profitable airlines in the world, making a profit of US$1.83bn in 2010. In the same year, it carried 60m passengers to 185 destinations, and had a fleet of over 260 aircraft, with a similar number on order. China Eastern Airlines (🖳 flychinaeastern. com) flies out of Shanghai, with additional hubs in Kunming and Xi'an. It flies to over 100 destinations and carried some 65m passengers in 2010. The largest and oldest airline of the three is China Southern (🖳 csair.com), founded in 1981 and based in Guangzhou. A member of the

SkyTeam Alliance, it has over 400 aircraft serving 120 destinations, and in 2010 carried over 76m passengers, making it the sixth-largest airline in the world in terms of passenger numbers and the largest in Asia. The bulk of its passengers fly on domestic routes.

In addition to the three major airlines, there are a large, and increasing, number of smaller airlines, some of which are grouped together in consortiums, such as Hainan Airlines, which now incorporates Shanxi, China Xinhua and Chang'an Airlines. The majority of these smaller airlines are owned by provincial governments. Since 2005, a small number of private airlines have started, of which Shanghai-based Spring Airlines (🖳 china-sss.com/en-us/airflights/index) was the first to begin regular scheduled services.

By and large, Chinese airlines have good safety records, particularly the big three, and in terms of seating, service and reliability they aren't much different from Western airlines, particularly the three national carriers. However, it's as well to check on safety and reliability if you're planning to use one of the smaller and less well-known airlines. Note that smoking is prohibited on all Chinese airlines.

Domestic Flights

For journeys of over 800km (500mi), it's usually quicker and easier to travel by air. The three main airlines use primarily Airbus and Boeing aircraft, and have a vast network of domestic routes covering the entire country. Some routes are now duplicated by smaller airlines, which also cover many regional routes, and on these there's been a move towards using 100-seat Embraer aircraft as well as other smaller planes.

There are no budget airlines in China offering low-cost fares, similar to the UK's Easyjet, but there are a number of regional airlines serving domestic and international routes. Hainan Airlines (🖳 global.hnair.com), based in Haikou on the southern island province of Hainan, is a highly regarded private airline, and the first in mainland China to receive a five-star rating from the Skytrax air travel research consultancy. It operates flights to 90 destinations, both in mainland China and further afield, with scheduled services to Berlin, Brussels, Seattle, Sydney, Toronto and Zurich.

Shanghai Airlines (🖳 ww1.shanghai-air.com/salnewweb-en/index.aspx) was merged with China Eastern in 2010, but has retained its branding and flies to 140 destinations from its twin bases at Shanghai's Pudong and Hongqiao airports. The majority of its routes are within mainland China and to neighbouring Southeast Asian countries, but regular flights to Melbourne were planned from summer 2011.

Established in 1984, Xiamen Airlines (🖳 xiamenair.com.cn) was the first privately owned airline in China, although it's now part-owned by China Southern. Based in the south-eastern port city of Xiamen, most of its 54 destinations are domestic, although it also flies to Japan, Malaysia, Singapore and South Korea.

Probably the busiest route in China is the one between Beijing and Shanghai, where five different airlines jostle for slots and there are flights every 30 minutes carrying a total of over 11,000 passengers daily. An innovative arrangement has been introduced on this route, whereby when you buy a special Beijing to Shanghai Express flight ticket that you can use on any of the five carriers serving the route.

The Civil Aviation Administration China (CAAC, 🖳 caac.gov.cn) has offices in all the major cities, often with a CAAC hotel adjacent, and airline tickets can be purchased from their offices, from travel agents or at the departure airport. Some airlines, e.g. Air China and Hainan Airways, offer the facility to book tickets online, therefore it's worth checking airlines' websites, some of which carry special offers.

Fares are fixed on state-run airlines, but if you're willing to travel at an unpopular time of day, or if a particular route isn't busy, some astonishing discounts can be obtained: up to 70 per cent in some cases. The ticket price of all flights is comprised of two components, the flight cost and tax, and it makes sense to ask if there's a discount available. Note that if you pay by credit card, you may be charged a 3.5 per cent surcharge.

The table oppostie shows the typical fares (in RMB) between Beijing and other major cities.

Flight Distances & Fares					
Destination	Distance	Flight time	Discount Fare Best	Standard	Official Fare
Guangzhou	1,881km/1,169mi	3 hrs 10 min	1,070	1,220	1,560
Harbin	999km/621mi	2 hrs	350	600	880
Kunming	2,115km/1,314mi	3 hrs 15 min	740	1,140	1,670
Shanghai	1,076km/669mi	2 hrs 10 min	650	650	1,130
Urumqi	2,421km/1,504mi	4 hrs 15 min	860	1,110	2,220
Xi'an	937km/582mi	1 hr 45 min	740	740	1,020

You must check in at least an hour before domestic flights, and check in usually closes 30 minutes before take-off; at this point, any vacant seats can be bought by passengers waiting on standby. Boarding is announced in Chinese and then in English. To board, you normally just have to show your boarding pass. Luggage is usually limited to 20kg plus one carry-on bag for economy class passengers, but many people ignore the restrictions and the overhead lockers get full quickly.

Hong Kong and Macau are treated as international destinations. If you fly to either, you must pass through immigration and, if you have a single-entry visa, must obtain a new one to re-enter China. Many people with short duration multiple entry visas fly to Hong Kong, then re-enter the country each time their permitted stay expires.

All flights serve non-alcoholic drinks such as tea, coffee and juice free of charge, and on flights lasting over an hour you usually receive a meal. These can be as little as a small packet of biscuits but a hot meal may be served on longer flights. The airline attendants distribute newspapers shortly after take-off, and many flights carry the China Daily for any foreigners on board.

Most seats are economy class, but many planes have a small business class section at the front of the aircraft. These seats are frequently empty and it's often possible to upgrade to one by paying a small sum, around 200 RMB, at the check-in desk. Not only are these seats wider, but they also offer more leg-room and can be a boon for tall passengers.

International Flights

The three main Chinese airlines fly to destinations throughout the world, including Europe, the US and Australasia. Most flights are in Boeing 747 or 777 or the larger Airbus aircraft. The seats are reasonably comfortable – the seat pitch is between 32 and 33in – the food is typical long-haul fare and drinks, including wine and beer, are served with meals free of charge. Duty free goods are carried on board, usually priced in US dollars, and films and music are provided.

Ticket prices are sometimes a little lower than those charged by overseas competitors and, as with domestic flights, it's worth enquiring whether discounts are available. If you're flying from China to Australia, all three Chinese airlines have routes to Sydney, but frequently one is considerably cheaper than the others.

If you're planning a flight to China, it's advisable to shop around using flight search engines and flight specialists (such as ☐ cheapflights.co.uk), as prices can vary considerably. In 2012, a one-month return ticket from London to Beijing cost between £500 and £700, depending on the airline. Some of the cheapest deals were with Air France, KLM and Russia's Aeroflot. Air China, meanwhile, had flights priced between £600 and £900, although if you took advantage of one of its promotional fares, the price dropped to around £550. Always check the cost of extras such as taxes and (e.g. fuel) surcharges, which can add considerably to the price.

Air China, China Eastern and China Southern all operate frequent flyer schemes and all three are members of airline alliances, so benefits can be used widely. To date all three, however, operate rather restrictive schemes and getting a response from them requires a great deal of patience.

Beijing, Shanghai and Guangzhou airports are also served by many international airlines and tickets for flights on any of these can be purchased at CAAC offices, larger tourist agencies or via the internet. Again, it's worth asking about alternatives as some airlines, notably KLM and Air France, offer discounted tickets at certain times of the year, although they may still be dearer than Chinese airlines.

There are now also a few low-cost Asian airlines such as Air Asia and Tiger Airlines flying into China, often to smaller airports such as Tianjin, which is just 30 minutes from Beijing by high speed rail. These airlines charge for each leg of the journey and sometimes work out cheaper if you're flying one way. For trips to Hong Kong it's worth checking for offers from the newly created Hong Kong Airlines. Bear in mind that for international flights, most airlines require you to check in two hours before the scheduled departure time and sometimes three hours.

Airports

The main three Chinese international airports are in Beijing, Guangzhou and Shanghai – the majority of overseas arrivals land at one of these three and they're the hubs at which passengers transfer to domestic flights. However, there are also international airports at many other Chinese cities including Chengdu, Chongqing, Dalian, Hangzhou, Harbin, Hohhot, Kunming, Qingdao, Shenyang, Tianjin, Urumqi, Xiamen and Xi'an. All are under the control of the Civil Aviation Administration China (CAAC).

Most of China's airports are being upgraded and extended and many facilities are under construction. Despite this, most are modern and well organised and little different from Western airports. In the check-in hall you'll find banks and currency exchange bureaus, ticket sales offices and left luggage facilities, as well as kiosks selling food, cigarettes and souvenirs, the usual fast food giants, and even a hairdresser. Once in the departure area there are bookshops, coffee bars and yet more kiosks selling souvenirs; most goods and services are much more expensive than outside the airport.

> It isn't difficult to find your way around a Chinese airport, as signs are posted in English as well as Chinese and staff are generally helpful, although English speakers are rare in the smaller airports.

One welcome free service is the provision of comfortable seats specifically for elderly and disabled people and for nursing mothers. For passengers travelling business or first class, there are private lounges with free coffee and snacks.

While waiting in the departure lounge you may notice smartly uniformed girls offering little booklets to waiting passengers. These are catalogues of hotels offering discount rates, and there are sure to be some in your destination city. It's worth taking advantage of them as the discounts are often 50 per cent or more on the usual room rate.

On arrival at any airport in China, collecting your luggage is straightforward. The way to baggage claim is clearly marked in English with boards indicating flight numbers and respective baggage carousels. Help yourself to a free trolley and wait for your baggage to emerge; it's usually remarkably quick, although there's often a scrum as people push to get at their bags. Hang on to your baggage receipt (stapled to your boarding pass) as staff will want to check it to ensure you aren't taking someone else's suitcase by mistake.

Beijing Capital Airport

The busiest airport in China – and the second-busiest in the world after Atlanta in the US – Beijing Capital Airport (bcia.com.cn) offers flights to over 120 destinations and in 2010 handled over 73m passengers. It's the main hub for Air China and a major hub for China Southern Airlines.

Beijing has three terminals. Terminal 3, which was completed in time to greet visitors heading to the Beijing Olympics in 2008, is the largest airport terminal in the world: larger than all five terminals at London's Heathrow combined. However, despite the airport's massive scale and huge passenger numbers, it's remarkably user-friendly and was voted the best airport in the world in 2009 by readers of *Conde Nast Traveller*, based on its cleanliness, efficiency and accessibility.

Terminal 1 is used by the Hainan Airlines Group as the base for their domestic flights, while terminal 2 caters for both domestic and international flights, including those operated by China Eastern and China Southern. Terminal 3 is the principal terminal for all Air China flights and is so vast that it's divided into three sub-terminals: T3C for domestic flights, and T3D and T3E for international flights. All check-ins are conducted at T3C; from there you can take a two-minute light rail journey to either of the two sub-terminals.

Terminal 3 is also the main hub for rail and road traffic, and there are buses to take passengers to Terminals 1 and 2. They run from 6am until 10pm; every ten minutes from 8am until 8pm and every 20 minutes at other times.

Beijing Capital Airport is 32km (20mi) northeast of the city centre and is connected via a light railway from Dongzhimen subway station in central Beijing. The journey takes 20 minutes and costs 25 RMB. It's also served by several expressways, and the taxi fare is around 100 RMB. Baggage labels issued at the airport are marked PEK for Peking.

Guangzhou Baiyun Airport

Although Pudong is further from Shanghai's centre than Hoingqiao, it's actually quicker to get to as it's served by the super-fast Maglev train (see page 128) which takes less than eight minutes. Hongqiao, meanwhile, can be reached by the Shanghai Metro – a journey time of around 30 minutes. There are bus shuttles to both airports.

One of the major frustrations for travellers is making the connection between an international flight arriving at Pudong and a domestic flight departing from Hongqiao (or vice versa), due to the distance between the two airports (25mi/40km). By road, the journey can take an hour or longer. The best way to travel is by metro, although the airports are at opposite ends of the line; you can reduce the journey time to an hour by switching to or from the Maglev at Longyang Road.

Guangzhou Baiyun Airport

China's second-largest airport and the hub for China Southern, Guangzhou Baiyun Airport (⌨ baiyunairport.com) handles over 41m passengers a year. It opened in 2004, replacing one of China's oldest airport terminals. Guangzhou Baiyun comprises two terminals, E3 (east) and W3 (west), both handling a combination of domestic and international flights to around 100 destinations. Work to expand its facilities and almost double its capacity commenced in 2011.

The airport is located around 28km (17mi) from the city centre. There are several bus services linking it to the city, the journey taking from 45 minutes and costing around 18 RMB. The Guangzhou Metro was extended to the airport in 2010. Baggage labels for Guangzhou Baiyun Airport are marked CAN (for Canton).

Shanghai's Airports

Shanghai has two airports (⌨ shairport.com). The older Hongqiao International Airport has served the city since the '20s but it was pushed into second place when Pudong International Airport opened in 1999. Hongqiao is just 13km (8mi) west of the city centre, compared with Pudong which is 40km (25mi) away, but the latter is now the third-largest airport in China with Hongqiao just behind.

Hongqiao was completely rebuilt in preparation for Expo 2010 and now has two terminals, with most traffic departing from the much larger Terminal 2. The airport handles over 30m passengers a year. In comparison, Pudong had a passenger throughput of 40.5m at its two terminals. To differentiate between the two, Hongqaio's baggage labels are identified with SHA for Shanghai, while Pudong's are marked PVG.

11.

MOTORING

The Chinese love their cars and buy more each year than any other nation; over 18.5m new vehicles were sold in 2011, of which 14.3m were passenger cars. However, the Chinese don't buy cars just to get from A to B; a car's a status symbol, a way to show your neighbours that you're someone of importance who can afford to spend many thousands of *yuan* on your own personal mode of transport. And it follows that your car should be as large and expensive as possible.

Very few of these shiny new cars ever travel beyond the city limits. Most people still use trains and planes for longer journeys, as they're reliable, inexpensive and avoid the problem of trying to find your way around unfamiliar territory. Decent road maps in China are almost non-existent. However, the cities were never designed to cope with so many vehicles and the result is never-ending traffic jams and a long, tedious search for a parking space. Before becoming a car owner in China, it pays to think long and hard about whether you really need one.

Until 1994, it was illegal for a private individual to own a car, which was a luxury reserved for party officials. However, the Chinese are now making up for lost time and the market for luxury cars has become the largest in the world, despite the fact that so few people can afford them. In 2011, the per capita disposable annual income for Chinese urban dwellers was just 21,810 RMB – around US$3,500 – while a basic Chinese-manufactured car cost 100,000 RMB – over US$15,000 – before additional costs such as registration and insurance were added. So a car can cost over seven times the average income.

In 2012, there were around 112m cars in China, compared with the US, a similar sized country, where there were 252m and the much smaller UK with 31m. The number of cars in China is predicted to rise to 200m by 2020, but for now the ratio of cars to people in China is still comparatively low. Statistics for 2011 show that while the US had some 812 vehicles per 1,000 people and the UK around 520, China had just 83 (although it won't seem like there are fewer in the cities!). Thus the potential market is

huge and, with few exceptions, all the major car manufacturers from Europe, Japan, Korea and the US have established joint ventures in China to build cars, and have been extending their facilities to increase production to meet demand. Those without a joint venture are exporting their vehicles to China.

Chinese manufacturers haven't been left behind. Major names such as Chery, Geely and BYD are turning out new cars at lower prices than their overseas competitors. Most are good quality and compare favourably with overseas models, although there are still some budget brands where the build quality is suspect.

Away from the cities, Chinese roads are pleasantly traffic free. Figures from the World Bank database show that in 2008, while the US had 38 vehicles (cars, buses and trucks) per km of highway and the crowded UK had 77, China had just 13. It's possible to drive for long distances without seeing another vehicle, other than the odd tractor, cart or bicycle. But in cities, it's a very different matter. The traffic jams begin as you approach the suburbs and continue throughout city centres. Parking is a perennial problem. Many residential areas were built in the '50s and '60s and have virtually no space for parking anything larger than a bicycle, while the small car parks built for supermarkets and department stores in the '80s and '90s are full by 8am. Public car parks are rare and many drivers simply park on footpaths.

The road traffic accident rate in China is over twice that of the US. In 2009, the official number of road deaths reported to the Chinese police totalled around 70,000; in the same year 33,808 people lost their lives on US roads and 2,337 were killed in the UK. The World Health Organisation (WHO) has disputed the accuracy of China's road death figures. In 2010, it published a report comparing road traffic mortality rates from police-reported data and death registration in China in 2007. According to WHO, the number of road-related deaths registered by China's health ministry that year was 221,135, compared with 81,649 deaths reported to the Chinese police. Based on its figures, the World Health Organisation estimates that the road death rate in China is increasing even though official police figures suggest otherwise. And in WHO's 3rd National Retrospective Survey on Causes of Death, the road death rate for 2005 (its most recent year) is stated as 15.3 per 100,000 population, three times higher than in the UK.

Whichever figures you believe, there's no doubt that China's roads are dangerous, but it's important to put the dangers into perspective. Most serious accidents happen in rural areas. In the crowded cities, traffic is forced to move at a gentle pace – notwithstanding the odd loony showing off in his new BMW – and most accidents are minor bumps. However, on the fast expressways and, particularly in the countryside, fatal accidents are a regular occurrence. It's the more vulnerable road users who come off worst. WHO reported that in 2006 only 5 per cent of those killed were car drivers; 25 per cent were pedestrians and 28 per cent were motorcyclists. In the countryside, many people still aren't accustomed to cars and are unaware of the dangers, and rural children are particularly at risk.

Car crime is minimal in China compared with developed countries. Car theft is relatively uncommon, probably because there aren't many thieves who know how to drive, and vandalism is rare, as is breaking into cars to steal valuables. If you do come back to find your car gone, it's more likely to have been towed away for being parked illegally than stolen.

☑ SURVIVAL TIP

Driving in China is undoubtedly challenging but it isn't as difficult as some expatriates claim. You must expect the unexpected and drive defensively but don't let this put you off. The important thing is to observe how the local people drive, and go with the flow.

Whether or not you decide to own and drive a car in China depends on where you live, the availability of public transport and parking, and how keen you are to discover the country. If your home and workplace are served by a subway or reliable buses, then a car may be a liability and more trouble than it's worth – as it is in London or New York – but if your public transport options are limited and you have somewhere to park at home and at work, it's worth considering. The enjoyment you can get from using a car at weekends to explore the countryside more than makes up for the hassle of driving into the city to work.

IMPORTING A VEHICLE

As most foreigners stay in China for a limited period of time, very few consider importing a car – or their household belongings. It's possible to import a vehicle; the Australian ambassador in Beijing drives a top of the range Holden that he brought into the country, albeit with the assistance of the General Motors manager; and some other ambassadors drive imported cars which represent their home countries' automotive trade. However, for most individuals, the hassle and expense involved means it isn't worthwhile.

The Chinese Customs Administration (🖳 english.customs.gov.cn) imposes a range of restrictions on the types of vehicles which can be imported, who can import them and for how long. Vintage and right-hand drive vehicles (e.g. from the UK) are unlikely to be approved; the Chinese drive on the right, and a right-hand drive car would be more of a liability than an asset. And then there's the issue of import duty and other taxes which can add up to over half of a vehicle's value. Joint venture companies can import vehicles tax-free, but permission doesn't necessarily extend to their employees. Rules change all the time, therefore if it's something that you're considering, you should talk to your employer about it and check the latest situation with a Chinese consulate and Chinese Customs.

Nearly every model of car made in the world is either made in China under a joint venture or imported, or you could ask a dealer to import a particular model for you. There are also some interesting cars produced by the fledgling Chinese motor industry.

TECHNICAL INSPECTION

Like many countries around the world, China requires older vehicles to pass an annual inspection to confirm that they're still roadworthy and not emitting too much pollution. Once a car is over eight years old, it must pass this test annually before its registration can be renewed and road tax paid. Although the test itself is a relatively simple check of brakes, steering, lights and bodywork, the entire process can take a whole day.

Before you can take a car for testing, you must obtain clearance from the traffic police, who use this opportunity to check whether you have any outstanding traffic fines; if you do, they must be paid at a branch of the Post Office Savings Bank before the inspection can take place. The next step is an emissions test. It costs just 2 RMB and, provided your car passes (most do), you receive a sticker to display in the windscreen.

Only after any fines are paid and a car's emissions approved can you visit the vehicle testing station, where your car is checked by a police driver on a rolling road. This takes around ten minutes. If your car passes you're issued with a certificate, which you take to another office where you pay to tax your vehicle for the forthcoming year. The total cost is 100 RMB and you receive a sticker to place behind your windscreen indicating that your car is taxed and road legal. If the vehicle has been regularly serviced and kept in reasonable condition it should easily pass this test. If it fails, you must get the fault fixed and take it back for a re-test before you can tax it.

The main problem with this procedure is the fact that the traffic police's headquarters, emissions and vehicle testing stations are often in different parts of the city, so you can spend several hours driving around.

If you fail to display an up to date registration sticker, your car can be impounded by the police and you'll face paying a storage fee of 50 RMB a day as well as a fine.

REGISTRATION & NUMBER PLATES

Buying a car is a major expense in China and the purchase price is only a part of it. All new cars must be registered and this can be eye-wateringly expensive. The fee depends on the size and value of the car, but to register an average family saloon or hatchback you should budget around 10 per cent of its purchase price: as much as 25,000 RMB for a medium-sized hatchback or saloon, e.g. a Ford Mondeo.

In some cities it's a struggle to get a new car registered at all. There are now so many cars coming onto the roads that the authorities are trying to restrict numbers by limiting the amount of new registrations. In 2011, Beijing set up a lottery for

drivers wishing to register a new car: there were 210,178 applicants and just 17,600 got number plates. As a result, the total registration of new cars in Beijing is now fixed at 20,000 per year and the waiting list has reached over one million. Anyone wanting to enter this lottery has to prove they have had a Beijing *hukou* (residency) or have lived and paid taxes in Beijing for at least five years. Meanwhile, Shanghai holds an auction each month at which drivers bid for a specific and limited number of registration slots; some people have paid as much as 50,000 RMB to register their car.

It's difficult to get around the system. In theory, if you live in Beijing or Shanghai, you could buy your car in another province or country where the restrictions don't apply and register it there – but you can only do this if you have a local address. Similarly, if you buy a car in one city and move to another, e.g. from Shanghai to Dalian, you must re-register your car at your new address and obtain local number plates.

With registration being such a headache, there's no point in buying a new car until you've secured the right to register it. If you're successful, the dealer will arrange the initial registration for you once you've paid a deposit on the car.

⚠ Caution

You cannot complete registration of a new car until you've obtained compulsory third party insurance, which costs around 1,300 RMB a year.

On initial registration, a credit card sized blue booklet is issued confirming the vehicle's specification, its registration number and the owner's name and address. This must be kept in the vehicle at all times and is the first thing the police ask to see in the event of a problem.

Registration is revalidated each year by payment of an annual road tax of 100 RMB, which also covers the cost of a technical inspection which is a requirement for all cars over eight years old (see above). On payment you receive a receipt which you should keep in the vehicle and a sticker to fix inside the windscreen on the offside (the driver's side). The sticker for compulsory third party insurance goes on the top nearside (the passenger's side).

Number Plates

Once you've managed to obtain a registration slot, paid the fee – and recovered from the shock – you can drive your new car home. You don't receive your number plates until registration is complete, and then not for a few weeks. While the plates are on order, you have yet another sticker to put in the windscreen indicating the car's registration number. The car is then road legal to drive while you wait for the plates to arrive. Some drivers wait for several months.

Each province has its own number plates, consisting of the name of the province (often a local nickname, e.g. in Henan province it's yu, meaning elephant) followed by a five or six figure number which incorporates an initial letter indicating the city of registration. This letter is important, as when the city police tow away illegally parked vehicles, they usually tow away non-local vehicles first!

Personalised number plates, e.g. LOV3R or B1GB0Y, aren't a big deal in China, although lucky numbers certainly are, and the Chinese will, if possible, choose certain number combinations for their number plate. You see few vehicles on the roads with a four in their registration number – it's pronounced the same as the word for death and is considered unlucky (you need all the luck you can get when driving in China) – but you'll see plenty with a six, eight or nine. All are considered lucky and the number eight stands for financial success and in today's China is the 'luckiest' number of all!

You can ask your dealer to choose a specific registration number for your car but none of the lucky numbers come cheap. If you see a Mercedes fitted with number plates bearing the number 8888, its owner may have paid more for the plate than for the car.

The police and the army have their own special number plates incorporating a small number of red characters on the left of the plate. It's handy to be able to recognise these, as both the army and the armed police (wu jin) teach their drivers how to drive fast in heavy traffic and if you come across a driver practicing this on a busy street you need to get out of his way pronto.

Change of Ownership

When a car changes hands, both the vehicle and the registration booklet must be taken to the traffic police. The police check for outstanding traffic fines and then issue a new registration booklet with the new owner's name in it. Cars over eight years old must pass a technical inspection first.

CAR HIRE (RENTAL)

Car hire (rental) as it exists in the West is unusual in China, where you must usually hire a driver along with a car. Self-drive hire is still fairly rare and with good reason: a foreigner new to China and the Chinese way of driving shouldn't really consider getting straight off a plane and into a hire car.

Major car hire names such as Hertz and Avis operate in China, as do a small number of local companies, but these are generally limited to the largest cities. Where self-drive is available, the vehicles offered are usually large luxury saloons and your chances of hiring an economy vehicle and driving it yourself are minimal. Agencies hiring out older cars, e.g. rent-a-wreck, don't exist in China.

If you do manage to hire a car and drive it yourself, you may only be permitted to drive within a restricted area, e.g. within a city's limits, and the rental charges are likely to be very high. Rental is subject to possession of a Chinese driving licence or, at the very least, an International Driving Permit (IDP); even though China doesn't officially recognise the IDP, most hire companies insist that foreign drivers have one. Always check the insurance cover carefully, and ensure that you have extra insurance to cover any excess in the event of damage to the car.

Hiring a car from an agency, complete with a driver, allows you to enjoy the journey without having to negotiate poor road signs and other drivers' bad habits. However, you aren't required to rent a car from an agency. There are thousands of taxi drivers in most cities, and you can negotiate to hire their services for a day. The charge depends on how long you want the vehicle and the distance you plan to travel, but it shouldn't be over 350 RMB a day. This is much cheaper than using a car hire agency, which can charge from 800 RMB a day for a mid-range car.

BUYING A CAR

There are no restrictions on foreigners buying cars in China, other than those imposed by the registration system, which applies to drivers of all nationalities. If you do decide to buy, China has one of the largest ranges of cars for sale of any country, and there are showrooms representing the major manufacturers on every corner to satisfy the Chinese desire for all things four-wheeled. Note that you need to possess a Chinese driving licence (see page 146) before you can buy a car.

The types of cars for sale can be classified into three groups:

♦ **Chinese models**: cars built locally by Chinese companies such as Chery, Geely, BYD and Great Wall.

♦ **Overseas models made in China**: many major foreign manufacturers are in joint ventures with Chinese partners, including General Motors, Honda, Hyundai, Toyota and Volkswagen.

♦ **Imported cars**: some models can be ordered from overseas – at a price!

Not so many years ago, Chinese cars were considered a bit of a joke, but not any more. They now compare (more or less) with most Western makes, and account for around half of all new car sales. Chinese models are also cheaper. In 2011, you could buy a new BYD F3, a compact four-door saloon not unlike the Toyota Corolla, for 59,800 RMB (around £5,635). They also look the part. Some designs are based on Western models; Shanghai Automotive Industry Corporation (SAIC) owns the rights to several Rover models and makes well-engineered cars under the name Roewe. And the Chinese aptitude for imitating top brands has resulted in some close copies of world-

famous makes, from the Smart car to the Mercedes CLK and even Rolls-Royce.

Cars made in China by a joint ventures are generally a little cheaper than the price of the equivalent model in the UK (British VAT included), but more expensive than cars in the US. You can buy a new Toyota Yaris for between 87,000 and 106,800 RMB (£8,198-10,064), compared with £10,040-13,280 in Britain. However, if a manufacturer anticipates high demand, prices rise accordingly. This is particularly the case with sports utility vehicles (SUVs), which are highly sought after – sales of which increased by over 100 per cent between 2009 and 2010 – and are 'priced for the market' at well over double or even treble the price they fetch in Europe.

Imported cars are by far the most costly option. The majority are in the luxury class and imported to order for China's *nouveau riche*, and their price tags reflect the high taxes they attract – sometimes well over a million RMB. Importing a car with an engine capacity of four litres or more attracts import duty of 25 per cent, plus local value added tax of 17 per cent and a consumption tax of 40 per cent, meaning that a Rolls Royce Phantom can cost from 6.6m RMB. Even some versions of the BMW X6 cost over 2m RMB.

In some respects it's a seller's market, and foreigners are often surprised to find a lack of choice when it comes to a new car's specifications. There are usually only a couple of options: a basic model with manual gears and no air-conditioning, or a top-of-the-range model with automatic transmission, climate control and leather seats, but nothing in between. So you must accept a car that lacks certain things that you would like, or go for one that has extras you don't really need.

Dealer prices include Chinese VAT at 17 per cent, but you must budget for the extras: the costly process of the initial registration, plus road tax and compulsory third party insurance.

Used Cars

The secondhand car market is growing in China but it's far smaller than the market for new cars. When the Chinese upgrade their car, they often give the old one to a relative or a member of their staff;

the Chinese are no keener on buying used cars than they are on buying pre-owned houses. So the practice of trading in an old vehicle for a new one is still in its infancy, although some new car dealers have a limited number of secondhand cars for sale.

The alternative is to visit a used car mart. The largest are in Beijing and Shanghai, although similar operations are now appearing in other large cities. The drawback of buying secondhand, whether privately or from a car mart, is that there's no way of checking a car's history, e.g. whether it's stolen, has payments outstanding on it or has been involved in a major accident, and you could easily end up buying a lemon. The Chinese drive their cars hard, and many used cars suffer from high mileage, worn gears and dented bodywork.

If you want to buy a used car, it's better to buy through an established dealer who's selling on vehicles for established customers and knows their history. There are (as yet) so few expatriates owning cars in China that the expat market is limited, although it may be worth looking at classified adverts in expat publications.

DRIVING LICENCE

You can drive on your home country's licence in China, but only for a short time. Within three months at the most, foreigners are expected to obtain a Chinese driving licence and without one you won't be able to buy or register a car. This isn't as daunting as it sounds and many foreigners have taken and passed the test.

The legal driving age is from 18 to 70. Drivers aren't allowed on the roads after 70 and you rarely see older women driving. There's a rumour that the Public Security Bureau (PSB) won't issue licences to women over 45 but this should be taken with a pinch of salt. Licences are issued separately for drivers of cars, motorcycles or trucks, and there are different tests for each type. Riders of electric bicycles don't need a licence, but petrol-powered scooters can only be ridden if you have a motorbike licence.

Licences are issued by the traffic section of the PSB and are initially valid for six years. Holders must undergo an annual medical examination and the licence is stamped by the PSB to this effect. If you complete six years of driving without using up your full quota of 12 penalty points in that time, your second licence is valid for ten years and is renewed every ten years thereafter, provided you don't lose all your points. The licence itself costs 70 RMB, contains a photograph and is contained in a credit-card-sized black booklet.

You apply for your test at the PSB. The first step is a medical examination including an eye test and a test for colour blindness. In addition, you must provide a copy of your overseas driving licence plus a Chinese translation and at least five photographs, which must have a white background and be 2.5 x 2.5cm (1 x 1in) in size, i.e. smaller than a passport photograph.

The written test takes around 45 minutes and is based on the rather dauntingly-titled *Reference Manual of the Road Traffic Safety Laws of the People's Republic of China* (a.k.a. the Chinese Highway Code) which can be purchased at any branch of the government bookseller Xinhua for 150 RMB. The book contains lists of multiple-choice questions and answers – similar to those used in the test – and is available in a number of languages including English. In some areas the test can be taken on a computer and you can elect to take it in either English or Chinese, but where it's only available in writing the PSB provides an interpreter. There's an extra fee of 100 RMB for his services, but it's money well spent as he usually tells you the answers!

The pass mark is high – 90 per cent – but if you fail, you can retake the test after a week and keep taking it until you pass. After this, the practical test is a no-brainer, usually involving a plunge into the nearby city traffic for around 15 minutes. There are no awkward manoeuvres to master, such as reversing into a parking space, just straightforward driving in traffic.

You're permitted to practice for your test on Chinese roads on your overseas licence until you pass. There aren't many driving schools in China and few drivers have ever had lessons. In fact, a considerable number have never taken the test or possessed a licence, including government officials. In 2009, newspapers reported a story about a local government officer who was involved in an accident and found not to have a driving licence. On closer inspection, none of the officials in his office had taken a driving test either, even though some had been issued with a licence and all drove government vehicles. When ordered to take the test, they complained that it was a waste of their valuable time and that if they failed, it would ruin their careers.

⚠ Caution

Drivers are required by law to carry their driving licence with them while driving. The car's registration booklet must also be kept in the car at all times.

As this story suggests, it's possible to obtain a driving licence without taking the test, and there are a number of websites targeting foreigners which claim to provide a driving licence within 10 to 20 days, provided applicants pay a deposit of 2,000 RMB. Since the cost of taking and obtaining a Chinese licence through official channels is 70 RMB (plus the cost of the medical exam), this isn't exactly a bargain.

Some sources suggest that you can travel to Hong Kong, pay HK$120 to have your licence converted to a HK licence and then go back to China, say Guangzhou, and have the Hong Kong licence converted to a Chinese licence. This may be an option if you keep fluffing the theory test.

Fines & Penalty Points

The Chinese police have two ways of fining bad drivers. If you're caught in the act you may receive a ticket on the spot, which must be paid within 14 days, usually at a special office of the traffic police. More likely, though, you'll be caught on camera – often located at traffic lights to catch those jumping red lights – and will know nothing about it until you go to renew your car's registration (see page 143).

Most 'minor' offences, such as exceeding the speed limit by a small amount or running a red light, incur fines of 200 RMB, although if you exceed a speed limit by over 50 per cent you could be fined as much as 2,000 RMB. Fines can mount up over a year and poor drivers are in for a nasty surprise at registration time.

There's also a system of penalty points. Drivers start with 12 and lose one or more for each traffic misdemeanour. Lose them all and your licence could be withdrawn for three months, although this is rarely enforced outside the big four cities.

The most serious traffic crime is dangerous driving, particularly when alcohol is involved. After a succession of appalling accidents in 2009 involving drunken drivers, which resulted in the death of a number of pedestrians, the PSB charged the drivers with 'endangering public safety'. Defendants found guilty of this charge can, in theory, receive the death penalty – in recent years several drivers have been sentenced to capital punishment, although none have been executed to date.

CAR INSURANCE

Car insurance is available from Chinese insurance companies and from branches of overseas insurance companies. However, other than compulsory third party insurance, which cannot be avoided, most drivers don't buy extra cover for their cars. The Chinese don't see much point in insurance; many believe that they'll never have an accident and, if they do, then it's easier to settle up in cash on the spot.

Third Party Insurance

In 2006, the government introduced a new law requiring owners of all vehicles (excluding bicycles and electric bicycles) to insure against the risk of causing death or injury to third parties or damage to their vehicles. Cover is up to a maximum of 180,000 RMB – though few insurers pay anything close to this amount – and policies cost between 650 and 1,300 RMB a year. You cannot register a car until it's been insured, and must display a valid sticker in the windscreen. The police are quite vigilant in checking that all vehicles, including parked ones, are insured, and those that aren't are often towed away and impounded

Note that third party polices don't include damage to your own car (where you're at fault) or cover against your car being stolen or set on fire (known in the UK as third party, fire and theft/TPF&T). If you want to insure against these possibilities you must take out comprehensive cover.

Comprehensive Insurance

Policies in China are similar to those in other countries. They should cover you for damage to someone else's vehicle or property, as well as damage to your own car, and most include cover for breakage of glass (e.g. windscreen), your medical expenses and theft of the car or its contents. Some policies also include a courtesy car if yours is off the road and legal assistance in the case of a dispute, although these may require you to pay an extra premium. Always check what you're covered for and any restrictions, e.g. who can drive the car and where it should be kept

comprehensive insurance policy for an average family car (such as a Ford Mondeo) cost 5,000 to 6,000 RMB a year. The majority of Chinese drivers, even those driving expensive cars, don't bother with comprehensive insurance.

Most insurance policies are only written in Chinese. If you want to fully understand them, you'll need to pay for a translation.

Excesses & No Claims Discounts

If you have to make a claim, Chinese insurance companies usually pay the full amount without deducting an excess (deductible) – if they pay anything at all. Overseas insurance companies usually insist on the policy holder paying a proportion, e.g. the first £100/US$150, of each claim. No claims discounts are minimal and only apply to the first year of a policy: if you've made no claim they might reduce your renewal premium by 10 per cent. However, for most motorists, the only benefit they gain from having an accident-free year is that the cost of their annual policy doesn't increase, as it otherwise would.

Motor Breakdown Insurance

This isn't available in China, although breakdown services are offered by motoring organisations (see page 156).

RULES OF THE ROAD

There are two 'rules' which aren't included in China's Highway Code but which are essential to know before venturing onto Chinese roads:

♦ Larger vehicles take precedence over smaller vehicles.

♦ The vehicle that gets there first has precedence over all other vehicles.

The Chinese adhere to these two unwritten 'laws' without exception, using speed and size to claim space in the road ahead of anyone else, and you ignore them at your peril.

However, there are also many official road rules which are outlined in the *Reference Manual of the Road Traffic Safety Laws of the People's Republic of China*, available from Xinhua bookshops. In most cases, the same rules, signs and road markings apply as in Europe or the US, the most important of which are shown below.

Note that in common with the US and most of Europe, the Chinese drive on the right. (During the Cultural Revolution, so it's claimed, this was changed temporarily to driving on the left, for ideological reasons.) If you're from Australia or the UK, where traffic drives on the left, this takes a little getting used to. The same applies if you're arriving from Hong Kong or Macau, where they also drive on the left. Take extra care when pulling out of junctions and one-way streets, and remember to look first to the left when crossing the road on foot.

Documents

You're required by law to carry your driving licence and registration document in your car at all times. It's also advisable to carry a copy of your insurance policies.

Drink & Drugs

Drink driving is a huge problem in China, where excessive drinking is encouraged at banquets (formal dinners) and many people (try to) drive home afterwards. However, the police take a harsh view of it, particularly after a spate of fatal accidents in recent years which resulted in the deaths of pedestrians, and you can be stopped and breathalysed at any time. So concerned are the authorities that they tightened up the law and increased penalties for drink drivers in 2011, and even being just over the blood alcohol limit can result in a conviction and a driving ban.

If you have over 20mg of alcohol per 100ml of blood you're officially classified as drunk. Your licence will be revoked and you'll be effectively banned from driving for five years. It's quite possible to register a 20mg/100ml reading after just one 375ml can of local beer, therefore drinking any alcohol before driving can put you at risk of losing your licence.

If your blood alcohol reading is over 80mg of alcohol per 100ml of blood, you're charged with drink-driving as a criminal offence, and risk an automatic jail sentence of between one and six months. Anyone convicted on this charge acquires a criminal record, which means they can be dismissed from their job in local government or, in the case of lawyers, stripped of their professional licence. How far this will apply to government officials, who are among the worst drink-driving offenders, remains to be seen.

⚠ **Caution**

Don't drink and drive in China. The blood alcohol limit is very low and just one beer could be enough for you to be changed with drink-driving, which will mean the loss of your licence and even your job.

It's also illegal to drive under the influence of drugs, although the use of illicit drugs in China is less common than in some Western countries and there's been little evidence of recent police activity centred on driving under the influence of drugs.

Junctions

There's no formal right of way at Chinese road junctions. A major road has precedence over a minor road but there are rarely 'stop' or 'slow' signs at junctions or crossroads. In theory, drivers should give way to traffic approaching from the right, but in practice they give way to the car that gets there first. This applies especially in the cut and thrust of crowded roads. If the car beside you has its nose just a centimetre or two in front of your car, its driver won't hesitate to cut in front of your car and it's up to you to avoid him. Cutting up other cars from either side is the normal Chinese way to drive, and the only response is to let them get away with it. If you challenge the manoeuvre and it results in a collision, the tell-tale sign of your paintwork on the side of the other driver's car will place you firmly in the wrong.

Lights

Headlights should be switched on after dark; however, most road users are loathe to use them. Most motorists wait until deep dusk before switching on their lights and bicycles rarely, if ever, have any lights to switch on. Riders of electric bicycles avoid turning their lights on to conserve battery power, and many buses are driven with only their internal lights illuminated. The use of side lights when parked is rare. Outside city centres, street lighting is minimal, if there's any at all, and you struggle to spot hazards such as pedestrians in dark clothing walking in the middle of the road. All this makes driving at night particularly dangerous.

Mobile Phones

The use of mobile phones while driving is forbidden by law, although you can use them if your car is stationary and the engine is switched off. This ruling is widely ignored, and many drivers simply slow down to a crawl (with no warning) to take a call and then speed up again once they hang up.

Overtaking

You should normally overtake on the left, but this can be impossible when a slow vehicle hogs the outside lane for several kilometres, as many do. In this case it's legal to pass on their nearside (the right).

Parking

A severe lack of parking spaces leads the Chinese to leave their cars anywhere there's space, including across doorways and on footpaths. Until recently, most got away with it but parking restrictions are creeping in. Most cities now have restricted parking and parking meters – although there are few public car parks – and charges are increasing. In 2012, Beijing introduced a wave of new parking charges across the city, based on the distance from the city. Parking within the third ring road cost 10 RMB for the first hour plus 15 RMB for each additional hour, and the penalty for over-staying on a meter was a steep 200 RMB. Parking between the third and fifth ring roads cost half as much. In third tier cities it's much cheaper: between 3 and 4 RMB for as long as you like and, provided you pay up before driving away, you're unlikely to be fined.

Illegally parked cars are sometimes towed to a car pound, where you're charged 50 RMB for each day – or part day – that the vehicle is in storage. Traffic police are quite loyal to local residents when towing cars, and usually tow those registered in other cities first!

Pedestrian Crossings

Zebra crossings, sometimes linked to traffic lights, are in use in most cities but are largely ignored. Only in Hangzhou in Zhijiang province does anyone give way to pedestrians on a crossing, and there it's only the buses that stop. Cars and taxis routinely overtake at speed, even when a bus is stationary at a crossing. In Shanghai, the problem is so bad that during rush hours uniformed 'police helpers' carrying a red flag and a whistle operate at junctions, halting cars with their flag to enable pedestrians to use the zebra crossing in safety. This system was launched for the 2010 Expo, and would be welcome in other cities.

Faced with heedless drivers, most pedestrians cross the road in stages, hopping from one lane to the next as space becomes clear. It isn't as dangerous as it looks – drivers are used to it – but you'd do well to cross with a group of hardened Chinese pedestrians rather than try it on your own. As a driver, you must always keep your eyes peeled for kamikaze pedestrians as if you hit one, the police will most probably take their side (particularly if you kill somebody!).

Road Markings

These are similar to markings in the UK or US. A solid white line (or two) in the centre of the road means don't cross the line, whereas a single broken line or one on your side of the road means that you may cross to overtake. In some cities, the lane nearest the kerb is reserved as a bus lane, which is marked (in Chinese) on the road surface and sometimes also by a solid lane line.

Roundabouts

Roundabout (traffic circle) rules are the same as in most other countries. You're required to go round them anti-clockwise, but if the roundabout is blocked by traffic, many drivers take the clockwise route.

Seatbelts

There's a legal requirement to wear seatbelts, but few Chinese cars have them fitted in the back. Most Chinese drivers prefer to ignore them, only hastily draping them across when approaching toll booths or when spotting the traffic police.

Signs

The majority of road signs are similar to those used in the West. There are far fewer signs than in most countries, and the majority indicate the speed limit, shown in kilometres per hour. Watch for 'no entry' signs which show the front of a car with a black diagonal bar across it, often indicating that you're at the wrong end of a one-way street. Some local governments interpret this sign exactly, so that cars must stop but buses can enter. It's hair-raising if you're driving the correct way down a one-way street only to see a large bus coming towards you. Most bicycles and electric bicycles routinely go the wrong way up one-way streets, and riders pay no attention to such signs (or any others for that matter).

Directional signs are excellent on expressways, where information is given in Chinese script and pinyin (and sometimes in English), but incomprehensible on minor roads where they're only in Chinese. If you're heading into rural China, it helps to memorise the Chinese characters for your destination or have them written down. Signs for expressways are in white on a green background, while those indicating tourist attractions are in white on a brown background.

Speed Limits

Speed limits are 30kph (19mph) on city roads, 40kph (25mph) on single carriageways and up to 80kph (50mph) on dual carriageways. On expressways the limit is 120kph (75mph) and there's a minimum speed limit of 50kph (30mph); slow-moving vehicles such as tractors aren't permitted to use them and neither are motorcycles. Official speed limits are shown in the table below.

Most drivers drive quite sedately in urban areas. They may do stupid things, such as overtaking while turning a corner, but they rarely exceed the speed limit while doing so. It's only when driving out of town and on expressways that speeding becomes a problem. To counter this, traffic calming strips ('sleeping policemen') are placed outside police and army barracks and to slow traffic before road works. The police also use lifelike statues of policemen at the side of the road as a deterrent to speeding motorists in places where speeding is commonplace.

Traffic Lights

There's an oft repeated joke that the traffic lights were changed during the Cultural Revolution to red for go and green for stop, but there weren't enough cars in China then to justify traffic lights. Now, however, they're used at many junctions and

Speed Limits	
Speed	**Application**
30kph/19mph	single lane roads within a city (i.e. one lane each way);
70kph/43mph	city roads with three lanes each way or a central divider. There's no specific rule for roads with two lanes each way.
80kph/50mph	national highways, i.e. main trunk roads;
100kph/62mph	expressways in cities;
110-120kph/68-75mph	intercity expressways.

crossroads, often incorporating illuminated arrows showing which lanes are open and which are closed, whether you're permitted to turn left or right and even the number of seconds before the lights will change. In many countries this would prompt a Grand Prix-style revving of engines, but surprisingly the Chinese pull away quite calmly, if quickly, and rarely display signs of road rage.

The traffic light sequence is red-amber-green-flashing green-red; only in Shanghai is amber used as a warning light. It's an offence for pedestrians to cross traffic lights once the green light has begun to flash prior to turning red. That said, stopping at a red light is often a matter of personal choice in the country or at night. Some drivers believe that the faster you drive through, the less chance there is of hitting someone. Note that in the cities, many traffic lights have cameras mounted on them to catch drivers running red lights.

CHINESE DRIVERS

The most important fact to bear in mind about Chinese drivers is that most are inexperienced and have little or no road sense. About half of all drivers on any stretch of road would be on L (learner) or P (probationer) plates in many Western countries, and the majority have less than three years' driving experience. In 2009, China issued over 22m driving licences to new drivers whose only previous road experience was gleaned from riding a bike, travelling on a bus or being chauffeured by a professional driver. A large number have no licence at all.

Another major factor is the lack of consideration for others that is part of the Chinese psyche. Witness the belligerence that many Chinese pedestrians exhibit when making their way along a crowded path, and you begin to understand why the Chinese drive as they do. They're particularly inept and inconsiderate when it comes to parking. Although parking bays are clearly marked and considerably larger than in Western cities, drivers struggle to manoeuvre even the smallest car into them and regularly park across two bays. They also park on the apex of blind bends, across entrances, on zebra crossings and often as much as a metre or more from the kerb. Not surprisingly, parking isn't included in the Chinese driving test.

Chinese drivers do things that other nationals wouldn't dream of, even the Italians. They think nothing of driving the wrong way up a road, even on expressways, if it saves time or gets them around a traffic jam. Many drivers, including motorcyclists, will race straight into a stream of traffic from a minor side road to take advantage of the smallest gap, relying on the lagging driver in the queue to somehow avoid hitting them.

Solid or double lines on the road are routinely ignored, and on a busy four-lane road you may find not two but three or even four lanes of traffic approaching you, and the only thing you can do is get out of their way. At traffic lights, drivers will cut across several lanes of traffic, forcing you to wait in order to make a left turn.

The avoidance of eye contact, a typical Chinese trait, is employed to great effect on the road when making unlawful manoeuvres. When a car pulls out in front of you, the driver deliberately looks anywhere but at you, putting the onus of avoiding a collision firmly on you. And if someone drives down the wrong side of the road towards you, the driver will studiously avoid looking you in the eye.

Many cities have banned the use of the horn within city limits, but that's a bit like asking a dog not to bark. Most Chinese drivers use their horn instinctively, rather than their brakes, and will use it to bully their way through thronged pedestrians, even on a pedestrian crossing.

Despite their assertive style of driving, displays of road rage, a growing problem in the Western world, are rare in China. When two cars are involved in a minor collision, the drivers get out and argue a little but then wait quietly and companionably for the police to arrive and sort it all out. However, the increase in traffic has led to a growing compensation culture, whereby some victims see road accidents as a way to make money. If a pedestrian or cyclist is knocked down but only slightly injured, they often lie there and pretend to be mortally wounded in the hope that the driver (or his insurer) will make a significant payment for their distress; for a rural farmer, this could be his once-in-a-lifetime opportunity to get rich. And if you hit a dog, don't be surprised if someone comes forward (not necessarily the owner) claiming it was a valuable beast and demanding huge reparation.

For some 'victims' this attitude has backfired, with horrific consequences. In recent years there were some chilling reports of drivers who, having knocked someone over and injured them, went back and made sure they were dead by driving over them again, repeatedly, or even finishing them off with a weapon. Drivers are only required to pay a relatively small one-off sum if they cause someone's accidental death, but in the case of a severe injury they may be obliged to fund treatment and pay compensation for many years. Therefore killing someone is cheaper!

As a foreigner making your first tentative forays on to Chinese roads, how do you survive in this unpredictable, alien and sometimes frightening arena? The only way is to go with the flow and drive as the Chinese do. If you stop and wait for a little old lady to stagger slowly across a zebra crossing, you'll get the full force of the other drivers' horns directed at you or, worse, be rear-ended by the car behind. You stand a far greater chance of an accident if you drive like a considerate Westerner, as other drivers won't appreciate or understand it. However, if you can learn to drive the Chinese way, you may actually find you enjoy it. And if you don't, there's no shortage of inexpensive taxis and reliable public transport to use instead.

CHINESE ROADS

China's road system stretches for 4 million km (2.5m miles), and away from major conurbations, they're comparatively traffic free. Even as a foreigner, there are few restrictions on where you may drive in China, although military installations, airfields and some border areas are restricted for security reasons. If you have the time and an adventurous spirit you can drive almost the entire length of the country, which stretches over 5,000km (3,000mi) from west to east and from north to south. Do this and you'll experience every kind of road, from broad, well-surfaced expressways to single-lane earth tracks strewn with rocks.

Over the last two decades, China's road-building programme has been one of the busiest in the world. As recently as 1989, there were just 147km (91mi) of motorways – known in China as expressways – but by the end of 2011 there were 85,000km (53,816mi)! The amount of new roads being built annually is equivalent in length to the entire UK motorway system, and it won't be long before the country has more roads than the US.

The best roads are in the eastern half of the country, and already it's possible to drive from Beijing or Shanghai to almost every major city in China, as far north as the Russian border north of Harbin and southwest to Kunming. By 2020, China plans to have over 95,000km (59,030mi) of expressway, with new roads providing a direct link from Beijing to less accessible destinations in the far west, such as Urumqi in Xinjiang province and Lhasa in Tibet.

Expressways carry a G prefix plus a number denoting their direction. G1 to G7 originate in Beijing; G11 and ensuing odd-numbered roads run north to south, while G12 and other even-numbered roads run east to west. Most also have names, e.g. the Jinghu Expressway (G2) from Beijing to Shanghai. The first expressway built was the Beijing- Tianjin-Tanggu Expressway which was completed in 1989. The longest expressway built to date is the G30 from Lianyungang (Jiangsu) to Horgos (Xinjiang) which stretches for 4,280km (2,675mi).

China's expressways are designed to the latest world-class standards. Most have two carriageways separated by a hedge, kerbs and

road junction, Hangzhou

two rows of steel crash barriers, while well-designed flyovers keep traffic moving at important crossings. Signposting is good and surfaces are smooth. Everything is designed to keep traffic moving, and there are special 'crawler' lanes for trucks on steep inclines. As a result, these roads are fast. The official speed limit is between 110 and 120kph (68 and 75mph), but many vehicles travel at 150kph (93mph) or more, despite regular patrols by traffic police.

There are some emergency phones along expressways but there are no lay-bys. If you need to stop in anything other than an emergency, you must pull into one of the service areas where you can buy fuel, get minor repairs and grab a bite to eat.

The road building frenzy is paid for, in part, by road users, as all expressways are toll roads. Drivers enter through a manned toll gate, take a plastic card and pay on exiting, where the card is used to calculate the tariff which must usually be paid in cash. The cost of journeys soon adds up, and on a 200km (125mi) trip, you can easily accumulate 60 RMB in toll charges. There are also tolls on the approach roads to many major cities, and on bridges.

The precursors of the expressways were China's national highways, which are similar to A roads in the UK. Many follow ancient routes, such as the Silk Road, and they're generally well maintained although they don't receive the same investment as the expressway system. Like expressways, highways carry a number denoting their destination; those beginning with 1 fan out from Beijing; those prefixed with a 2 run north to south and those prefixed 3 run east to west.

The quality of national highways is usually good and the advantage for drivers is the lack of tolls, except for those on the approach to cities, and the comparative absence of traffic police. Road surfaces can be challenging, however, particularly on provincial and county highways, which may be single lane or poorly surfaced.

In rural areas many roads are just dirt tracks, one car wide and mainly used by farm vehicles. They're usually made and maintained by hand by local villagers. Road signs are rare, and there are unexpected hazards, particularly in the harvest season when farmers use them to dry their crops. Sesame and corn are often laid over half the carriageway and protected by large rocks, but wheat may be laid across the full width of the road up to half a metre deep so that cars and trucks must pass over it and, in doing so, provide a free threshing service to separate the wheat from the chaff! Watch out for pitchforks left lying around.

China has a variable climate, and weather can severely affect driving conditions, particularly in the north where snow and ice make winter driving hazardous, while some areas, particularly Hebei, Henan and Shandong provinces, are prone to thick fog. Take extra care when driving in fog, as most Chinese drivers don't adjust their speed but rather advertise their presence by switching their hazard warning lights on and blinding you with their headlamps on full beam.

TRAFFIC POLICE

The main role of the traffic police is to keep China's traffic moving and reduce the number of jams. During rush hour, most major junctions are manned by traffic policemen (and women) with whistles and white gloves, briskly directing the traffic, and you're more likely to incur their displeasure by holding up the flow than by going too fast. Although they can issue tickets for speeding and other misdemeanours, speed traps are rare, but you should take care on main roads between city centres and airports, which is where many drivers are caught on camera.

Chinese traffic police aren't equipped for high-speed chases. Many drive Volkswagen Jettas or ride 250cc twin cylinder Yamahas. Like many officials, they occasionally take advantage of their position and you'll see police motorcyclists without their helmets on (even though all riders are legally required to wear one). They wear helmets in winter to keep their ears warm but in summer they swap them for peaked caps. If you see a police car driven by a young woman, chances are she's a policeman's wife using the car to go shopping or do the school run!

If you're stopped by the traffic police, it's probably because you look foreign. In most cases, they're unwaveringly polite and simply want to check your driving licence and your vehicle's registration booklet to see if you have any outstanding fines. If you do, they'll issue a ticket and you must pay this (at a special office) in cash within 14 days.

⚠ Caution

Even if you're relatively fluent in Chinese, it doesn't pay to flaunt it. Most traffic police cannot speak English and find it such a hassle to explain what you've done wrong that they often give up and send you on your way with just a warning.

MOTORCYCLES

China isn't the best place to ride a motorcycle. They're banned from expressways (the Chinese think all motorcycles are too slow) and from many city centres; you cannot ride one within the city boundaries of Guangzhou and Hangzhou, while both Beijing and Shanghai have forbidden them in their central business districts. Add to this the lack of consideration which most car drivers have for motorcyclists, and riding a motorcycle in China is a dying occupation in more ways than one.

Locally made motorcycles are surprisingly cheap: just 3,000 to 4,000 RMB buys you a brand new 125cc machine. If you want a larger capacity bike, you can buy an imported Japanese model or you can try a locally made sidecar outfit modelled on the Russian Cossack 750cc twin. Imported large capacity machines are rare; many have been illegally imported, and most aren't suitable for the roads on which you're allowed to drive them, i.e. rougher rural highways. However, Russian-style sidecar outfits are tough, if slow, and safer in traffic, and can be purchased new for 16,000 to 20,000 RMB.

You must be aged 18 to ride a motorbike and must pass a special test; if you only have a car licence, the only powered two-wheeler you can ride is an electric bicycle.

Despite the apparent antipathy towards motorcycles, there are occasional competitive events; road races take place in Macau and Zhuhai and there's even MotoGP in Shanghai. One Chinese company, Zhongshan, has raced in the World Endurance series, albeit with bikes supplied by Suzuki, and there are rumours that Chinese manufacturers are considering building larger capacity machines. However, if the Chinese want to travel on two wheels with minimum effort, they buy an electric bicycle.

ELECTRIC BICYCLES

Cheap to buy and cheap to run, motorised bicycles are enormously popular, and it's been estimated that there are four times as many e-bikes on the road as there are cars. This is good news for the environment as they're clean – they run on a battery – and quiet. However, there are now so many buzzing around the cities that some local governments, e.g. central Beijing, have been forced to ban them.

This is unlikely to put off the Chinese, who regard them as the perfect compromise for anyone who cannot afford a car but prefers to avoid public transport. They're fully automatic (no gears). Anyone can ride one – some riders are as young as 12 – and there's no driving test, no annual registration or insurance required, and no law requiring riders to wear a helmet. They travel with the bicycle traffic, frequently along footpaths where their silent motors can be a problem for pedestrians.

There are two principal types of electric bicycle: the most popular is shaped like a ladies' bicycle and costs around 1,200 to 1,600 RMB, or you can buy one which resembles a motor scooter, e.g. a Vespa, with all enveloping bodywork for between 2,300 and 3,500 RMB. The latter look 'cooler' and are popular with younger owners.

Both have a battery-powered electric motor that forms the hub of the machine's rear wheel. This is charged using a trickle charger which can be plugged into any mains socket. A full charge takes several hours, and bikes can travel for up to 50km (31mi) at speeds of up to 40kph (25mph) on a single charge. If the battery goes flat, there's a secondary chain drive powered by pedals. The pedals remain in place on the cheaper models, and are handy when moving off, as pedalling relieves the load on the battery.

Electric bicycles are well equipped with full lights, speedometer (which also shows the battery's charge level), horn (of course!) and, usually, a top box for storage. They're powerful enough to cope with a pillion passenger (and a couple of children), although the brakes are less reliable when they're fully loaded. They can be parked at any bicycle park but are easily stolen, therefore you should always lock your machine.

If most of your travel is short distance and you're comfortable riding a regular bicycle, it's worth investing in an electric bicycle for the commute to work. They can be purchased at cycle shops and supermarkets and are serviced by bicycle repairers. They're also incredibly cheap to run. The main drawback is that riders can be vulnerable to the foibles of other road users, but if you ride defensively and stay aware, you shouldn't have any problems.

 Caution

Electric bicycles shouldn't be confused with regular petrol-engine scooters. They look similar but the latter, which cost more and are much faster, have all the complications of a motorbike, i.e. you must have an appropriate licence, wear a helmet and ensure that the vehicle is registered and insured.

BICYCLES

Before cars, buses and electric bicycles, everyone in China rode a bike, and for many people, including rural folk and migrant workers, it's still the most popular way to get around. Once you've seen the rivers of cyclists flowing calmly along China's city streets, you may be tempted to join them. However, cycling is transportation rather than recreation, and the rules which govern Chinese cyclists and their place in the traffic may be different from what you're used to.

In China, it's okay to ride on the footpath; in fact it's encouraged, and there are dropped kerbs at every junction so it's easier to cross the road. In major cities there are wide cycle paths running alongside the main roads, although if the traffic is held up some drivers won't hesitate to drive along them, sounding to their horns at cyclists to force them out of their way. In 2010, a foreign woman on her bicycle in Beijing took exception to this and blocked the cars with her bicycle, only for a motorist to deliberately drive over it!

But by and large, drivers and cyclists get along quite well. Most drivers give cyclists a wide berth – in an accident, the police mostly blame the driver – and most accidents involving a car and a bike stem from the cyclist taking ridiculous risks. If you stay with the flow of cyclists and remain alert, cycling is perfectly safe.

One of the main hazards arises from the amount of building work; there are screws, nails and many other sharp objects littering Chinese roads, and punctures are commonplace. However, if you get one, there's usually a cycle repair man nearby who'll repair your wheel for a couple of *yuan* while you wait.

Riding a bike takes care of the parking problem. Within built up areas there are numerous parking bays for bicycles, usually with a middle-aged lady standing guard, and the parking charge is just two *jiao* (0.2 RMB). Outside built-up areas, it's best to leave your bike locked to an immovable object such as a fence or lamp post. Stealing bicycles is big business in China, and an unattended bicycle is easily lifted into the back of a van.

ACCIDENTS

If you're involved in an accident you're obliged to stop and leave your vehicle where it is – even if it's in the middle of the road – until the police arrive. Moving your car could be construed as leaving the scene of the accident, and lead the police to treat it as a hit and run, and if you're caught and charged with this you could be banned from driving for life. If anyone is hurt, you must contact the emergency services by phoning ☎ 120 for an ambulance and ☎ 110 or 122 for the traffic police.

In China, it's the traffic police who have the authority to decide who's to blame in an accident, based on the vehicles' position and any damage. In most cases, they work on the basic premise that the larger vehicle was at fault. So if a truck hits a car it's the truck's fault, if a car knocks over a motorbike it's the driver's fault and if an electric cycle ploughs into a pedestrian it's the rider who's to blame. It's important for blame to be apportioned accurately, as it affects the amount of money payable under the compulsory third party insurance. The victim receives ten times more compensation than the road user who's liable for the accident. As in the West, it's advisable to keep quiet even if you know you were at fault. It's down to the drivers to contact their insurers once they've obtained the police report.

Never try to bribe a traffic cop. Unlike in some developing countries, the Chinese traffic police are well paid and would be insulted by an offer of money, however large. They aren't, in many cases, interested in the damage to your vehicle or your nerves; all they want is to get the traffic moving again.

FUEL

Chinese petrol stations are vast and cater to an army of cars and trucks. Many belong to the major Chinese petrochemical companies, such as Petro China or Sinopec, but in recent years Total, BP and Shell have all opened petrol stations in joint ventures with Chinese companies, particularly in the southern provinces. Some petrol stations on busy routes are open 24 hours a day, seven days a week.

All petrol on sale is unleaded and comes in three grades of 90, 93 and 97 octane; 93 is the most commonly used and costs around 7.5 RMB a litre. Diesel cars are unusual in China, and some taxis run on liquid petroleum gas (LPG), which can only be bought at special LPG filling stations. In some provinces, some grades of petrol are sold containing 10 per cent ethanol, e.g. E93. According to China's Ministry of Science and Technology, this is perfectly safe to use in a regular petrol car, but the decision is up to you.

Drivers usually buy petrol by value rather than volume, e.g. 200 *yuans'* worth at a time. There's no need to get out and man the pumps yourself as most filling stations have attendants, frequently young girls, but the service ends there. If you want a receipt you must go into the office and ask for one, which will be handed over begrudgingly. There's no free water or air – you must go to a tyre repair shop for that – no sandwiches, drinks, magazines or tired looking bunches of flowers. The only facility besides fuel is a toilet, and you'd do well to avoid it.

GARAGES & SERVICING

When buying a car in China, always bear in mind the local servicing facilities. It's much easier (and cheaper) to gets spares and repairs for a Chinese-made car or one of the foreign marques built by a joint venture in China, than a rare imported model, particularly one from the US.

Getting your car serviced can be a hit-and-miss affair, largely depending on what model you drive. When Volkswagen set up joint ventures with two Chinese companies, it was one of the first overseas motor manufacturers to major on quality control, and it had the foresight to set up a chain of garages around China to service its vehicles, with in-house trained mechanics; so if you own a VW group car (including Audi and Skoda), you can make use of one of these excellent service depots. Each has up to 30 service bays, all spares in stock and service while you wait, without any need to book. It's to be hoped that the other major manufacturers, both joint venture and Chinese, will follow suit.

There are garages servicing all makes and models of cars in most cities, so getting repairs isn't usually an issue, although the standard of workmanship and parts does vary. Usually you can just turn up and the service is done on the spot. Most garages expect payment in cash, and if you don't have enough money on you, they'll hold the registration booklet as security while you go and get the funds. Servicing is much cheaper than in the West, and costs between 100 and 300 RMB for most cars, plus parts.

MOTORING ORGANISATIONS

In all major cities there are motoring clubs, even including one boldly named the Royal Automobile Club of China. They offer a range of services to members, including getting your car to a garage and you home in the event of a breakdown or accident. One of the best known is the China Automobile Association (CAA, ☎ 010-6595 1380 or 400-818 1010, 💻 caa.com.cn). It offers 24-hour roadside rescue and towing services, and vehicle management services, including inspections, insurance and claims handling. As a foreigner, it can be useful to have some help with China's motoring bureaucracy, and membership costs around 200 RMB a year. CAA is part-owned by Australian insurance group IAG and its main office is in Beijing.

Shanghai

12.

HEALTH

The Chinese attitude to health is different from that of the West. According to Traditional Chinese Medicine (TCM), disease isn't seen as a set of distinct symptoms leading to a defined condition but as a result of an imbalance in the body which prevents it from functioning as it should, and treatment seeks to restore the body's natural harmony using not just drugs, but also physical treatments such as massage and acupuncture. The history of TCM dates back some 2,000 years and is still widely practised and taught across China today. Many Western practitioners also use elements of TCM and some go to China to learn it.

Another way in which the Chinese view of health differs from orthodox medicine is in its focus on food. In China, you really are what you eat and people firmly believe that food and drink can have a profound effect on their health. This isn't as simple as cutting out food groups which may be unhealthy, such as sugar and fat, but they believe that there's a direct physical or medical benefit to be gained from eating or drinking specific foods. This has led to lurid tales of the Chinese eating things that aren't to Western tastes, such as fish lips or dog meat, for their perceived health benefits. It has also created a demand for animal parts which are considered therapeutic, such as bear bile or sharks' fins, but which many Westerners regard as cruel and unnecessary. It may sound bizarre, but there's a lot of good sense in much of the Chinese folklore concerning diet and health, even if it isn't to everyone's taste.

TCM and diet aren't the only options. Western medicine is just as important in modern China, which has top quality hospitals and some of the most advanced medical research facilities in the world. China is at the forefront of stem cell research, for example; it isn't unusual for Chinese doctors to use both Western and Chinese medicine side by side, prescribing whichever they think is most appropriate for a patient's welfare, and you may have the opportunity to benefit from both. The key is to keep an open mind.

By and large, the Chinese are healthy people, although some Western afflictions such as obesity are starting to have an effect as people become wealthier and more open to outside influences. People eat more meat and fish than they used to – it's more available and affordable – and fast food restaurants such as McDonalds and KFC are gaining ground.

People live as long in China as they do in many developed countries. The average life expectancy is 74.84 years, with women living to 77.11 and men to 72.82. This seems low in comparison with, for example, the UK, where the average woman lives to 82.40 years and man to 78.05 years, but it's higher than the worldwide average and above that of some Eastern European and Middle Eastern countries.

Certain diseases are less prevalent in China than they are in the West – breast cancer, for example – but others pose more of a problem, in particular hepatitis and tuberculosis. The Chinese addiction to smoking and the high levels of pollution in many cities mean that lung- and heart-related diseases are among the major contributors to ill health.

There's a distinct two-tier system of healthcare in China. While most city-dwelling Chinese, and foreigners on even a modest income, have good access to health facilities and the funds to afford treatment, people in rural areas often live too far from a medical facility to benefit from it and cannot afford even the low fees charged for medical care. For many, a spell in hospital can decimate a family's life savings. It's the country's failure to provide good healthcare across the board which drags it down in world health rankings. In the last World Health Organisation's ranking of health systems in 2000, China came 144th out of 190 countries, although the general health of its people was ranked 61st. It was also ranked a lowly 139th for its per capita health expenditure, which isn't so surprising given the sheer size of the population.

A yardstick often used to measure the quality of a country's health care system is its infant mortality rate: the number of children who die before reaching one year old. The CIA World Factbook estimated that in 2012, there were 15.62 deaths per 1,000 live births in China, compared with a world average of 38.48; the UK figure was 4.62 and the US 5.98. However, children born in Hong Kong have a better chance of survival than even British babies – only 2.90 in 1,000 die – therefore it appears that the figures are skewed by the number of infant deaths in rural China.

One of the major problems China now faces is in providing an all-embracing and affordable healthcare system across the entire country. There's a system of social insurance covering employees, but many smaller private organisations fail to contribute to it and it's estimated that even in the cities, as few as 40 per cent of workers are covered by such a scheme. In the countryside, where many people are subsistence farmers, it doesn't apply at all.

To address this problem, in 2005 the government set up the New Rural Co-operative Medical Care System (NRCMCS) to part-fund medical care for rural people. By 2007, around 80 per cent of the rural population (some 685m people) had taken it up. However, the amount of funding provided to individuals wouldn't even cover the cost of a prescription in the UK. Each recipient is entitled to 50 RMB of health care per year of which 20 RMB is contributed by the state, 20 RMB by the provincial government and 10 RMB by the patient. It's only sufficient to cover fairly rudimentary treatment in a local clinic and not a major operation, which only a city hospital could provide.

The NRCMCS, while a welcome initiative, isn't sufficient, as the high rates of depression and even suicide in the countryside testify, particularly among the wives of farmers and particularly in areas populated by the ethnic minorities. Not surprisingly, many people are forced to turn to folk remedies or tempted by 'wonder cures' advertised heavily on television rather than visit a clinic or hospital.

Foreigners, on the other hand, find China a wonderfully cheap place in which to be ill. Treatment in public clinics is prompt, effective and amazingly affordable, and if you want a bit more luxury, some state hospitals have a VIP (*gaogan bingfang*) floor reserved for wealthier Chinese, such as Communist Party members, where foreigners can be treated. Many expatriates find that private health insurance isn't really necessary, but those who do take it up – or have it provided by their employers – can be treated in an international hospital by English-speaking doctors. The treatment may be no better, but the surroundings may be considerably nicer and the much higher cost is picked up by the insurers.

EMERGENCIES

If you need an ambulance in an emergency, call ☎ 120. However, be aware that most Chinese ambulances are taxis for getting to hospital rather than life-saving units on four wheels. There are no paramedics and most ambulances arrive with just a driver and a young nurse – you (or somebody else) must assist in getting the patient out of the house and into the transport. There's a charge for using an ambulance, with public ambulances being considerably cheaper than private ones, although the charge for calling a public ambulance is still around 200 RMB. If you live close to a hospital it's often easier (and cheaper) to call a taxi or drive the patient there yourself.

Major cities such as Beijing and Shanghai have private ambulance services linked to major private hospitals and are geared more towards foreigners. You can phone for an ambulance from the United Family Hospital by dialling the emergency number: ☎ 010-5927 7120 in Beijing or ☎ 021-2216-3999 in Shanghai. More emergency service contacts are provided in **Chapter 7**.

Major hospitals have an accident and emergency (A&E) department or emergency room, and emergencies are treated immediately. Treatment isn't free but at least patients' families aren't expected to pay in advance.

> ## ☑ SURVIVAL TIP
>
> Keep the 'cards' for any hospitals or doctors you use, both by the phone and in your wallet, so that you have the numbers handy and can show the address to a taxi driver in an emergency.

HEALTH RISKS

Traditionally, the Chinese have eaten a fresh, healthy if limited diet and are probably healthier than many Westerners. Certainly, obesity has long been regarded as a Western affliction; just 50 years ago, many Chinese struggled to get enough

respiratory viruses such as avian (bird) flu and SARS.

There's always a small risk, as in most developing countries, of encountering a number of infectious diseases, such as tuberculosis and hepatitis – both significant in China – and, less commonly, typhoid and cholera.

Not all of these health issues directly affect foreigners, but some do, and the following section lists those which you should be aware of.

Smoking

It's claimed that over 3,000 people die every day in China from smoking-related diseases and that this could increase four fold over the next 40 years. More than two-thirds of all males aged over 15 are smokers, and a third of all the cigarettes produced worldwide are smoked in China. In the West, most smoking-related deaths are from heart attacks or lung cancer, but in China they're more often linked to tuberculosis, emphysema, and stomach and liver cancer. Studies have suggested that a third of young Chinese men will die as a result of smoking. It's predominately a male problem. Men smoke an average of 10 to 15 cigarettes a day; women rarely smoke (other than bar girls), although this may change as the cigarette companies increasingly target younger women. Pipes and cigar smoking are unusual, and chewing tobacco is non-existent.

The government faces a particularly awkward situation as it tries to combat smoking. It controls a monopoly on the growing of tobacco – China produces over 40 per cent of the world's cigarettes – and this industry forms the backbone of employment in many rural areas. Despite this, there have been efforts to ban smoking in public places. It's officially banned on all aircraft, express trains and buses, and there are pilot schemes to ban smoking in the workplace in Chongqing, Harbin, Lanzhou, Nanchang, Shenyang, Shenzhen and Tianjin. This follows attempts by Beijing and Shanghai to ban smoking in many public places prior to the 2008 Olympics and the 2010 Expo.

However, it's an uphill struggle in a country where cigarettes are still socially acceptable – luxury brands are often given as business gifts, and even handed out at weddings to boost the bride's chances of conception! Some of China's most celebrated icons were smokers, including Mao Zedong and Deng Xiaoping, and the majority of doctors smoke. The problem is exacerbated by the low cost of cigarettes. Over 50 per cent of smokers pay less than 5 RMB for a packet of 20, which is far less than what they cost in the UK and many other countries. It seems inevitable that

food. However, the popularity of electric bicycles and the spread of car culture in China's cities means that fewer people are riding bicycles, which traditionally provided involuntary daily exercise for so many citizens. Meanwhile the lure of global, often fattening food, is difficult to resist.

According to the World Health Organisation, only 5 per cent of China's population is classed as obese. It's a condition which mainly affects city folk and is literally a growing problem among younger, more affluent Chinese. Most of the 'fatties' you see are 'little emperors', the children of relatively wealthy parents who can afford to over-indulge themselves at foreign fast food outlets. The Chinese government has acknowledged the problem by building more playgrounds and increasing the amount of physical education in schools, in an attempt to prevent0020a further increase in obesity-related diseases. Even so, there are some 100m Chinese with high blood pressure and 26m diabetics.

The rapid increase in the number of cars and the surge in industrialisation have also had a detrimental effect on Chinese health. Many cities are heavily polluted, with Linfen in Shanxi province, at the heart of the coal-mining belt, frequently cited as the most polluted city in the world. Beijing is not much better. Local folklore has it that spending a year in China's capital has the same effect on your body as smoking 20 cigarettes a day. Many cities have 'oxygen bars' where you can pay to breathe in pure O^2 to counteract the effects of the pollution, or you can take to the streets wearing a surgical mask as some Chinese do. The countryside is free of smog, but the age-old custom of literally living with livestock and poultry – often in an adjoining room – has led to increasing problems from flu-type the government will be forced to raise taxes on cigarettes, as this may be the only way they can persuade many smokers to quit without losing too much revenue.

If you're a non-smoker you may find China a difficult place in which to live; smokers often ignore bans on the habit and fines are low, so passive smoking is a serious problem. If you're a smoker, however, it's a non-judgmental country in which to light up.

Rabies

Although there are strict regulations requiring dogs to be vaccinated against rabies (hydrophobia) in all Chinese cities, it's believed that only 3 per cent of all dogs in China have the jab. As a result, the risk of contracting rabies from a dog bite, although lower than in India, is a very real concern. In Beijing alone, almost 70,000 people a year seek treatment for dog bites and between 2,000 and 3,000 people die from rabies in China each year. The most badly affected provinces are Guizhou, Guangdong, Hunan and Sichuan, and rabies is a major hazard in Tibet where there are packs of feral dogs. It isn't only dogs that can infect you with rabies – you can also contract it from a bite from a monkey or a bat – but you're much more likely to come into contact with dogs.

▲ Caution

Don't get too close to any dog in China and never stroke or pat one, even a friend's pet.

Rabies is transmitted via saliva and other bodily fluids so you can be infected if bitten or even licked on an open wound. If this happens, wash the affected area thoroughly then go straight to a hospital and ask for the human diploid cell vaccine. **It's absolutely vital that you do this immediately.** Rabies is a deadly disease and

it must be treated as quickly as possible. The incubation period ranges from a few days to over a month, but once symptoms develop, there's no cure.

Dangerous Wildlife

Although there are tigers, bears and elephants in the more remote corners of China, you're unlikely to see them, let alone be attacked by one. You may encounter a snake in Sichuan or Yunnan province and some varieties are venomous, but the greatest risk is from mosquitoes which can transmit deadly diseases such as malaria (see **Mosquito-borne Diseases** on page 164).

Respiratory Diseases

The Chinese seem particularly prone to infectious respiratory diseases. The invasive pollution and addiction to smoking are major factors, along with the widespread habit of spitting. Everyone spits, men, women and children, in the street and even in supermarkets, and you must be careful where you put your hands, particularly on handrails in public places. If you hear some loud throat clearing, it's as well to step smartly out of the way!

Even if they don't openly spit, people rarely use a hand and handkerchief to contain coughs and sneezes. As a result, influenza and the common cold are almost endemic in winter for locals and expatriates alike, and more serious diseases such as tuberculosis (TB) are fairly widespread, despite vaccination programmes. The World Health Organisation's rates for TB show that the incidence in China was 98 per 100,000 people in 2007. In the UK it was just 15 per 100,000 people.

In 2002, China became the breeding ground for a new flu-like infectious disease called severe acute respiratory syndrome (SARS). This was first identified in Guangdong province and for a while created panic across the globe. Around a third of all SARS cases occurred in China, where over 340 people died, and many people blamed the southerners' habit of breeding wild creatures such as civet cats for food, which led to more restricted menus. A vaccine was created, but by 2004 the epidemic was over and WHO declared China to be SARS free.

Unfortunately, avian (bird) flu has been harder to combat and outbreaks still occur from time to time in China, which has had two-thirds of all reported cases. A WHO report in 2011 documented that there had been 40 confirmed cases of avian flu A (H5N1) and 26 deaths since 2003. Bird flu is a problem across Southeast Asia, particularly in neighbouring Vietnam, partly as a result of people living in close proximity to poultry. China has supplies of the antiviral drug Tamiflu –

the drug was formulated from Chinese ingredients including star anise – to combat bird flu, therefore treatment is available. The government takes all forms of influenza very seriously, and each year it urges people to have an inoculation against it. This is something to consider if you're older or in poor health.

It's highly unlikely you'll contract SARS or bird flu, but you're almost guaranteed to suffer from heavy and frequent colds during winter. You can buy over-the-counter cold remedies, but many Chinese swear by 'dropping'. The doctor comes to your home, inserts a needle in the back of your hand and a sterile saline solution is allowed to drip slowly into your bloodstream. It sounds a drastic solution for the common cold but works amazingly well.

Hepatitis

Hepatitis causes inflammation of and sometimes permanent damage to the liver. There are two main types: hepatitis A is the most common, and is transmitted through poor hygiene and contaminated food; while hepatitis B, which is more serious, is passed on through direct contact with an infected person's bodily fluids, e.g. unprotected sex or dirty needles. Less common strains include hepatitis C, D, E, F and G. All are present and relatively widespread in China.

Approximately 300m people worldwide have hepatitis A or B and, of these, around 120m are Chinese; it's thought that a tenth of the population may be carriers. Even though they display no symptoms, carriers can pass the disease on to others and for this reason, it's unwise to drink from the same glass or cup or to share a cigarette with anyone unless you know them very well.

The state takes the problem seriously, and until recently, those identified as having the hepatitis virus were refused employment in government services.

The best protection is vaccination, and there's a combined vaccine called Havrix which works against both hepatitis A and B. It requires two initial injections and a booster later. If you're unlucky enough to contract hepatitis, you'll be unable to drink alcohol for at least a year.

Stomach Bugs

Despite the Chinese penchant for eating some extraordinary foods, the risk of a stomach upset, e.g. vomiting and diarrhoea, is lower in China than in many Southeast Asian countries. However, you should still guard against risks such as eating food which may contain or have been washed in contaminated water or not properly washed at all. Giardiasis, a particularly virulent intestinal infection, is present in some areas, particularly Tibet. Spicy food can have an unpleasant effect if you aren't used to eating it and not everyone can cope with the chilli-heavy diet enjoyed by people in Sichuan province. Rather than diarrhoea, many Chinese are preoccupied with constipation, possibly a result of their starch-laden diet of noodles and rice, and a well-known greeting directly translates as, 'Did you evacuate your bowels today?'

Weather Warning

The wide range of climates in China makes for some regional health hazards, from sunburn and heat exhaustion in the tropical south to hypothermia in the northern winters. Altitude sickness is a problem in Tibet, where the average elevation is 4,900m (16,000ft) – rated as 'very high altitude'. Once above 4,000m (13,120ft), you should watch for symptoms such as a severe headache, impaired coordination and blurred vision. If any occur, get to a lower altitude as soon as possible and seek immediate medical help.

Contaminated Food

One of the major health risks in China is from eating food or drink that has been contaminated during production and then (often knowingly) sold to the public despite containing additives or other substances harmful to health. Sadly, some manufacturers put profit before public health and in some cases local government has assisted in concealing their wrongdoing. It's only when the media unearths the story or when people start falling ill, that the facts become public knowledge.

In 2008, there was a major scandal involving one of the largest milk suppliers in China which was found to be adding melamine – a chemical used in the production of plastics – to milk products that had been previously diluted with water in order to raise 'protein' levels and fool testers into believing it met the required standards for milk. This was covered up for months by the company concerned, aided and abetted by local government officials, and it only came to light after the effects were published on the internet. Six infants died from kidney problems after drinking affected milk and a further 860 were treated in hospital; it's thought that several thousand suffered less serious sickness. The Chinese milk scandal, as it became known, severely dented the faith of both the public and overseas importers, with many refusing to touch Chinese-produced milk products. The officials who connived at the cover up were 'punished' but didn't lose their jobs.

This was by no means an isolated case. In 2010, similar reports emerged, again on the internet, about a 'luxury' cooking oil which was found to contain five times the legal maximum of a well-known carcinogen. The discovery was made in December 2009 but the manufacturer continued to sell the product until March 2010, putting out some 42,000 contaminated litres. Only 33,000 litres were ever recalled and the remainder is presumed to have been ingested by unsuspecting consumers with, as yet, undocumented results. Once again, the state colluded with the manufacturer to cover up the scandal, which left Chinese consumers with a nasty taste in their mouths.

There's little individuals can do to protect themselves against greedy businessmen in such situations, other than to give processed products a wide berth or opt for imported goods. Since the milk scandal, many Chinese have been buying imported baby milk in preference to home produced products.

Water

The Chinese never drink water straight from the tap. There's no guarantee that it's safe to drink and every so often there are outbreaks of cholera, usually in rural areas, which can be traced back to unsafe drinking water. Follow the locals' lead and stick to bottled water or boil tap water before drinking it. All water provided in hotels, restaurants and public transport is usually pre-boiled, and water served in thermos flasks is safe to drink.

Mosquito-borne Diseases

China's southern provinces are in a sub-tropical zone where mosquitoes are a major problem. They aren't just an irritant but also carry diseases such as malaria – a particular problem in Hainan – Japanese encephalitis and dengue fever. If you're planning to live anywhere south of the Yangtze River, it's advisable to discuss the risks with your doctor. There's an inoculation against Japanese encephalitis but not for dengue fever, and you may not want to take anti-malarial medication long term. The best protection is not to get bitten, and long sleeved clothing, mosquito nets and insect repellents are your best defence. Bug repellent is sold at every supermarket.

Sexually-transmitted Diseases

When the People's Republic of China was declared in 1949, one of its first successes was a ban on prostitution, but the world's oldest profession isn't easily proscribed and it's now a major problem again, particularly in the major cities. As a result, sexually transmitted diseases are on the increase in China, as is HIV/AIDS. The number of people affected is thought to be at least 1.5m, and official figures put the death rate from AIDS at 7,000 people between January and September 2007. However, HIV/AIDS is a taboo subject and estimates are conservative. The state is being forced to acknowledge and deal with the problem, albeit unwillingly, by offering counselling, testing and support to those affected.

The best prevention is to practice safe sex and be wary of any procedures using needles (see box). A large proportion of HIV-positive Chinese are thought to have contracted the disease through contaminated blood.

Note that China is very intolerant of foreigners who are positive for HIV or other sexually transmitted diseases. Part of the process of staying long term in the country involves tests for these conditions, and hospitals are required to report test results to your employer who's obliged to inform the Public Security Bureau. Expatriates who test positive are subject to deportation.

 Caution

The dangers of catching disease from contaminated blood or dirty needles shouldn't be ignored in China. Always ensure that new needles are used for any injections, including local anaesthetic at the dentist – make sure that they're unwrapped in front of you – and avoid invasive procedures such as tattoos. If you're heading into rural China, take a supply of needles with you.

Vaccinations

Chinese children are vaccinated against tuberculosis and smallpox with the BCG serum, and also inoculated against polio, diphtheria, pertussis, tetanus, measles, rubella, mumps and meningitis A and C under the EPI (Expanded Programme for Immunisation) scheme, free of charge.

For foreigners travelling to China, no vaccinations were required by the authorities in 2012, although you should check the latest situation with a Chinese consulate and with your doctor. Hepatitis (Havrix), tuberculosis and typhoid are among the recommended vaccinations, although it depends where you're going and for

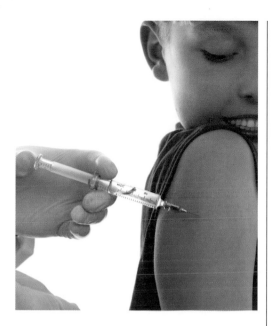

how long, and others may be advisable if you're going off the beaten track. Make sure that your tetanus protection, which only lasts ten years, is up to date.

THE DISABLED

China is a difficult country for people with disabilities. Other than in the most recently built hospitals, there's little provision for the disabled. Many government buildings are only accessible by stairs or steps, and lifts are rare. Subways are almost impossible to access if you cannot manage an escalator. The same is true of most department stores and supermarkets, although some, such as Carrefour, provide moving walkways between floors rather than escalators, making them easier to navigate.

Wheelchair users have an easier time of it on the street, where the presence of countless bicycles and electric bicycles has led road builders to construct ramps between roads and footpaths at every junction, so you rarely need to negotiate kerbs. Most cities also incorporate a row of ribbed paving stones into the pavement (sidewalk), providing a surface which blind and partially sighted users can easily detect and follow. However, anyone with a disability is at a distinct disadvantage when trying to cross the road, where it's every man/woman/pedestrian/cyclist/driver for himself.

China can be socially awkward, too, for disabled people and you'll have to get used to people staring, pointing and openly asking about your disability. Signs designed to help are often lacking in political correctness, especially as the Chinese have a habit of translating the word 'disabled' incorrectly, and you may find yourself using toilets or seating set aside for 'deformed' people.

PUBLIC HEALTH CARE

There's no all-embracing system of public healthcare in mainland China; no Chinese version of America's Medicare or Britain's National Health Service. There's a form of social insurance which applies to some city workers, although many employers avoid making contributions on behalf of their staff, and the only ones who are guaranteed some cover are government employees. Migrant workers are rarely included in such schemes. Meanwhile, the New Rural Co-operative Medical Care System (NRCMCS), which was established in 2005 to provide limited healthcare for rural people, only provides 50 RMB of cover a year.

Even within these schemes, benefits can be difficult to access and many are only available for in-patient treatment in a hospital, e.g. surgery. People seeking outpatient services such as diagnostic or drug therapy have to foot the bill themselves. For the great majority of patients there's no alternative to paying in full for treatment, and if they cannot afford professional help, they do without it, even in an emergency.

Foreigners aren't covered by any social insurance schemes, as these are solely for Chinese citizens. If you're lucky, your employer will provide health cover for you; if not, you must either pay in full for treatment or take out private medical insurance (see page 179). Fortunately, healthcare isn't expensive – at least by European or US standards – and a consultation with a doctor in a public hospital can cost as little as a litre of petrol, i.e. between 5 and 10 RMB, while you can have an operation followed by a short post-operative stay for around 2,000 RMB. Therefore, provided you aren't struck down by a major illness or accident, you should be able to afford to pay for health care as you need it.

PRIVATE HEALTH SERVICES

As well as the public hospitals, there are many private health facilities in China. These range from small clinics located in schools and universities, within factories and even at four- and five-star hotels, to Western-style international hospitals with Western prices to match.

In-house clinics frequently provide free primary health care to students, teachers and workers, although in hotels you usually have to pay. There are also countless private clinics, sited within housing estates as well as on the streets, providing primary care, with a doctor or small group of doctors and nurses always on call. For minor illnesses or small injuries these provide quick and inexpensive skilled attention, without the hassle of fighting your way through the crowds at a public hospital. At some clinics there's no fee at all for seeing a doctor, although you'll be charged for any drugs prescribed, and drugs will certainly be prescribed as this is how some doctors make a living.

There are also many private hospitals in China, some of which focus on Chinese patients – some are set aside for specific sectors of the population, such as army or police personnel – and others which cater to foreigners and 'VIPs'. The latter includes so-called international hospitals (and clinics), some of which are run by foreign joint venture operations, which are far beyond the pockets of ordinary Chinese, although China's growing *nouveau riche* use them. Fees are at least ten times as high as in a state hospital and the care isn't necessarily any better. A *Rough Guides* report revealed that a walk-in consultation at one top Shanghai clinic cost 4,375 RMB (around £420/US$700).

The widest choice of international hospitals is in major cities such as Beijing and Shanghai (see box). The best hospitals are similar to a good private hospital in Europe or the US, and resemble hotels with medical facilities. Many, though, are more basic and not all have English-speaking staff. A number of private hospitals specialise in Traditional Chinese Medicine (see page 169).

If you have private health insurance, either through your work or taken out privately, the insurer may have an agreement with one of the well-known international hospitals and insist that you use it, even though the charges are excessive by Chinese standards. Note that you may have to pay for treatment and then reclaim the cost.

International Hospitals & Clinics

There are a number of international hospitals and clinics to choose from in China, and those listed below are among the most popular with expats in Beijing and Shanghai, although inclusion in this list doesn't necessarily constitute a recommendation.

Beijing

◆ United Family Hospital (☎ 010-5927 7000, 🖥 unitedfamilyhospitals.com/en/bj). There are also United Family Hospitals in Guangzhou,

Shanghai (see below) and one scheduled to open in Tianjin.

◆ International SOS Clinic (☎ 010-6462 9112, emergencies 010-64629100, 🖥 internationalsos.com). International SOS has further clinics in Hong Kong, Nanjing, Shekou (Shenzhen) and Tianjin.

◆ International Medical Centre at the Lufthansa Centre (☎ 010-6465 1561, 🖥 imcclinics.com).

◆ Hong Kong International Medical Clinic (☎ 010-6553 2288 ext. 2345/6/7, 🖥 hkclinic.com/en).

Shanghai

◆ United Family Hospital (☎ 021-2216 3900, 🖥 ufh.com.cn/en/sh).

◆ Parkway Health (☎ 021-6445 5999, 🖥 parkwayhealth.cn/medical-center-locations.php). Parkway runs several clinics in Shanghai, including specialist clinics for dental treatment and women's health.

◆ Huashan Hospital (☎ 021- 6248 9999 ext. 2531, 🖥 huashan.org.cn). This is a Chinese state hospital with some English-speaking staff and is recommended by some expats.

Most embassies publish lists of doctors, clinics and hospitals on their website. These are for guidance only, but they're a good place to start if you're new to China and need medical help. Visit the British Embassy website (🖥 ukinchina.fco.gov.uk/en/help-for-british-nationals) or that of the US embassy (🖥 beijing.usembassy-china.org.cn/acs_health.html).

DOCTORS

The ratio of doctors to the population in China is high – about one doctor to 950 people, three times as many as in Western Europe – but the vast majority choose to practise in the cities where opportunity and income are higher. Occasionally, you'll find an excellent doctor in a rural area; one who grew up there, became a doctor despite his background, and returned to his home town to serve the people he grew up with. However, there's a great shortage of doctors in rural China, and it's been estimated that a further 500,000 are needed to make up the shortfall.

There are very few foreign doctors practising in China. You may be treated by one in a top-flight international hospital, but even there the majority of medics and nurses are Chinese. Medicine is one of the professions of choice for academically gifted students, and China trains thousands of doctors each year. Many end up practising abroad. Younger doctors often speak some English, but in a state-run hospital or local clinic you're likely to be seen by a more mature doctor. Many of those at consultant level have been doing their job for years, sometimes after their normal retirement age, and few speak English.

There's no GP system in China. You select your clinic or hospital and see the most appropriate doctor there, depending on your problem, and this requires a degree of self-diagnosis. The majority of Chinese go directly to their nearest state hospital, as it's by far the cheapest option. Don't dismiss state facilities in favour of a private hospital. If you can get a native Chinese speaker to accompany you, you'll receive good treatment at a very reasonable cost. If it's essential that you consult an English-speaking doctor, then you must seek one out at an international clinic or hospital. Some advertise in expatriate publications, although a flashy one-page advert is no guarantee of expertise.

There's no need to make an appointment to see a doctor – just turn up at their clinic or the appropriate hospital and wait your turn. Hospitals are open seven days a week, although most doctors only work five days and some have more limited hours. The majority are general hospitals but there are many specialist hospitals dealing with, say, gynaecological disorders, gastric (stomach) problems or broken bones. Many

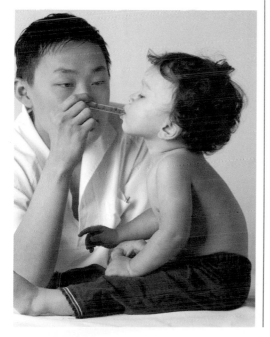

Chinese doctors specialise in one area – and they can be very specialised, dealing with, for example, just leg injuries or fractured skulls – but there are some general physicians if you need a diagnosis first.

At a state hospital, the reception area displays a series of photographs of the doctors working at the hospital, with details of their background and areas of expertise (in Chinese). Patients pick the one they feel will help them best and queue up at a payment counter. On payment you're given a receipt and told where to find your chosen doctor. Wait outside their room until it's your turn, hand over your receipt, describe your problem and the doctor will then examine you. Once he has diagnosed your problem he prescribes treatment: this may be orthodox medicine or, possibly, a traditional Chinese treatment. A trainee doctor writes out a prescription which you take back to the reception area. You pay for your prescription at a different counter and collect another receipt, which you take to the hospital's in-house pharmacy where you collect your medicine.

If you're used to having a one-to-one consultation in a private room, seeing a doctor in China may be a slightly uncomfortable experience, particularly in a state hospital. He (or she – around half of all doctors are female) may be accompanied by up to three junior medics, there to learn the ropes, and the door may be left open so that patients waiting nearby can stare at the foreigner and wonder what is wrong with them. Remember that the Chinese concept of privacy is very different from a Westerner's.

Once the doctor has examined you, he may prescribe tests or treatment. If you need an injection or an x-ray, you must usually visit different departments, paying in advance of each procedure, before returning to the doctor's room; you might, for example, be sent to the pharmacy to obtain medicine and a sterile needle so that the doctor can administer an injection.

Don't be surprised if you're prescribed Traditional Chinese Medicine and given some guidance as to your diet. To the Chinese, food and health are closely linked, and most doctors take a holistic approach in treating not just your symptoms, but also the underlying cause. A doctor trained in Western medicine will prescribe a course of acupuncture or a herbal remedy if he feels it's the best course of treatment, while a TCM doctor may feel that Western drugs are the best approach. Sometimes, your treatment will be a combination of orthodox and TCM. In China you can have the best of both worlds.

The Chinese respect doctors but they aren't afraid to challenge them or ask for a second opinion if they aren't happy with the diagnosis or treatment. Many Chinese are concerned that doctors prescribe too many drugs and that some receive kickbacks from the drugs companies. It's unlikely that you'll leave a consultation empty-handed.

If you're just too ill to make it to a clinic or hospital, a doctor can come to you. There are state-run district clinics in most cities and you can phone and request a home visit. The doctor will come to your house complete with a nurse, diagnose your problem and possibly prescribe/sell you the appropriate medicine. This service costs around 50 RMB.

HOSPITALS & CLINICS

Most towns and all cities have at least one hospital and several clinics, some of which are private: just look for a sign with a white cross on a red background. In larger cities there may be a dozen or more state-run hospitals, with at least one specialising in Traditional Chinese Medicine. In a provincial capital there will be at least one modern, general hospital equipped with all the very latest technology, such as MRI scanners.

Many clinics are one-doctor affairs and comprise a waiting room, consulting room and examination room. They're usually spotlessly clean, and for straightforward primary care for minor problems they're fine, and usually inexpensive. In many ways these clinics take the place of GP surgeries in the West.

You can visit either a clinic or a hospital to consult with a doctor (see above) but if you need surgery or in-patient treatment this takes place in a hospital. Most modern hospitals come as a pleasant surprise. They're clean and well run and have signs in both Chinese and English – even though there are few English speakers – with floors accessible by lifts and escalators. There are bright, well-furnished waiting rooms, and even the car parking is efficient and cheap. Wards are also modern and there are no long dormitories with a dozen or more beds; most patients are accommodated in two-bedded rooms, each with its own en-suite toilet (with a proper WC) and a television, for which you must pay.

Older hospitals are less impressive. Those built two or three decades ago may lack modern facilities, such as en-suite rooms, although the government is working to upgrade every hospital to the most modern standards. Those which are located on cramped, inner city sites usually have insufficient parking, so you must arrive early if you want a space.

All state hospitals work strictly on a pay-as-you-go basis. This means that you receive a bill every few days and are expected to pay as soon as you're able to. There's a kiosk where payments are made. Cash is preferred but most hospitals accept international credit cards. This can be difficult if you're confined to your bed, therefore you need someone to do the running around for you. However, there are few restrictions on visiting hours and many patients have a family member with them from morning to night. It isn't unusual for a patient to have a relative bring in not only their lunch and supper, but their breakfast also!

MEDICINES & PHARMACIES

There are very few Western-style chemists in China, except for the Hong Kong-based chain Watsons, which has outlets in the larger cities. Chinese chemists are pharmacies first and foremost; they don't sell cosmetics, toiletries or babies' nappies or develop films. You cannot buy female hygiene products such as sanitary towels at a pharmacy; for these you must go to a supermarket, and tampons are almost impossible to find in China. Pharmacies (*yaodian*) are there to sell medicines and medical equipment such as blood pressure monitors and even wheelchairs.

☑ SURVIVAL TIP

If you're on regular medication, bring a good supply with you as it may not be available in China (and make arrangements to obtain more from overseas if necessary). Ask your pharmacy or doctor for the generic name so that you can obtain an alternative brand if necessary. It's advisable to carry a copy of your prescription as well as keeping your drugs in the original packaging. If you get stuck for a specific drug in China, there's a good chance you'll find it in a pharmacy in Hong Kong.

Pharmacies are identified by a green sign with the pharmacist's name in white letters, and are generally open seven days a week from 8am to 7pm, although those in or near to hospitals may close later. Many have a section selling TCM products, such as dried seahorses or 'tonic 'wines containing the remains of dead lizards and snakes. However, you can also buy many medicines that are well known in the West, either locally manufactured or imported and in their familiar packaging (the latter cost more), although aspirin can be difficult to find and isn't a particularly popular drug in China. You can buy most drugs over the counter, i.e. without a prescription, including antibiotics – a course of antibiotics costs around 100 RMB. It's better to stick with the larger pharmacies, as some of the smaller ones sell counterfeit drugs.

Large pharmacies often have a resident doctor who can give you a check-up and medical advice for a reasonable fee: perhaps as little as 5 or 10 RMB.

TRADITIONAL CHINESE MEDICINE

The Chinese firmly believe that life is all about balance and harmony, and therefore good health is achieved by ensuring a well-balanced body. We all have a life force, called the *qi* (pronounced 'chi') which flows throughout the body along set paths called meridians. There are 12 main meridians, each of which is connected to one of the main organs of the body. The meridians are further classified as being either yin, which are protected by their location, or yang which are exposed. The yang meridians are believed to resist disease, while the yin meridians help to nourish the body. Achieving balance in the body is done by stimulating the flow of *qi* along the meridians using techniques such as acupuncture, herbal medicine, diet, massage or specific exercises. These are the main principles behind Traditional Chinese Medicine (TCM).

A patient in the West with a painful knee joint would undergo a series of x-rays or scans resulting, possibly, in knee replacement surgery, as his doctor sought to cure the source of the pain. However, a TCM practitioner would try to find out why the pain had occurred in the first place and look for reasons why the patient's body had lost its natural harmony. Diagnosis consists of not just asking about your symptoms but also examining your appearance – especially your tongue, eyes and fingernails – and checking your pulse. TCM treatment is more measured and may involve a range of different therapies, and no one expects an overnight cure, but the entire process is far less invasive.

Some Western scientists claim that many Chinese herbal medicines or TCM techniques, such as acupuncture, have no proven scientific basis for their use but, rather like the bumblebee that shouldn't be able to fly but does, many patients swear that TCM works. So much so, that its efficacy has been officially recognised by the World Health Organisation (WHO), and it's

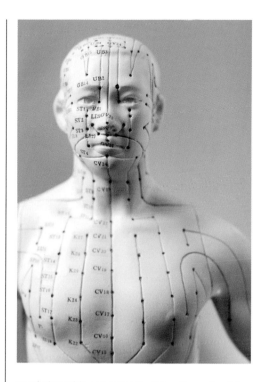

used alongside orthodox medicine throughout the world.

The links between TCM and Western medicine are strong. Many Western medicines are based upon naturally occurring materials from trees and plants, e.g. digitalis which is derived from the foxglove and used in drugs to treat heart problems, or natural processes such as the formation of mould, e.g. penicillin.

If you need medical treatment in China, it's likely that you'll be offered some therapies based on TCM. The main four types of therapy are listed below. For information on learning some of the skills of TCM, see page 122..

Acupuncture, Moxibustion & Cupping

These physical techniques are used to stimulate the flow of *qi* along the body's meridians. Acupuncture involves the insertion of very fine needles through the skin at specific points along the meridians. It isn't as painful as you might expect; it may sting a little, but often you don't even feel the needles go in and, once in, they're not painful at all. The needles are inserted up to 15mm (1/2in) into the body and left in place for up to 45 minutes. The doctor may manipulate them from time to time or he may attach electric wires to a few of them and pass low voltage electric current from a battery into your body from one needle to another, causing the affected area to twitch – again, this isn't painful. The aim is to increase the flow of *qi* along that part of the meridian.

Moxibustion is often used in conjunction with acupuncture to boost its effects. Small boxes containing a plant called mugwort (wormwood) are placed close to but not touching the skin and set alight to smoulder, heating both needles and the affected area. The box containing the mugwort is insulated with towels to concentrate the heat (the smell is quite pleasant).

Cupping is used to treat localised pain that's thought to be caused by the *qi* moving too slowly. A small glass jar is held with the open end pointing downwards, a lit taper or match is held under it to create a vacuum within the jar which is then placed on the skin where the pain is strongest. The skin is pulled up into the jar as it tries to fill the vacuum and this movement, which is completely painless, is believed to help to get things moving below.

Herbal Medicine

Over the centuries, the rural Chinese have acquired an extensive knowledge of which plants and other natural substances can be used to treat a wide variety of sicknesses. Some, such as honeysuckle buds, are remarkably effective, especially for treating lung conditions. Other more controversial ingredients, such as powdered tiger's bones, are based on superstition and have little effect, although the fact that a patient believes in their effectiveness may in itself have a positive result.

TCM physicians prescribe herbal medicines for many conditions, and the prescription will be filled by a trained herbalist who carefully measures the prescribed mixture. It may well consist of several ingredients, each with a different purpose, which together provide a comprehensive path to a complete although slow cure.

The herbal preparation, packaged in a brown paper bag, must be boiled to create a liquid medicine which you then take as directed. Often the medicine needs to be taken for a few weeks before its effects become apparent.

Caution

Don't take your herbal medicine for longer than prescribed, as some of these potions can be toxic when taken in excess.

Tuina

Therapeutic massage or *tuina* is used to treat a specific physical problem, such as stiff and painful joints or sports injuries, e.g. water on the knee, and plays a fairly large part in the armoury of a TCM physician. This kind of massage is often carried out in a small *tuina* hospital, and the masseurs are frequently highly skilled blind people who have developed a particularly keen sense of touch.

Tuina massage is very different from the type of massage available at beauty parlours, where the aim is to leave you feeling relaxed. No oils are used and patients are usually massaged through their clothing. It's also much cheaper. A relaxation massage at a beauty parlour could cost as much as 200 RMB for an hour, but 45 minutes of *tuina* by a trained practitioner usually costs no more than 30 RMB. That said, you may need several sessions to overcome a problem.

Taijiquan & Qigong

Taijiquan (often referred to as *tai chi chuan* In the West) and *qigong* have their roots in Chinese philosophies such as Taoism and Confucianism, and are believed to have beneficial effects on both mental and physical well-being. *Taijiquan* is based on martial arts, and consists of a series of exercises which aim to make the blood and the *qi* flow better and to increase flexibility. They're a way of life for many Chinese, and you often see groups of people, particularly older folk, performing these exercises in the parks in the early morning, sometimes to music, all moving in synchrony.

Because the movements are slow and deliberate, and appeared to be performed mainly by retirees, they can look like special exercises for the elderly. However, it takes great strength and concentration to perform them properly, and some studies have shown that it consumes as many calories as surfing or brisk walking. The words 'tai ji quan' translate as 'supreme ultimate fist', which gives an idea of its potency, and to become even partly competent in these skills takes many years of practice.

CHILDBIRTH

Most Chinese women give birth in a hospital, attended by doctors rather than midwives, and it's a fairly clinical experience. In a country where many couples are limited to having only one child, birth is an extremely important event and nothing is left to chance. It's government policy for women to give birth in a well-equipped medical facility where there are experienced staff on hand in case of complications. In rural China, many women give birth at home, but it's unlikely a city-dwelling mum would choose to do this or that her doctor would allow it.

Husbands and partners rarely attend the birth, but families offer a great deal of support, and pre-natal and post-natal classes are available if required. The cost of giving birth in a hospital is between 4,000 and 5,000 RMB. If it's necessary to have a Caesarean section, it will add around 2,000 RMB to the bill. Pain relief such as epidurals is uncommon. The hospital provides the birth certificate, which is necessary to add the child's name on the family's hukou (registration) at the Public Security Bureau.

Having a baby is inexpensive in China, compared to the cost in the US, but the expense of bringing up a little emperor is rising fast, and the average age of first-time mothers is increasing: it rose from 27.1 in 2006 to 28.2 in 2009. Meanwhile, as many as 20 per cent of all couples choose not to have children at all.

Contraceptives are easily obtained in China. State-run family planning services are available in every city and condoms are sold at supermarkets. Abortion is legal and in some cases mandatory if the parents already have a child. A sad consequence of the one-child policy is that healthy female foetuses are sometimes aborted in the hope that the next child will be male.

DENTISTS

Dental treatment is widely available and cheap in China. There are dental practices in all towns and cities, ranging from small one-dentist offices to dental hospitals – sometimes they're contained in a wing of a general hospital. You don't need to make an appointment and can simply turn up, check in at reception and wait your turn. In dental hospitals you may feel as if you're on a production line, as there are rows of dental chairs, sometimes ten in a room, and these accommodate a line of patients each attended by a qualified dentist and two or three trainee dentists, supported by an army of nurses. Despite this, the quality of care is good – the dentist does the important work, while the trainees may follow up with scaling and polishing – and you can expect the hospital to have the latest equipment and materials.

Most dentists have both Chinese and foreign materials, and you may be asked whether you want an imported anaesthetic or filling. Local brands are cheaper but not by much. Costs are low, in any case, compared with a Western dentist: an extraction costs around 100 RMB and a filling 200 RMD, while a crown costs 600-800 RMB and a full upper-plate of dentures just 1,000 RMB. Most dental hospitals have their own in-house facilities for making false teeth, crowns and similar items, and can make and mend them quickly.

If you're dental phobic, you can ask to see a children's dentist, most of whom are gentle.

OPTICIANS

All major hospitals have a department which deals with optical problems, and you can have an eye examination and buy glasses or contact lenses direct from the hospital. Alternatively you can visit a high street optician. There are many of these, catering to a growing market: the Chinese are prone to poor eyesight and many wear spectacles or contact lenses. Opticians usually offer the eye test for free – you must pay for it at a hospital – and have up-to-date equipment and a wide range of glasses. Prices range from around 300 to 1,500 RMB for glasses, frames included, although the sky's the limit for fancy designer frames. Most lenses are imported from Thailand, although the most expensive are made in Germany. A set of contact lenses costs from 150 RMB. You may struggle to find good sunglasses in China, where few people wear them except for tourists and gangsters.

FOOT CARE

Chiropody is widely available in China, and there's sometimes a chiropodist available at public baths or steam rooms. You're expected to bathe your feet prior to treatment, and the chiropodist then works on them with miniature chisels to gently trim nails and hard skin. Treatment is skilful and isn't expensive – expect to pay around 20 RMB.

Even if you have no foot problems, it's well worth indulging in a foot massage, sometimes called reflexology, which is popular in China – and across most of East Asia – and some claim it has health benefits similar to those of acupuncture. The zones of the feet are supposed to be linked to the body's main organs by the meridians, thus massage can stimulate more than just the feet. Whatever its health benefits, an hour of lying back and having your feet washed in steaming water and then manipulated and massaged with pungent oils is the ideal antidote to a day's sightseeing or shopping. Most shopping centres have a foot massage booth tucked away, and an hour's massage costs between 50 and 80 RMB.

⚠ Caution

In China, most massage on offer is exactly what it purports to be: a therapeutic or relaxing experience with no sexual innuendo. However, there are 'massage parlours' offering less salubrious services, and the presence of young, scantily-clad masseuses should be a 'warning' sign.

COUNSELLING

Formal counselling is a relatively new concept in China. Professional counsellors have done notable work helping people in the aftermath of disasters such as earthquakes and mud slides, but most Chinese prefer to keep their problems within the family. Thus parents help their children with problems, and turn to their own parents when they need help. Teachers also take on the role of counsellor to their students.

DRUG & ALCOHOL ABUSE

Drug abuse exists in China, but to a far lesser degree than in many Western countries. There's a relatively small drug problem in the larger cities, centring on dance halls, but there's virtually no 'drug scene' at high schools or universities as is so common in the West. Yunnan province has the largest drug problem in China, due to its location adjacent to the 'Golden Triangle' of

drug-producing countries (Myanmar, Laos and Vietnam), and it's often a conduit for the entry of drugs into China. However, the government is ruthless in its determination to keep illegal drugs out, and punishment is draconian, with the death penalty imposed regularly on drug traffickers.

Alcohol is freely available, and the excessive drinking of *baijiu,* the local high proof spirit, is a feature of many meals or 'banquets' in restaurants throughout the country. Toasting is an important part of banquets, and there's a thoroughly unhealthy practice of coercing others around the table to drink too much. There are regular reports in the newspapers of drinkers dying from alcoholic poisoning as a result, and of incidents of drink-driving leading to the deaths of innocent people. The government has reacted strongly, pressurising the police to crack down on drink-driving, but the practice of drinking too much at banquets continues unabated. However, the Chinese are social rather than solitary drinkers, and alcoholism is largely confined to these occasions. You rarely see a drunk on the street.

DEATH

When someone dies, it must be certified by a doctor and reported to the Public Security Bureau (PSB) so that the family's *hukou* (registration) can be amended accordingly.

Undertakers collect the body and arrange for its cremation. Funerals are low-key affairs and strictly for family; there's far more emphasis on remembering the dead later than on seeing them on their way. The deceased's ashes are released to the family who either scatter them in a well-loved place or have them interred in a vault at a crematorium. There's a charge for this, which is renewable every ten years.

Burial is forbidden by government decree because it uses valuable land resources. If the deceased's family are very wealthy, they may be able to purchase a site for a grave (tomb) within a cemetery, but this can cost as much as 150,000 RMB, not including the tombstone. In rural areas, many people ignore the ban on burials and inter their dead on farmland. When this happens, there's a proper funeral and everyone follows the coffin through the village to the burial site, all wearing white clothing or white armbands and sometimes singing. After the burial, the grave is decorated with silver paper wreaths and plastic flowers.

The procedure is the same for foreigners, although the home country's consulate should also be informed.

Tomb Sweeping Day

On April 5th the Chinese celebrate the dead with
Qing Ming Jie (Tomb Sweeping Day). This is a
public holiday, and on the evening before, it's
customary for people to burn funerary objects to
their ancestors. These include paper money and
even cardboard models of items which were dear
to them, from cars to iPods. On the day itself,
people visit the grave site or crematorium to pay
their respects to the departed, often leaving food
at the tomb and letting off firecrackers.

13.

INSURANCE

Insurance is an alien concept to the average Chinese person. They don't see the point of it, nor do they trust the organisations that provide it. That's not to say they don't worry about future and unforeseen catastrophic circumstances, but rather than arming themselves with policies to protect their home, car, health and even the family dog, they stockpile money instead. The Chinese are firm believers in saving for a rainy day, and if their own funds prove insufficient then they trust that their family will step in to help.

That's not to say that you cannot buy insurance in China. There are many Chinese insurance companies, both state-run and private, while a fair number of overseas insurance companies now have offices in China.

Insurance is a relatively new business in China. Until two decades ago, there was only one insurance company: the People's Insurance Company of China (PICC), which was created by the state in 1949. At the time China joined the World Trade Organisation in 2001, allowing the formation of new insurance companies and permitting foreign ventures to enter the business, the PICC was the market leader. In 2002, it had over 75 per cent of the non-life insurance market and two-thirds of the life market. A decade later and the market has expanded to include around 100 insurance companies, with Chinese companies accounting for some 60 per cent of business. Of these, the largest are China Life (🖥 chinalife.com.cn), China Pacific (🖥 cpic.com.cn), PICC (🖥 piccnet.com.cn) and Ping An (🖥 insurance.pingan.com/index.shtml).

Despite this, penetration of the potential market is still weak. In 2006, just 2 per cent of the population had a life policy, while less than 1 per cent had any other kind of insurance. Foreign insurers were finding it particularly difficult to attract customers; they accounted for fewer than 6 per cent of life policies and just over 1 per cent of non-life policies. Royal and Sun Alliance's premiums totalled just US$13.8m and Zurich just US$20,000, compared with China Life which could count its income in billions of dollars.

Many financial experts believe that the insurance market will boom over the next two decades, as the Chinese adopt more Western attitudes, but it looks like an uphill struggle. Ordinary people are averse to the principle behind insurance: the idea of pooling their hard-earned savings with other people's savings, only for those funds to be used by people they don't trust to help people they don't know, seems inherently stupid to them. Why would they do that when they've worked hard to save money which they can access at any time, at their own discretion, without having to ask anyone else?

This attitude – that everyone should look after himself, if necessary with help from his relatives – pervades society in China. In a country with so many people, a man must look after his own destiny or he'll fail to progress. Most people also believe that there are some things that no one can do anything about, such as earthquakes, and that to try to safeguard against them is a waste of time.

Unlike the US and, increasingly, Western Europe, China isn't a litigious country. Very few people pursue legal action against another individual or organisation for the simple reason that they don't expect to win; most believe that if the party you're seeking redress from is wealthier or better connected than you, then you're doomed to failure. Insurance is treated with a similar level of suspicion. Most people believe that the insurance companies always ensure that the organisation and its owners benefit from any profits, rather than the policy holders, thus there's little point in taking out insurance unless they absolutely have to. (Many Westerners, having struggled to obtain payouts from insurers in the wake of a car accident or disrupted travel plans, may well agree with their viewpoint.)

To date, there's little compulsory insurance in China. Employers are supposed to fund social insurance for employees, although many don't, and car owners must by law take out third party car insurance. However, all other policies are optional. As a foreigner, there's nothing to stop you insuring your car, home, life and health – and you should certainly consider health insurance if your employer doesn't provide it – but you'll be in the minority.

> ### ⚠ Caution
>
> Never assume that Chinese law is the same as that in your home country or your previous country of residence. In many cases, it isn't.

INSURANCE COMPANIES

There are plenty of insurance companies to choose from in China. If you prefer to insure with a well-known name from your home country, it's worth checking whether they have a branch in China or in Hong Kong which covers mainland China. Some foreign insurers operating in China include American Insurance Group (AIG, ☎ 400-820 8858, 💻 chartisinsurance.com), Allianz (☎ 020-8396 6788, 💻 allianz.cn/en/home_page) and Royal Sun Alliance (RSA, ☎ 021-3855 4828, 💻 rsagroup.com.cn).

Alternatively, you can take out a policy with a Chinese insurer. Both Chinese and foreign insurers have branches in every city, and most offer a fairly wide range of policies to cover most of life's contingencies, including home and property, health, life and travel insurance. Chinese insurers provide a wide range of accident and disability insurance – reflecting, perhaps, the high road traffic accident rate and poor health and safety standards in the country – and also sell policies targeted at students and at parents wishing to safeguard their child. Some insurers also sell private pension plans.

Major Chinese banks sell insurance policies and you can also consult with a broker. The largest Chinese insurance broker is Chang An, and the three largest international brokers are Aon (💻 aon-cofco.com.cn), Marsh (💻 marsh.com.cn) and Willis (💻 willis.cn/indexen.asp).

A quote from a Chinese company is usually always cheaper than one from an overseas insurer, but this could be a false economy if you cannot fully understand what you're covered for. Chinese companies generally only issue their policies in Chinese, therefore it's difficult to understand the fine print and check for limitations and exclusions. This could cost you dear if you need to make a claim. Also bear in mind that Chinese can be vague and is much less precise in its meaning than many European languages and that some clauses may not be clear cut. If you need to be certain about the fine print of a policy, it may be better to take out insurance with a well-known foreign insurer.

Even the major names in the insurance sector haven't managed to avoid the shadow of scandal that dogs some Chinese businesses. In 2011, the *China Daily* newspaper reported that the national auditor had found issues of 'financial misconduct' in relation to two major Chinese insurers, China Life and PICC, amounting to over 3bn RMB in 2009 alone. This 'misconduct' was said to include bogus invoices and extensive expenses fraud, false premium increases and fake claims settlements. In addition, a number of secret accounts had been set up from which millions had been siphoned off directly into staff members' pockets. A total of 352 employees were reported to have been punished and some dismissed.

With such murky goings on, it isn't surprising that many people prefer to create their own financial insurance than deal with a major organisation. Bear in mind that you need to take care which company you do business with. If you don't know which insurer to use, ask your employer or other expats for their recommendations.

CONTRACTS

Nearly all insurance policies are issued for a year and must be renewed annually. Usually, insurers contact you prior to renewal with details of the next year's premium and any changes to the policy. The policies issued by Chinese insurance companies are set out and worded in a similar way to their overseas counterparts – albeit in Chinese – and, as well as being signed, they're usually stamped with the company's seal. No policy is valid without such a seal.

When you receive your policy, you usually get a small plastic card detailing your policy number, plus details of who to contact in case of an emergency or claim.

Claims

If you need to make a claim, the first step is to call the insurer. The claim line is usually manned 24 hours a day and you should call as soon as the necessity for a claim arises. If you're insuring with a Chinese company, don't expect the helpline to have English-speaking staff. Always confirm the full details in writing and/or obtain a claim form and return it promptly.

If your claim is for theft, it's essential to report it to the police and, if possible, get the number of the policeman you reported it to and the address of his police station. Without this, the insurer may refuse to pay out. The same applies in the event of a traffic accident, and you should never move your car before the police arrive as this may have a bearing on your liability and on how much compensation you receive.

Health insurance can be particularly tricky to claim against. Some insurers insist on your using particular clinics and hospitals, and most have a strict procedure which must be followed if you need treatment or are making a claim. Often there's a specific number to call first. Insurance companies are in business to make money and, if you fail to comply exactly with their conditions, they'll use this as a reason not to pay your claim.

Policies Issued Overseas

It's worth checking any policies you have in your home country to see whether they offer cover while you're abroad. If you're taking an extended break in China, there are long-stay travel policies which take care of medical issues, repatriation, loss and theft, and these may offer sufficient cover for your purposes. Some credit card companies offer similar limited cover while you're overseas. If you have a property in your home country and it's covered by a home insurance policy, check whether it includes all-risks cover for personal belongings such as cameras, laptops and even bicycles, which you can use while in China. You may find you can claim if your bicycle is stolen from a Chinese street – not an uncommon occurrence. The best way to check is to read the fine print and call the insurer direct.

▲ Caution

You may not be covered by home insurance in your home country if you aren't living in a property. Many insurers insist on being advised if you let the property or leave it unoccupied for more than a short period – as little as 30 days. Failure to notify them could result in your policy being invalidated.

SOCIAL SECURITY

China's social insurance system covers five basic areas: old age pension, health, unemployment, work-related injury and maternity pay. However, it's very limited and only a minority of the population are covered by it. Those who work for a state-run organisation should have contributions made on their behalf by their employer, although these account for only a small percentage of the employee's wage. Those who work for private employers are less likely to be covered, and the vast majority of migrant workers and rural people have no social insurance at all.

Under normal circumstances, foreigners are outside the scope of the Chinese social security system (small as it is) and there's no way, short of acquiring Chinese citizenship, that you can become eligible, although this could change in the future. A new social security law came into effect in 2011 and is an attempt to put China's social insurance into a national rather than a local framework. It's hoped this will make it easier for employees to transfer pension and medical insurance contributions between locations, e.g. if they change jobs, and put more pressure on employers to make contributions on their employees' behalf.

This law may also draw some foreigners into the social security system, although to what extent is unknown. According to a report by international tax advisors Ernst & Law, much depends on whether involvement is mandatory for foreigners and even on how a foreigner is defined. It may be that only those foreigners working for Chinese-owned companies will be affected. Whatever the outcome, it's something to bear in mind when considering a job in China.

Barring any changes in the law, the only circumstances under which you may be able to claim social security in China is if your employer has taken out a policy to cover you while you're working for him, although such policies may only apply to citizens of the employer's country. Thus if you're British and working for a UK-Chinese joint venture based in China, you should be covered to an extent by the UK's social security system, e.g. contributions towards your UK state pension should still be made. However, if you're an Australian working for an Italian company based in China, the company's social security policy may only cover Italians under Italy's social security system and be of little use to you.

It's important when taking a job in China that you find what provisions are made to cover your health care, pension and compensation in the event of an accident or work-related disability – and if necessary to take out extra cover yourself. Some countries, including the UK, expect overseas residents to keep up payments into their social security system if they wish to benefit from it in the future.

State Pension

The Chinese are entitled to a state old age pension – men qualify at 60, women at 55 – provided they or their employer has made sufficient contributions. However, only Chinese citizens can receive a Chinese pension and it isn't designed to provide anything more than a very frugal existence. Ordinary workers receive just 1,320 RMB a month, although government employees receive considerably more. For many Chinese, their children are their pension and traditionally, people have expected to be looked after by their children and family in their later years. As in many Western countries, the ratio of older people is growing – partly as a result of China's one-child policy – and this is likely to put a great deal of pressure on the government in the future when it's forced to provide more care for its elderly citizens.

Overseas Pensions

Expatriate pensioners living in China are entitled to a state old age pension from their home country, but the rate you're paid and how easily you receive the payments depends on where you come from. Americans can move to any other country and receive their state pension at the same rate as if they were still living in the US. However, for others, such as Australians, who are subject to means testing, their pension continues unchanged for the first six months after they leave Australia, but can change after that date if their financial circumstances change.

UK pensioners have their state pension index-linked to inflation, but only if they live in certain countries. Move to China and your pension will be 'frozen' at the amount that was paid on the day you left the UK and remain at that figure unless you move back to the UK or move to a country with a social security agreement with the UK. Countries where your pension increases in line with UK inflation include all EEA as well as some outside Europe. For the latest information, see 🖥 dwp.gov.uk/international/social-security-agreements/list-of-countries.

British pensioners also have to negotiate a complex and antiquated system that reflects the worst of both Chinese and British bureaucracy in order to receive their pension payments. The UK government refuses to pay pensions direct to a recipient's Chinese bank account by electronic transfer, allegedly because China's currency isn't fully exchangeable. Rather, they post a cheque to your Chinese bank. However, the bank is unwilling to accept this because the cheque states the issuers as the UK Paymaster General, rather than a named bank, thus you have to visit the bank and sign the cheque to authorise it, after which the bank posts it back to the UK for the pensions' authority to verify that your signature is valid and then posts it back to China again. Only then can it be paid into your account, some eight to ten weeks after it first arrived in China.

You're charged for this process. The Chinese bank deducts around £5/US$7.50 of the value of the cheque **and** imposes a further 60 RMB charge. With an electronic transfer, there would be no charges. The only way to avoid this rigmarole is to have your pension paid to you in the UK, but this could make you liable for tax in the UK in addition to being taxed in China.

☑ SURVIVAL TIP

If you marry in China, don't forget to inform whoever is providing your pension or pensions that you have a spouse. This may mean that your state pension is increased and that, in the event of your death, your spouse can continue to receive pension payments. The same applies if you have life insurance.

PRIVATE PENSIONS

In most cases, working for an overseas employer based in China, such as a joint venture or non-governmental organisation (NGO), shouldn't affect your private pension. And if it does, your contract should make this clear. If you earn more than you did in your home country, your new base salary (excluding local allowances) will be used to calculate both your and your employer's revised contributions and you'll carry on building up your pension fund.

However, if the organisation has set up a subsidiary in China and you're transferred to work directly for the subsidiary, this may result in the suspension of your pension for the duration of your time in China, with a resulting reduction in your final pension. You must check this carefully with the personnel department or an independent pensions advisor before accepting the job, because a few years without contributions can considerably reduce the pension you receive.

Of course, if you begin work as a new employee with a China-based foreign subsidiary or with a Chinese company, the organisation may have no pension scheme at all and you'll have to fund your own private pension. Pensions are available from Chinese banks and insurers, and many overseas financial organisations offer expatriate pensions.

Whatever you plan to do, it pays to take independent expert advice before committing to any pension, particularly a private pension fund. Bear in mind that the first year's contributions are often eaten up by fees, and that there's a huge difference between the best and worst-performing pensions.

PRIVATE HEALTH INSURANCE

Many employees seconded to China have private health insurance included as part of their remuneration package. In the event that you need treatment, your employer can assist with contacting the insurer and you'll no doubt be whisked to the smartest hospital in town. However, if you work for a Chinese employer, such as a school or university, are self-employed, or you're in China studying, then you may wish to take out your own health insurance policy.

There are two schools of thought on this. One is that China is a relatively safe place to live and healthcare costs are low, therefore you might be better off putting some funds aside to use if you do need medical care; this may apply if you're young and healthy and planning a shorter stay in China. However, anyone who's approaching middle age, has health issues or dependants and is staying long term should consider taking out a health insurance policy. A major accident or chronic condition could be costly to treat, even at Chinese rates, and in the unfortunate event that you need to be repatriated to your home country, the cost will run into many thousands of pounds

Health insurance is never cheap, and the older you are, the more it will cost. If you need comprehensive cover, expatriate policies are available from major overseas providers such as BUPA and AXA PPP. However, these organisations often deem China to be a high-cost destination, possibly because they insist that policy holders use specific international hospitals, where charges are high, rather than relying on the state health system. Their policies also include repatriation, if necessary by air ambulance, to your home country or to facilities in Hong Kong, which adds considerably to the premium. If you're happy to be cared for at a Chinese clinic, even in a major emergency, local insurers are considerably cheaper. Premiums vary enormously, according to your age, state of health and the type of cover you need, but as a rule of thumb overseas insurers' charges are around 20 per cent higher than those of Chinese insurance companies.

China Life, China Pacific, Ping An and the People's Insurance Company of China all offer health insurance policies. In fact, this is one area of insurance which is selling well, both to locals and expats. The Chinese government is quite keen for people to take out health insurance, presumably to alleviate some of the pressure on the state system.

Although all Chinese insurers offer straightforward long-term health insurance, some also have policies specifically covering life-threatening diseases and injuries, and if you don't succumb to these risks after a certain number of years then you can reclaim a proportion of your premiums. The Chinese treat these policies a little like a savings plan, with a built-in health benefit.

When comparing different insurers, there are a number of factors which you should consider, including the following:

♦ Does the policy cover you for outpatient treatment, e.g. consultations with specialists, diagnostic tests, etc. or just inpatient treatment, i.e. operations? Some insurers have a wide range of ancillary costs, e.g. dental cover, psychiatric and stress counselling, physiotherapy, even prescriptions, which can only be covered by payment of an additional premium.

♦ Is there a limit to the amount that the insurer will pay out for each illness or incident?

♦ Will they cover any pre-existing conditions?

♦ Is there an upper-age limit, after which the policy cannot be renewed? And by how much are the premiums likely to increase each year?

♦ Can you choose which hospitals and clinics to visit or are you limited to those nominated by the insurer? This could be a problem if you live a long way from major cities such as Beijing and Shanghai, where many of the top international hospitals are located.

♦ Are you covered for treatment by Traditional Chinese Medicine practitioners, e.g. acupuncture? Most Chinese policies include this, but overseas insurers may treat it as an ancillary cost.

♦ Does the insurer settle direct with the doctor/hospital, or do you have to pay and then reclaim the costs? Is there an excess (deductible)?

♦ If it's a family policy, at what age are your children deemed to be adults (and no longer covered)?

♦ If it's an expatriate policy, does it cover you for places you don't plan to visit? Some overseas policies automatically include cover for the US, where medical treatment is incredibly expensive, and this increases the cost of the policy.

Unlike in the West, it often isn't possible to check all the details (and costs) of a policy by visiting the company's website, or to take out a policy online. Many Chinese insurers' websites are only in Chinese, and they require applicants to visit a branch office to discuss the options and sign up in person. Bear in mind that in China it's okay to haggle, and some polite negotiation may secure you a discount on the quoted premium.

Dental Insurance

Separate dental policies aren't usually available from Chinese insurers. Dental expenses may be covered by an expatriate policy – or you may pay an additional fee – but as dental treatment is inexpensive in China, such cover isn't really necessary.

BUILDING INSURANCE

Surprisingly in a country where earthquakes, floods and mudslides occur quite frequently, most Chinese have no insurance for the structure of their homes. The smart modern apartment blocks which are going up throughout China are usually uninsured. Residents pay a monthly levy to the estate management company, but it's rare for this to include building insurance – as service charges do in the West – and no one seems particularly worried about this. Most residents take the attitude that if a natural disaster does strike the government will pay some compensation, but that the chance of such a mishap happening is so remote that there's no point in stressing over it.

If you prefer to insure your home or your mortgage lender insists on it, then there are buildings policies available from overseas and Chinese insurers. The annual premium is based on a percentage of the property's value.

HOME CONTENTS INSURANCE

When it comes to ensuring the security of their personal possessions, the Chinese are more pragmatic. The first line of defence for most residents of apartments and villas is to install good locks to external doors and even window bars, particularly on ground (US, first) and first (second) floor windows. However, even these don't deter the more dedicated thieves – there are stories of thieves abseiling down from the roof to gain entry to flats on higher floors, therefore those with valuable possessions sometimes take out home contents insurance. The majority of Chinese insurers offer these policies to both homeowners and tenants, and they cover your belongings against fire, flood and other unforeseen disasters, as well as against theft. If you want to insure items taken outside the home, e.g. a camera, laptop or bicycle, you must nominate and insure them separately from the other contents.

PERSONAL LIABILITY INSURANCE

Personal liability insurance is increasingly common in Europe and the US where people are more likely to sue each other for damages. As yet, the Chinese have (thankfully) not adopted this mentality so this type of insurance is rare. If you must have it, companies such as China Life offer cover.

LIFE INSURANCE

This accounts for almost three-quarters of all policies sold in China and works exactly as it does in the West, by providing a payment to provide security for dependents in the event of the policy holder's death. All major Chinese insurers sell it.

HOLIDAY & TRAVEL INSURANCE

Until recently, few people had the money or opportunity to travel abroad, but as the package holiday industry takes off and more Chinese want to study abroad, so insurers are now offering travel insurance and long-term study abroad insurance. The main aim of these policies is to cover the high cost of medical treatment overseas, particularly in Australia, Europe and North America. If a Chinese person wants to travel to one of these destinations, they may well have to show proof of insurance in order to obtain a visa. Most Chinese insurers offer policies, and insurance agents often have offices located close to foreign embassies. Low cost insurance for students is also offered locally in some countries.

If you're staying in China and want to take a trip to another country, e.g. Thailand, you can buy a simple travel policy from a local insurer.

14.

FINANCE

The Chinese are a nation of savers, not spendthrifts. Most take money very seriously: acquiring it, investing it and seeing it grow. They also enjoy spending it, not least on property and art, but the lack of a reliable social security system and the sweeping changes which are affecting the country mean that most people feel it's essential to make provision for life's vicissitudes, their child's education and their later years by saving as much as they can.

As a result, they're always on the lookout for ways to make money. Chinese banks pay a poor return on investments, and inflation, while fairly low, means the value of cash kept under the mattress buys less and less. So many people, from the very rich to the aspiring middle classes, seek alternative places to invest their savings. This is the reason for the prolonged property boom which has been waxing since the late '90s and for the wild gyrations on the Chinese stock exchange. Deng Xiaoping famously said, 'To be rich is glorious', and many of his countrymen are now doing all they can to follow his advice.

China's economy is growing at a rapid rate. It has reported domestic growth of between 7 and 11 per cent every year since 2000, and its nominal gross domestic product (GDP) for 2011 was US$7.30 trillion. However, when set against the size of the population, it lags well behind most Western countries, and there's a wide gulf in prosperity between Beijing and the bustling cities of the east coast, and the vast rural areas. In 2009, GDP per head for Shanghai – which apart from Hong Kong (and Macau) is China's most affluent city – was just 23 per cent of that of Australia. In remote Gansu province it amounted to just 3.6 per cent of Australian GDP. Despite its meteoric recent rise, the majority of the population hasn't yet enjoyed a share of the economic good times.

Another concern centres on rising prices. Following the 2008/9 priming of the Chinese financial system by the national government, when billions of RMB were pumped into the economy and banking went on a lending spree, inflation began rising again for the first time since the late '90s. In late 2010 it had crept up to just

over 5 per cent, however, by late 2012 it had fallen to 1.7 percent. There has been a huge surge in property prices since 2003 – they rose by an average of over 11 per cent countrywide between November 2009 and April 2010 – and although in late 2012 prices were stable, many people fear that China's fast-inflating 'asset bubble' could burst, with catastrophic results.

Unlike countries in the West, China is still a largely cash society. Credit – and debt – is avoided whenever possible. Hire purchase only recently became available and is almost solely used to buy cars. Banks are lending money to enable people to invest in increasingly over-priced housing and a privileged few take out bank loans to finance overseas education for their offspring, but most ordinary people are debt-free. The prudent Chinese save as much as half of their household income, in comparison with the Americans who put aside just 4 per cent.

The principal banks issue debit and credit cards but they're much less popular than in the West. Credit cards account for just a tenth of all cards in use, and although the number issued rose by a third in 2009, the total number in circulation amounted to just 186m or around one card for every 700 people. The major disadvantage of plastic is finding places that will accept it – this is largely limited to major hotels, department stores and supermarkets – and even then it can be a tedious process with staff claiming, almost as a matter of course, that your card won't work in their machine (even if it did the week before). It's even harder to persuade traders to accept foreign credit cards.

Most people simply carry cash, and there's a great deal of paper money in circulation.

People carry wallets bulging with notes, and banks and businesses are forced to keep large amounts of cash on their premises. This creates a security issue, as literally tons of banknotes are transported around cities every day by numerous armoured trucks. Each is protected by guards who are armed to the teeth with submachine guns and are a threatening presence as they line up outside banks while the cash is being transferred.

If you see armed guards waiting outside a bank, cross the road and walk past them at a distance, and if you spot an armoured car in your rear-view mirror, move over and let it pass. These people are dangerous. They won't hesitate to use their guns if they believe their money is under threat, and there have been cases of innocent people being shot for getting too close or not obeying instructions.

One of the good things about living in China is that you aren't ranked by the amount of credit you've built up or bombarded by people trying to sell you financial services. One of the negative things is that if you do get into financial difficulty, you're on your own. There are no debt-counselling agencies or citizen's advice bureaus to help you out. However, you can learn a lot from the cash-conscious Chinese about how to acquire money and make it grow, and even if you don't end up 'gloriously rich' it'll be a fascinating experience.

FINANCIAL NUMBERS

The Chinese have created a special set of characters which are used on all financial documents, such as mortgage agreements, to prevent anyone tampering with them and adjusting the figures. The regular characters for numbers are simple and just as it's easy to change the number 3 to an 8, so you don't have to be a master forger to amend several Chinese characters. Wikipedia (see ▱ en.wikipedia.org/wiki/chinese_numerals) has an excellent example of this, showing how you can change 30 (三十) to 5,000 (三十) with just a few strokes of the pen. Financial characters are far more complex and cannot be easily amended.

The different numbers and their characters are shown below.

COST OF LIVING

The cost of living in China varies hugely depending not just on where you live, but also on how you live. You can just about get by on around

Financial Numbers				
Number	**English**	**Pinyin**	**Character**	
			Chinese	Financial
0	zero	*ling*	〇	零
1	one	*yi*	一	壹
2	two	*er*	二	贰
3	three	*san*	三	叁
4	four	*si*	四	肆
5	five	*wu*	五	伍
6	six	*liu*	六	陆
7	seven	*qi*	七	柒
8	eight	*ba*	八	捌
9	nine	*jiu*	九	玖
10	ten	*shi*	十	拾
100	hundred	*bai*	百	佰
1,000	thousand	*qian*	千	仟
10,000	ten thousand	*wan*	万	萬
1,000,000	million	*bai wan*	佰	萬

Don't worry about having to learn these numbers. They're only used relatively rarely, and all banks keep a card available so that you can copy them if necessary.

3,000 RMB a month (around £300/US$450) although it will be quite a frugal existence, whereas you can live in some comfort on between 6,000 and 9,000 RMB. Much depends on whether you have to pay for your own accommodation, as rent takes a large lump out of the monthly budget.

In one of the first-tier cities, such as Beijing or Shanghai, you could pay twice as much rent as you would for a comparable apartment in a tier-two city such as Dalian or Tianjin, and up to five times as much as in one of China's less popular (but equally pleasant) third-tier cities such as Kunming or Xi'an; it's accommodation, more than any other expense, which makes China's major cities so expensive. Food, clothes and household goods also cost appreciably more in the major cities, because shopkeepers are paying the same high rents (although goods can also cost a lot in remote parts of China due to the expense of transportation).

The major cost of living indices usually rate Beijing as one of the most expensive cities in the world. Mercer's Cost of Living index for 2010 (🖳 mercer.com) ranks China's capital in 12th place, just above London and Paris, while Shanghai is ranked 25th, on a par with Sydney and Rome. However, many expatriates who live there rent free would disagree.

It's how you live which is the most important factor. Teachers find life in China incredibly cheap, even in Beijing or Shanghai, provided they live rent-free, while expat executives at major companies often find they can save more than they spend. It all depends on how much like the locals you're prepared to live. If you shop at local markets, eat at noodle bars, travel by subway (or bicycle) and drink Tsingtao beer (moderately), China can be as cheap as chips. However, if you're into fine dining and cocktail bars, insist on eating imported foods and want the luxury of driving your own car, it's considerably more expensive. Factor in private schooling for your children and a nice gated villa and the Mercer rankings begin to make sense. One of the major

problems of settling in Beijing or Shanghai is the temptation. There's far more to spend your money on, from designer clothes to imported cheese, than there is in, say, Chengdu.

China has been self-sufficient for millennia, relying on exporting goods rather than importing them to get by, and it's those 'essentials' from overseas which cost dear. A Chinese beer costs as little as 3 RMB for a 375ml bottle in a supermarket, while imported beer costs around 20 RMB for a similar-sized bottle. Locally grown tomatoes cost 1.5 RMB a *jin* (a little over a pound or 500g in weight) but avocados, which must be imported, are as much as 90 RMB a *jin*.

Many necessities of life are much cheaper in China, namely electricity, state medical care, public transport and petrol: in 2012, filling up your tank cost only half as much as in the UK, but twice as much as in the US. However, a few things are surprisingly expensive. A good cup of coffee, for example, is dearer than in Europe or the US, despite that fact that Yunnan province is a major coffee producer.

A foreigner can never live quite as cheaply as the Chinese. There are unavoidable expenses such as phone calls home, foreign language books and newspapers, the irresistible yearning for a bar of imported chocolate, and the cost of flying home occasionally to see family and friends. However, the majority of everyday essentials, from steak to Levi's jeans, are often (possibly a lot) cheaper than abroad. Even a retiree, living on a state pension, can get by quite nicely in one of China's smaller cities, and if you're earning a salary, however modest, you should be able to live well and save.

CHINESE CURRENCY

The Chinese unit of currency is the *renminbi* (RMB). This translates as 'people's money' although it's also often called the *yuan* or, in slang, the *kwai* (piece). *Renminbi* is the term used for the currency as a whole (like sterling) while people often refer to a monetary unit as *yuan* (like the British pound). Each RMB is split into ten *jiao* – the slang is *mao* as in Chairman Mao – and each *jiao* is worth ten *fen*. The symbol for RMB is written in two ways; one is similar to the Japanese Yen, a capital letter ¥ with either one or two lines crossing the stem, but it's more commonly written as 元.

Chinese coins are available in denominations of 1 and 5 *fen*, 1 and 5 *jiao* and 1 *yuan* or RMB. Most coins are made of aluminium and are coloured 'silver'; only the 5 *jiao* coins are 'gold' in colour. Notes are taking over from coins in many places, with the latter only needed for phones and vending machines, and you may never see a *fen* as these coins have negligible value.

Notes are issued in values of 1, 2 and 5 *jiao* and 1, 2, 5, 10, 20, 50 and 100 RMB. The latter is only worth around £10 (or US$15). All RMB notes carry the face of Mao Zedong on one side and a Chinese scene on the other, and the values are shown in numbers as well as Chinese characters. Notes also vary in size according to their value, with the 100 RMB note being the largest and the 1 RMB note the smallest. The colours of the notes are as follows:

Chinese Banknotes	
Value	**Colour**
100 RMB	red
50 RMB	bright green
20 RMB	brown
10 RMB	blue
5 RMB	purple
2 RMB	dark green*
1 RMB	pale green

* These are rare as printing ceased in 2004.

The *jiao* notes are smaller still and often very crumpled and well used; one way of distinguishing them is that unlike *yuan* notes they don't carry Mao's portrait.

The largest denomination note, the 100 RMB, is usually bundled into thick wads of 100 notes with a total value of 10,000 RMB; this is known as a *wan*. The Chinese measure things in *wan*, i.e. values of 10,000, rather than 1,000 as is common in other countries. Be careful of this, as it's easy to miss the final zero and miscalculate.

Traditionally, the RMB was pegged to the US dollar but since 2005 it has been allowed to float more freely, albeit in a fairly narrow band set by a basket of other currencies. China hopes it will become a world reserve currency but its use is still fairly limited outside China, with the exception of major trading partners such as Australia and the United Arab Emirates.

The RMB appreciated by 25 per cent against the US dollar between 2005 and 2012, but its value is still considered to be artificially low – as much as 40 per cent too low – by competitors such as the US and European Union who think its low value encourages people to buy Chinese goods rather than their home countries' products. In late 2012, its official (not tourist rate) value stood at 6.25 RMB to the US$, about 8 RMB to the € (euro) and around 10 RMB to the GB£ (see 🖥 xe.com for the latest rates).

There are quite a lot of forged notes in the Chinese system, particularly 50 and 100 RMB notes, and some are very skilfully made. When you hand one of these notes to a trader, the recipient often examines it carefully, sometimes passing it through a machine to check its authenticity. If you have a note rejected, there's no point in taking it to a bank as they'll confiscate it without reimbursing you for its value.

Outside of China, it can be difficult to acquire *renminbi*. Because the currency isn't fully convertible, many Western banks either don't hold it or impose high fees. You may find it easier to obtain RMB through a currency exchange bureau or travel agent. One of the best rates of exchange can be found in the local 'Chinatown' in your home country, which is also a good place to sell surplus RMB.

As China works to make its currency more fully convertible, the government has made agreements with a number of neighbouring 'countries', such as Hong Kong and Macau – which are Special Administrative Regions of China with separate currencies – and Singapore, to trade using RMB, and it's easier to buy or exchange the currency in these countries.

FOREIGN CURRENCY

Obtaining foreign currency in China isn't straightforward. Changing RMB into sterling or dollars is a bit of a rigmarole which involves visiting a nominated branch of a particular bank and producing your passport as identification. All transactions are recorded on a central register with the State Administration of Foreign Exchange so that China can keep tabs on the amount of foreign money, especially US dollars, within its monetary system. This is also a precaution against money laundering.

There are limits on the amount of foreign currency that can be deposited or withdrawn from a foreign currency account on any one day: you can deposit up to US$5,000 (or its equivalent in another foreign currency) and withdraw up to US$10,000. There's also an annual limit on the amount of dollars/foreign currency which can be changed into RMB or vice versa: US$50,000 worth of foreign currency or a maximum of 50,000 RMB.

Faced with this level of bureaucracy and with people keen to get their hands on Western currencies, particularly dollars, it isn't unusual for someone to sidle up to you outside a bank and ask if you want to change some money, an offer which you should decline. Friends and acquaintances may also ask you, but you should only change money for people if you know them very well. Foreign exchanges which take place outside the banking system are against the law.

⚠ Caution

Never change money in the street. Not only is it illegal – it's a ploy used by some 'businessmen' to launder 'hot' money – but there's a good chance that you'll receive counterfeit notes!

In an emergency, it's sometimes possible to withdraw foreign currency from a Chinese bank account against a foreign debit or credit card. Only certain banks do this, e.g. CITIC Bank or the Bank of China, and they may only supply a limit amount of cash, e.g. US$100 and are sure to charge a high fee.

Buying & Selling Foreign Currency

As a foreigner, you can open more than one bank account and it's advisable to have two: one for RMB and the other for foreign currency, e.g. sterling, dollars and euros. You cannot easily pay RMB into a foreign currency account or vice versa, but you can pay different currencies into a foreign currency account. Many people open a Chinese account for daily transactions and also have a foreign account into which their salary is paid or to receive money from abroad.

Your bank may be willing to change small amounts of foreign currency into RMB, but if you wish to change RMB into, say, dollars or sterling, or withdraw cash from your foreign account, you must visit a specific bank. All foreign transactions take place at a designated branch of the Bank of China in each town, which is the only bank which holds large amounts of foreign currency and the only bank with the authority to conduct foreign exchange. Even if you have a foreign account with another bank, you must still visit the foreign branch of the Bank of China to withdraw your foreign cash.

5 RMB note

Unlike most banks, it only opens five days a week – most banks are open every day – and closes for a lengthy lunch. You must produce your passport as well as your bank book – the teller will make a photocopy of its key pages as a record of the transaction. This takes a while, so don't try to do it when you're in a hurry on your way to the airport.

You can pay overseas cheques into your foreign currency account but they take an inordinately long time to clear – it's often more than a month and sometimes up to three months before you can access the funds – so it's better to have funds paid into your account, e.g. pension payments or regular transfers from home, by electronic transfer.

There are limits on the amount of cash – foreign or Chinese – which you may bring into China. If you're planning to bring in a large amount of foreign cash, e.g. over US$5,000, you must declare it on arrival. For more information, contact the Chinese Customs Administration (☎ 010-6519 4114, 🖳 english.customs.gov.cn).

Cash Transfers

You can send money to or from a Chinese bank account using an electronic transfer such as SWIFT. Banks and building societies in the West can arrange cash transfers, although charges vary and transfer times can be from a few hours to a week or more. It's important to have the money transferred into a foreign currency account, e.g. sterling to a sterling account, as it makes withdrawals easier.

One of the problems of arranging cash transfers from abroad is that a bank may need your signature as authorisation. You can download the transfer form online but still need to sign and post it to them before the transfer can be made, although this isn't usually necessary.

However, you don't have to use banks to make transfers. There are a number of online money transfer agencies such as Moneybookers (🖳 moneybookers.com). In order to use them you must set up an account to which you upload money from your UK account and then download it into your Chinese account. Fees are lower than those for a SWIFT transfer – around £5 as opposed to around £20 – and transfers can be completed in a few days, although your Chinese bank may impose their own fees on top.

The FX Compared website (🖳 fxcompared. com) allows you to compare different charges and timescales for cash transfers to China from the UK, the US, Australia and many other countries. Another alternative is a telegraphic transfer, e.g. via Western Union (the quickest, safest and most expensive method). You can also set up regular overseas transfers with companies such as Travelex (⌨ travelex.co.uk) or Currencies Direct (⌨ currenciesdirect.com) which are ideal if you have a fixed monthly amount to transfer, such as private pension payments.

If an organisation insists on sending you money by cheque, you must be prepared to wait a long time before the funds are available (see above). Note also that Bank of China's anti-money laundering precautions require that all paperwork involved in cashing overseas cheques clearly shows the name of the bank, e.g. Barclays. British pensioners have particularly difficulty in cashing state old age pension cheques because these bear the name of the UK's Paymaster General, rather than the name of a bank, and they must be sent back to the UK for verification and clearance before a Chinese bank will accept them.

It's even more complex sending money abroad from China, as you first have to change it into foreign currency (see above). Once you've done that, the bank can wire your funds to a designated bank account. It isn't worth doing this for small amounts as the transaction charge is around 200 RMB.

CREDIT RATING

The demand for credit in China is low. Most people would rather save than borrow and if they need a loan, they approach family and friends before they consider borrowing from a bank. Credit rating agencies aren't established in China and there's no system whereby individuals have credit rating imposed on them or their credit history (correct or otherwise) held on a computer database somewhere.

If you need a loan, e.g. to buy a home or car, or you want to apply for a credit card, you approach the bank direct. Alternatively, the developer or car dealer will have a finance agreement which you can sign up to. Generally, they check out your creditworthiness the old-fashioned way, by asking questions and examining your bank balance, income and outgoings, and you're charged a loan establishment fee to cover these costs.

BANKING

Banking has a long history in China, dating back some 1,000 years; the first paper money was printed in Sichuan province in the 11th century. However, it's only in the last 30 years or so that banking has been modernised and it's now similar to that of Europe and the US. The financial sector is one of China's most profitable areas with

Chinese coin of good luck - Dragon & Phoenix

branches of major Chinese banks in every city, offering services which, increasingly, resemble those available in the West.

Innovations such as electronic banking are catching on, albeit slowly. However, the Chinese are cautious about money, and many transactions are still conducted on a face-to-face basis and involve considerable manual processing. You cannot arrange foreign transactions online, e.g. exchanging RMB for dollars or transferring funds to an overseas account.

This caution has its advantages. The global financial crisis of 2007 and the resulting recession caused concern in China but it didn't lead to near financial meltdown as it did in the many Western countries. The national aversion to borrowing and the state's control of many banks meant that China has emerged from the credit crunch relatively unscathed.

Banks

There are five 'big banks' in China. These are Bank of China (BOC, ⌨ boc.cn), the China Construction Bank (CCB, ⌨ ccb.com/en/home/index.html), the Industrial and Commercial Bank of China (ICBC, ⌨ icbc.com.cn/icbc/sy/default.htm), the Agricultural Bank of China (ABC or AgBank, ⌨ abchina.com/en/default.htm), and the Bank of Communications (BoCom, ⌨ bankcomm.com/bankcommsite/en/index.jsp). All are owned by the national government, but also have shareholders and are quoted on the stock exchange.

Founded in 1912, Bank of China is the oldest bank and has the most overseas operations, with branches in 27 countries including Australia, the UK and US. However, it isn't the largest bank in

China: this distinction goes to the Industrial and Commercial Bank of China, which has some 18,000 branches, both domestic and overseas.

There are many more banks to choose from, some of which are state owned and some privately owned. These include second-tier commercial banks such China CITIC Bank, China Merchants Bank and Guangdong Development Bank, and more localised city commercial banks, such as Bank of Beijing, most of which also trade outside their immediate region.

Foreign banks are allowed to operate in China, but they're few and far between. Those with the largest presence are HSBC, Standard Chartered, Bank of East Asia and Hang Seng Bank, although they only have around 110 main branches between them in the whole of mainland China. Unless there's a branch near you and it has the authority to conduct RMB business, foreign banks aren't much use to private customers, although businesses may find them valuable. The country's central bank, overseeing China's finances, is the People's Bank of China, and banks are supervised by the China Banking Regulatory Commission.

Which bank you choose is down to personal preference, and it's worth asking other expats about their banking experiences. While Chinese banks don't bombard you with products, they aren't as tuned in to customer service as Western banks, and then there's the language barrier to overcome. However, the big five all offer online banking, plus a large number of branches and automatic teller machines (ATMs), and probably provide the widest range of services and the best security for your money.

Building Societies & Credit Unions

There are no building societies or credit unions in China, where all lending is done by the banks.

Post Office Banking

China Post has a banking division called the China Postal Savings Bank (⌨ psbc.com), although this is nothing like Europe's post office banks. It's located separately from post offices and you cannot use it to pay bills or transfer money. It's strictly a savings bank.

Business Hours

Most banks are open seven days a week from 9am to 5pm, remaining open at lunch time and even opening on public holidays other than the first few days of Chinese New Year. There are no 'bank holidays' in China. The exceptions to this are the special 'foreign currency' branches of Bank of China, which have more limited hours,

usually five days a week from 9am to 12noon and from 2.30pm to 4.30pm.

Electronic Banking

Electronic banking includes automatic bill payment, ATMs, smart cards, electronic funds transfer, telephone and internet banking. This is still in its early days in China where many transactions are still done manually, but the Chinese penchant for technology means it's catching up fast.

All major Chinese banks now offer internet banking (sometimes called e-banking) via their websites, which allows you to access your account via a computer or with an internet-enabled mobile phone, even from abroad. Services provided include obtaining details of account balances and recent transactions, checking interest rates earned/charged, and downloading statements, paying bills and transferring money to recipients in China. However, you cannot move your money between different currency accounts online, or arrange overseas cash transfers. Some websites are better than others but in most cases, you can select the 'English' option to navigate a website, although some of the translations are puzzling to say the least!

To set up an internet account, you must visit a branch of your bank and complete a form. To access the account, you're usually provided with a 'security key', a small device which generates a new password each time you log on to the banking website.

Telephone banking provides access to your bank 24 hours a day, seven days a week, although calls may be answered by a recorded message and quite possibly in Chinese, making it awkward unless you can speak the language.

If you don't already have one, it's advisable to set up an online account with your bank in your home country so that you can manage your finances at a distance.

⚠ Caution

You must take care to protect your password and other details when using online banking in China, where hackers are a particular problem. It's advisable to avoid using online banking at an internet café, where hackers sometimes implant devices into computers to record passwords and PIN numbers.

Current Accounts

It's fairly easy to open a bank account in China. All you need is your passport for ID and some money to deposit. You can open a *renminbi* account with as little as 100 RMB but may need a larger deposit when opening a foreign currency account. Some banks may require you to have a Chinese name (see page 81).

When opening a current (cheque) account you may be offered the choice of a bank book in which transactions are recorded or a debit card. Go for the bank book. Chinese banks don't issue monthly statements to individual customers so the bank book, which is updated whenever you visit the bank, is the only way you can retain a printed record of transactions (unless you can access a statement online). A week after receiving your bank book you can request a debit card.

On opening an account, you set up a six-digit personal identification (PIN) number that you're required to enter into a machine at the counter, sometimes more than once, when making a transaction. (This is separate from the four-digit PIN used with your debit card.) Your money is handed over as a large bundle of notes. Most bank counters feature a machine for counting banknotes so that you can check the sum requested. Just taking out a small sum of money can be a bureaucratic business, and you'll appreciate having a debit card so you can use ATMs and cut out the queuing.

Note that joint accounts are regarded as highly unusual and, if you want one, you may find it difficult, if not impossible, to persuade the bank staff to open one.

Bank Charges

Provided you keep your account in credit, you shouldn't pay any bank charges. Unlike many European and US banks, Chinese banks don't impose an annual fee for maintaining your account, provided you maintain your balance above a certain level, although if it drops below this threshold then charges may apply to certain transactions – check when opening an account. If you go overdrawn, you're charged for the facility and expected to pay off the overdraft as soon as possible.

Cheques

Banks don't issue chequebooks to private customers. Cheques do exist but are only used in conjunction with business accounts. If you receive a cheque and wish to pay it into your account, it must be for the same currency, e.g. a dollar cheque into a dollar account, and clearly state the name of the issuing bank. Even then, you may have to wait several weeks for it to clear.

Traveller's cheques can also be difficult to change in China, although as a secure way of carrying 'emergency' money, they're invaluable. Bank of China may be willing to cash them, but a posh hotel will only accept them if you're staying there, and most retailers and smaller banks dismiss them out of hand. You should also buy them from a well-known issuer such as American Express, who have offices in Beijing, Shanghai, Guangzhou and Xiamen where you can cash cheques.

Deposit Accounts

The Chinese love to save and all banks offer deposit accounts. Most pay fixed interest provided you leave your money on deposit for a fixed period; withdraw it early and you lose some, if not all, of the interest 'earned'. Interest rates were low at around 2.5 per cent in 2011, when many investors were shunning banks in favour of stocks and shares or property, but had risen to 3.25 by late 2012. Most banks also pay interest on the balance in current accounts, although at a negligible rate. Any interest earned is recorded in your bank book annually, together with an automatic 20 per cent deduction for income tax.

Debit & Credit Cards

All the larger banks issue debit and credit cards and they're becoming more popular. There were over 2.5bn in circulation in 2012, of which fewer than 10 per cent were credit cards. The Chinese are adapting to the convenience of paying by card but they're less keen on the concept of using a card to borrow money.

But even debit cards are by no means universal in China, where the number of places accepting them is still small – as few as 2 per cent of merchants by some estimations. Bank of China claims to have 60,000 points of sale for its bank cards, which is only a fraction of the total number

of retailers and service providers in China. Debit cards are most useful for withdrawing money from your bank's ATMs. It's also possible to obtain a debit card for use abroad: Bank of China's Great Wall Card is a Maestro card in sterling which can be used in most UK ATMs and at outlets displaying the Maestro/Switch symbol.

Credit cards can be used to pay for purchases and services at participating retailers, e.g. hotels, airlines and restaurants, or to make purchases online within China (in RMB), although, like debit cards, they aren't accepted everywhere. You can also use credit cards to withdraw cash, although it's expensive. There's a charge of 30 RMB for each 3,000 RMB or part thereof that you withdraw, thus a 3,500 RMB withdrawal can cost you 60 RMB in charges.

☑ SURVIVAL TIP

Most Chinese credit cards can only be used in China, due to the non-convertibility of the *renminbi*. However, there are dual currency cards which can be used in conjunction with RMB and one other currency, e.g. dollars or euros, which are useful when you're travelling abroad. You can nominate different currencies but only one at a time, e.g. Australian dollars if you're making a trip to Oz, and must have the card activated for use with that currency by your bank.

Some credit and debit cards carry the Union Pay logo, an interbank network based in China but with overseas affiliations, meaning it can be used in over 100 countries worldwide. In the UK it's aligned with the LINK network, therefore you can use your card to withdraw cash from ATMs showing the LINK logo.

You must provide proof of identity and income when applying for a Chinese credit card. Most are linked to either Visa or MasterCard and can be used throughout China. The annual fee is around 100 RMB, although this may be waived if you use the card at least six times a year. Interest is charged at around 0.05 per cent a day.

It's possible to use a credit or debit card from your home country to withdraw RMB from a Chinese ATM, provided it carries the Visa or MasterCard logo and/or there's an agreement between the issuer and the bank. For example, Bank of America has an arrangement with China Construction Bank which allows BoA card holders to withdraw cash from CCB ATMs with no fees,

other than a charge for currency conversion. However, in most cases you're charged a transaction fee and commission, or even interest on cash withdrawals, so check with your card issuer. Note that if you don't tell your bank that you plan to use your debit card in China, they may think it's been stolen and block it.

If you cannot use your overseas card to withdraw cash from an ATM, you can usually use it over the counter, although banks often impose a 3 per cent transaction charge and offer a poor rate of exchange.

You should ensure that you know your card issuer's emergency telephone number in case your card is lost or stolen.

Payments & Transfers

By far the easiest way to pay for something is to visit the store and pay cash. If you need to send money to another city in China, China Post has a service which allows you to send cash via the postal system. To use it, you visit a special counter at the post office and fill out a form and the money is transferred in a couple of days. This is easier and less bureaucratic than using a bank. If you have regular payments to make, e.g. utility bills, it's possible to set up a direct debit with your bank.

Debit and credit cards can be used to pay for goods and services ordered via the internet. Some websites allow you to input your bank details, in which case your bank does the transaction. Alternatively, you can use Alipay (🖥 alipay.com) which is the Chinese version of PayPal.

Automatic Teller Machines (ATMs)

There are over 200,000 ATMs in China, so it isn't difficult to withdraw cash. However, most debit cards can only be used at the same bank's ATMs and not at those of a different bank, e.g. Bank of China cards can only be used in Bank of China ATMs.

If your card has a Union Pay logo, it can be used in any bank's ATM displaying the same logo, although you're charged a fee for a withdrawal if it isn't made at a branch of your own bank. Within the same province as your bank the fee is just 2 RMB, while in another province it's 1 per cent of the amount withdrawn.

ATMs usually have instructions in both Chinese and English and operate in the same way as ATMs in other countries. Some also accept deposits and you may be able to print transactions in your bank book if it has an electronic band on the back cover for this purpose.

Many ATMs are located within banks, often in a small room at the front of the bank which you can access out of hours by swiping your card through a slot by the door. This is more secure than using an ATM on the street, and it's less likely that the machine will have been tampered with.

Complaints

There's no banking ombudsman or other consumer associations dealing with complaints about banks. If you have a problem you must take it up with your bank manager. There's also no deposit guarantee scheme in China.

MORTGAGES

As an expatriate, you can obtain a mortgage as easily as the locals, provided you can offer sufficient security to make the payments. There are no 100 per cent mortgages in China where the government, in an effort to cool the housing market, has set a minimum deposit of 40 per cent. Anyone purchasing a second home – not an option for foreigners – must put down 50 per cent of the asking price.

If you're buying a new apartment, the developer will have arranged a mortgage package with a particular bank, although there's nothing to stop you making your own arrangements.

Mortgages typically run for between five and 15 years, although it's sometimes possible to obtain a 20-year mortgage. Most are basic repayment mortgages and the interest rate is normally fixed for the period of the loan. The interest rate is set by the government and was around 7 per cent in 2012, although the rate can be discounted by 15 per cent for Chinese first-time buyers – useful if your spouse is Chinese – while short-term mortgages, i.e. for five years or less, may also attract a discount. The rates offered by developers are sometimes a little higher, so it's well worth shopping around.

An arrangement fee applies when taking out a mortgage, and you may have to take out life assurance to repay the loan if you die before it's paid up.

TAXATION

The Chinese tax system is complex and includes over 25 separate taxes, but unless you're the boss of a reasonably large company, you're unlikely to encounter most of them. The main ones which affect foreigners are income tax, capital gains tax, property taxes, vehicle/road taxes, customs duties and value added tax/consumption tax. All are direct taxes except the last category, which is incorporated into the price of goods and services.

The government receives a large slice of its income from taxation, although less than many Western countries; tax revenue accounts for around 17 per cent of GDP. In 2009, tax revenues were 6.31tn RMB, according to the State Administration of Taxation, a 9 per cent increase on the previous year. Tax applies not just to individuals and businesses but also to provincial and local governments, which pay taxes to the central government.

Although the Chinese prefer not to pay taxes unless absolutely necessary – hence the unwillingness of some landlords and service providers to issue an official receipt (*fa piao*) – tax evasion is rare, at least among ordinary folk. The penalties are just too high. In the UK you might receive a fine for fiddling your taxes, whereas in China you're more likely to end up with a lengthy prison sentence.

> ## ☑ SURVIVAL TIP
>
> Like that as in most countries, Chinese tax law is constantly changing and evolving, and this section is intended only as a general guide. For the latest information – particularly if you're self-employed or setting up a business in China – you should consult a tax professional.

Tax Number

If you're self-employed or a business owner and need to register with the tax authorities, you can do this at the local tax office for your area. There are no specific tax numbers. Chinese tax payers are identified by their ID card number, while foreigners use their passport number.

Using an Accountant

If you're self-employed or setting up a business, your local chamber of commerce can usually help with tax advice and recommend an accountant. A Chinese accountant charges around 200 RMB an hour, although if you employ an accountant from a multinational company such as PricewaterhouseCoopers, your bill will be significantly higher.

INCOME TAX

Individual income tax applies to anyone working and earning money in China, whether Chinese or foreign, subject to any exemptions to which they may be entitled and to the terms of any double taxation agreements.

For the vast majority of foreigners seconded to China by their employer, or working for a joint venture or Chinese organisation such as a school, income tax is deducted at source from your salary by your employer. Only if you're self-employed or running your own business do you need to calculate and pay your own income tax.

Domicile & Residency

Generally, foreigners are taxed in China on any income generated there, or generated for a Chinese organisation while overseas. This applies from the time you start earning until you've resident for three years, after which you're liable to pay Chinese tax on your worldwide earnings, including dividends from shares or rent from properly owned abroad. The rules on where you pay tax are complicated, and depend on your domicile and/or residency (they aren't the same thing – you can live in one country but be domiciled and liable to pay taxes in another). It's important to find out how the tax laws will affect you (both in China and in your home country) before moving to China, particularly if you have income from different sources. In this case you should obtain advice from a tax advisor who's an expert in the tax law of all the countries involved.

Double-taxation Agreements

These are to ensure that individuals don't end up paying tax twice on the same income, e.g. in China and in your home country. China has such agreements with some 90 countries including Australia, Canada, New Zealand, South Africa, the US and most European countries, including the UK. Usually double-taxation agreements allow you to offset taxes paid in one country against your tax liability in another country.

Citizens of most countries are exempt from paying taxes in their home country when they spend a minimum period overseas, e.g. a year. Americans are a notable exception and can obtain advice from US embassies. If you're in doubt about your tax liability in your home country, contact your home country's tax authority or consult an accountant.

Taxable Income

Individuals in China are liable for income tax on all income over a specified amount. In 2012, the annual tax-free allowance for foreigners was 57,600 RMB a year – or 4,800 RMB a month. The Chinese must pay tax once they've earned in excess of 2,000 RMB a month. This doesn't sound a lot, but bear in mind that incomes are low by Western standards and that many ordinary Chinese can only dream of earning such a magnificent monthly wage! If you work as a teacher, you're unlikely to earn much over 4,000 RMB and may not be paid for the full 12 months, so you're unlikely to be liable for income tax, although employees of overseas and joint-venture companies who are paid in China may well end up paying tax.

Not all the 'perks' you receive are taxable. For example, accommodation and utility bills paid by your boss don't count as income; neither does a company car, although this is a rare benefit in China. Remuneration for relocation expenses, plane tickets home and any travel allowance you may receive at the end of your contract also aren't deemed to be taxable income.

Should you receive your salary in separate payments, e.g. your basic salary, an overseas allowance and a local living allowance, you only pay Chinese income tax on the element which is paid in China; for many seconded employees this is just the living allowance, as the remainder is paid into their home bank account. However, once you've been resident in China for three years, you're taxed on your worldwide income.

You don't pay tax on pension, insurance compensation or redundancy payments, or prize money won in government sponsored lotteries.

As an employee, your tax payments are deducted at source by your employer and there's no need to complete a tax return unless you have taxable income from other sources.

Allowances & Rebates

The only allowance against income is the annual allowance specified above. There are no allowances for married couples, dependent children, etc. There are a number of allowances or incentives for businesses established in certain regions, e.g. away from the eastern hotspots, where the authorities are keen to attract investment. The local chambers of commerce can advise about these.

Income Tax Rates

Taxable income per month	Tax rate	Tax paid/RMB	Cumulative tax/RMB
Up to 500 RMB	5%	25	25
501 to 2,000 RMB	10%	150	175
2,001 to 5,000 RMB	15%	450	625
5,001 to 20,000 RMB	20%	3,000	3,625
20,001 to 40,000 RMB	25%	5,000	8,625
40,001 to 60,000 RMB	30%	6,000	14,625
60,001 to 80,000 RMB	35%	7,000	21,625
80,001 to 100,000 RMB	40%	8,000	29.625
Over 100,000 RMB	45%		

Tax Rates

There are nine progressive tax rates from ranging from 5 to 45 per cent. They apply to Chinese citizens and foreigners and are levied on any income earned above the initial tax-free allowance (see table above).

Self Employed

The self-employed pay tax on their income, less any deductible expenses, at the same rate as employees and receive the same tax-free allowance, but they must submit an annual tax return (see below). The regulations pertaining to tax law for the self-employed and businesses are complex, and it's important to obtain expert advice before establishing a business or starting work as a self-employed person in China.

Sole traders and small family businesses are taxed across five grades (rates), ranging from 5 to 35 per cent (see table below).

Company Tax

The corporate tax rate in China is 25 per cent, although some smaller companies pay only 20 per cent.

Tax Returns

The Chinese tax year runs from January to December, and the self-employed and business owners are required to submit an annual tax return by May 31st of the following year. Tax returns can be submitted on paper or online. It's all in Chinese so you'll probably need an accountant to help you.

Payment

If you're required to file a tax return, you must also make advance payments against tax, Individuals must do this monthly, while foreign businesses must file reports and make interim payments every three months. If there's any tax due at the end of the tax year, you'll be billed by the tax authorities after they've checked your report. Fines are imposed for unpaid tax or late payments.

PROPERTY & LAND TAXES

In 2011, only businesses were required to pay property tax and this was on commercial, as opposed to residential buildings, while municipal

Small Business Income Tax Rates

Grade	Annual taxable income	Tax rate	Tax paid/RMB	Cumulative tax/RMB
Grade 1	Up to 5,000 RMB	5%	250	250
Grade 2	5,001 to 10,000 RMB	10%	500	750
Grade 3	10,001 to 30,000 RMB	20%	4,000	4,750
Grade 4	30,001 to 50,000 RMB	30%	6,000	6,750
Grade 5	Over 50,000 RMB	35%		

governments and developers paid land tax. There was no tax to pay (national or local) for individual property owners – no rates or council tax. However, the upward surge in property prices has led the government to review the situation, and it's quite possible that a residential property tax may be imposed in the not too distant future, although how it will be calculated is anyone's guess. In Shanghai, where property has risen more sharply than in any other part of China, the municipal government has been trialling an annual tax based on 0.4 to 0.6 per cent of a property's value. This would mean that an apartment worth 2m RMB – quite modest by central Shanghai standards – would attract a not inconsiderable tax of 8,000 to12,000 RMB per year. This is something to keep an eye on if you're thinking of investing in Chinese property.

When buying property in China you must pay a deeds tax and stamp duty, which together amount to between 3 and 5 per cent of a property's value.

CAPITAL GAINS TAX (CGT)

CGT is applicable on all gains in excess of 50 per cent of the original purchase price, and applies when you make a gain on anything substantial such as property. The rate of CGT starts at 30 per cent and increases up to 60 per cent on a gain exceeding 200 per cent of the original purchase price. There's no indexation to take into account any rise due to inflation. No CGT is payable on a gain on a private dwelling that you've owned for five years.

GOODS & SERVICES TAX

Value added tax (VAT) at 17 per cent is included in the price of virtually all goods in China with a few exceptions, e.g. books and newspapers, cooking oil and water bills, where the rate is 13 per cent. In addition to VAT, a consumption tax is added to certain goods, such as alcohol, tobacco products, cosmetics, jewellery, fireworks and motor vehicles, which varies from 1 to 50 per cent. However, as with all indirect taxation, the tax is included in the sales price and you aren't aware of it, although it explains why some things, e.g. cars, are more expensive in China than you might expect.

All goods which are exported attract a 100 per cent rebate, therefore no VAT is paid on them. However, there doesn't appear to be any arrangement whereby VAT on goods purchased by an individual can be reclaimed on departure from China, as is common in some other countries.

SAVINGS & INVESTMENTS

Even the best savings bonds in Chinese banks don't pay much interest: around 2.5 per cent at the most. Some foreigners can take advantage of offshore accounts, but these are more a way of reducing your tax liability than seeing your money grow. Bear in mind that while you may be able to receive interest tax-free – depending on your resident status in your home country – you must still declare it, and may end up giving at least some of it to the taxman. It's advisable to check your tax situation with your tax advisor before opening an offshore account.

So what are the alternatives? The Chinese have a national obsession with making money, plus there's an awful lot of 'grey' money looking for a good home, so they're targeting different ways of investing their funds. The three most popular are property, stocks and shares, and art and antiques, described below.

Property

Many Chinese see property investment as the number one way to increase their wealth, and there are queues for new housing developments in 'hot' parts of China. As a foreigner, you're at a disadvantage. One, you can only buy one property and, two, you cannot do that until you've lived continuously in China for over a year. But don't dismiss the idea. Luxury apartments in the major city centres may be beyond the pockets of most people, but the smart money is now targeting second- and third-tier cities, where property is still comparatively cheap, particularly when compared with many countries overseas. If you're looking for somewhere to live or even to invest, consider the

current RMB-US dollar exchange rate. This has been gradually rising since 2005, and is unlikely to fall again, so that further appreciation will make owning a property in China a progressively better investment if you sell it and convert the proceeds into another currency.

> If you buy a property as an investment to let out, rather than to occupy, you'll be liable for income tax on the rent received. If it's a commercial property, you'll have to pay property tax and this may be extended to include residential property in the future. However, owning a desirable property in any sizeable Chinese city is unlikely to lose you money, and could prove to be an excellent long-term investment.

Shares

Investing in shares in China is very different from buying shares in the West. For a start, China's stock exchanges are unusually volatile. Between early 2006 and mid-2007 the market rose by over 200 per cent, resulting in incredible price/earnings ratios averaging almost 70:1 across the entire 1,487 shares listed on the Shanghai Stock Exchange. By late 2007, some shares had reached a p/e ratio of over 300:1. However, this couldn't last and share prices collapsed almost as quickly as they had risen. By early 2011 they had fallen to less than half their 2007 peak and have drifted ever since.

In China there's a blurred line between investing in shares and gambling. Genuine investors are rare; most are day traders who know little about the stocks they're buying and often choose them for their stock exchange number. The Chinese, inveterate gamblers to a man, buy shares with an eight or a six in the number purely because they're lucky numbers. Therefore investing in the stock exchange is like putting money on a horse: a quick thrill in the hope of an overnight windfall rather than a serious investment for the future.

An additional problem is that there's very little transparency in the shares' market and you're often, literally, investing in an unknown quantity. Thus it's a brave foreigner who plunges into the market.

There are three stock exchanges in China: Hong Kong, Shenzhen and Shanghai, which is the largest in China and the sixth-largest in the world based on turnover. The Shanghai Stock Exchange (SSE) was closed in the early days of the People's Republic of China and only reopened in late 1990. It has two share indices, covering type 'A' and type 'B' shares, and publishes their current values daily, as well as publishing the current value of a combined 'A' and 'B' shares list called the Shanghai Composite Index. It's this index that most people refer to when talking about the Chinese stock exchange.

While foreign-owned companies and institutions can buy shares, individual foreigners can only buy them through a licensed dealer in securities. You're limited to buying type 'A' shares through either a Qualified Foreign Institutional Investment (QFII) scheme on the Shanghai or Shenzhen Stock Exchange, or through Exchange Traded Funds (ETFs) on the New York Stock Exchange. Alternatively, you may buy 'H' shares via the Hong Kong Stock Exchange, which is how the celebrated Mr Warren Buffett was able to make his huge investment in the BYD car company. 'H' shares are shares in mainland-based companies that are listed on the Hong Kong Stock Exchange, but there can be a large difference in the price of 'H' shares of a mainland company and the same company's 'A' shares, with 'H' shares being much more expensive.

Shares on the Hong Kong Stock Exchange are traded in Hong Kong dollars; 'A' shares are traded in Shanghai and Shenzhen in *renminbi*, while 'B' shares are traded in US dollars on the SSE and in HK dollars in Shenzhen. Both mainland stock exchanges are open five days a week from 9.30 to 11.30am and 1 to 3pm.

Antiques & Art

With the stock market so unstable and the government attempting to dampen down investment in real estate, the Chinese are turning to art and antiques as alternative investments. Valuable paintings can fetch extraordinary amounts, and genuine ancient porcelain or jade artefacts and real Ming era furniture are almost beyond price.

Chinese bidders are gaining a reputation for pushing up prices at overseas auction houses; in November 2010, they drove up the price of an 18th century Qianlong vase to 40 times its estimate during bidding at a small London auction house – the vase had a guide price of US$1.9m and sold for US$70m, the highest price ever paid for a Chinese artwork sold at auction. This is by no means an isolated case. There's now an art 'stock exchange' in Tianjin where investors can buy shares in paintings, and in some instances investors' enthusiasm has seen the value of paintings increase 50 fold.

Sadly, the chances of finding a genuine antique are rare. Chinese craftsmen have been copying valuable items for many centuries, and it's now probably easier to find the genuine article in

New York or London than in Beijing or Shanghai. It would probably be considerably cheaper in the West. However, if you see something you like and can afford it, buy it. It may be a 17th century copy of a 15th century vase but it will still have a value, and as more antiques go into collectors' hands, so the value may well increase.

Even if you don't plan to invest, it's worth using your time in China to learn how to distinguish between a genuine antique and a copy. If nothing else, you can use this knowledge when you return to your home country, and you may even discover a Ming vase going for a song at a local auction or car boot/yard sale (it has happened).

Well-known artists enjoy almost celebrity status in China, and works by such artists as Zhao Wuji, Cui Ruzhuo, Fan Zeng and the late Wu Guanzhong can easily fetch over 1m RMB. However, paintings, like antiques, are the subject of skilful copiers, therefore it can be difficult to identify a valuable original.

Art schools turn out thousands of painters each year, all of them taught how to produce paintings in two quintessentially Chinese styles: either a black and white landscape with stylistic mountains and foaming rivers with just a tiny splash of a bright colour, usually red, highlighting a roof or a boat, or a small branch of a flowering tree with a single colourful bird. There are millions of both types of art on sale throughout the country, some very valuable, some worth nothing, but it takes years of study to distinguish the good from the bad.

Truly original art is rare. Tourists snap up so-called 'farmer's art' paintings – charming pastoral scenes of rural folk – but these are passed over by Chinese collectors who are focused on the more classical styles. Street scenes, particularly of places such as Beijing's *hutongs*, are gaining in popularity and aren't yet excessively expensive, so if you see one you like, buy it. You'll be pitting your judgement against that of expert collectors but, who knows, it could turn out one day to be the star turn at an auction. And it'll be more attractive to look at than your bank savings book.

Ming dragon jar

15.

LEISURE

Leisure is only a recent concept for many Chinese. Rural people busy on their farms have little time for relaxation, but for city dwellers the relatively recent introduction of a five-day working week, plus annual and public holidays, has opened up new possibilities for recreation, and leisure and tourism are fast becoming some of China's most important industries.

More and more foreigners are keen to discover the mysteries of a country which was long closed to the outside world; according to the World Tourism Organisation, there were almost 56m overseas visitors to China in 2010, making it the third-most visited country after France and the US. However, the domestic tourism market is equally important. In 2009, Chinese tourists made 1.9bn trips – 15 per cent up on the previous year – and contributed 1.26tn RMB (US$185bn) to the country's economy.

The attractions of China are many and diverse. It has innumerable areas of outstanding beauty, from the karst landscapes of Guilin to the waterfalls of Jiuzhaigou. There are sacred mountains, caves decorated in ancient Buddhist art, remote deserts, rare wildlife such as Sichuan's giant pandas, and some of the mightiest rivers in the world.

China has one of the oldest civilisations on earth and there's history and culture in abundance around every corner, with even the most industrialised centres preserving part of their ancient past. There are 40 UNESCO World Heritage Sites in China – only Italy and Spain have more – which include many man-made cultural treasures, such as the Great Wall, the Terracotta Army in Xi'an and the Temple of Heaven in Beijing.

Much of China's appeal lies in its living history. Cities like Pingyao in Shanxi province appear little changed since the days of the Ming Dynasty, while Beijing's *hutongs* provide a glimpse into the more recent past. Old customs and art forms still play a large part in people's lives, from calligraphy and comedy 'cross talk' (*xiangsheng*) to Chinese opera and *taijiquan*. And many of the main causes for celebration are based on old traditions, from

Tomb Sweeping Day (*Qing Ming Jie*), an ancient ritual for paying respects to ancestors, to Chinese New Year which has its roots in Taoist mythology.

As China becomes more prosperous and a middle class emerges, so Western-style leisure pursuits are developing, and new entertainment centres, galleries, museums, opera houses and sports facilities are being built, bringing high quality art, music, dance and opera to the people, as well as new recreational opportunities. Every town and city has its own tourist centre and tourist agencies serving both Chinese and foreign visitors. Meanwhile, many places of interest are being spruced up – although they're sometimes over improved at the expense of their original charms – in anticipation of increased tourism.

▲ Caution

If you can, avoid visiting popular attractions during public holidays when they're literally swamped with sightseers. It can sometimes feel as if the entire population has descended upon your chosen palace or temple all at once. It's better to visit during weekdays or out of holiday season where possible.

One of the major dilemmas for tourists is how to narrow their list of must-see places. China is an enormous country and it would take years of travel to see every place of interest. Some cities, such as Beijing, have dozens of fascinating attractions, enough to keep you busy for several weeks. However, once you've had your fill of history and culture, you can chill out in Sanya on Hainan Island, which has beaches as scenic as any in the world, or head northwest to the Kunlun Mountains, said to be the setting for the fictional Shangri La in James Hilton's *Lost Horizon*. Whatever diversion you're seeking, you'll find it in China, where every day holds the possibility of adventure and nothing is ever quite what it seems.

TOURIST INFORMATION

There's no shortage of information for tourists in China, whether in print, online or in person. You'll find tourist offices in every city and town; some are branch offices of the China Travel Service (CTS, 💻 chinatravelservice.com) or China International Tourist Service (CITS, 💻 cits.net), while others are run by the local provincial or city government or by private organisations. There are also travel agents working in large hotels.

Tourist offices can provide information about accommodation, transport, local attractions, restaurants, leisure activities and specific events, as well as arranging tickets and tours. Most offices are open between 9am and 5pm and have English-speaking staff.

If you're making plans in advance of your visit, the China National Tourist Office (💻 cnto.org) has offices around the world, including Frankfurt, Hong Kong, Kathmandu, London, Los Angeles, Madrid, New York, Osaka, Paris, Seoul, Singapore, Sydney, Tokyo, Toronto and Zurich. Britons can also contact the China Travel Service and Information Centre in London (☎ 020-7439 8888, 💻 chinatravel.co.uk).

For inspiration, there are national magazines such as *China Pictorial* (💻 chinapictorial.com.cn) which carry beautifully illustrated articles about places of unusual interest, while the *China Daily* newspaper regularly publishes travel features, and the main English-language television channel on China Central Television, CCTV News (channel 15), shows well-presented travelogues each night.

There are a great many tourist guide books about China. For English speakers, the best include the *Lonely Planet*, *Rough Guide* and *Dorling Kindersley* series, all of which are regularly updated. The best Chinese tourism websites include China Highlights (💻 chinahighlights.com/travelguide), China Tourist (💻 chinatourist.org) and the Travel China Guide (💻 chinahighlights.com/travelguide).

If you have little time and want to experience the real China and not spend all your time totally discombobulated (great word), then hire a mobile 'concierge' – fancy word for a guide – for around £100/US$150 per day (try 💻 atyourside.asia).

HOLIDAY & SHORT-TERM ACCOMMODATION

The standard of accommodation in China ranges from five-star hotels to backpacker hostels and everything in between. Until recently, there were restrictions on where foreigners could stay, but since China opened up to the West, you can find accommodation in most destinations. The only places you might have difficulty finding a room for the night are the more remote parts of the north and west, such as Inner Mongolia and parts of Sichuan province.

The greatest choice is provided by hotels, from two stars upwards, although there are some tourist guesthouses in popular areas, like the old parts of Beijing, as well as backpacker hostels in well-travelled destinations such as Lijiang and Yangshou. Camping opportunities are rare, unless you join a tour and stay in a Mongolian yurt.

Most hotels with three or more stars have a travel agency in house and can arrange trips to local places of interest, but do a little research first. Many tours are no different from those offered by a travel agency in town, but book them via a five-star hotel and you pay considerably more. Ask around town and see what excursions are on offer, and for how much, before letting your hotel book them.

A sleeper carriage on a train can be as comfortable as a three-star hotel bed, and travelling by rail for longer journeys saves you the cost of an overnight hotel stay.

Hotels

Most large international hotel groups are represented in China, including Ramada, Holiday Inn and Days Inn. If you want a relatively inexpensive yet familiar brand of hotel, Accor Group's Ibis hotels are well represented throughout much of the country. However, you aren't limited to Western hotel chains. The

Japanese, in particular, have several top class chains, such as Gloria Hotels, and there are plenty of Chinese hotels at all levels, which are more than satisfactory and usually a little cheaper than their Western or Japanese equivalents. Popular Chinese budget hotel chains include Jin Jiang (🖳 jinjianghotels.com/portal/en/index.asp), Motel 168 (🖳 motel168.com) and Home Inns (🖳 homeinns.com/index/index.aspx).

Room rates vary according to the location and season. The most expensive are in Beijing (see box) and Shanghai, particularly in central business areas and close to major tourist attractions. Rates drop dramatically in smaller, less popular towns, and you should be able to haggle down the price of a three-star hotel room to around 400 RMB a night or less. Expect to pay more during the main tourist months of May to October. In Hainan, in the far south, it can be cheaper mid-summer and more expensive in winter due to the climate, while the opposite is true in northerly Heilongjiang.

Note that rates are per room rather than per person, so there's no supplement for single occupancy of a double room.

Beijing Hotel Rates

Star Rating	Cost (RMB) Typical	Discount
2	280	180
3	540	260
4	820	410
5	1,980	770

The discount prices can be obtained by booking through one of the hotel booklets handed out at airports (see below).

Hotels display their rates at the reception desk but they're for guidance only and it's usual to ask for a discount – the receptionist expects it. However, you usually get the best discount if you pre-book your accommodation through one of the booklets given away at airports (see page 138), when you can get as much as 70 per cent off the regular rate. There are a number of websites with a facility to book hotel rooms, such as China Hotel (🖳 chinahotel.com) and Sino Hotel (🖳 sinohotel.com), but online booking isn't necessarily any cheaper than using one of the discount booklets, and if the price is posted in dollars rather than RMB it's often a sign that you're paying 'tourist prices'. For more information about hotels and rates, see **Hotels** on page 200.

Facilities

Most rooms have twin beds with distinctly firm mattresses; soft mattresses are rare in China and many Westerners take some time to adjust. If you want a double bed, you must ask for it. Otherwise rooms have most of the facilities you'd expect in a Western hotel, including central heating or air-conditioning, a television and, sometimes, a small kettle plus sachets of tea and coffee or, in a budget hotel, a flask of freshly boiled drinking water.

Virtually all hotels of three or more stars have an en-suite bathroom, although some two star hotels have only a shower. Toilets are sit-down, European style. Hotels with any pretensions provide free toiletries such as soap, razor, toothpaste and toothbrush, bath cap and shampoo, but beware of the occasional bottle of bath gel in the basin area as these are for sale, and if you sample it the cost is added to your bill.

Nice touches include two pairs of towelling slippers (free to keep) and, in posh hotels, towelling bathrobes (not free to keep!). There may be a small safe in the room or a line of safety deposit boxes close to reception, where it's advisable to store your valuables.

Breakfast, particularly in two- and three-star hotels, is usually of the Chinese variety which means starting the day with rice porridge and fried bread sticks. Western breakfasts are served only in top class hotels.

Keys are being replaced by swipe cards which you leave in a slot inside the door to activate the electricity supply. Sometimes, you can also use the card in a computer in the reception area to get an hour of free internet access each day, although a broadband connection in your room or even free wi-fi throughout the hotel are becoming increasingly common.

Checking In

Some aspects of the check-in process may be different from what you're used to. Hotels sometimes require you to pay a deposit amounting to at least one night's stay, and three-star hotels expect to be paid in cash, although more upmarket establishments accept credit cards. Make sure you're given a receipt for the payment and retain it, as you'll need it when settling your bill.

All hotels are required by law to register their guests with the local Public Security Bureau (PSB), and there's usually a lengthy form to complete. This isn't just for foreigners, but also applies to Chinese guests. It's easier to hand over your passport and let the receptionist complete the form for you.

Guesthouses & B&Bs

These are far less common than in the West, although there are guesthouses in Beijing and Shanghai and other cities popular with tourists. However, the term usually applies to small boutique hotels, often within historic buildings, rather than rooms in a family-owned boarding house, and prices can be higher than in a three-star hotel. At the other end of the scale, some 'guesthouses' are hostels. There are a number of websites offering guesthouse accommodation, including Bed and Breakfast in China (🖳 bb-china.com) and Guest in China (🖳 guestinchina.com/index.html).

Self-catering & Serviced Apartments

With hotels costing far less than in the West, self-catering accommodation isn't as in demand as in more expensive countries. However, it's possible to rent an apartment short term in major cities, either direct from the owner or through an agency. Some foreigners choose a serviced apartment rather than a hotel while they're finding their feet in China, as this provides them with more space and cooking facilities. Many are in prestigious blocks with high prices to match – as much as 1,000 RMB a night – but others can be rented for no more than the cost of a hotel room. Websites offering this kind of accommodation include the Self-catering Directory (🖳 selfcatering-directory.co.uk/results.asp?country=China), Serviced Apartments China (🖳 servicedapartmentschina.com) and Sublet (🖳 sublet.cn).

Homestays

Staying in local people's homes is usually an option when you're taking a language course and of huge benefit as it forces you to practice. Homestays are also available for travellers, and offer a unique opportunity to mix with local people and see another side of China. Homestay Booking (🖳 homestaybooking.com.cn) is a source of home stays throughout the country, even as far as Xinjiang province.

Hostels & Other Budget Accommodation

There's an expanding hostel scene in China, though it's aimed more at foreign travellers than Chinese and concentrated in popular destinations. Hostels fill a useful gap between tourist hotels and budget accommodation targeted at the Chinese. The latter ranges from hotels for business travellers (one star) which sometimes have en-suite rooms, to unlicensed boarding rooms known as *zhusu* (no stars) where you get a bed but no privacy, security or facilities. Both are usually off limits to foreigners.

Hostels, however, are usually clean and comfortable, with English-speaking hosts – often expatriates with good local knowledge – and offer the opportunity to catch up with other travellers and enjoy 'home' comforts such as Western food. Some are members of the International Youth Hostelling Association, while others are independent.

> ### ☑ SURVIVAL TIP
>
> Hostels aren't the only budget option for foreigners. It's possible to get a bed in a university dormitory during holiday periods, while some martial arts schools, e.g. those in Shaolin, provide accommodation.

Facilities

Some hostels are on a par with or even better than guesthouses and smaller hotels. As they're aimed at travellers and backpackers, they have useful facilities such as a laundry service, internet access, a library of games, books and DVDs, bicycle hire and reasonably priced food. Sometimes there's a kitchen where cash-strapped youths can cook their own meals. Many also act as mini travel agencies, arranging excursions and transportation to your next destination in the hostel 'network'. The downside is that they insulate travellers from the 'real' China, and you may not want to spend the evening listening to Aussies and Americans discussing their Great Wall experiences while eating toasted sandwiches and watching *Star Wars* on DVD. They can also be a paradise for thieves (usually other guests) and it's important to secure your valuables in the lockers provided,

Accommodation & Costs

All hostels offer budget dormitory accommodation, sometimes in single-sex dorms, but many also have private en-suite rooms. Prices start from around 40 RMB per person for a bed in a dormitory or around twice as much if you want a private room. This doesn't include breakfast, and in some hostels you may have to pay extra to hire sheets. Hostels in popular destinations fill up quickly, therefore it's essential to book in advance, which usually requires you to pay a deposit that's deducted from your final bill. There are a number of websites where you can book, including Hostel China (⌨ hostelchina.com), Hostelbookers (⌨ hostelbookers.com) and Hostelz (⌨ hostelz.com).

Youth Hostel Association

While many hostels are privately run, the Youth Hostel Association (YHA) has over 100 hostels in China, from Beijing to Lhasa. The organisation maintains strict standards in its hostels worldwide, therefore quality and safety should be guaranteed. Prices at YHA hostels start from around 25 RMB per night but can go up to 130 RMB or more, depending on the location and facilities. You must be a YHA member to stay at some hostels, which can be arranged on the spot or in advance (members may receive good discounts). Fees vary depending on where you are in the world, but in the UK the annual fee is £15.95. All YHA hostels can be booked through Hostelling International's website (⌨ hihostels.com) or via the YHA's China website (⌨ yhachina.com).

CARAVANNING & CAMPING

The Western obsession with motor homes and caravans hasn't caught on in China. There are no laws covering trailers and no ball hitches fitted to cars for hooking up a caravan. Besides which, most hotels are so cheap that there's no need to take your accommodation with you. Camping is unpopular for similar reasons. Although there are miniature tents on sale in supermarkets, most Chinese would much rather stay in a comfortable hotel, and the few campers are invariably foreign. If you set up your tent in the wilds of China, you may be approached by curious locals who feel sorry for you and offer you a bed for the night. It's important to note that camping is often regarded as suspicious behaviour by the police, and could even be dangerous.

PARKS, GARDENS & ZOOS

The Chinese make great use of their open spaces and there are many to explore, from the glorious national parks to city parks and gardens which provide an urban oasis in every town.

China has no fewer than 208 national parks, of which 183 are also recognised as 'geoparks' or areas of outstanding geological interest. The greatest number can be found in Zhejiang and Guizhou provinces, each with around 20 parks. Many parks surround sacred mountains or important rivers or lakes. Among the largest and oldest is Taihu Park in Jiangsu province, not far from Suzhou or Wuxi. It gained national park

status in 1982 and covers an area of 3,091km² (1,193mi²), much of which is taken up by Taihu Lake (Tai Hu means Grand Lake), which at 2,250 km² (869mi²) is the third-largest freshwater lake in China. Some national parks have been awarded World Heritage status, including the three peaks of Mt Sanqing in Jiangsu province and Mt Emei in Sichuan province, home to the largest stone Buddha carving in the world. For a list of national parks, see the national parks website (⌨ nationalparkofchina.com).

There are many public parks and green spaces in urban areas, some of which charge for admission (only around 5 jiao), where bicycles must usually be left outside parks. These parks are the people's playgrounds and are fascinating places to stroll around and watch the Chinese at play. In the early morning, they're the backdrop for groups of people practising taijiquan (Tai Chi), playing musical instruments or enjoying old-time dancing to the accompaniment of a portable CD player, and as the day progresses you may see troupes enacting Chinese opera, old men admiring their caged birds and people engaged in frenetic games of mahjong. At weekends there may be a temporary exhibition, perhaps of a new housing estate being constructed in the local area, so you can examine cut-away models of the apartment blocks.

Many parks feature lakes on which couples can hire boats, and there may be a pool where you can fish for tiddlers, a small fairground (perhaps with dodgem cars or a Ferris wheel) or even a mini-zoo or aviary.

There are also quieter places where you can enjoy a peaceful break from the crowded streets, and watch a father showing his child how to fly a kite or a young couple quietly talking and dreaming as they saunter by, wrapped in their own company.

Although many of the flowers, shrubs and trees grown in the West originated in China, there are officially only eight botanical gardens in China, of which the one in Beijing is the most interesting. Established in 1955, it has over 6,000 species, including indigenous plants such as peonies and camellias. The camellia is a member of the same family of shrubs as the bushes from which tea is picked and, in the hills of Sichuan, tea bushes grow as large as trees.

Modern China is a land of apartment dwellers and gardening as a recreation is unknown. Most private gardens were systematically destroyed by the Red Guards for being 'bourgeois' during the madness of the Cultural Revolution and today there are few left. However, a few remain, mostly in local government care. These include the elegant Yu Gardens in Shanghai and the delightfully named Humble Administrator's Garden, one of many classic Chinese gardens in Suzhou.

Zoos aren't seen in quite the same light as they are in the West, and most Chinese adults wouldn't consider visiting one unless it's for a child. As a result, local government ranks them pretty low down in importance, so they tend to be old and neglected, with rusting cages and a smell of ammonia. Many contain small funfairs and special sections where you can pay to see a performance, such as an exhibition of snakes. However, as prosperity spreads, zoos are being smartened up; old cages are being replaced by more animal-friendly compounds, larger aviaries and modern aquariums, and the emphasis is on conservation rather than entertainment. Beijing Zoo is home to many endangered species endemic to China, such as tigers, snow leopards and, of course, the giant panda. Even more interesting are the breeding facilities such as the giant panda sanctuaries in Sichuan province – nominated as a World Heritage Site – and the Siberian tiger park near Harbin.

Ornithologists will no doubt be aware that China is situated on one of the major migration routes for many species of birds, and bird watching is something that you can enjoy throughout the country (wetland areas are outstanding), even in the cities. One of the best places is the Zhalong Nature Preserve in Heilongjiang province. This 2,175km² (840mi²) marsh hosts over 300 species, including storks, herons and the rare Red-crowned Crane. For information, see the China Bird Watching Network website (🖵 chinabirdnet.org).

Finally, river cruising provides a unique view of the scenery and is a popular pastime with Chinese tourists. Number one on their list is the famous Three Gorges cruise along one of the most stunning sections of the Yangtze River. There are many boats plying this stretch of the river and the quality varies considerably, as do the ticket prices. Shop around to ensure that you get a well maintained boat with a good level of service and good food at a reasonable price.

MUSEUMS & GALLERIES

With a recorded history stretching back five millennia and a rich artistic culture, China is almost a living museum. Stroll through Beijing's *hutongs* – narrow alleyways with fascinating courtyard houses – or explore some of China's beautifully preserved settlements, such as the town of Lijiang in Yunnan province with its narrow waterways and stone-built houses, or the circular earthen *toulous*, Fujian province, home to the Hakka tribes, where the past feels but a breath away.

The same is true of China's many temples – Buddhist, Confucian and Taoist – where history meets religion and people come to worship as well as to view. Among the best known are the Temple of Heaven in Beijing and the Shaolin Temple where monks perfected their skills at *gong fu* (kung fu). However, there are lesser known gems such as the White Horse Temple outside Luoyang in Henan, which many believe to be the first Buddhist temple in China, and the Hanging Temple which clings precariously to the side of a cliff in Mt Heng, Shanxi province.

⚠ Caution

Some of China's most revered temples and spectacular views are situated at the peak of the country's many sacred mountains, and it takes some dedication to climb them. In some cases, the route can be distinctly dangerous, notably Mt Hua, east of Xi'an in Shanxi province, where the combination of ice and narrow wooden walkways on the side of precipitous cliffs makes it suitable only for the most fit and fearless.

Museums abound in China, where there are almost 3,000 in total, featuring over 20m exhibits. Beijing alone boasts over 100, of which the Palace Museum, otherwise known as the Forbidden City – home to China's emperors for some 500 years – is probably the most iconic. However, there are many more in the capital, including

Forbidden City

from 9am to 5pm. They're usually spotlessly clean and well organised, with exhibits labelled in Chinese and English, and the larger ones have lifts and escalators, providing easy access for disabled and elderly people.

CINEMA

Despite the availability of newly released films on cheap (pirated) DVDs, Chinese cinemas do good business and attendance is increasing. Modern cinemas are opening across the country, many are multi-screen complexes with comfortable seating – some even have overstuffed armchairs and sofas rather than rows of seats – but there are still plenty of old fleapits where the seats are cramped if you're taller than 6ft (1.83m).

The majority of films on general release are Chinese made. There's a limit on the number of foreign films which can be imported each year – in 2012 it was just 20 films – and therefore the only ones that make it are the major Hollywood blockbusters such as *Titanic* and *Avatar*. These are frequently dubbed into Chinese but carry English subtitles. However, in the major cities, where large numbers of expatriates live, there are cinema clubs where you can watch overseas films in their original language, including smaller-budget productions and art films.

Chinese films are often characterised by their gorgeous cinematography and their sad endings; most conclude with the hero and heroine either dead or dying and a Chinese film with a happy ending is rare, although there are also comedies, action adventures and even horror films. Well known directors include Ang Lee (*Crouching Tiger, Hidden Dragon*, *Lust, Caution*), Zhang Yimou (*Hero*, *House of Flying Daggers*) and Feng Xiaogang (*Aftershock*). Well-known actors and actresses include Jackie Chan, Gong Li and Zhang Ziyi, all of whom have appeared in Chinese and overseas productions. For more information about Chinese cinema, there are a number of good websites including Film in China (💻 china.org.cn/english/features/film/84528.htm) and the Chinese Movie Database (💻 dianying. com/en).

The main cinema chains are Wanda Cinema (💻 wandafilm.com), UME Cineplex and the Polybona chain. Some cinemas have websites, and all print leaflets detailing what's on and when, while local papers also print details of films (but

the fascinating Military Museum of the Chinese People's Revolution and the splendid Museum of Natural History. Aircraft buffs will enjoy a trip to the China Aviation Museum in Changping County, around 64km (40mi) north of the city; built on an old fighter airstrip with entry along a taxiway, it's a great day out. Shanghai, too, is good for museums, and the eponymous Shanghai Museum has one of the best collections in China.

Most museums display collections of artefacts which were locally made or unearthed, including bronze, jade, embroidery, porcelain and pottery – Xi'an's Terracotta Army is one of China's most visited museums – but there are others which commemorate important events and people, such as the Sun Yat-sen Memorial Hall in Guangzhou. There's also a wealth of museums dedicated to subjects as diverse as tea, silk, coal and even dinosaurs. What's amazing about Chinese museums is the extraordinary amount of ancient artefacts on display, many of which have only been discovered in recent years, and the exquisite quality of the workmanship.

China also has many galleries, both public and private, of which the premier draw is the National Art Museum of China in Beijing (💻 namoc.org/en). The Chinese are avid collectors of art, and there are displays of paintings and photographs in most cities, as well as crafts such as paper cutting and calligraphy. Many exhibits are for sale, although most are expensive, and you must employ your best bargaining skills if you wish to buy one for a reasonable price.

Most museums charge a relatively low admission price. For example, it costs around 60 RMB to visit the Palace Museum, but most charge only a third of this price and some are free. Discounts for children and older people are often available. Museums and galleries are open not the screening times). You can book tickets in advance, although it's rarely necessary.

Cinema tickets cost between 25 and 80 RMB and there are discounts at less popular times. Eating in cinemas is allowed – and yes, you can buy popcorn – but smoking is prohibited and if your mobile phone rings, the etiquette is to leave the auditorium and ring the caller back.

⚠ Caution

There's no system of film classification in China and no age restrictions. In theory, you can take a five-year-old to see the goriest horror film. It's up to you to check that the content of a film is suitable for younger viewers.

TELEVISION STUDIOS

There are a surprising number of television studios in China, and joining the studio audience, particularly in studios outside Beijing, isn't difficult. Every provincial capital city has at least two TV studios, and seats are usually available and free – just enquire at the gate – so you can watch programmes being recorded, from game shows to soaps. It's fascinating seeing the sometimes flimsy scenery used to provide lifelike effects, and if you have teenage children you'll have trouble dragging them away.

PERFORMING ARTS & MUSIC

There are two essentially Chinese performing arts which have been around for several centuries: Chinese opera and shadow play. The latter is an ancient art which uses articulated puppets behind an opaque screen to tell stories, but while it can still be seen in some provincial theatres, it has been largely consigned to history by the advent of cinema and television. Chinese opera, on the other hand, is flourishing. Unlike opera in the West, it has universal appeal and even has its own dedicated television channel.

Chinese opera uses a combination of music, theatre, acrobatics and dance to tell stories based on popular legends and folktales and featuring much loved characters, such as the Monkey King in *Journey to the*

West. Occasionally, it bases its performances on Western classics, e.g. Shakespeare's *A Midsummer Night's Dream*. Foreigners sometimes mistakenly refer to it as Beijing opera but there are many regional variations, and an aficionado can easily distinguish between, say, Shanghai opera and Shanxi or Cantonese opera. Equally, to a foreign ear it can seem boring and overlong, but it's worth persevering – tune in to CCTV's channel 11 for a taster – as some of the skills of the performers, such as the way they change their faces at lightning speed, are fascinating to watch, and some of the music is quite beautiful.

Straight theatre is far less popular. In 2010, there were just 36 theatres in China – four of which were opera houses – which hosted a variety of performances, including Chinese opera, ballet, music concerts, martial arts performances and, occasionally, theatrical productions from overseas. However, there's a move to build modern entertainment and arts centres in many cities and the number of theatre venues will increase.

China has its own national ballet troupe which performs both Western and Chinese dance. Most performances, however, revolve around the half dozen ballets produced during the time of the Cultural Revolution at the behest of Mao Zedong's last wife, Jiang Qing. Designed to replace the bourgeois entertainment of the West, they're overtly political but still entertaining and some have become classics, such as *The Red Detachment of Women*, the story of an all-female troupe in the Red Army, which was famously performed during the 1972 visit by US President Nixon, and *The White Haired Girl*. Part of the fun is hearing the audience cheer so spontaneously when the heroes triumph and the villains are overcome.

Concerts are also popular. The programme often includes both Western compositions and Chinese works such as the *Butterfly Lovers* concerto, one of China's best-loved classical pieces. During the interludes, there's often a

National Centre for the Performing Arts, Beijing

Chengdu Opera Theatre

chance to hear music played on ancient musical instruments. There are also performances by world-famous artists and groups, as well as Chinese stars such as singers Liu Huan and Fei Yu Qin and the Hong Kong rock band Beyond, which take place in sports' stadiums. Tickets are expensive by Chinese standards but a bargain for expatriates.

Finally, there are the circuses and acrobatic performances. Many Westerners have seen the incredible feats of the Shaolin monks who display their *gong fu* (martial arts) skills on worldwide tours, and similar shows are performed throughout China. Circuses are also popular, where the emphasis is on acrobatic skills rather than performing elephants or lions – few circuses include animal acts – and include juggling, balancing and trapeze work. These shows are a huge hit with children, especially as some of the performers are as young as nine or ten years old.

PHOTOGRAPHY

China is extraordinarily photogenic. Its geography encompasses a cornucopia of landscapes, from the terraced rice paddies and tea gardens of the south to the great mountain ranges and deserts of the north and west, while its people display a wide range of features. In many ways, it's a photographer's dream, other than on days when pollution renders the landscape misty or invisible.

Many keen snappers head for Guilin in the southern Guangxi region where the landscape, dotted with mini-mountains, is outstanding. Where else in the world can you find a teachers' training college with its own mountain in the grounds or a karst mountain that you can climb for a stunning view of the surrounding city? Guilin is unique and a trip up the River Li to Yangshuo is a must, although there are many lesser-known places to focus on. Xikou, 60km (37mi) south of Ningbo in Zhejiang province, provides some stunning historic subjects. This was the birthplace of Chiang Kai Shek, leader of the Kuomintang nationalist party and an opponent of Mao Zedong; the view from his house, overlooking vast areas of terraced mountainside rice paddies, is outstanding. Not far away, nestling in the middle of a lake, is the delightfully pretty home of one of his girlfriends. Amazingly, none of these buildings were damaged by the Red Guards during the Cultural Revolution and all are very photogenic. However, these are just two examples; wherever you go in China, there's always something or somebody beautiful or unique which demands to be photographed.

⚠ Caution

There are some subjects which you must avoid. Never take photos of anything to do with the Chinese armed forces. The police may also object to you photographing places that could be considered as strategically important, such as bridges or railway stations. They can also be annoyed if they see you photographing anything that they feel could be regarded as derogatory to China and its people. The Chinese are proud of their country and, like most people, don't like being criticised

The Chinese, many of whom have fascinating faces, make wonderful subjects, especially some of the ethnic minorities with their colourful costumes. Most don't mind being snapped, although it's polite to ask someone first, by gestures if need be. If they decline, don't push it.

Camera equipment and film is available in China, although not to the extent that it's in the West. Cameras, whether imported or made by overseas companies in China, such as Olympus, cost much the same as they do in Europe or the US. You can buy them in department stores or supermarkets, although if you're looking for a specific lens you must visit a specialist camera shop. The same applies to repairs.

There are two major Chinese camera manufacturers: Phenix and Seagull. Phenix produces SLR cameras for use with film as well as digital models, and both are widely available. Seagull has had problems and it isn't easy to locate new stock, although secondhand models can be found. Other than these two, there are a number of other companies producing 'point and shoot' film cameras that are inexpensive.

China is one of the last bastions of film cameras, as apposed to digital. Both locally-made Kodak and Fuji film is on sale everywhere, together with two or three local manufacturers' products. Most film sold in China is ASA 100 colour film, but ASA 200 is becoming more popular and ASA 400 can be obtained. Black and white film or films for slides are usually only sold in Beijing or Shanghai. Film processing is quick and cheap but places which can print from the memory card of a digital camera are more limited. Print-it-yourself machines are rare outside major cities.

SOCIAL CLUBS

There are a number of private clubs in China, some of which are exclusive and expensive to join. Members enjoy facilities such as restaurants, swimming pools, gyms and saunas, and sports such as table tennis; some even have a fishing lake or gardens. They're aimed at Chinese businessmen who use them for meetings and while foreigners can join, they find themselves socialising almost exclusively with Chinese members.

There are also expatriate clubs, based mainly in cities with a large expat population. Well-known organisations include the Rotary Club, Hash House Harriers and the American Club, all of which have branches in China. Chambers of commerce can put you in touch with clubs catering for people from your home country, while your embassy may also have details. There are also many smaller clubs, which may advertise in expat publications, on websites and on notice boards.

CELEBRATIONS

For many people, the most important leisure activities centre on national holidays, especially Chinese New Year. For some migrant workers, this is their one chance to travel home, while many city dwellers take advantage of the extended break to go on holiday.

Chinese New Year (*Chun Jie*), and the Spring Festival which follows it, takes place in late January or February – depending on the lunar calendar – and lasts for up to 15 days. It's as big a celebration as Christmas is in Western countries. The entire country begins to shut down in the run up to New Year; houses are swept, new clothes purchased and lucky signs displayed on front doors. At midnight, the coming year is ushered in to a salvo of firecrackers; the crescendo of noise is intended to drive away bad fortune.

Chinese New Year is a time for families to get together. Special food is served, such as dumpling 'purses', and the emphasis is on creating an auspicious atmosphere which, it's hoped, will last throughout the coming year. It culminates in the Lantern Festival, when people take to the streets, with children carrying red paper lanterns with candles inside to illuminate the months ahead.

New Year isn't the only Chinese festival. China has seven national holidays and all have a special significance – there's a list of dates in **Chapter 2**. There are also some important days celebrated in certain areas or by specific sections of the population (see box).

NIGHTLIFE

There are few places quieter than a Chinese city after 11pm. Shops and workplaces are closed

	Special Holidays	
Date	**Holiday**	
February	Tiancang Festival. Farmers set aside this time to pray for a good harvest in the coming year.	
March	Guanyin's Birthday. This goddess of mercy is revered by Buddhists and Taoists with celebrations at temples.	
Mid-April	Water Splashing Day. An important time in Yunnan province. when people throw water over each other to ensure a fresh, clean start to the coming year.	
May 4th	Youth Day. This date commemorates the uprising in 1911 which marked the shift of power from the emperor to the people. Many people lay flowers on memorials.	
July 1st	Chinese Communist Party Day. A celebration of the founding of the CPC.	
Aug 1st	Army Day. This date marks the establishment of the People's Liberation Army.	
August	Ghost month. The Chinese version of Halloween; August is considered to be a bad month to travel or get married.	
Sept 28th	Confucius Festival. The great man's birthday is celebrated in all Confucian temples, but particularly at his birthplace in Qufu, Shandong province.	

and families are at home, and the streets are empty apart from road gangs repairing potholes. However, this is an illusion. Behind closed doors the bars are doing a roaring trade, many not closing until the last customer leaves. Discos and dance halls are full of young people and the karaoke bars are just getting into their stride.

Many Chinese cities have a lively nightlife, although it only attracts a small percentage of the population. There are plenty of bars (see below), but if you want to see and be seen or attract the opposite sex, there are discothèques and dance halls playing the latest music, although anyone aged over 30 sticks out like a sore thumb. Clubs range from smart and sophisticated to jam-packed and deafening, and most don't get going until after 10pm. Entrance fees vary depending on the club's prestige but you could pay up to 150 RMB to get into a top city nightclub, although women are sometimes admitted free (but not men). Night clubs are a hotspot for drug dealing and are subject to checks by plain clothes police. They're also the haunt of 'working girls' and not all female attention is genuine.

The other late night destination is karaoke bars, although these also open during the day. The Chinese love karaoke, which involves singing the lyrics to hit songs, both Chinese and Western, to words displayed on a screen. A great voice isn't a prerequisite – some 'singers' are totally out of tune – although the Chinese take it quite seriously. Most bars have private soundproofed rooms where groups can sing together, although hiring one isn't cheap. Daytime prices start from 25 RMB an hour, and at night the price shoots up to 200 RMB or even higher.

Most karaoke bars provide alcohol to loosen the vocal chords, as well as female 'hostesses' to loosen other parts of your anatomy. These are called *san pei xiaoji* which literally means 'three company girls': they provide company while you sing, company while you eat or drink, and company in bed. They're a major part of many karaoke bars' business, but be warned that an evening in their company ends up costing much more than the price of a few beers!

GAMBLING

Since 1949, gambling has been illegal in China, but the Chinese are great gamblers and many cannot resist the opportunity to bet on a game of chance. For most, this is limited to penny stakes on card games or mahjong, and you'll see people trying their luck at tables set up on footpaths or under trees in a park in warmer weather. It's usually just a game of fun, although gambling addiction is a growing problem. The government has estimated that as much as 1tn RMB may be staked each year on illegal gaming, from 'private' card and mahjong clubs to gambling websites.

Mahjong

Legal gambling is available in Hong Kong and Macau, and many mainlanders travel to these autonomous regions to get their fix. There are 26 casinos in Macau, while Hong Kong has a jockey club and two racecourses. The largest and most prosperous punters at these gambling venues mostly come from the Chinese mainland.

The internet has created further opportunities for gambling via electronic betting. Gaming websites are firmly on the government's list of undesirable influences, and there are repeated crackdowns on any based in China, although overseas sites pop up as fast as the state can block them.

There are signs that, in a small way, restrictions on gambling are beginning to relax. Since 2004, there has been horse racing at a course in Wuhan, and Beijing now has a Jockey Club. However, it's treated as a sport rather than a betting opportunity, and there are no lists of runners and riders printed in newspapers.

The only legal gambling in China is provided by official lotteries. These are run by state or provincial governments, with tickets sold at tobacconists and kiosks, with the proceeds going to fund sports and welfare programmes. They're low-key affairs and aren't widely advertised, although the prizes can be enormous – one lucky winner scooped over 83m RMB.

BARS & PUBS

Although most large hotels have bars, the busiest bars and pubs are usually independent and located on a street where every building is a bar. Most have background or live music and/or huge TV screens showing sport, and sell beer, spirits and simple food to soak up the alcohol. Despite recent laws to curb smoking in public places, in many bars smoking is rampant.

There are no licensing laws in China and bars can stay open all day, although most don't get busy until around 9 or 10pm. Drinks aren't particularly cheap unless you turn up at 'happy hour' early on in the evening.

In expat bars, beer is by far the most popular drink and some serve draught beer with a glass usually costing between 15 and 25 RMB. It's worth asking around for suggestions for good bars, as some can be rather seedy and drinkers prey for bar girls, some of whom are little different from the 'three company' girls who hang out in karaoke clubs.

Some bars cater mainly to Chinese patrons, although for most Chinese alcohol is best consumed over a meal, and standing up at a bar and downing beer after beer isn't for them. Nonetheless, many Chinese do drink too much, when it's common for friends to rally round and steer them quietly out of the bar and, if possible, into a taxi (although many insist on driving, which is a serious problem in China). It's something which the police are cracking down on and is very risky, as you stand a good chance of being stopped and breathalysed.

Beer

The best-selling beer in China is called Tsingtao. It's a German-style lager that was originally brewed by the Germans when they had a concession in Qingdao in Shandong province in 1903 and is still produced there today and sold worldwide. Tsingtao has the same alcohol content as Budweiser beer and is sold on draught, or in 330ml cans and bottles as well as 375 and 750ml bottles. In Qingdao you can also buy it by the kilo, and you see people walking down the street with a plastic bag full of beer.

Tsingtao has many imitators and a good, drinkable lager style beer is brewed in almost every large city in the country. In a supermarket, beer costs between 3 and 3.50 RMB for a 375ml bottle whereas in a bar it costs five or six times as much, although many smaller restaurants charge a lot less for a beer than you would pay in a bar.

Most of the large international breweries have entered the Chinese market, often via joint ventures with Chinese brewers, and locally-made San Miguel beer, for example, is available in many places costing not much more than Tsingtao. It's also possible to find imported beers in supermarkets, but these tend to be expensive at 12 to 20 RMB a can.

If you aren't a fan of lager, some local brewers produce a dark beer that some drinkers enjoy, but it's best to steer clear of beer made from bitter melon. This is alleged to have health properties but tastes unlike any other beer anywhere in the world, and definitely isn't designed for Western palates.

Beijing's Bier Keller

Paulaner, the Munich brewer, has a small restaurant and micro-brewery in the Lufthansa Building on the East Third Ring Road in Beijing, as well as several branches around the country. Here, you can eat sausages and sauerkraut washed down with a cold wheat beer brewed on the premises and served by a Chinese girl dressed in a dirndl skirt. It's a bizarre experience, but both the beer and the sausages are excellent.

Wine

The Chinese have moved into wine production in a big way, and some experts predict that it could become the world's largest wine producer in the next 50 years, a suggestion that will send a shiver down the backs of most French vignerons. A Chinese wine (Jia Bei Lan from He Lan Qing Xue vineyards) won the award for 'Best Bordeaux Variental' in 2011 at the Decanter World Wine awards – appalling its grand French rivals – who probably won't turn up next year! In 2009, China produced 72m cases of wine, up 28 per cent on the previous year, and is now the sixth-largest producer in the world. As yet, much of the 'wine' made in China is awful: sweet grape juice, totally unfermented. However, a number of the larger and better established producers have learned how to make a perfectly acceptable wine, particularly reds based on the Cabernet Sauvignon grape.

Geographically, much of China is on the perfect latitude for wine production, and many wineries have been established in Shandong province. Among the largest producers are Chateau Chengyu, Great Wall and Dynasty, all of which produce a huge variety of different wines at widely varying prices. Of the smaller vineyards it's worth keeping an eye open for Dragon Seal, a winery with vineyards not far from Beijing. A joint venture with Remy Martin, employing an Australian vigneron, Dragon Seal produces a drinkable Cabernet Sauvignon and Chardonnay, which costs around 60 RMB a bottle in supermarkets.

How well the wine industry develops in China is dependent on the Chinese taste for wine, consumption of which is increasing, although it's seen as an upmarket drink. Many Chinese quaff wine like beer and there's a belief that Europeans only sip wine because they cannot afford to drink it quickly, whereas the wealthy Chinese can pour it down their throats!

Other Drinks

The Chinese national spirit is *baijiu*, a clear spirit made from rice, sorghum or millet, drunk from tiny glasses in one gulp. Toasts, which punctuate meals and banquets, are an essential part of Chinese culture and can be a risky business for unsuspecting foreigners. The quantities seem small but *baijiu* is high in alcohol. The two best known producers are Maotai and Wuliangyu, although there are countless other brands and shops that sell nothing but *baijiu* in every town.

Western spirits such as whisky and gin are much less popular. The only one to make a real impact in China is brandy, partly because XO quality brandy is very expensive and therefore makes an impressive gift for someone of importance (rare malt whisky has a similar cachet).

There are plenty of non-alcoholic drinks. Cola is universal, but the Chinese make some pleasant and interesting soft drinks from unlikely sounding ingredients such as apricot stones and lotus roots that are definitely worth trying.

Licensing Laws

There are no clear licensing laws in China, and beer and alcohol may be sold anywhere and at any time and, apparently, to anyone, although there seems to be a general view that alcohol is for those aged over 18.

CHINESE FOOD

China is often said to be home to one of the world's great cuisines, but in fact it's home to a number of different cuisines. There are several distinctive traditions of Chinese food, of which four take prominence. Cantonese food from the south of China emphasises freshness and quality and aims to appeal to the eye as well as the palate: this is the home of *dim sum*, tasty morsels artistically presented. Shandong cooking from the north is more substantial, with its reliance on noodles, breads and dumplings, well-seasoned with garlic and soy sauce. Shanghai food is sweeter and richer and makes great use of its coastal location by serving up a great variety of seafood and fish. The most fiery food is cooked in western Sichuan province, where the eponymous pepper is used to great effect in chilli-hot dishes such as Kung Pao chicken, named after a former provincial governor.

There are restaurants in China serving Western food, but they're overwhelmingly outnumbered by Chinese restaurants. The Chinese eat out a lot. Every family event,

celebration and business transaction involves a trip to a restaurant. People regard their home as private, therefore if you're invited for a meal, nine times out of ten it will be in a restaurant. This makes it difficult for a foreigner to sample Chinese 'home cooking', although it still gives you the opportunity to experience a wide range of incredible foods.

Chinese food in China is usually very different from the 'Chinese' food that your local take-away sells at home. Apart from sweet and sour dishes, most Chinese food served overseas is but a pale imitation of real Chinese food, and has been adapted to suit local tastes and available ingredients. Most food is either boiled, steamed or stir fried, although other cooking methods are used. China's most famous dish, *Beijing kao ya* (Beijing roast duck), is roasted into crispy skinned perfection, while grilled kebabs are a staple in the Muslim Xinjiang region.

It's a fallacy that the Chinese only eat rice. It's only in the south, where rice is grown, that it's the staple starch; in other parts of China, noodles, dumplings and even bread are eaten instead, and you can usually order alternatives from the menu.

The Chinese don't just eat things because they taste good. They attribute health properties to almost every dish and ingredient, and while their diet lacks many foods that Westerners rely on, such as butter and cheese, it's remarkably healthy. There are a great many elderly Chinese who have thrived on a very restricted diet.

Stories that the Chinese eat the most extraordinary things are exaggerated. While it's true that in the south, in Guangdong especially, people have a taste for foods that appear very strange to many foreigners, such as scorpions, snakes, frogs and crocodiles, most people (most of the time) eat simple dishes of vegetables with small quantities of meat or fish with rice or noodles. You may, on occasion, be offered something unusual, such as shark's fin (called shark's wing by the Chinese) soup or sea cucumber (sea slug or *beche de mer*), which you'll probably find unpalatable or even repellent. These are a real treat for Chinese diners – both dishes are very expensive – and they'll be presented to you as an honoured guest, not as a trick to make the foreigner squirm. The most appropriate response is to eat a little bit to acknowledge your host's kindness and then push the rest around the plate.

Meat

The most commonly eaten meat in China is pork, which finds its way in a multitude of ways into many dishes. Virtually every part of the pig ends up on a plate – even the ears and genitalia – and if a dish is described as containing 'meat' it usually means pork. Lamb and mutton are popular in Muslim restaurants and beef is also widely eaten, as is chicken. In many cases, meat is cut into small pieces – which are easier to handle with chopsticks – and fried quickly over high heat (stir fried). The downside to this is that few Chinese are able to cook or appreciate a good steak. Most steaks, even expensive imported beef, are beaten to a pulp before being (over)cooked and ruined.

Fish

Fish is more expensive than meat, and a large fish, cooked whole, often forms the centrepiece of a meal. Many, however, are river fish, farmed locally and full of bones. Watch out for this; filleting out fish bones with chopsticks isn't easy. Shellfish are also popular, with prawns available year round and crab best in the autumn months.

Vegetarian Food

Vegetarianism isn't an alien concept in China, where poorer people still eat a largely vegetarian diet. As a result, while there are specialist vegetarian restaurants in China, you can select vegetarian dishes in most restaurants. Try mushrooms with green vegetables (*qing cai mogu*) or one of the many eggplant (aubergine) dishes, which are usually well prepared and tasty. The humble soya bean has an honoured place in Chinese menus and protein-rich tofu (*dofu*) is served in many ways, e.g. fried, boiled and even raw. It makes an excellent alternative to meat.

On occasion, vegetable dishes may be 'enriched' with a meat-based stock or even slivers of meat, so strict vegetarians should check beforehand. One way of guaranteeing that you won't be served any meat (or chicken or fish) is to say that you're a Buddhist ('*Wo xin fuo*').

RESTAURANTS & CAFES

Eating places run the whole gamut from 'greasy spoons', where the very simplest and cheapest dishes are served in less than hygienic circumstances, to the most elegant restaurants. Some, such as Quanjude and Bianyifang which hold the 'trademark' for Beijing roast duck, are deservedly world famous. Most restaurants are large and noisy but, in addition to the main dining area, there a number of private rooms if you prefer a more intimate atmosphere. Eating out of doors, European style, is unusual.

The menu is invariably in Chinese, although some restaurants also provide pictures of dishes. The only way to be certain about what you're ordering is to eat with a Chinese friend or learn the characters for certain foods such as pork (猪肉), chicken (鸡肉) and fish (鱼肉). Menus rarely include the names of the dishes in pinyin. It's easier to order in simple workers' restaurants as you can simply point at what you want.

Alcohol is usually available, even in the cheapest eateries. Beer, in particular, is often cheaper in a restaurant than in a bar, but bringing your own wine isn't a local custom. For non-drinkers there's often yoghurt or fruit juice available.

> All restaurants serve either tea or hot water as a matter of course. If you want cold water you must ask for it, as the Chinese don't drink it, regarding it to be bad for the digestion.

Western-style Restaurants

There are a limited number of restaurants that specialise in non-Chinese food, with by far the largest selection available in major cities to cater to the tastes of expatriates and wealthy Chinese diners. Italian dishes such as pizza and pasta are the easiest to find, but there are also some serving German, Indian, Japanese, Korean, Thai and Turkish food – the food of the Uyghur people in Xinjiang province, with its kebabs, breads and soups, is similar to Turkish cuisine. Argentinian and Brazilian restaurants, which specialise in

a far cry from the slick and impersonal American coffee chains. They're often large and seat as many as 200 people on comfortable sofas, but in the mid-morning or afternoon they provide an oasis of calm and peace, with unobtrusive but attentive service. Even in the evenings, when they're much busier, coffee houses are still relaxed places, unlike the noisy hustle and bustle of most restaurants. The main clientele are well-off businessmen or young executives entertaining their girlfriends; children and old people rarely visit them.

barbecued meat, are popular with expats as an alternative to badly cooked steaks.

Fast Food

Western fast food franchises are gaining ground in China, although their menus often have a Chinese twist. Kentucky Fried Chicken (KFC) is China's largest fast food franchise (it makes half its revenue in China) and has extended its menu to include Chinese style dishes such as congee (rice porridge) on its breakfast menu, as well as some interesting teas. Pizza Hut also offers an extensive menu full of dishes unavailable in their restaurants elsewhere, including crispy squid and snails. McDonalds is less attentive to local tastes and serves up its international menu. Incidentally, many Chinese believe that the singer Madonna is somehow related to McDonalds, probably because both words are pronounced the same. At all three franchises, the core products taste exactly as they do anywhere else in the world.

Not to be outdone, Chinese chefs have created their own versions of US-style fast food. The two major chains are Dicos which serves up burgers and chips plus a short menu of Chinese dishes, and Mister Lee which majors on Chinese dishes such as noodles. Both are great value when you need a quick bite.

Possibly the fastest and cheapest food of all is on sale at roadside stalls. Chinese street food is freshly prepared and often delicious, and includes stuffed steamed buns, barbecued meat on sticks, dumplings and, of course, the ubiquitous noodles.

Coffee Houses

Chinese coffee houses are quite unlike cosy European cafés and coffee bars, but are equally

The coffee is individually ground to order and excellent, but isn't cheap, often costing 30 to 35 RMB a cup. There's usually an extensive menu of Chinese and faux Western dishes and drinks, but you should ignore these and concentrate on the coffee or, if you fancy trying something different, try one of the fruit teas. Often flavoured with grapefruit or pomelo (a similar citrus fruit), they come in fat little glass teapots, kept warm over a tiny heater, and frequent top ups of hot water are included in the price, which is much lower than a cup of coffee.

Teahouses

Tea is China's national drink and the tradition of the teahouse goes back many centuries. Today, however, many teahouses are visitor attractions – aimed at Chinese tourists as well as foreigners – and expensive ones at that. The tea ceremony, which is now rarely performed in people's houses, involves sampling a variety of teas from tiny cups, presented on a wooden board. It's conducted by girls dressed in traditional *qipao* dresses who tell you about the different teas. It's an enjoyable and instructive way to while away a few hours, although you're paying for the experience and the atmosphere rather than the tea: typically a visit to a teahouse costs between 60 and 100 RMB per person. At the end of the ceremony, the girls try with great charm to persuade you to purchase some tea to take away with you. This costs many times more than it would in the local supermarket, so check the price carefully before agreeing to buy.

Prices

The size of the bill depends on where you eat, but you can enjoy a bowl of noodles with meat for just 7 or 8 RMB in a workers' restaurant, whereas a full meal in a smart restaurant costs 50 to 100 RMB per person. Prices don't include alcoholic drinks. Coffee houses serve simple meals for around 40 to 60 RMB, and a burger at a fast food chain is considerably cheaper than in Europe, a Big Mac costing just 15 RMB.

Only top-end restaurants add a service charge, usually around 10 per cent. In most places, however, service is included in the price of the meal and you aren't expected to tip.

▲ Caution

Never leave a tip in a restaurant. It isn't expected and is embarrassing for the staff.

Opening Times

Workers' restaurants open early to catch the breakfast trade, and you can eat from around 6am in the morning. Many places remain open all day, although in smaller towns restaurants may close in the afternoon and reopen again at around 6.30pm for dinner. As a rule the Chinese don't eat late, and many places stop serving at 9pm. If you want to eat later, you must go to an up-market hotel, where they're more attuned to foreigners' strange eating habits, or to a coffee house or street stall.

Bookings & Dress

Booking is rarely necessary, although people eat their evening meal early and if you arrive much after 6.30pm, you may have to wait for a table. As for dress, there are no strict rules; just use your common sense. Jeans are okay if you're popping out for dumplings or noodles, but if your boss invites you to a banquet, you should dress up for the occasion.

16.
SPORTS

C hina isn't a particularly sporting nation, despite its excellent achievements at the 2008 Beijing Olympics, when its athletes won exactly 100 medals, including 51 golds – the highest gold-medal tally in the competition, and 15 more than the second-placed USA. Most Chinese prefer a second (or third) class ride to a first class walk, and many view the effort that foreigners put into jogging as slightly deranged. Setting aside time to work out is not part of the Chinese psyche and many people disdain the concept of organised sports.

However, most people are aware of the importance of exercise, good breathing and a properly balanced diet, and most are quite possibly fitter than the populations of more developed countries. For the Chinese, exercise is a way of life, something which they incorporate into their daily lives for practical and social reasons. The vast majority still labour in the fields and get around by bicycle, and many city dwellers enjoy group activities such as martial arts or old-time dancing in the park.

China's favourite form of exercise is derived from martial arts. Early morning, rain or shine, every park is dotted with people, often in groups, practicing the basic movements used in *taijiquan* and *gong fu* (respectively called Tai Chi and Kung Fu in the West), two of the most popular martial arts. These surprisingly strenuous exercises, which are usually performed very slowly, have been developed over centuries and help to build and maintain muscle strength and flexibility, and to instil a sense of relaxation and calm. Many participants are elderly, but perform them with ease as they've been doing them all their lives.

The state supports exercise, and in the mid-'90s initiated a nationwide physical fitness programme. Money was set aside for gym equipment, available to all, and most parks have open-air fitness centres featuring strong metal exercise bars and weights machines, usually painted bright yellow and tough enough to withstand the elements. These are in use, all day every day, by people of both sexes from the ages of eight to 88. Many parks also have concrete ping pong tables where the Chinese can indulge their passion for table tennis.

Apart from the Olympics, there are a number of regular sporting tournaments which take place in China, including the Asian Games. The premier domestic event is the National Games of the People's Republic of China, a tournament for top athletes which takes place every four years. The All-China Sports Federation (⌨ sport.org.cn) oversees individual sports associations across the country, while the government body in charge of sport is the State General Administration of Sports.

Despite the positive attitude towards fitness and the admiration that is heaped on to sporting heroes, there's little encouragement and enthusiasm for amateur sports. There are no public football pitches or golf courses, and in many cities there's just one sports centre catering for up to 4m people. As a result, there are few amateur football or hockey teams except for those organised by expatriates.

Chinese schools include physical exercise in their curricula and most have a yard with basketball hoops, although playing fields are a rare luxury and organised inter-school competitions are rare, not least because Chinese children spend most of their time studying. Facilities at universities are better. Many have football and basketball pitches, tennis courts and a gym, plus amenities for table tennis and badminton, and sometimes a swimming pool and running track. However, once again, the pressure of work means that organised matches against other universities are staged infrequently, although most establishments hold a sports day in the summer.

For those who want to make sport their career, there are special academies and some have turned out international sporting stars, such as basketball's Yao Ming and table tennis dynamo Deng Yaping. However, most Chinese, once they leave full-time education, view amateur sport as a frivolity for which they have little spare time. Those that do take part are often upwardly-mobile young people who favour more exclusive sports such as skiing, or those which have the potential to enhance their earning prospects, such as golf or tennis.

☑ **SURVIVAL TIP**

For many foreigners, joining a local sports team is a great way to meet and keep in touch with their fellow countrymen (and women), and most of the major cities have clubs you can join. In many instances, it's the embassies and consulates that organise matches and provide many of the players. However, social clubs, expat bars and workplaces also field teams, and if you keep your eyes and ears open it's possible to take part in many different sports while in China.

AERIAL SPORTS

Private aviation isn't encouraged in China, where there are tight restrictions on airspace and a lot of no-fly zones. Consequently, it has fewer than 300 private aircraft in total, a tiny number compared with the 230,000 plus in the US. Cessna has recently built a factory in Shenyang to manufacture the Cessna 162 Skycatcher aircraft and these are now being sold mainly overseas including to the USA and will be used primarily to train commercial pilots. In 2012, Cessna reached agreement to use their Shenyang factory to also produce small business jets. In China it has now become possible to both hire a business jet and to learn how to fly but the requirements for obtaining a private pilot's licence are extremely complex. Many business moguls can afford and would like to have their own plane and restrictions may be eased in the future, but currently China isn't a great destination for amateur pilots.

Opportunities for hot air ballooning are also restricted, probably for the same security reasons. This is a pity, as it offers unparalleled views of the amazing scenery. As it is, the only regular hot air balloon flights are those between Guilin and Yangshuo in the karst mountain region around the Lijiang River. There's also an annual ballooning festival in Langfang, Hebei province, in August, which attracts around 20 balloons.

If you want to get into the sky, your best opportunity is to take a flight in a microlight aircraft, although first you must find one; ask at your local airport; if you're near Beijing, the Flying Man Club offers microlight flights (💻 flying-man. com). For seasoned pilots, it's possible to build your own microlight; a supplier in Chongqing can supply the complete kit, ready to assemble, for a Nova-1 microlight (imported from the US) at a cost of US$10,000.

For a slightly less elevated flight, parasailing (where you're towed by a speedboat) is available at various coastal locations around China, including Qingdao, Sanya on Hainan Island and Gulangyu Island off Xiamen in Fujian province.

BASKETBALL

Basketball has captured the imagination of many Chinese. Much of the sport's popularity is down to one man, Yao Ming, the 2.20m (7ft 6in) tall player from Shanghai who's excelled as a player for the Houston Rockets in American's National Basketball Association (NBA). Many schools and universities have basketball courts, and basketball hoops are available in public parks and the car parks of business premises. Probably more hours of basketball, usually from the NBA, are shown on Chinese television than any other sport, and the NBA has opened several stores in the major Chinese cities.

There are a number of basketball leagues of which the most important is the Chinese Basketball Association (CBA, 💻 cba.gov.cn), which comprises 17 professional teams based in major cities, including Beijing, Dalian, Dongguan, Fuzhou, Guangzhou, Hangzhou, Jilin, Shanghai, Tianjin and Xian. The most successful are the Bayi Rockets from Ningbo and the Guangdong Southern Tigers. There's also a women's league, the China Women's Basketball Association (CWBA), and a university league, all of which play regular competitive games. The national teams dominate the Federation of International Basketball (FIBA) Asian tournaments, but haven't yet made their mark on the world championships.

CLIMBING & CAVING

China has a great many mountains to challenge climbers, including one face of Mt Everest (*Qomolongma Shan*) in the Himalayas, therefore if this is your sport you'll find excellent opportunities for testing climbs of every grade.

You're strongly advised to climb as part of a group. Many mountains are in isolated regions, and a number of people have died in climbing accidents which might have been avoided had they been accompanied, and the authorities advised of their plans. If you're attempting a serious climb, it's essential to inform the national park authorities and the local Public Security Bureau (PSB), and make sure that you know how to call for help if you get into trouble.

There are a number of so-called sacred mountains, places of pilgrimage for devout Chinese, and all can be climbed by amateurs by following a designated route, although some can be rather dangerous. Climbing to the peak and descending can take between four and eight hours, and for most people there's a real sense of achievement in reaching the summit. However, you need to be prepared for several hours of negotiating sharp slopes, precipitous steps and even ladders to reach the top, and then marvel at how the vendors of water and biscuits – often elderly ladies – manage to do it every day!

If you prefer to head underground, the areas around Guizhou and Guangxi are particularly rich in caves. The Huanglongdong (Yellow Dragon) cave in Zhangjiajie, Hunan province is the longest in Asia, featuring underground rivers and waterfalls, and has been explored by the British Cave Research Organisation. Expeditions to other caves and canyons have been undertaken by teams from France, Japan and the UK.

Some of China's caves can be visited as a tourist attraction, while others require full expedition gear. If you're doing the latter, ensure that someone, including the local PSB, knows about your plans.

CRICKET & CROQUET

Surprisingly, these two quintessentially English sports are gaining popularity in China. Cricket is played in some 150 schools, and matches are organised on a regular basis in Beijing, Chongqing, Dalian, Guangzhou, Jinan, Shenyang, Shenzhen and Tianjin, although the oldest club is in Shanghai where leather first hit willow in 1858. China's cricket association is a member of the International Cricket Council (ICC), and the country has fledgling national teams for both men and women who represented China at the 2010 Asian Games, and although no medals were won the women's team finished fourth. Nevertheless, it hopes to field a test team by 2020.

Foreigners are fairly well catered for in mainland China with a number of expat cricket clubs, but the finest pitch is that of the Hong Kong Cricket Club at Wong Nai Chung Gap in Hong Kong.

Croquet is a popular sport among the not so young, who play on smooth sand 'greens' located close to housing developments. The Chinese play with smaller balls, mallets and hoops than those used under Hurlingham rules, but the game requires the same cunning, skill and dirty tricks that it does in the West.

CYCLING

Cycling is still seen by the Chinese as a means of transport rather than a sport, but most cities have cycling clubs with organised weekend runs on public roads, and there are also expatriate clubs for cyclists in Beijing and Shanghai.

The Chinese compete on a national and international level in different types of cycle sports, including road cycling, speed cycling and mountain biking. Coverage on television of the Tour de France and the 2008 Olympics spurred an interest in competitive cycling, and in recent years the Chinese have staged a series of similar road races. The best known is the Tour de Qinghai Lake (⌨ tdql.cn/english/index_en.htm) which covers over 1,500km (930mi) in one of the most picturesque parts of the country and attracts riders from many countries.

In September 2010, the first ever Tour of China took place over 11 days, starting in Xi'an and finishing in Tianjin, a distance of over 1,800km (1,118mi). It attracted 14 overseas teams and offered a total of US$200,000 in prize money. This race has been repeated annually and in 2012 China entered its first professional team of cyclists in the race. The team didn't win but the race is

becoming a popular international event in which a number of the teams and riders from the Tour de France are beginning to compete.

Certainly, China's stunning scenery and comparatively traffic-free open roads make it a great venue for two-wheeled touring. There are a number of websites which offer tips, ideas and routes, including Bicycle Adventures (💻 bicycle-adventures.com/cycling-in-china.html) and Bike China (💻 bikechina.com/index.php).

Good quality bicycles are available in China at reasonable prices. Many cities have 'bicycle' streets where the choice of bikes and accessories is huge. An ordinary 26-in wheeled bike, complete with prop stand, front basket, rear carrier and lock (but no gears) costs around 300 to 500 RMB. Mountain bikes start from 600 RMB. There's a wide range of accessories, including a battery-powered horn that perfectly imitates the squawk of a police car, although they're a tempting target for thieves. Theft of and from bicycles is rampant, which is one reason why so few bicycles have lights.

EXTREME SPORTS

Adventure sports such as skydiving, cliff climbing and bungee jumping are practised in China, although their appeal is limited to wealthy thrill seekers or foreigners. According to skydiving website Dropzone (💻 dropzone.com), there's a skydiving club based at Shahe Airport in Beijing's Changping district, where the country's national skydiving team train, and it's possible to book a diving experience there. For a different type of airborne experience, there are several paragliding clubs in China, including Beijing's Flying Man Club (💻 flying-man.com), which also supplies equipment and training for kite surfing, windsurfing and other adventure sports. As testament to the popularity of paragliding, the third Paragliding World Cup took place in Linzhou, Henan province, in 2010. Meanwhile, Shanghai hosts the annual X Games Asia, featuring sports such as BMX, skateboarding and aggressive inline skating.

China's many mountains and caves offer challenging ascents and descents, although you can take a safer route up one of the indoor climbing walls in the major cities. One of the most unique climbing experiences is up the mast of the Macau Tower, a dizzying 338m/1,109ft (💻 macautower.com.mo/en/home/index.html). The tower is also the venue for the world's highest bungee jump, a 233m (732ft) fall at speeds of up to 200kph (125mph).

FISHING

Just as they love eating fish, so the Chinese enjoy catching them, and fishing is a popular recreational sport. Fishing equipment can be purchased cheaply in sports shops throughout the country, and many people spend their weekends waiting for a bite. Inland, the majority of fishing takes place at man-made pools, where you're charged per kilo for the fish you catch and keep. Some fisheries consist of a row of pools, side by side, each stocked with a different breed of fish, so you can choose which type to fish for. This way of fishing seems a bit sterile but it makes sense as many of China's rivers and canals are highly polluted and the fish, if they survive, may be full of toxic substances. Some river fishing takes place on major rivers such as the Yangtze and Yellow River, often from boats or bridges, but you cannot just throw your line in anywhere. Fly fishing is rare and most fishermen use bait.

On the coast, fishing from the beach in the evenings is popular, and in one or two places you can hire specially equipped boats for game fishing, although this is strictly for the well heeled.

The vast majority of fish at sea and inland are caught by professional fishermen, and it's big business; China is the world's largest exporter of fish, although much of it's farmed. However, old methods still exist – one of the most fascinating sights in China is that of the fishermen in their small boats on the Lijiang River in Guilin, using trained cormorants to catch fish.

cormorant fishing

FOOTBALL

Football (soccer) is one sport that China has really taken to heart – they even claim to have invented it some 2,000 years ago! However, despite producing some football talent – there are Chinese players in England's Premiership, Germany's Bundesliga and in a number of other European leagues – on the world scene, China has yet to make an impression.

The league system is well organised, consisting of three tiers of teams with the Chinese Super League (CSL) at the top. There are 16 clubs in the CSL, and in recent years, Beijing Go'an, Dalian Shide and Shandong Luneng have tended to dominate. Most play at modern, high-capacity, stadiums and are generally well supported; many matches are shown on national television (Channel 5) during the season.

Chinese footballers are well rewarded – by Chinese standards – and a top player can earn 4m RMB a year, while a few make it onto the international arena. Sun Jihai has played for the English clubs Manchester City and Sheffield United, while Zheng Zhi had a spell at Scottish club Celtic. However, overall, the sport has failed to produce any outstanding stars in the mould of Yao Ming, and its international performances have been largely forgettable. The national team failed to qualify for all recent World Cups, with the exception of the 2002 competition where China failed to score a single goal, and in 2011 it was ranked 77th in the world by FIFA.

A lack of facilities at amateur level may be one reason why Chinese football lags behind much of the world. There are hardly any public (or private) pitches, so few youngsters take up the sport. (Table tennis, which can be played just about everywhere, shows just how successful the Chinese can be at a sport if amateurs have the right facilities to develop their skills.) Many universities have a football pitch, but inter-university matches are few and pitches tend to get used for knock-about games rather than serious matches.

Chinese football hasn't been helped either by repeated allegations of match fixing, bent refereeing and betting coups in recent years, with a number of senior personalities being charged by the police. There have been a series of 'clean ups' but the situation remains less than satisfactory. Despite this, the fans have remained remarkably supportive, although many are fans of football, rather than Chinese football. The major European clubs have countless followers, and you see far more people wearing Barcelona or Manchester United shirts than those of Beijing Go'an or other major Chinese teams. There's extensive coverage (in Chinese) of European league matches on both CCTV and cable channels.

> If you'd rather play than watch, there are many expatriate clubs in the major cities and foreign teachers are welcome to join ad hoc games with university students. Don't worry if you aren't too skilful as neither are most of the other players.

Other types of football have a more limited following. A few games of American football (gridiron) have been organised in Beijing, as demonstrations by visiting teams or among American expatriates, but it hasn't caught on with the local population, possibly because it's a very aggressive contact sport. Australian Rules football is played by around six organised teams in China, such as the Beijing Bombers and the Shanghai Tigers, competing annually for the 'China Cup' on ANZAC day. The players are mostly Australian expatriates (mostly from Melbourne or Adelaide where the game is a religion rather than a sport), and they play regularly at the Xiaowuji Sports ground in Beijing. Information about games is published in free expat magazines.

Rugby union is also a minority sport, although a few universities have teams, notably the Agricultural University in Beijing. The World Sevens circuit has staged events in Shanghai and Hong Kong – the Hong Kong Sevens is considered by many to be the best and the most important Sevens tournament in the world calendar – but rugby has yet to take off among the Chinese, although expats in Beijing and Shanghai sometimes get together to play against local universities. Rugby is popular in Japan where there are literally hundreds of clubs, and the wealthier ones employ foreign players (mainly Australians) to strengthen their teams, so it may yet become popular in China.

GOLF

Many Chinese play golf for its prestige value rather than as a sport. It's seen as an excellent way to nurture business connections, so much so that several business colleges include golf tuition in their curriculum! Although the construction of new golf courses, which require large amounts of land, is technically illegal, it hasn't hindered their construction as many provincial cities regard them as prestigious and profitable, and simply ignore the law. All the major cities have at least one golf course and several driving ranges, but in China golf is a sport for the rich (as it is in most other countries).

Nowhere is this more true than at Mission Hills (⌨ missionhillschina.com/home.aspx), which is the largest golf complex in China (and possibly the world). Situated close to Shenzhen, it has a dozen 18-hole courses, each laid out by a famous golfer, and annual membership costs from around 320,000 RMB for the cheapest grade up to 2m RMB (US$300,000!) for the top tier, which allows unlimited play on all 12 courses. Even at a much less prestigious course in a provincial capital, annual membership can easily exceed 350,000 RMB, while a non-member wanting to play a round of 18 holes pays around 1,000 RMB for the day. You can treble these prices for even an indifferent course close to Beijing or Shanghai.

In China, golf is very much a luxury sport which comes with all the trimmings. Most caddies are attractive girls, and electric golf carts proliferate – it isn't a game played for its health benefits. Courses and driving ranges are professionally maintained, and many clubhouses have excellent facilities, including restaurants. In spite of the upmarket facilities and high membership fees, at some courses the major water hazard doubles as a swimming pool, with golfers stripping off for a quick dip on hot days!

A number of tournaments are held in China, including the WGC-HSBC Champions in Shanghai and the Volvo China Open. To date, few Chinese have been successful on the international circuit (in 2003, Zhang Lian-wei was the first Chinese golfer to win on the European tour), but with so much money being poured into the sport it can only be a matter of time before a Chinese golfer breaks into the top echelon.

GYMNASIUMS & FITNESS CLUBS

There are gyms and fitness clubs in all major cities. Many have good equipment, such as Nautilus machines, weights, parallel bars, treadmills and exercise bicycles, and they also run classes, e.g. aerobics and Pilates. However, membership isn't particularly cheap; expect to pay between 500 and 1,200 RMB a month, plus a further 1,000 RMB if you want a personal trainer. As an alternative, some of the top hotels have 'health clubs' which are open to non-residents for a fee.

There's no need to pay for expensive gym memberships in China. You don't have to pay anything to use the fitness equipment provided in public parks. The only drawback to this is the audience you may attract. Some bystanders cannot resist staring at you while you work out, simply because you're a foreigner.

HIKING & WALKING

Walking costs nothing and you can do it anywhere. Pounding the pavements of the major cities isn't very rewarding, due to the pollution, crowds and traffic, although there are some interesting walks in and around Beijing and Shanghai.

Beijing's *hutongs*, close to Dongdandajie, are a series of narrow lanes between ancient courtyard houses which can easily by explored on foot; they're Beijing as it used to be before the developers started tearing everything down. The side streets around Tian'anmen Square are also well worth a stroll – if you're lucky, you may catch a wedding at one of the churches, complete with white limousine and confetti – as is Xidan, parallel to Wangfujing where the locals shop. It has some brilliant pharmacists where the huge bottles of 'tonic wine', full of dead reptiles, are a sight to behold. The pleasant countryside of the Fragrant Hills is only a bus ride away.

In Shanghai, a stroll along the Bund in the cool of an autumn or spring evening, the promenade alive with Chinese families, the lights glittering off the Huangpu River and the little snack bars doing a roaring trade, make for a memorable walk, and from the northern end of the Bund you can carry on to the equally enjoyable surroundings of the old French Concession.

In Guangzhou, a walk around Shamian Island, with its glimpses of old colonial architecture and its magnificent ancient trees, is highly recommended. Just across the canal from Shamian is the Qing Ping market which sells an amazing cornucopia of herbs, spices and strange foodstuffs. Until the advent of SARS in 2006, this was where Guangdong people purchased exotic wildlife to eat, and

while most of the stalls have since been closed down, you can still sometimes come across unusual culinary items such as small live crocodiles.

Many city street maps can be misleading. Not only is the information printed in Chinese – although some maps also show it in pinyin – they aren't always to scale, and distances can be greater than they appear on paper. You can find organised walks, as well as hikes out of town, arranged by travel agents or expat clubs, often advertised in the free expat magazines. You may have to pay a small fee, but it's a good way to walk in interesting company.

If you want to walk further afield, there are many opportunities for hiking across China's great open spaces, which is a great way to relax and enjoy the real China, far from the (madding) crowds and factories. At heart, this is still an agricultural society, and its rural corners reveal unforgettable sights, such as crops being collected by hand, sweet corn hanging on walls to dry in the sun and oxen pulling ploughs on tiny, terraced fields.

A popular destination for hiking is the Great Wall and, in places such as Jinshanling and Simatai, where the wall is much less trodden and in some cases still unrestored, this can be glorious – the hike from Jinshanling to Simatai is spectacular (although the latter was temporarily closed in 2011 due to a village building project). You must be fit to do this as there's some scrambling, and it can be dangerous in places and shouldn't be attempted on your own.

Other popular destinations for hiking include Tiger Leaping Gorge in Lijiang province, the area around Kanas Lake in the Altai Mountains, Xinjiang province, and the trek to the Mt Everest base camp in Tibet. Note that some routes can be very testing and are only suitable for fit and experienced hikers.

▲ Caution

If you go hiking in any rural areas, it's wise to do it in a group. Many locals assume that all foreigners are rich – and compared to most farmers, you are – and there have been a few incidents in which tourists have been threatened and robbed of their money or belongings by rural folk. On one occasion, this resulted in a death. Such events are extremely rare, but lone hikers are much more vulnerable; few thieves will target a group.

Running & Jogging

Competitive marathons are organised in many cities, with the largest taking place in Beijing in October. Starting from Tian'anmen Square, with the huge painting of Chairman Mao looking down benevolently on the contestants, the Beijing Marathon winds its way around the surprisingly hilly city to finish with a lap around the track at the Workers Stadium. If you cannot manage the full 42km (26mi) distance, there are the options of a half marathon and both 10 and 5km races along part of the same course and run at the same time..

Jogging has been slow to take off in China, and virtually every jogger you see is a foreigner. If you'd rather run in company, a number of cities have active branches of the Hash House Harriers – the oldest in Beijing. Typically, Beijing members meet at a bar on Sunday morning then put in around 12km (7mi) around a course laid earlier in the city, before finishing back at the bar where a refreshing beer puts back any weight shed during the run. For a list of Hash clubs (called kennels) and contacts, see the organisation's China website (🖳 hashchina.com).

HORSE RIDING

Horse riding is available in a number of places, most notably in the hills around the Great Wall outside Beijing and on the outskirts of Shanghai. There are some well organised stables, and many offer group-hacking through fine countryside, but experienced riders should note that the horses are often old and not very lively.

Although horse riding is a minority sport in most of China, it's a central part of Mongolian culture; Mongolian horses are stocky and strong and their riders are exceptionally skilful. A trek through the grasslands of Inner Mongolia is an unforgettable experience, while a trip to one of the annual Naadam festivals in late July/early August to watch the younger riders compete at picking up objects from the ground at full gallop is a great spectacle.

INDOOR & TABLE SPORTS

Both chess and Chinese chess (*xiangqi*) are widely played in China, and in international competitions Chinese teams frequently achieve a top three placing. However, regular chess is a poor second to *xiangqi* which uses a different board and pieces marked with Chinese characters rather than knights or pawns. It has the status of a sport in much of the Far East, and is contested at the Asian Games where Chinese competitors usually take the medals. If you can learn the rules of Chinese chess you'll quickly make friends with the locals.

Another incredibly popular activity is mahjong, a game of skill and strategy not dissimilar to gin rummy but played with carved tiles rather than playing cards. Invented in China, supposedly by Confucius, mahjong is played by young and old alike. However, it's also the main attraction at many illegal gambling clubs, so can have a slightly seedy aura, similar to poker in the West.

Snooker has grown in popularity in recent years, bolstered by the success of Ding Junhui who was ranked number five in the world in 2010/2011. There are snooker and pool tables everywhere, even in the smallest villages, although some are outdoors and exposed to the weather: China may be one of the only countries where you can pot balls in the rain!

Darts is played in many bars, although it's seen as more of an expats' game. In Beijing, there's an inter-embassy darts league where competition is intense, although not all of the players come from the countries they represent. You can buy darts and dartboards in sports shops and supermarkets.

CHINESE SPORTS

China has some unusual indigenous sports. Chief among these is *jianzi* which consists of a small metal disc with coloured feathers attached to it – similar to a shuttlecock – which players must keep in the air using their feet. Children play *jianzi* by throwing the disc in the air, catching it with the heel of their shoe and kicking it back up again, the winner being the child who can keep the *jianzi* up in the air longest without it hitting the ground – a bit like 'keepie uppie' with a football. Adults turn it into a serious game, not unlike volleyball played with your feet. There are two players on either side of a net and the *jianzi* is kicked over the net and caught on the foot of an opponent who kicks it back. This requires a lot of skill.

Less energetic but no less skilful is *kongzhu*, sometimes called Diabolo. It's a reel-shaped disc which is balanced on a cord and the object is to keep both disc and cord spinning and to perform various tricks (a sort of Chinese version of yo-yo). An ancient skill, dating back some 2,000 years, it requires stamina, flexibility and excellent coordination.

Kite flying is practiced by young and old in any open space, and in the windy springtime you can see dozens of kites fluttering above Tian'anmen Square. The sport originated in China over 2,500 years ago, when they were made from bamboo and silk, and used for measuring distances and sending messages, as well as for recreation. There's an annual international kite festival in Weifang, Shandong province, as well as the largest kite museum in the world exhibiting some extraordinary kites. The cheapest kites cost less than 10 RMB but the larger ones, which can perform stunts, are between 60 and 150 RMB. If you want an unusual but typically Chinese present to take overseas, a kite is light, folds up small and can be very beautiful.

MARTIAL ARTS

Although Westerners regard martial arts as combat sports, in China they're viewed as an art: a collection of strategies and skills developed for defence, in which mental and spiritual strength is as important as physical ability.

Chinese martial arts date back centuries to a time when the country endured centuries of strife, from invading forces, disputes between warlords and civil wars. Each group of people, whether villagers or the supporters of a temple or shrine, sometimes had to be able to defend themselves, sometimes with fists and feet, sometimes with spear or staff, therefore a variety of martial arts were developed in different locations, taking many different forms.

Foreigners often think immediately of kung fu but the correct name is *gong fu* – the 'kung'

resulted from an old method of transliterating Chinese into English. Along with *taijiquan*, *gong fu* is the most widely practised of Chinese martial arts.

The collective term is *wushu* and there are two main forms of *wushu*: 'external' forms (*waijia*), e.g. *gong fu*, which mainly encompass muscular strength, and 'internal', e.g. *taijiquan*, which concentrate on increasing tendon power, improving breathing and using the body's natural energy (*qi*) to overcome an aggressor. Inevitably, both forms overlap; you cannot make your body strong if you haven't mastered the art of breathing properly.

Nowadays the Chinese concentrate much more on the health benefits of *wushu* rather than on employing it for self-defence or aggression. For many people, performing *taijiquan* exercises in the early morning is a ritual which sets them up for the day.

> Shaolin temple in Henan province is considered by many to be the birthplace of martial arts in China and, especially, of *gong fu*. It's visited by millions of Chinese and foreign tourists every year, and has the most photographed temple floor in China, with indentations caused by the kicks and blows of the monks over the centuries. Shaolin was where Bodhidharma, the 28th incarnation of the Buddha, settled after arriving from India in 527AD. He completed nine years of solitary meditation in a cave before founding Buddhism in China, and you can still see the faint outline of his figure, where he sat motionless, on the cave wall. Bodhidharma is credited with inventing the form of hand-to-hand combat known today as *wushu*.

If you want to learn martial arts, there are many opportunities to do so, either at one of the universities or by visiting temples such as Shaolin. For more information, see page 123.

MOTOR SPORTS

China has two major motor racing venues: the old Grand Prix circuit in Zhuhai and the new track in Shanghai, where both Formula 1's Chinese Grand Prix and motorcycling's Moto GP are held. In addition, there's the old street circuit in Macau. Despite the cachet of hosting motor racing events, attendance at the Shanghai International Circuit hasn't been as high as had been hoped and F1 has yet to fire the Chinese public's imagination. China also hosts some long-distance rallies, including the Hong Kong to Beijing rally, and

Beijing is also the destination of several Paris to Peking events for vintage cars.

Local radio stations often organise treasure hunts or navigational rallies for keen motorists, while there are regular motorcycle trials in the mountains of Central China, which draw competitors from overseas as well as local riders. News of forthcoming events can usually be found in the free expat magazines available in bars and hotels.

RACQUET SPORTS

One of the most popular racquet sports in China is badminton. The Chinese regard it as a 'Chinese' sport, one at which they expect to win, and their players usually oblige (at the 2012 Olympics, China scooped eight of the 15 available medals). Its success is due to its simplicity. Badminton doesn't require any fancy equipment or even a proper badminton court. People play each other wherever they can, on a footpath, in a car park, anywhere. Like table tennis, it's an example of an amateur sport which breeds champions.

In contrast, tennis must be played on proper tennis courts. There are courts available at many universities, a number of embassies, some large hotel complexes and, occasionally, on residential estates, but few public courts. And while there are tennis clubs in the major cities, membership fees are too high to make this a universal sport.

China has had its own tennis association since 1953, and some women players have done well on the international circuit: in 2011, Li Na won the women's singles at the French Open, the first Asian to win a Grand Slam singles title. Male players have yet to make their mark, although the state is pumping money into the game. China hosts several major tournaments, and tennis is one of the most popular sports on TV after football and basketball, so it's odds on that Chinese players will become much more prominent in this sport. If you want to play you can buy good quality rackets and equipment, while the free expat magazines include details of clubs and forthcoming tournaments.

Most squash courts in China are part of hotel complexes. In Beijing, there are squash courts at the Jade Palace, Sino-Swiss, Kempinski, Lido Holiday Inn, Hilton and China World hotels, as well as at the East Lakes Club in the well-known villa complex. The fee to play ranges from 80 to 200 RMB an hour. In Shanghai, see Shanghai Squash (🖳 shanghaisquash.com) for links to courts in the city.

TABLE TENNIS

Ping pong, as the Chinese call it, is China's national sport and one in which it leads the world. It's incredibly accessible – there are ping pong tables everywhere, made from plywood, steel or even concrete, in schools, hotels, office blocks and parks – so there's always an opportunity to play it. As a result, it's very popular among amateur players and some 300m people are said to take part.

China dominates the sport at the international level and won every gold medal for table tennis at the Beijing Olympics, and frequently sweeps the board at world championships. Even the US national table tennis team employs a Chinese coach, and most of the players in other Asian countries' teams are also Chinese.

Players such as Wang Hao and Deng Yaping enjoy a similar status in China to David Beckham or Tiger Woods in the West, and many youngsters aim to emulate their success. You often have to queue to use a table – at a sports centre, an hour's hire costs 10 to 20 RMB, although in public places tables are usually free – and while you're waiting you'll be amazed by the skill of the players, and may feel embarrassed at your own.

Ping Pong Politics

Ping pong has also played a role in China's diplomatic relations. In the early '70s, members of the US table tennis team were invited to visit China, the first American sportsmen to do so since the founding of the Peoples Republic in 1949. The two countries found a common ground in the sport and table tennis is sometimes cited as an element in the thawing of relations between the two powers, which lead to President Nixon's meeting with Mao Zedong in Beijing in 1972.

WATER SPORTS

Although China has a long coastline and many rivers and lakes, water sports aren't high on the Chinese list of sporting pursuits. This is partly due to the cost of equipment, but also because most people aren't very comfortable in water and many Chinese cannot swim. Their reluctance is understandable given the polluted state of many waterways, but even in a public pool you see a great many 'swimmers' bobbing about encircled by giant rubber rings. Breast stroke is the standard stroke taught, and few master even that to any degree.

Pools are by far the safest places to swim (see box below) and admission is inexpensive. Most charge 30 to 40 RMB per session, and are best visited in late evenings or during school time if you want to swim some peaceful lengths.

Most pools insist on the wearing of swimming caps in the water and sandals around the pool; the latter is a guard against infections such as 'grey nail', an unpleasant if harmless fungal disease which you can catch in public pools. All pools have lockers and showers and sometimes even a sauna, in which you're expected to keep your swimming clothes on at all times. Note that most pools are only around 2m (6ft 6in) at the 'deep' end, therefore diving isn't recommended!

There are limited opportunities for sailing or wind surfing in China, and while small boats and windsurfing equipment can be hired on some lakes outside Beijing, or at Qingdao in Shandong province and resorts on Hainan Island, water sports aren't a major draw and there are no marinas crammed with boats for hire. If you're a keen sailor you need to head for Hong Kong with its large expat community and greater boating opportunities.

The largest marina in mainland China is at Qingdao, where the Olympic sailing events were held in 2008. It has the capacity for 700 yachts, but only 300 berths were filled by 2011, suggesting that the sport is very much in its infancy. China builds boats but most are toys for the nouveau riche rather than yachts for amateur sailors, and sailing is clearly a rich man's 'sport', reflected by the high prices charged at Qingdao. A regular mooring costs around 150,000 RMB a year plus compulsory membership of the Qingdao Yinhai International Yacht Club, which adds a further 300,000 to 600,000 RMB to the cost. Some boats moored at the marina cost as much as 200m RMB.

Other water sports are limited. There's some boogie boarding available at Sanya in Hainan but no surfing scene in the Western sense, while white water rafting takes place on the Mengdong River in the Zhangjiajie National Forest Park (not far from the town of Wulingyuan in Hunan province, near the Jutian cave) and you can take a trip on a bamboo raft near Wuyi Shan mountain in Fujian province. Note that the latter two experiences can be hazardous.

⚠ Caution

Most lakes are okay for swimming provided the water is clear, but the poor controls on industrial pollution means that many rivers are highly polluted with heavy metals and other contaminants. In the south, you might even meet an alligator in the Yangtze River or one of its tributaries. In the sea around Hainan there are venomous sea snakes, sharks and jellyfish. While there have been no reports of any of these coming close to the shore, there are no nets protecting bathing beaches.

WINTER SPORTS

China experiences very cold winters in the north. Beijing receives quite heavy snowfalls most winters, and Harbin in Heilongjiang province is famous for its ice festival, where people create astonishing ice sculptures. It can snow as far south as the Yellow River, but most winter sports opportunities are confined to the northern provinces and are mainly limited to skating and skiing.

Ice skating is popular in Beijing. People gather at lakes within the city, such as Kunming Lake in the grounds of the Summer Palace, and skate to the sound of martial music played over loudspeakers. The sight of thousands of rugged up Chinese walking, sliding and skating joyously across the huge lake is one that you'll never forget, and similar scenes take place in all the northern cities. If you want to join in, skates can be hired on the spot for a few RMB and the experience is huge fun, although you should expect a few bumps. For year-round skating, there are ice rinks in a few cities, while some have concreted areas set aside for roller skating. Skates can be hired for next to nothing.

Skiing is far less accessible than skating and few Chinese have the time or money to devote to it, although the snow conditions in some parts of the country were made for winter sports. According to the China Ski Association, around 5m ski trips were made in 2010 and it predicts an increase to 20m by 2014, although this seems highly unlikely.

There are ski slopes in Hebei province, within easy driving distance of Beijing, but these are mainly for beginners. More experienced skiers and snowboarders should head to Jilin province where there are good facilities at the resorts of Beida Hu, Songhua and Changbei Shan, and to Yabuli's Sun Mountain, some 200km (125mi) from Harbin, where there's a resort run by Club Med offering almost 20 different runs and the longest toboggan run in the world. These destinations provide opportunities for beginners and intermediate skiers as well as cross-country runs. A full day's skiing at either location costs 600 to 700 RMB per person and equipment can be hired in resorts.

It's also possible to book skiing and snowboarding package holidays further afield in Qinghai province or even Tibet. Resorts in these regions are still in the early days of development and facilities may be rudimentary, but they reward the more adventurous skier with astonishing scenery.

Shopping Mall, Beijing

17.

SHOPPING

Shopping in China is very different from shopping in most Western countries. Many items are manufactured by the state so there can be a limited range of brands and styles to choose from – you either buy the only government-designed watering can or you go without. However, at the same time there are innumerable goods available in China that you cannot buy elsewhere, particularly unusual and beautiful handicrafts.

Another overriding difference is the haggling culture; with few exceptions (e.g. supermarkets, food markets and larger shops), prices are negotiable and bargaining isn't just possible but taken for granted. This adds a new dimension to your shopping, but also means that if you aren't comfortable haggling then you'll often pay well over the odds.

Mainland China has many excellent department stores, supermarkets and smaller shops. There are well-known names such as Parkson and Carrefour but they don't dominate the retail market as they do in some countries, and the large out-of-town shopping malls beloved by Americans and Britons aren't common. Much daily shopping is done at markets; not just street markets but also in purpose-built market halls.

Although China manufactures and exports a wealth of products to the rest of the world, the sheer range of choice that Western shoppers have come to expect isn't always available in China, therefore you must be prepared to compromise or to travel further afield. Wealthier shoppers fly to Hong Kong to buy big-ticket items, such as a top-of-the-range camera, that aren't available on the mainland. If you see something you really want, snap it up without hesitation. If you go away to think about it, chances are it'll be gone when you return and you may never see anything like it ever again.

Prices depends very much on where you shop. Markets sell cheaper goods than supermarkets and supermarkets have lower prices than department stores. Apart from expensive imported goods, prices are generally much lower than in Europe or the US, and discount shops, such as the 'pound' shops that proliferate in the UK, aren't

necessary in China where shoppers expect to get a discount on almost everything they buy.

Even the price of foreign goods has decreased since China joined the World Trade Organisation (WTO) in 2001. Prior to this, many luxury items were hit with an import duty of 30 per cent and the equivalent Chinese-made products were overpriced to match, particularly cars. Membership of the WTO opened up the market to overseas companies to set up joint ventures with Chinese companies and manufacture goods in China, resulting in wider availability and lower prices. Today, many overseas brands are built in China, from cars to televisions, and cost much less than they did in the '90s. However, imported goods are still heavily taxed and accordingly expensive.

Foreign delicacies such as German ham, Australian Cheddar cheese and American cereals cost much more than Chinese foodstuffs, but even the price of locally produced food can vary quite wildly. A dry or cold spring can result in the price of vegetables soaring, while a safety scare, such as the milk scandal in 2008, can cause a run on alternative products, pushing up prices. Most Chinese only buy Chinese goods because they cost less, but will quickly switch to imported brands if there are concerns over safety.

Regrettably, adulterating foodstuffs isn't uncommon and can be difficult to detect. The use of chemicals to make meat look redder or pesticides to make vegetables grow larger and faster is widespread. In 2011, many farmers in Jiangsu province lost their watermelon crop when the fruit exploded due to excessive use of growth chemicals.

The Chinese are infamous for their skills at copying/counterfeiting foreign products. There are copies of everything from designer clothes to computer software, CDs and DVDs being sold quite openly in established shops, despite regular crackdowns by the government. Whether you buy or not, it's as well to be aware that pirated DVDs may be blank, the bottle of phony perfume may smell very different from the tester bottle, and the fake Tag Heuer watch you cannot resist may stop ticking the minute you get it home.

☑ SURVIVAL TIP

Counterfeiting also extends to the world of antiques and collectibles, where copying is big business and it's almost impossible to find a genuine item for sale. All you can do is buy something because you like it and accept the fact that it was probably made the previous year in the 'Something-zhou Antiques Factory'. Just make sure you pay the right price.

Despite the strangeness, shopping in China is fun. There's the joy of actually finding something you've searched for everywhere, and the satisfaction of getting it for less than you expected by skillful haggling. And then there's the sheer excitement of exploring exotic markets and discovering items so uniquely Chinese that you won't find them anywhere else in the world.

SALES & NEGOTIATING A DISCOUNT

Seasonal sales are rare in China where discounts are down to the individual store. They can take place at any time when there's stock to shift, and you often find 'sale' goods alongside other merchandise being sold at (apparently) full price.

Reduced prices are indicated by a single number, e.g. 3 or 7. This doesn't mean that the goods displayed are discounted by 3 or 7 per cent or even by 30 or 70 per cent. Rather it means that they're on sale at 30 or 70 per cent of their original price, so the lower the number, the larger the discount. The number 5 means they're effectively selling at half price. As in the West, some of these discounts aren't strictly true – a jacket marked down to 30 RMB didn't necessarily start off costing 100 RMB – but they do make you feel as if you're getting a bargain.

Even with sales goods, you have nothing to lose by asking for a further reduction. Just ask the sales assistant 'Is this your best price?' and you might get even more deducted. It's also worth doing this for items which don't have a discount tag.

There are few places where you cannot negotiate the price. Supermarkets and some large chain stores have set prices, but at individual shops and stalls it's possible to reduce the price by up to a fifth – or in some cases considerably more – by some polite but firm haggling. A surprisingly good copy of a Gucci handbag offered at 300 RMB can be haggled down to 150 RMB, whereas you'd pay 15,000 for the genuine article at the Gucci store in Wangfujingnandajie. It isn't usually possible to haggle over food prices – most food markets sell at the lowest possible price – but with clothes, household goods and, particularly, 'antiques' and collectibles, it's advisable and even expected. At markets which cater to the tourist trade it's even more necessary, as the mark-up on goods may be three, five or even ten times higher than their 'real' value; e.g. a watch priced at 100 RMB may only be worth 20 RMB, but if someone's gullible enough to pay 50 RMB for it, then both sides will be happy.

Finding out the 'right' price is the hardest part of haggling. If you see something you'd like to buy, it's best to display no interest and get a Chinese friend, one who isn't obviously shopping with you, to ask the vendor for his best price. There's usually a huge difference between the price offered to a foreigner and that given to a local, although vendors sometimes also try it on with Chinese shoppers.

There's an etiquette which you should follow when haggling so that both sides are happy with the outcome and no one ends up losing face. Your first offer is the most important and you cannot reduce it once the bargaining starts, so think hard about how much the item is worth to you and offer no more than 50 per cent of the asking price. In touristic markets you could bid as little as 25 per cent. If the vendor comes back with a counter offer, you can either raise your bid or, if you think it's still much too high, walk away. He will then, quite possibly, call after you and agree to your price. If he doesn't, then you really were offering too low. Don't lose your temper with stallholders, no matter how obstinate they are, or haggle for fun, i.e. if you don't intend buying. The ideal negotiation should be concluded with smiles on both sides.

Once you've secured your bargain, never check the price of a similar item on another stall. You may find it's even lower than the price you just paid, discount included, and will end up feeling cheated rather than triumphant. The time to check out prices from different vendors is before making your initial offer.

With the exception of antiques, everything for sale in China is brand new (many 'antiques' are also new!). Old things have little appeal, and people want to be the first to own something, hence the focus on buying new cars and new apartments. There are no secondhand shops or charity shops – old clothing is usually handed down to children or chopped up as rags – and the only garage sales are held by expatriates who are preparing to leave the country.

SHOPPING HOURS

Most retailers are open seven days a week, even on public holidays. Smaller family shops may close during Chinese New Year/Spring Festival so that the proprietors can take their annual holiday, but larger stores stay open to benefit from the holiday trade. This includes department stores and supermarkets; the French chain Carrefour proudly advertises that its supermarkets are open 365 days a year.

However, opening hours vary. Markets open early, some from 6am, all by 8am, but they also close early, perhaps by 4pm, particularly food markets. Smaller shops usually open at 8 or 8.30am and close around 5.30 or 6pm, but opening hours aren't dictated by local government and most stay open until the last customer leaves. There's no early closing day and no lunch hour, although some rural shops may shut for a couple of hours at lunchtime.

Supermarkets open around the same time but close later, not before 9 or 10pm. In the major cities, some supermarkets open 24 hours a day, although these are rare. Department stores are usually the latest to start trading. In second- and third-tier cities, many don't open until 9 or 9.30 am, while in larger cities 10am opening is common, although like supermarkets they don't close before 9 or 10pm.

DEPARTMENT & CHAIN STORES

There are well-known chain stores in China, such as Shuang Hui, a chain of mini supermarkets specialising in meat, and the clothing store San Qiang. Such stores may have one or two outlets in many cities, but aren't omnipresent on every high street. Some foreign chains have penetrated the market, such as the British DIY retailer B&Q and the Hong Kong based drugstore Watsons, although most are in the supermarket sector.

Most cities have at least one department store. Some are one-off quality stores such as Yan Sha Yo Yi on Beijing's East Third Ring Road – China's answer to Harrods – while others are children with

branches in several cities, e.g. Parkson, although none have the widespread coverage that Marks & Spencer has in the UK, or the major US chains. One of the oldest department store chains is that of the Friendship Stores (Yo Yi). They date back to the early '90s, when foreigners were barred from using RMB and instead were issued with foreign exchange certificates which could only be exchanged in exclusive government-run Friendship Stores. They were known for stocking hard-to-find items which foreigners craved, and although they've since been privatised and are open to everyone, they're still worth visiting for goods that you cannot buy elsewhere, such as English-language books. There are Friendship Stores in most large Chinese cities.

Chinese department stores aren't dissimilar to those in the West, consisting of different floors devoted to different types of goods, e.g. cosmetics on the ground floor (called the first floor in China), women's fashions on the next floor and so forth, all linked by escalators and lifts. There's often a supermarket in the basement, and while few department stores have a coffee shop, many contain in-house branches of the ubiquitous McDonalds or KFC. Most stores rent space to individual brands such as Burberry or Adidas, as well as to small retailers, so that there are usually many smaller shops within a department store. There are regular promotions of individual brands and seasonal campaigns. In October, many stores feature an entire floor of winter clothing.

SHOPPING CENTRES & MALLS

There are small shopping centres in most cities, often featuring a Carrefour supermarket and limited parking, but Western style complexes set over several floors, featuring one or two major department stores and dozens of smaller shops, aren't that common in China, and large out-of-town malls with vast car parks are rarer still.

Some malls have been opened to great fanfare but have failed to attract many shoppers. The New South China Mall in Dongguan, Guangdong province, which opened in 2005, claims to be the largest in the world and resembles a retail Disneyland – it even has its own rollercoaster. However, the majority of its 2,350 retail outlets remain empty. The Golden Resources Mall in Beijing, which was the world's largest until the New China Mall was built, suffers from a similar lack of custom. The reasons are a combination of location – neither is easy to get to without a car – high prices, and the fact that the Chinese prefer to shop locally.

Those malls which do attract shoppers are usually in central locations, and designed to tempt wealthier Chinese and foreign customers with luxury goods, such as the China World Mall at the World Trade Centre in Beijing (💻 cwtc.com/cwtc/mall/cmall.jsp).

MARKETS

There are markets for food, clothes, pets, flowers, art and antiques and much more, and more people shop at them than anywhere else. Markets are local and convenient, cheap and friendly, and they stock the range and quality of goods that most people want to buy. They don't necessarily consist of stalls set up in an open space, and many are in fixed locations, sometimes within large halls; many stallholders specialise in one kind of produce, with shoppers visiting several adjacent markets to complete their daily shop.

The majority of markets sell food (see page opposite), but there are also markets selling clothes, linens and textiles and a range of other specialities. Most clothes markets sell pirated copies of famous brands and 'seconds'; but if you're discerning, there are some real bargains to be found.

Capital Markets

There are some excellent markets in Beijing. The Russian Market sells top-end garments, such as leather and fur coats, secreted in among the usual array of fakes, while the Hongqiao Pearl Market specialises in pearls, gemstones, antiques and collectables. The Panjiayuan Market is the one to visit for 'antiques', and the Silk Market (Xiu Shui) has clothes made from every fabric (not just silk), including copies of popular brands. Shanghai's most interesting market is Yu Yuan near the gardens of the same name.

Pet markets are frequently called bird markets in China, although you can buy every kind of creature, including cats, dogs, rabbits, turtles and tortoises, crickets (kept for their 'singing' voices) and exotic fish, as well as pet paraphernalia such as cages, tanks and food. The caged birds are often the star attractions, and include not just budgerigars and canaries, but also wild birds such as owls or hawks. One of the most popular birds is the bai lin niao or 'bird of one hundred songs': similar to a thrush, with a lovely liquid voice.

Flower markets, often housed in immense greenhouses, sell not only plants and freshly cut flowers, but also fill the role of garden centres, selling small trees, fertiliser, seeds, garden tools, lawnmowers and decorative rocks, together with every shape and size of vase and flower pot you could wish for.

Markets selling art and antiques are packed with curiosities, but you need to take care what you buy. There are unlikely to be any genuine antiques, and if someone sidles up to you and offers an 'ancient' vase covered in dirt (which was dug up only yesterday), it should arouse your suspicion. More recent collectables are just as much fun: look for the statuettes of characters from Chinese ballets made during the Cultural Revolution or the posters from '20s Shanghai, which cost far less than a supposed antique and are genuine vintage collectables.

Finally, night markets which take place in the evenings in many cities sell a vast range of goods, from clothes to souvenirs, although most people visit them for the entertainment and eating rather than the shopping.

FOOD

There are few immigrants in China, therefore foreign food influences have barely touched the plates of most ordinary Chinese. Apart from a small number of international restaurants in major cities and the relentless march of the US fast food chains, Chinese food dominates. This also applies to food shopping. There are many strange and unidentifiable ingredients for sale in markets and supermarkets, but you can also buy familiar foodstuffs, from meat and poultry to yogurt and eggs.

It's perfectly possible to cook Western food using Chinese ingredients. China may have some bizarre and exotic dishes, such as sharks fin or birds nest soup, but many of these are delicacies and not everyday fare. The average diet isn't so dissimilar to that eaten in the West, consisting of many variations on the meat-and-vegetables theme. The main difference is that that the Chinese eat far more vegetables than meat, and bulk up with rice or noodles rather than potatoes.

The quality of food in China is generally good, but there are far fewer regulations governing food safety than there are in the West, and some vendors aren't above doctoring their goods to improve the appearance, e.g. brushing red dye onto meat to make it look more appetising. Supermarket food is generally safe and reliable, and it's in the street markets that you need to be alert. Market traders often employ the canny trick of putting damaged or old fruit into a box under a layer of their carefully selected best produce, therefore it's wise to check the entire contents.

There are a few specialist shops, such as butchers, fishmongers, greengrocers and bakers, and most food shopping is done at food markets and supermarkets.

Food Markets

Meat markets usually sell every type of meat and poultry, with chicken and pork particularly popular. They also sell more unusual meats such as rabbit, pigeon and donkey. Dog meat is sometimes on sale in regions where it's popular, e.g. Southern China, but usually at a specialised market. The consumption of dogs is becoming less socially acceptable, with a number of Chinese campaigning against the practice and the government is planning to outlaw the practice. Some markets cater to one section of the community; e.g. Muslim markets, which sell halal meat such as lamb and goat and definitely no pork. Most meat sold at markets is good and fresh and much cheaper than that purchased in a supermarket. Locally produced fillet steak sells

for around 18 to 20 RMB a *jin* (around 500g or 1lb in weight), compared with 45 to 65 RMB a *jin* at a supermarket.

Fish markets are fascinating, although they can be wet and messy – don't visit wearing your best shoes. The fish couldn't be any fresher; many are still swimming in tanks and are sold still wriggling, to be carried home in plastic bags like goldfish won at a funfair. The bags are half-filled with water and pumped up with oxygen so the contents are still alive – and super-fresh – when you get them home. Prawns are sold in the same way. Every part of the fish is eaten, and fish heads fetch more than fillets as they're considered to be particularly nutritious. The fish market also sells other creatures, including massive bullfrogs and snakes, which are destined for the wok, plus insects such as cicadas and scorpions, which are believed to have medicinal properties.

Vegetable markets sell a far greater variety of vegetables and fruit than supermarkets, and some unusual seasonal produce, such as *huai hua* (tree blossoms) and *kukucai* (dandelion leaves), can only be bought at a market. Vegetables are as fresh as can be and the prices are low. There's no price control, so walk around and check out the produce before you buy; it's infuriating to buy tomatoes only to find better quality ones for a lower price a few stalls away. Fruit ranges from the familiar to the exotic. China produces excellent apples as well as bizarre delicacies such as the durian, which has a unique flavour but an 'aroma' which foreigners often compare to dog poo.

Vegetable markets also sell pulses and dried fruits – some more unusual fruits, such as persimmons, are delicious when dried – freshly made noodles, and eggs; not just chicken's eggs, but also duck eggs, quail eggs and 'hundred year old eggs'. The latter are preserved eggs which are usually no more than a few weeks old, although they're an acquired taste. Eggs are sold by weight

rather than size, and white eggs cost more as the Chinese prize them above brown eggs.

Supermarkets

Supermarkets have a large slice of the food retail market and vary in size, from huge branded hypermarkets to small local convenience stores. The Chinese supermarket giant Beijing Hualian probably has the largest number of outlets, but there are a number of major foreign competitors, including Carrefour (France), Walmart (US), Lotus (Thailand) and, more recently, Britain's Tesco, which trades under the name Hymall. There are also branches of the German cash and carry warehouse Metro, although you must be a member to shop there. Of all these, only Carrefour has fully understood the Chinese market, and it provides a range of goods that the Chinese public wants in a way that appeals to Chinese shoppers. It's also popular with expatriates, as it stocks a wide range of imported goods.

Supermarkets sell the same range of products as they do in the West, including toiletries, stationery, household goods and, in the larger stores, hardware, linens, kitchen utensils, electrical goods, clothes, shoes and bicycles. However, their main lines are food and drink. Some produce is strictly aimed at the local market, e.g. dried meats and dumplings, and a lot of space is given over to Chinese staples such as vinegars and pickles.

There's plenty of fresh food on sale, including noodles and tofu (*doufu*), and many varieties of fruit and vegetables, although not as many as markets sell. There's far less choice on the dairy aisle – most Chinese are averse to dairy products, and some are allergic to them – but you'll find prodigious quantities of yogurt, both plain and fruit flavoured. Butter, margarine and milk are also sold, although milk often comes in small cartons for toddlers. Many people regard milk and dairy products as children's food. The only cheese readily available is 'plastic' slices of bland processed cheese – the sort that goes in hamburgers – and if you want good cheese you must visit a large supermarket and pay through the nose for imported Australian cheddar, which costs around 50 RMB for just 200g.

Another disappointment is bread. Most supermarket bread is sweet tasting and soft, rather than crusty. Unless you can cultivate a taste for Chinese bread, such as steamed *mantou* or hard but tasty round breads called *shao bing*, you're better off investing in a bread-making machine and making your own. Dried yeast and flour is widely available.

Most supermarkets have a good range of fresh meat, although the choice of deli-style cold meats and cured meats such as bacon is limited, and the imported versions are expensive. However, fish is as fresh as can be – usually still swimming in a tank – along with fish offal (bladders and brains are popular), shellfish such as prawns, crabs in season (autumn) and even large, unappetising looking bullfrogs.

The emphasis on cooking fresh food means that the contents of the freezer section are disappointing. There are no racks of frozen pizza, ready meals, fish fingers and frozen desserts. There are, however, countless frozen dumplings!

The check-out process is similar to that in Western supermarkets, with goods bar-coded and recorded by laser gun by check-out girls who stand at their tills. The main difference is that most people pay in cash. Some supermarkets accept debit and credit cards, but neither staff nor most customers are particularly familiar with their use, and a groan often goes up in the queue in anticipation of a delay when a shopper produces one.

It's advisable to take your own bags when shopping. Carrier bags are provided, but a government initiative to reduce the amount of plastic bags suffocating China by encouraging shoppers to reuse them, means that supermarkets charge for them.

Labelling

Most packaged foods are properly labelled with a list of ingredients plus nutrition advice, such as the calories and fat content. The only snag is that labelling is invariably in Chinese. Note that organic food isn't widely available, and that fruit and vegetables should always be thoroughly washed and/or peeled before cooking and eating to ensure that any traces of chemicals or fertiliser are removed.

ALCOHOL

The Chinese rarely drink alcohol at home, preferring to consume it with a meal at a restaurant. However, you can buy beer, wine and the popular Chinese spirit *baiju* in supermarkets and specialist shops. There are a great many shops selling nothing but *baijiu*. It's an acquired taste and very high in alcohol – as much as 70 per cent proof – and is frequently used for toasting honoured guests rather than pleasurable quaffing.

Wine

Grapes have been grown for wine in China since before the Qin Dynasty, but it's only recently that the process has become industrialised. As China prepares to take on the world in wine production, it's now easier to buy in supermarkets and specialist wine shops. The main labels are Dynasty, Great Wall and Chateau Changyu – the latter has built a French-style chateau outside Beijing where you can enjoy a wine-tasting session. Imported wines are also available, and you can buy a bottle from Australia, Chile, France, Germany, Hungary, Italy, South Africa or the US for only a shade more than it costs in its country of origin. It may be better to stick to imported white, as the Chinese haven't yet got the hang of making a good white wine although their reds can be drinkable. If you're a wine connoisseur, it's possible to buy fine wines from France, although they can cost up to 8,000 RMB a bottle and are mainly purchased as gifts to oil the wheels of business.

 Caution

Just as they copy designer clothes and DVDs, so some enterprising Chinese are turning out fake Australian wines. You need to be wary of familiar-sounding labels such as Benfolds Grange, which has nothing to do with the Penfolds winery's famous Shiraz and tastes nothing like it, either.

Beer

The best-known beer in China is Tsingtao, a pleasant lager-type beer which is best drunk cold.

There are local versions of this brew throughout China, all very similar – the one brewed in Harbin is particularly good. Beer is sold in cans and bottles, and can be bought in supermarkets and shops selling alcohol, although the cheapest place to buy it is from a street market where it can be found for less than 2 RMB for a 375ml bottle. Supermarket prices are a tad higher – up to 3.50 RMB a bottle– but both are as cheap as chips compared with bars, which sometimes price it as high as 25 RMB.

CLOTHES

The quality of clothes varies hugely in China, from high-end designer boutiques on Shanghai's Huai Hai Lu to cheap and cheerful T-shirts in one of the many markets. But the same cannot be said about sizing. The Chinese are shorter and more lightly built than most Westerners, and any man taller than 6ft (1.83m) or heavier than 14 stone (89kg) will find it difficult to buy clothes. Women taller than 5ft 7in (1.7m) or larger than a size 14 will have problems finding something to fit. Shoes can also be a problem, as men's shoes only go up to a size 9 and women's to size 6.

The Chinese follow the continental sizing system (see **Appendix D**), but you should always try clothes on before buying, as the sizing isn't always standard. Most sports clothing is sized by letter, and ranges from small (S) to extra-extra-large (XXL), but it's still advisable to try items on, as one retailer's XL may be another shop's M. Where neck sizes are used, e.g. men's shirts, it doesn't always follow that the chest size has been increased proportionally.

COUNTERFEIT GOODS

The Chinese attitude to counterfeit goods is that they fill a much-needed gap in the market. People have little sympathy for the (usually Western) designers, drug companies and owners of intellectual property rights because they believe them to be excessively greedy. Thus they see nothing wrong in purchasing affordable Chinese-made imitations of well-known brands of DVDs, computer software, clothes, leather goods, pharmaceutical products and much more. The government regularly initiates crackdowns on the manufacturers and sellers of pirated goods, and there are photos in the newspapers of them being crushed, to act as a warning to other traders and purchasers. However, the problem will continue as long as the genuine articles are so expensive.

The major cities offer more choice, but elsewhere you may be limited to shopping for sports clothing and trainers, which are usually available in larger sizes. There's no shortage of jeans, sweatshirts, T-shirts and sports shoes, which are practically a uniform among Chinese youth. Prices in markets are satisfyingly cheap, although many items are fakes and most are emblazoned with logos.

For smarter clothes, there's the option of having outfits tailor-made; you can have a suit made-to-measure for a fraction of the price you'd pay in the West. There are tailors in every town that can make up clothes in record time. However, to ensure you get what you want, take a photo from a magazine or an item of clothing for them to copy.

There are a number of Western fashion stores with branches in China, including H&M, C&A and Zara, but they're aimed at Chinese shoppers and, once again, size is often an issue for foreigners. Many clothes in the West carry the 'made in China' label, but it doesn't follow that you can buy them in China as they're strictly for the export market. One exception to this is the British store, Marks & Spencer, which sells some of its overseas range at its store on Shanghai's Nanjing Road. If you have the time and money, a shopping trip to Hong Kong can be worthwhile, as there's a greater variety of fashion on sale in the region, often at lower prices than the mainland.

It can be difficult to find traditional Chinese attire such as the qipao (often called a cheongsam in the West), a skin-tight dress, or the tangzhuang, a high-collared slim-fitting jacket worn by both sexes. These elegant garments, often made from silk and highly embroidered, are rarely worn by ordinary Chinese except as part of a work 'uniform', e.g. the girls who welcome diners to restaurants are frequently dressed in a qipao. You can have such items made, but you may look rather foolish in them. The qipao is particularly unforgiving unless you're tall and slender.

There's one Chinese fashion house, called Fish, that makes clothes incorporating the best of Chinese fashion, and their shops are well worth visiting as they stock more practical sizes for Western figures and aren't outrageously expensive.

⚠ Caution

Think twice before buying fake designer handbags, particularly if you plan to take them abroad. Not surprisingly, some countries are unhappy at the number of high quality copies the Chinese are turning out; if you try to enter France or Italy carrying one, it could be confiscated and you can also be heavily fined.

One area of attire in which the Chinese excel is winter clothing. Northern winters can be bitter, and every autumn heralds great displays of thermal underwear such as long johns, quilted coats and trousers and other clothing that emphasises comfort over style. Fur coats go on sale, as well – the Chinese have no qualms about wearing animal fur – and as the temperature plummets, department stores erect great quilts over their entrance doors and turn up the heating.

High summer sees the arrival of another unusual fashion, as many people take to the streets wearing their pyjamas. This is particularly true in Shanghai, where temperatures can climb above 32°C (90°F). These are special pyjamas designed for wearing outdoors and some, especially those made from silk, manage to be comfortable and glamorous at the same time.

Most children's clothes sold in China are locally designed and produced, and aren't expensive, particularly when bought from markets. Specialist stores include the British Mothercare chain, which has several outlets in China.

NEWSPAPERS, MAGAZINES & BOOKS

The Chinese buy a vast number of newspapers, although there isn't much available in English. Some Chinese newspapers carry a small English-language section, but the only nationwide paper printed wholly in English is the China Daily. Published six days a week in Beijing, it's available in every province. China Daily costs 1.5 RMB, although you can often pick up a free copy in hotels. It's owned by the Communist Party of China, therefore it isn't the most entertaining of reads, but it includes reasonable coverage of international news and sport, as well as national business and politics, and it has a comprehensive website (🖥 chinadaily.com.cn).

A competitor called the Global Times is published in English in Beijing and Shanghai but not countrywide. If you live in Guangdong province, you can easily get hold of the Hong Kong published South China Morning Post, which suffers from less censorship than mainland newspapers but is no more exciting to read.

Some Chinese newspapers have online editions in English and several other languages, including the top-selling People's Daily (🖥 english. peopledaily.com.cn) and the Shanghai Daily (🖥 shanghaidaily.com). Most foreign newspapers and magazines have online versions, some of which require a subscription to be paid, but some websites are blocked, such as the BBC. You can, however, access blocked websites if you install a proxy browser such as TOR (🖥 torproject.org) on your laptop before arrival.

Foreign language newspapers such as *The Times*, *The Asian Wall Street Journal* and *USA Today* are available at news kiosks in five-star hotels, although the editions are often a few days out of date. You can also pick up magazines such as *Time*, *Newsweek* and *The Economist*.

The easiest way to obtain your daily paper is to ask the postman to deliver it. You must pay him in advance, but this guarantees a newspaper on your doormat, along with your post, every day without fail.

All magazines published in China are for the Chinese market. Many are Chinese versions of well-known titles such as *National Geographic* and *Cosmopolitan*, but there are no English versions on sale. The government-owned news agency Xinhua publishes the occasional magazine for foreigners, extolling the virtues and the opportunities available in China; but other than that, the only other magazines are those produced by expats for expats. These include the *Beijing Review* and *Beijing this Month*, as well as Beijing and Shanghai *Metro*. There are also local editions of *City Weekend* published in Beijing, Guangzhou and Shanghai, and other expat magazines come and go. They mainly feature classified advertisements and what's on listings, although some have interesting articles. Most have an online edition which saves you tracking down the real thing. If you want any magazine from overseas, you must take out a subscription with the publisher.

One of the major frustrations for foreigners in China is the lack of English-language books. There are government-run foreign-language bookshops in most large cities, but the choice of titles is usually limited. Most stock no fiction other than copies of classic novels written by long dead authors, and most of the books consist of dry treatises on subjects such as architecture. Exceptions are the Foreign Language Bookstore in Wangfujingdajie in Beijing, where there's a whole rack of contemporary novels and biographies, albeit headed by left-wing heroes such as Che Guevara, Karl Marx and Fidel Castro, and there's also a broad selection of books on Chinese culture and cookery. In Shanghai, Charterhouse in Huai Hai Lu sells only English-language books.

Expats in Beijing, Chengdu and Suzhou can visit The Bookworm (: chinabookworm.com), a small but expanding chain of English-language bookshops opened by an enterprising foreigner. They don't just sell books but also have a members' lending library, serve tea, coffee and beer, and even have a small restaurant. They also invite authors to give talks. Apart from these shops it's sometimes possible to find a limited number of English-language books on newsstands in five-star hotels, in larger Friendship Stores and at museum shops, e.g. the Shanghai Museum shop is outstanding.

To get hold of particular titles, you must order your books from overseas, either by buying from an online retailer such as Amazon or via a book club or friendly bookshop in your home town. Hong Kong based Paddyfield (🖥 paddyfield.com) has a good selection. Most books turn up in the post with no problem, although Chinese customs officials can take exception to some titles. Anything to do with pornography is banned, as are books which criticise the Chinese government, past or present. Don't imagine that your order will slip through the net, as packages are often opened and examined.

ANTIQUES & COLLECTIBLES

China is a shoppers' paradise, and Westerners are drawn to its unique arts, crafts and collectibles. Many are utterly different from anything in the West, and because they're often run of the mill to local people, they can sometimes be purchased at bargain prices. Even some brand new objects, straight from the factory, are desirable, such as musical instruments and bird cages. This section highlights some of the areas which collectors find irresistible, along with tips on what not to buy.

What to Buy

Bamboo Carvings

The Chinese are adept at carving lengths of bamboo into Chinese characters or country scenes. These are unique to China, and aren't expensive; around 50 RMB buys a good example.

Bird Cages & Feeders

The wooden cages in which the Chinese display their pet birds are beautifully proportioned and often ornate, yet cost next to nothing: between 100 and 250 RMB buys a beautiful cage which doesn't need a bird to be decorative. Just as desirable are the small porcelain bowls used to hold birdseed or water. Some are lavishly decorated with coloured figures, flowers, fish and dragons, all on a tiny scale. A new bowl can cost as little as 1 or 2 RMB, while a rare antique might fetch 3,000 RMB, which would be highly prized in the US.

Bronzes

There must be hundreds of thousands of copies of bronze spear or arrow tips and cooking vessels on sale in antique shops and markets, supposedly dating back thousands of years. However, the odds of finding one which is genuinely ancient are remote.

Calligraphy

One of China's most arresting sights is that of an elderly man, with a metre long brush and a bucket of water, 'painting' Chinese characters in water on the pavement. The characters are gone in minutes but he paints for the practice and to demonstrate his talent. The Chinese admire the art of calligraphy, and many people aspire to achieve beautiful handwriting or display proverbs or poems written in Chinese characters as they would a painting, for its artistry as much as for its meaning.

The calligraphy industry produces inks, brushes, ink stones and special paper, all of which are sold in art shops, frequently located close by or within antiques markets. Ink stones – small mortars for the grinding and holding of ink – can be works of art in themselves.

Cameras

During the early days of the People's Republic, Mao Zedong's wife Jiang Qing commissioned the Shanghai Camera Company to make 200 copies of the Leica M4 and Hasselblad under Chinese names, as proof that China was as skilled as the West. Many were gifted to visiting politicians, and the few which remain in China fetch ridiculous prices. However, the same company also produced many copies of Leica 3 and Rolleiflex cameras, and these can still be unearthed in shops and markets. A Chinese Leica 3 would set you back 300-1,000 RMB.

Chinese Opera & Martial Arts

Almost completely unknown outside China, the opera plays a huge part in Chinese culture. It uses a decorative range of clothes, masks, beards and make-up, fans and miniature drums, which are sold by specialist shops. The drums are used to accompany the actors' movements and also by practitioners of *taijiquan*. If you're a fan of this martial art, you can buy one of the loose white suits which people wear while practising the movements from the same outlets.

Cloisonné

This is an old technique whereby metal wires are brazed onto a copper plate or vessel to form the outline of a pattern and the spaces filled with enamel or gemstones. The process is still practised today and, regardless of what a vendor might tell you, 99.9 per cent of cloisonné work on sale in China is modern. However, it's very decorative and smaller objects aren't expensive if you haggle – as little as 20 RMB for a small dish.

Cultural Revolution Souvenirs

Busts and plaques of Mao Zedong are everywhere, as are Chairman Mao lapel badges; there are over 200 varieties of badge, which are popular with collectors. Also collected are the pretty porcelain figurines of characters from revolutionary ballets such as *The Red Detachment of Women* and *The White Haired Girl*. Some are modern copies but most are delightful. They sell on eBay for between US$25 and $50 but are much cheaper if you spot one in an antique shop or market in China.

Other interesting memorabilia from this period include khaki military satchels with Chairman Mao's picture emblazoned on them, revolutionary troops' caps, old field telephones and much more. Very few items are as old as they're made out to be, but they're often very good copies.

Dinosaur Eggs

Farmers have been selling fossilised dinosaur eggs to collectors for decades. Surprisingly, many are genuine but you should think hard about buying one, as officially this trade is illegal and you could run into problems if you wanted to take your egg out of China, as antiques cannot be exported without a permit. The eggs can also be very heavy.

Embroidery

Just 50 years ago, clothing was often elaborately embroidered by hand and older items are works of art. If you can find an old piece, when framed it makes a lovely picture. Most modern embroidery is done by machine, which is also sometimes sold as 'art', and ranges from naff pictures of kittens to some pleasant landscapes and studies of birds and flowers.

Furniture

Items of 'antique' furniture are almost certain to be copies, but even copies often display intricate craftsmanship and are valuable. The Chinese produce exquisite lacquered furniture, often black and inlaid with mother of pearl or painted with designs in gold, and this can be relatively inexpensive, considering the artistry; a chest or desk can cost between 1,500 and 5,000 RMB and sellers can organise shipping overseas. Ming Dynasty style chairs and tables have a solid yet simple style that's very attractive.

Ivory

The trade in ivory is banned or restricted in many Western countries to protect elephants, but the Chinese still collect it and there are many beautiful items for sale. However, if you buy it, be aware that it may be confiscated by customs in many countries. A more ecologically correct alternative is to seek out items made from bone or horn. However, don't buy an 'oracle bone'. These are pieces of bone or turtle shell that were heated and cracked for the purpose of divining messages during the Shang Dynasty and while some still exist, most are fakes.

Jade

You can buy this beautiful green gemstone everywhere, even in supermarkets, although a great deal of the 'jade' sold in street markets is plastic. If you handle some genuine pieces you should be able to discern the difference. Jade is highly valued and pieces are priced according to the quality, colour and the workmanship of the carving. The only way to evaluate a piece of jade is to study a range of similar pieces, although unless you're an expert this isn't easy. If you find a piece of jade that you like and the price seems fair, buy it and don't worry too much about the value.

Lacquerware

Lacquerware is a process whereby metal dishes and small vessels are covered with repeated coats of paint or varnish, usually red, to a thickness of perhaps 2mm, then carved or inscribed with intricate designs. It dates back to the Shang Dynasty and antique examples are much sought after and valuable. Some modern pieces are available, made using the old techniques, but there are also many factory-made copies in which plastic has been substituted for the lacquer.

Money

Old banknotes and coins are for sale in every antique market. Some notes from the early days of the People's Republic are attractive and collectible, as are those featuring past political leaders such as Chiang Kai Shek or Sun Yat-sen.

None are very expensive. Notes from the 19th century or earlier are much rarer. You also find notes from other currencies; pre-Gulf War Iraqi dinars bearing the likeness of Saddam Hussein are a best seller among Chinese collectors. Early coins were crude and easy to copy, therefore many offered for sale are counterfeit; be especially careful of 'silver' coins.

In Beijing's Liulichang district, you can track down the original certificates for shares in some of China's railway lines, dating back to the early 20th century when the money to build them was raised overseas. They have no monetary value, but are decorative and make interesting framed prints.

Musical Instruments

The Chinese have a number of unique musical instruments, such as the *erhu*, a two-stringed instrument played like a fiddle, and the *pipa*, resembling a ukulele. These aren't necessarily antiques – many are still manufactured and played today – but if you're musical, they're reasonably priced and interesting acquisitions. They're sold in specialist music shops.

Paintings

Many Chinese paintings are in a very distinct style. Those by the most sought-after artists sell for many thousands of *yuan*, but it's difficult for Westerners to judge their quality, and you need to study the medium carefully to stand a chance of picking up a good investment. Modern wall hanging paintings are inexpensive and decorative. For more information on investing in Chinese art, see page 196.

Porcelain

Although many people think China is named after the china that was sent to Europe centuries ago, this is incorrect – the name came from the Qin (pronounced 'Chin') Dynasty, centuries earlier. However, china, or more accurately, porcelain, originated in China and pieces which were fired in one of the five original imperial kilns of Ding, Ge, Guan, Jun and Ru are valuable today. The imperial kilns in Jingdezhen in Jianxi province are also famous for the blue and white porcelain that was produced there centuries before it reached Delft in Holland.

Any antique shop or market in China is full of porcelain and pottery, most of it dusty or dirty. Blue and white are the predominant colours but there are many others. Yellow was used for a long time, but only on porcelain for the Emperor, and tends to be difficult to find.

People have been copying porcelain since the first piece was fired, and the vast majority of objects on sale are copies. However, a good copy is worth more than a poor copy, and an antique copy is worth more still. Most good porcelain has a square 'chop' mark on its base, identifying the Emperor at the time it was made. There's no guarantee that it actually dates from the time indicated by this mark – the chop mark can also be copied – but it helps to identify the porcelain and its source.

☑ SURVIVAL TIP

The feet of the dragons which decorate porcelain provide a clue to the quality of the piece. If they have four claws on each foot, it was intended for everyday use by ordinary people, but five claws indicate that it was imperial quality and made for one of the ruling classes. Of course, forgers knew this also, and there's a lot of fake 'imperial' porcelain on sale.

The study of porcelain is a major task, and a good book, perhaps from somewhere like the Shanghai Museum, will help you to understand the different techniques and styles used in different eras.

Posters

Some of the most valuable and collectable posters are from the time of the Cultural Revolution. They picture sturdy, handsome soldiers leaping forward, rifles in hands, or happy, red cheeked girls driving tractors. They may have been intended as propaganda, but it's gloriously colourful propaganda. The genuine article should show its age, with creases, turned corners or little rips, although more recent copies have been skilfully 'aged'.

Easier to track down are posters from '20s and '30s Shanghai, featuring languid ladies with shingled hair, dressed in 'flapper' fashions and smoking cigarettes in long holders, which were used to sell cigarettes and soap. Although older, they're more widely available and far cheaper than posters from the Cultural Revolution period. The latter can cost up to 500 RMB but you can pick up a '20s poster for 10-20 RMB.

Seals

If you look at a Chinese painting you can usually find a small red square in one corner containing several Chinese characters. This is how painters sign their work, using a seal dipped in a red ink slab or pad. The actual seal is a short length of beautiful or unusual rock or stone, square in section, on the bottom of which is carved the characters that make up the owner's name; the top may be carved to represent a dragon or a lion or, if the stone is exceptional, left in its natural state. Seals can also be made from wood, particularly oak, and even from porcelain. Most places that sell antiques can carve one for you in around ten minutes, providing you with a unique 'Chinese signature' for between 20 and 200 RMB, depending on the type of material chosen.

Shadow Puppets

In the countryside, long before the arrival of television or the cinema, people entertained themselves with puppet shows. Often the puppets were behind a screen backlit by a lantern and the audience watched their shadow antics. Shadow puppets, made from semi-translucent card or animal skins, can still be found. Some are amazingly complicated, with every joint articulated, and yet they aren't expensive, costing from 100 RMB, or up to 500 RMB for a more elaborate figure on horseback. Mounted in a picture frame, they make a real conversation piece.

Snuff Bottles

Small, clear glass bottles, around 7cm (3in) high, were used by the Chinese long ago for snuff or perfume. Many have scenes painted on the **inside** the bottle. Most are less than 100 years old but are decorative and desirable. However, like most 'antiques', most are modern copies.

Watches

The Chinese began making wrist watches in the '50s. Early examples had mechanical movements, and people are just beginning to realise their worth. One especially collectable timepiece, which reflects recent history, is the watch which features the head of a helmeted Chinese soldier on the face. These were issued to soldiers as a form of campaign medal, and can be purchased for around 200 RMB.

Where to Shop for Antiques

Every city of any size has an antiques building, home to scores of separate dealers. In some places, there are also government-run antique shops where prices tend to be higher, although the articles on sale are a little more authentic. Then there are the private antique shops, often in a street with many similar antique dealers, or located in an upmarket hotel, where prices reflect the clientele rather than the value of the artefacts. Many museums have shops. The one at the

Shanghai Museum is excellent although, even here, the articles are mostly copies.

Finally there are the street markets, which can be real fun, although the items on sale have a less authentic pedigree and the initial prices may be ridiculously high. If you're willing to haggle and haggle well, you may buy something for a third, a quarter or even a tenth of its original price.

Panjiayuan is the main antiques market in Beijing, although the Hongqiao Pearl Market is the most interesting market, as it has so much more besides antiques. In Shanghai, a good place for antique hunting is Guang Dong Street in the Huang Pu district, where a daily antiques market is held, or Dongtai Lu and Fangbang Lu at weekends. In Guangzhou there's Longjin Xilu market.

Don't expect the 'antiques' in any of these places to be well presented. The Chinese think that a dusty or earth-encrusted article looks more genuinely old than something that is clean, and that is how they're usually displayed.

FURNITURE

Most department stores have a furniture section, but the choice is limited by the space available. For a much wider selection, visit the nearest 'furniture city': a cluster of warehouses with each floor divided into separate showrooms for individual furniture manufacturers. Each building may contain the products of over 100 manufacturers, allowing you to compare different brands for comfort and prices, which are consistently lower than you would pay in the West.

There's a 'furniture city' in every town. Most showcase Chinese manufacturers' wares,

but there are also joint ventures with Italian and Scandinavian companies, therefore it's possible to find some well-designed pieces. (Chinese design is improving, although there are still some ugly three-piece suites that look as if they were designed for a very large Buddha with a penchant for bling.) If you like the Scandinavian look, the Swedish homes warehouse IKEA has several stores in China offering well-designed furniture and accessories at a reasonable price.

Once you've made your selection at 'furniture city', you can order direct from the showroom. Delivery is usually with a week, and in some cases your new sofa will arrive the same afternoon, occasionally on the back of a three-wheeled bicycle! Delivery may be included in the price (check first), and the delivery men are generally helpful, assembling your dining table or installing your light fittings as part of the service.

For curtains and blinds, there are numerous showrooms or you can visit a textiles market, buy the cloth and have your curtains made up by them. Either way, allow two weeks for delivery and installation, which is usually included in the price.

Fitted carpets are unusual in China. Most homes have tiled or wood floors, with perhaps some scatter rugs or small carpets. Floor boards made from laminated strips of bamboo look and wear well.

Not for Sale

Some items are difficult if not impossible to find in China, and it's worth bringing a supply with you from home. These include:

- aerosol deodorants: roller-balled deodorants are the only ones available

- aspirin

- bras & underwear in larger sizes

- Marmite

- tampons (Chinese women don't use them)

HOUSEHOLD GOODS

Everyday necessities, from mops and dustpans to spoons and plates, are sold in supermarkets and (more cheaply) in markets. There are several different types of suppliers of electrical appliances. The widest choice of fridges, washing machines and televisions, etc., is offered by large electrical goods retailers such as Gome, which sell nothing else. Larger supermarkets have a smaller range of appliances, while department stores sometimes sell imported electrical equipment as well as Chinese products.

Although the Chinese do most of their cooking on a hob, you can buy top quality ovens, both gas and electric, in specialist stores.

Many of the 'foreign' goods are actually made in China by joint-venture companies. Philips manufacture virtually their entire range of products in China, while Siemens make excellent washing machines and refrigerators, and the quality is every bit as good as those manufactured in Europe. However, don't dismiss Chinese white goods manufacturers such as Haier, which make excellent products at competitive prices.

Whatever you buy and wherever you buy it, don't expect much after-sales service. Although officially, goods are covered by a warranty (see below), few retailers are willing to offer a refund if there's a problem, although they'll happily put you in touch with someone who can fix it.

HAIRDRESSERS & BARBERS

The Chinese are proud of their strong black hair and take the trouble to care for it. Men, especially, are fussy about their crowning glory, and many start dyeing it as soon as they see the first signs of grey. There are hairdressers and barbers on most streets; some are ladies' hair salons offering beauty as well as hair treatments, but there are also many salons that cater to both sexes, usually identifiable by a rotating striped pole outside. A man may find himself having a trim sat next to a woman having a permanent wave, and the hairdresser may be male or female. Whoever cuts your hair, it will take longer than you might expect, often an hour or more.

The experience begins with a wash and shampoo. You then move to the barber's chair, where the hairdresser takes great pains to cut your hair into the required style. It's then back to the basin for another wash, before a final trim and blow dry. The final bill comes to between 10 and 40 RMB, depending on how posh the salon is, although more extensive treatments such as perms and highlights and the attentions of a top stylist will increase the price. There's no need to tip, and it isn't expected.

Although most hairdressers use cut-throat razors to trim hair at the nape of the neck and around the ears, very few have the skill to give you a shave. This is something outside their experience, as Chinese men have sparse facial hair and few need to shave on a regular basis.

HOME SHOPPING

It's possible to shop by mail order or online in China, although home shopping is still in its infancy, and many people are suspicious of it because of the dubious quality of goods and inadequate consumer protection. However, internet shopping is catching on among younger people, with the most popular website Taobao (💻 taobao.com/index_global.php), which is similar to eBay. The Chinese version of eBay is Eachnet (💻 eachnet.com).

The major drawback (insurmountable?) for foreigners is that these websites are only available in Chinese. However, if you can get a Chinese friend to help you, then it can be a good way of tracking down hard-to-find items. Payment is usually by debit or credit card, e.g. Visa, or through Alipay (💻 alipay. com), the Chinese version of PayPal. Deliveries are via China Post or, for an additional fee, private courier.

There are a great many international shopping websites, such as Amazon, and these are a great way to obtain goods from your home country, although the high cost of postage to China can make them expensive.

DUTY FREE ALLOWANCES

On entering mainland China from overseas (Hong Kong and Macau count as overseas), you're permitted to import the following goods duty free:

♦ 400 cigarettes – 600 if you're staying for over six months;

♦ 2 litres of alcoholic drinks;

♦ a 'reasonable' amount of perfume for personal use;

♦ one film or digital camera, video camera, tape recorder and laptop;

♦ 50g of gold or silver. Officially, you're supposed to declare any amount in excess of 50g.

There are no restrictions on the value of gifts. For more information about restricted or prohibited items, see page 62..

CONSUMER RIGHTS

There are laws protecting consumers, but many shops interpret them to their own advantage and you'll struggle to get a refund if an item is faulty. Retailers are far more like to offer you a replacement or an alternative item of the same value. Furthermore, this only applies in larger stores such as supermarkets and department stores, and small traders are often unwilling to admit there's a problem or offer any recompense. The moral is, always check goods carefully before parting with your money, and make sure it's something you really want to buy. You cannot just exchange something because you don't like it.

If you feel that you've been badly treated by a shop or service provider, you can take your complaint to a government-run consumers' organisation (*xiaofeizherxiehui*). You're unlikely to receive a refund, but using this route can sometimes persuade a reluctant retailer to replace a faulty item.

⚠ Caution

If you plan on taking something back to a department store or a supermarket, you must provide proof of purchase, e.g. a receipt, and file your complaint within seven days.

Yading, Chuanxi

18.
ODDS & ENDS

This chapter contains miscellaneous information, in alphabetical order. Although all topics aren't of vital importance, most are of general interest to anyone planning to live or work in China, including everything you ever wanted to know (but were afraid to ask) about tipping and toilets.

CITIZENSHIP

It's rare for a foreigner to become a citizen of China. Many Chinese face considerable difficulty travelling the world and must usually obtain visas to visit other countries, particularly those in the West; most would be amazed if someone was willing to swap the 'freedom' of a Western passport for life as a Chinese national, although they'd be honoured it you did.

Foreigners can apply for citizenship, but it's a long and complex process requiring a great deal of documentation at many different levels, from the local Public Security Bureau (PSB) right up to the Ministry of Public Security in Beijing, which makes the final decision.

Marriage to a Chinese citizen doesn't confer automatic citizenship and you cannot even begin the application process until you've been married for five years. It's also possible to apply as the widow or widower of a Chinese citizen or if you're technically 'stateless'. But consider carefully. Unlike most European countries and the US, China doesn't recognise the state of dual nationality – unless you're a resident of Hong Kong with a British overseas passport – and you'd have to give up your original nationality. Americans might find renouncing US citizenship to be nigh on impossible as the US authorities are unlikely to take your request seriously!

The alternative to citizenship is the acquisition of a Foreigners' Permanent Residence Card. These allow the holder to live long-term in China without a visa, and to work without restrictions, but the application process is long and complicated and few permits are issued.

CLIMATE

China is a similar size to the US and experiences a comparable range of climates, from the sub-Arctic chill of the north to the semi-tropical south.

The hottest place in the country isn't on the southern coast, however, but in China's remote northwest. Turpan (*Tulufan*) in Xinjiang province sits in a basin surrounded by desert and endures summers as hot as 50°C (122°F) in the shade. It's also the driest place in China with an average 300 days a year without rain. The wettest place is *Emei Shan*, a mountain in Sichuan province which gets 2,034mm (80in) of rain a year, but the east and south can also be very soggy, particularly during summer.

China's coldest spot is said to be Mohe county in Heilongjiang province, where temperatures as low as -52°C (-62°F) have been recorded. However, anywhere north of the Yellow River can get snow, and you certainly need central heating during the chilly winters. Snow further south is rare, although in early 2008 freak snowstorms crippled much of eastern China as far south as Guangdong province, damaging property, cutting off power supplies and even halting flights at Guangzhou's airport.

Average temperatures and rainfall (precipitation) are shown in the table overleaf, but temperatures can and do vary widely from these figures.

Newspapers provide remarkably accurate weather forecasts, and television and radio broadcasts are also excellent; the most detailed daily weather forecast is shown on China Central Television's Channel 1 at 7.30pm each evening.

Due to its size and location in relation to certain tectonic plates and weather systems, China suffers many natural disasters. Typhoons (*tai feng*) and cyclones are common along the south and east coasts during spring and autumn, which (as well as wind damage) can spark widespread flooding, not just on the coast but also in areas

Average Temperatures & Rainfall in Major Chinese Cities		
City	High/Low °C (°F)	Annual rainfall in mm (inches)
Beijing	31/ -10 (88/14)	619 (24)
Chongqing	35/5 (95/41)	1,088 (43)
Guangzhou	36/12 (97/54)	2,286 (90)
Guilin	32/8 (90/46)	1,284 (51)
Harbin	29/-25 (84/-13)	983 (39)
Hong Kong	31/13 (88/55)	2,169 (85)
Jilin	31/-18 (88/0)	711 (32)
Kunming	29/8 (84/46)	967 (38)
Lhasa	24/-10 (75/14)	457 (18)
Shanghai	32/1 (90/34)	1,168 (46)
Shenzhen	32/11 (90/52)	1,928 (76)
Urumqi	28/-22 (82/-8)	330 (13)
Wuhan	34/1 (93/34)	1,257 (49)

close to major rivers and dams. The flooding which devastated many central provinces in 1931, resulting from a combination of cyclones and torrential rainfall, is still ranked as the world's worst natural disaster, with a final death toll estimated as high as 4m. At the other end of the climactic spectrum, drought is a problem in the western provinces of Yunnan and Guizhou, leading to crop failures and forest fires.

Earthquakes occur in the more mountainous central and northern provinces. They aren't as frequent as in neighbouring Japan, but the high population densities mean they can lead to serious loss of life. There have been a number of devastating earthquakes in China, include one centred on Shaanxi province in the 16th century which claimed 830,000 victims – the deadliest earthquake in history. Other serious quakes have affected the areas around Ningxia and Hebei provinces and, in 2008, Sichuan province was hit by a quake measuring 8 on the Richter scale and which killed over 68,000 people. Sichuan has been particularly badly affected by earthquakes, and has experienced more than a dozen measuring over 6 on the Richter scale since 1900.

Earthquakes and flooding often result in further catastrophes such as landslides and epidemics, of which hydrophobia (rabies) and Japanese encephalitis from infected mosquitoes are among the most dangerous.

There's little you can do to minimise such risks, which are inherent in some parts of China, but you should be aware that they exist.

North & Northeast China

These regions, which encompass Beijing and all points north, have glorious autumns, especially in Beijing which is on almost the same latitude as New York and has a similar climate. Winter begins in early December and lasts until late March, during which it can be intensely cold with frequent snowfalls. The night-time temperature in Beijing can fall as low as -20°C (-4°F), while during the day it hovers close to freezing; bitter winds from further north make it feel much colder. Further north, in Heilongjiang province and Inner Mongolia, the thermometer may sink as low as -40°C (-40°F) and it can stay well below freezing all day.

Spring is a brief interlude before the heat of summer. In Beijing, it lasts just five or six weeks but the temperature is perfect, around 25°C (77°F), and the skies bright blue. There's a chilly wind, and people dust off their kites. Further north, spring comes later and the mercury only reaches 22°C (72°F), but it's still pleasant.

Summer is the wettest time of the year in Beijing, with temperatures rising to 31°C (88°F), and on some days it's unpleasantly humid. Another weather hazard is dust or sand storms that blow in from Mongolia's Gobi Desert during late spring and summer; visibility can be reduced to zero and cars are shrouded in dust.

Throughout these regions, most offices and homes have central heating, but it's often connected to a district heating plant and only operates during winter months. An alternative form of heating is advisable.

Northwest China

This region, bordering Outer Mongolia and Kazakhstan to the north and Tibet to the south, is one of climatic extremes and much of it's near-desert .The total rainfall in Urumqi, the capital of Xinjiang province, averages just 330mm (13in) a year and temperatures in the low 40s (above 100°F) aren't uncommon, although it's a dry heat and therefore isn't unpleasant. However, there's nothing to retain the warmth in the winter, so from mid-October to mid-March when the wind sweeps down from the north it can be bitterly cold. In Xinjiang, the average maximum winter daytime temperature is around -10°C (14°F) and it can fall to -40°C (-40°F) at night.

Central & Eastern China

On the central plains of China, through which run the Yangtze and the Yellow Rivers, the summers can be long and very hot. The cities of Chongqing, Nanjing and Wuhan, all on the Yangtze, are called the 'three furnaces', where the average maximum summer temperature is 34°C (93°F), although on many days it's considerably higher. Shanghai, at the mouth of the Yangtze and at about the same latitude as Cairo, New Delhi and Houston is hot and humid at this time of year and many locals go about wearing pyjamas, the coolest outfits they own. Shanghai has roughly twice the rainfall of Beijing at an average of 1,168mm (46in) a year, with the heaviest precipitation between April and September.

Winters are short in these regions but can be almost as cold as in Beijing; Shanghai can be particularly grey and unpleasant, particularly as central heating isn't common in the city. Winter also brings fog to many areas, particularly the provinces of Henan and Shandong.

Southern China

The Tropic of Cancer passes through Yunnan, Guangxi and Guangdong provinces, therefore much of the south enjoys a tropical climate. Guangzhou, the largest city in the south, is on the same latitude as Cuba and Calcutta, and it rains there every month of the year, from winter drizzle to heavy, tropical summer deluges when several inches fall in a single day. The area also suffers from the ravages of cyclones and typhoons in late summer and early autumn. However, when the clouds clear it can be lovely, despite the humidity.

While the mercury doesn't hit the temperatures reached in the northwest, it can still reach 38°C (100°F) on occasions. Winters are short and mild. The official average minimum temperature is a heady 12°C (54°F), although after so much heat it can feel pretty cold at times.

Further south, Hainan Island, China's second-largest island after Taiwan, has similar weather to Guangzhou, although the sea breezes make it feel much more pleasant.

Tibet

Tibet is totally dry from October to mid-May, so while winters are bitterly cold there's little snow. Instead, the wind, driving across Tibet from the north, creates sand or dust storms. Summer brings glorious sunshine. The capital Lhasa enjoys almost 3,000 hours of sunshine a year, earning the name Sunlit City. Summer also brings rain and heat. The official average maximum temperature of 24°C (75°F) in June and July is misleading, as it can reach 38°C (100°F) on some days. However, even when it's baking hot during the day, Tibet's extreme elevation means that it can still be freezing at night.

CRIME

China is generally very safe. Most crime consists of minor offences such as theft and pick-pocketing and white collar crimes such as fraud – corruption is rife among government officials, developers and business people. The Chinese aren't aggressive, and while you may witness altercations involving

Dali City, Yunnan Province

raised voices, pushing and shoving, they rarely escalate into a fight. Serious crimes against the person, such as assault or violent robbery, are rare. Violence against foreigners is rarer still.

A major trigger for crime is the vast difference in income between city dwellers in the more prosperous east and south, and those who live deep in the rural centre and west of China. It's a two-tier society, and in spite of the state's efforts to improve it, the disparities are getting worse. Workers arriving in the booming cities are poorly treated by their employers and sometimes turn to petty crime just to get by. Foreigners are visible and easy targets for small-time thieves, and you need to take care to protect your belongings.

Take particular care in crowded places, such as railway and bus stations, as these are favourite places for pick-pockets and thieves. Take particular care of your passport. They're a popular target for thieves who 'recycle' them to provide fake ID documents, and replacing them can be a lot of trouble. Thieves sometimes use razor blades to slit bags to get at passports and other valuables, therefore it's safest to carry them in an inside pocket or a money belt concealed under your clothes.

Avoiding petty theft is mainly common sense. Don't invite trouble by doing things you wouldn't do at home, such as flashing wads of cash in public places or walking alone through a 'rough' area after dark. Foreigners are rich in comparison with most Chinese – a foreign teacher's monthly wage is equal to the annual income for a rural

family – and that has the potential to make you a target for a desperate and unscrupulous thief.

The Chinese go out of their way to protect their belongings. Bicycles, motorcycles and cars are always locked, even in private car parks, and houses often have bars on the windows. Always lock your bicycle or vehicle, even when you're just nipping into a shop.

Many expatriates have lived in China for years and never lost a thing or had a nasty moment through luck or, more likely, common sense. If you're unfortunate enough to be a victim of crime, report it to the Public Security Bureau and ask them to complete a report to enable you to make a claim on your insurance (if applicable).

Sexual Harassment

This is rare in China, where women are treated with respect. However, you must also behave respectfully and avoid revealing clothes such as short skirts and low-cut tops, which can invite unwanted male attention. If you dress in an overtly sexy manner, people may think you're a 'working girl' and proposition you. You should also treat invitations with caution. For example, if a businessman invites you to a karaoke bar after a meal, he may well have more than singing in his mind.

In China, foreign men are more likely to be harassed than women. Prostitution is a growing industry, and prostitutes even ply their trade in the public rooms of top hotels. In 2010, a famous five-star hotel belonging to an international chain was demoted to four stars due to the presence of so many prostitutes within its environs.

If you're a man staying alone at a hotel and you want a good night's sleep, take the telephone off the hook. It's common for women to telephone your hotel room at all hours of the night offering 'massage services'.

Corruption

This is unlikely to affect you, as a foreigner, as it primarily occurs between those looking for favours and those capable of dispensing favours. The most serious corruption takes place between developers of real estate and government officials responsible for the allocation or sale of land, and many offenders get away with it. A recent investigation by the Supreme People's Procuratorate, China's highest prosecution agency, into state functionaries convicted of such crimes between 2005 and 2009, revealed that almost 70 per cent had received a reprieve or been exempted from punishment after intervention by their superiors.

If you work in a position where your decision could help someone, e.g. you have responsibility for placing contracts, purchasing on behalf of your employer or recruitment, you may be offered bribes. Teachers, too, can face awkward situations when parents, seeking better results for their child, make offers in return for extra 'help', and it can be difficult to refuse them diplomatically.

Drugs

Illegal drugs aren't a major issue in China, although the problem is growing. Heroin trafficking takes place, mainly in Yunnan province which adjoins the drug-producing countries of Laos, Myanmar and Vietnam, and ecstasy is sometimes peddled at clubs, but the drugs scene so common in the West hasn't (yet) taken hold in China. Don't even contemplate bringing drugs, even cannabis, into China. The law is very tough on drug offenders, with dealers, manufacturers and smugglers all facing a possible death sentence, and drug users forced to undergo rehabilitation. Foreign users are usually deported at lightning speed.

Between 2008 and 2010, almost 600 foreigners were arrested and charged with drug offences. The majority were from Africa and Southeast Asia, but some Westerners were involved. Every year a number of people, Chinese and foreign, are summarily executed for drug offences. In 2010, a British citizen was executed after being found guilty of attempting to smuggle heroin into China. Currently there are other foreigners awaiting sentence for drug offences and some will almost certainly face the death penalty.

Taboo Subjects

No one spies on foreigners in China anymore and the notion that you could be accused of political crimes, a fantasy espoused by some expats, is mainly paranoia. However, if you do something blatantly contrary to local customs you risk being reported to the police.

Foreigners can be asked to leave the country for talking too vigorously about their views on politics or religion. Both subjects are taboo in China, so even if a Chinese person raises them, it's best to change the subject or remain silent. Don't try to be a missionary for your religion or criticise Chinese politics too openly, however strongly you feel. Bear in mind that you're a guest in China and keep your views to yourself.

FLAG & ANTHEM

China's national flag dates back to 1st October 1949 when it was first flown in Tian'anmen Square to declare the People's Republic of China. Known as the Five Star Red Flag (*Wu Xing Hong Qi*), it commands respect, and people still turn out to see it hoisted and lowered each day in Tian'anmen Square.

The flag features five yellow stars on a red background. The red symbolises the blood of the martyrs of the revolution and is the colour of Communism worldwide, while the stars also have an important significance. The large one represents the Communist Party of China, while the four small stars denote the four social classes which made up the country at the time the flag was first flown – the workers, the peasantry (or farmers), the petite bourgeoisie (small businessmen) and the city bourgeoisie (officials and leaders) – all looking to the CPC for leadership.

> The national anthem was written in 1934 and is called *The March of the Volunteers* (*Qilai buyuan zuo nuli de renmen*). It became the country's anthem in 1949, although it was only made official in China's constitution in 2004. Most Chinese people know all the words, having sung it every morning before lessons at school.

GEOGRAPHY

With a land area of 9,596,961km^2 (3,705,407mi^2), China is generally accepted to be the fourth-largest country in the world, after Russia, Canada and the United States. However, if disputed territories such as Taiwan and Aksai Chin on the Indian border were included, it would nudge ahead of the US. Its geography is characterised by extremes. In the southwest it lays partial claim to the highest mountain in the world, Mt Everest (*Qomolongma Shan*), which towers 8,850m (29,035ft) over the Tibetan highlands, and the country is bisected by the River Yangtze (*Chang Jiang*), at 6,400km (3,920mi) the world's third-longest river after the Nile and the Amazon. Elsewhere its topography takes in high plateaus and sweeping grasslands, hostile deserts – the largest is the Taklamakan in the far west of the country, some 270,000 km^2 (100,000mi^2) in area – and lush tropical rainforest.

China's land border of 22,117km (13,743mi) is shared with 14 countries. From south to north these are Vietnam, Laos, Myanmar, India, Bhutan, Nepal, Pakistan, Afghanistan, Tajikistan, Kyrgyzstan, Kazakhstan, Mongolia, Russia and North Korea. Its 14,500km (9,010mi) coastline adjoins the China Sea and South China Sea and, beyond them, the Pacific Ocean.

The landmass of China slopes from west to east, with the highest mountains and plateaus in the Western half of the country, where much of the land is over 4,000m (13,123ft) above sea level. Mountains are incredibly important to the Chinese, who believe that many are sacred (see box) and make regular pilgrimages to their peaks. Other mountains of note include Mt Huang (*Huang Shan*) in Anhui province at 1,864m (6,115ft), considered by many to be the most beautiful of all China's mountains, while the karst limestone peaks around Guilin and in parts of Sichuan, although not particularly high, are amazing in shape; just like a Chinese landscape painting.

China's Sacred Mountains

Some 2,000 years ago, Taoists nominated the Five Sacred Mountains (listed below), chosen for their position rather than their height, which are places of pilgrimage for many people.

- North: Mt Heng (*Heng Shan Bei*), Shanxi province, 2,017m (6,617ft)
- South: Mt Heng (*Heng Shan Nan*), Hunan province, 1,300m (4,266 ft)
- East: Mt Tai (*Tai Shan*), Shandong province, 1,533m (5,030ft)
- West: Mt Hua (*Hua Shan*), Shaanxi province, 2,160m (7,087ft)
- Central: Mt Song (*Song Shan*), Henan province, 1,500m (4,921ft)

The Buddhists later designated four sacred mountains of their own, termed the Four Famous Buddhist Mountains:

- North: Wutai Mountain (*Wutai Shan*), Shanxi province, 3,058 m (10,033ft)
- South: Mt Jiuhua (*Jiuhua Shan*), Anhui province, 1,335m (4,380ft)
- East: Mt Putuo (*Putuo Shan*), Zhejiang province, 297m (974ft)
- West: Mt Emei (*Emei Shan*), Sichuan province, 3,099m (10,167ft)

It's possible to reach the summit of these mountains, either by cable car or, in some cases, via a long, steep and sometimes dangerous route of steps, ladders and narrow walkways.

Snowmelt and ice from glaciers on the mountain ranges, including the Himalayas, feed over 50,000 rivers. Of these, the most geographically important are the Yangtze and the Yellow River (*Huang He*), so called because of its enormous silt content, which flow west to east, the Mekong (*Lancang Jiang*) and Salween (*Nu Jiang*) rivers which flow from Tibet into Myanmar via Yunnan province, and the Pearl River (*Zhu Jiang*) which cuts through the southern Guangdong province towards Hong Kong. These rivers, and the vast flood plains which surround them, form the agricultural hub of China, and are where its population first settled and prospered, from the Han civilisation to the modern day.

There are many lakes in Tibet, but the largest in China is Qinghai Lake (*Qinghai Hu*) at 4,489 km^2 (1,733mi2), a saltwater lake on the edge of the Tibetan plateau.

GOVERNMENT

China's modern and often frantic pace of life can appear at odds with its politics, for despite its breakneck progress in recent years it remains one of the last true communist states. There are other political parties, but the Communist Party of China (CPC) effectively runs the country, overseeing all its administrative and legislative decisions; it appoints China's judges, manages its military, supervises its media and employs a large proportion of its people. It even provides China's head of state.

But it's a modern form of communism with a strong socialist edge. Since reforms began in the mid-'70s under the leadership of Mao's successor Deng Xiaoping, China has espoused many socialist beliefs, and its constitution even describes it as a 'socialist state under the people's democratic dictatorship'. The constitution also contains articles setting out civil rights such as freedom of religion and freedom of speech, and while some might question the level of freedom, it's clear that modern China is a very different place from its neighbour North Korea.

Central Government

In China, power is divided between three bodies: the Communist Party of China (CPC), the state, and the military, i.e. the People's Liberation Army (PLA). The highest power in the country is the Politburo Standing Committee, an elite group of CPC members which makes all the important decisions. In 2012, this committee comprised seven members, including President Xi Jinping and Premier Li Keqiang.

The state also consists of three organs: the National People's Congress (NPC) which is the only elected body, the State Council which consists of a premier (prime minister), vice premier and ministers – similar to the cabinet in a Western democracy – and the president. China's

Mao Tse Tung portrait from Tienanmen square

president has much more decision-making power than many Western presidents, not least because the position usually goes to the CPC's general secretary, and for a long time he was referred to as the chairman. (Note the word 'man': there are no high-ranking female politicians.) The president and premier can serve for up to ten years, and both Hu Xi Jinping and Li Keqiang were elected in November 2012.

The National People's Congress (NPC) is elected by the people, although not directly. NPC delegates are elected by the Provincial People's Congress (PPC) which, in turn, is elected by a lower level congress, who themselves are elected by a local people's congress which is elected by the electorate. Anyone over 18 is eligible to vote. In most cases, the number of candidates is limited. In the case of the NPC, only 110 candidates can contest each 100 seats, while for the PPC 120 candidates can contest each 100 seats. On the lower tiers, an unlimited number of candidates can compete for a maximum of 50 per cent of the seats.

The NPC meets with the Chinese People's Political Consultative Congress (CPPCC) each year at the Great Hall of the People in Tianan'men Square. At the most recent meeting in 2012, 2307 deputies attended and were elected for five years. The CPPCC is made up of delegates from various political parties, and plays a similar role to the House of Lords in the UK or the US Senate, while the NPC is more comparable to the House of Commons or House of Representatives. In practice, however, both are heavily influenced by the CPC. Around 70 per cent of NPC delegates are CPC members, while the bulk of the CPPCC's membership is from the party.

Local Government

Power is much less centralised in China than in many countries, and local government authorities play a large part in the country's administration. There's a system of devolving power down through different levels, from the provinces at the top to the village councils at the bottom.

The highest level is the provincial government, of which there are 34, comprising the 22 provinces plus one claimed province (Taiwan), the five autonomous regions (Guangxi, Inner Mongolia, Ningxia, Tibet and Xinjiang), the four municipalities (Beijing, Chongqing, Shanghai and Tianjin) and two Special Administrative Regions or SARS (Hong Kong and Macau). The second level is occupied by the 333 prefecture governments, most of which represent large cities or urban areas. There are 2,862 third-division governments representing counties and districts reflecting the administrative areas which China has been divided into for over 2,000 years. Below these are the 41,636 township administrations, which are similar to municipalities or communes in other countries. At the bottom of the ladder, but still powerful, are the village or neighbourhood committees; there are a total of 704,386 committees, each representing up to 20,000 people.

Political Parties

There's effectively only one party in China: the Communist Party of China. The CPC is the largest political party in the world, with some 82m members in 2012. However, it does recognise other political parties up to a point, and the following eight have, between them, around 500,000 declared members:

♦ China Association for Promoting Democracy

♦ China Democratic League

♦ China Democratic National Construction Association

♦ China Peasants and Workers Democratic Party

♦ China Zhi Gong Party

♦ September 3 Society

♦ Revolutionary Committee of the Guomindang (Kuomintang)

♦ Taiwan Democratic Self Government League

Candidates from these parties regularly stand for election to the local people's congress and are sometimes voted in, but the present system doesn't allow them to progress any higher.

There are five other political parties that aren't recognised by the CPC which means that they're effectively banned. All are based outside China, and have names that include the words 'democracy' or 'nationalist'.

LEGAL SYSTEM

The law in China is a form of civil law, and has some similarities to France's Napoleonic Code under which defendants are presumed guilty unless they can prove their innocence. The process of criminal law begins with the Procurator's Department of the police, which primarily decides whether an accused party is guilty and what offence they should be charged with. The accused's lawyer provides the defence.

The courts are presided over by a judge and two jurors, appointed by the National People's Congress, and it's their job to hear the case and decide the verdict, although the courts largely follow the Procurator's Department's lead; their principal role is to decide on the appropriate penalty. Penalties range from fines to imprisonment, although when serious crime occurs, punishments can be severe. There are over 60 offences for which the death penalty can be imposed – execution is either a bullet in the back of the head or a lethal injection.

Laws are promulgated under the aegis of the National People's Congress or the State Council. Officially, laws apply nationwide, but provincial courts often interpret them differently, so while there may be a sound legal system, not all citizens acknowledge that it applies to them. It sometimes seems as if many people, particularly local government officials, ignore the law if it doesn't suit them or use it to cover up misdemeanours and awkward situations. Local governments are judged, in part, by the number of complaints that are filed against them, and some try to present a good record by preventing people from registering complaints. This is a situation that has regularly led to social unrest and the frequent exposure of errant officials and police. However, national government is doing its best to tighten up the legal system and prevent individuals from using it to their advantage, and as a result, more people are seeking redress through the courts.

There are four levels of courts, with appeal cases being seen at the next highest level. At the bottom are the People's Courts, dispensing justice at county level. These have no jurisdiction over matters involving foreigners, who must apply to the next level, that of the Intermediate Courts. Above the Intermediate Courts are the High Courts, which operate at provincial level, and, at the very top, the Supreme People's Court, which is the final point of appeal. All courts handle both civil and criminal cases.

Officially, both Chinese and foreign plaintiffs should be treated equally, but this isn't always the case and local interests are sometimes allowed to colour judgements.

☑ **SURVIVAL TIP**

If you get into legal difficulties, you must seek help from a lawyer as soon as possible. Many English-speaking lawyers advertise in the free expatriate magazines, although it's best to choose one based on recommendations. Alternatively, contact your home country's embassy or consulate. The British Embassy's website includes a list of English-speaking lawyers (🖥 ukinchina.fco.gov.uk/en/help-for-british-nationals/when-things-go-wrong/if-you-need-lawyers).

Tucked away in the small print of most contracts there's usually reference to arbitration, and the China International Economic and Trade Arbitration Commission (🖥 cietac.org/index.cms) offers an arbitration service as an alternative to going to court. The advantage is that the proceedings can be carried out in English or another foreign language, provided both parties agree, and that foreign lawyers, normally barred from Chinese courts, can take part in arbitration proceedings.

MARRIAGE & DIVORCE

The age of consent is 22 for a man and 20 for a woman, and statistics show that, on average, Chinese men marry when they're 23 or 24 and women at 22. The Chinese firmly believe in marriage and the family as the key to a happy life, and while arranged marriages are rare, families still wield considerable influence over their son or daughter's choice of life partner.

There's no custom of engagement, and neither is it common for couples to cohabit prior to or instead of getting married. 'Living in sin' is frowned upon by most parents and by society in general.

If your landlord discovers you're living with your Chinese girlfriend or boyfriend, he may try to evict you for 'offending morals'.

The attitude to cross-cultural marriages can also be unfavourable, particularly if you're black or of mixed race. Many older Chinese feel that marrying or even just dating a foreigner is improper and that going out with a black foreigner is very wrong. There were riots in Nanjing a number of years ago when some local girls dated students from Africa.

Most marriages take place in the Chinese equivalent of a registry office, the local office of the provincial government's Civil Affairs Department, although some Christian Chinese couples marry in church. The ceremony itself is quite low key and inexpensive, although it's often followed by a lavish wedding feast for family and friends. This is usually held at a hotel, often around midday, and involves a meal and much toasting in *baijiu* by a master of ceremonies (MC). This event can cost many thousands of *yuan*. Guests bring a little red envelope containing money (*hong bao*) as a wedding gift, and the bride and groom eventually escape to the sound of exploding firecrackers set off by the guests.

Marriage between a foreigner and a Chinese citizen is uncommon, but isn't particularly difficult to arrange. You must notify the Civil Affairs Department in advance and book your slot, as they usually only conduct foreign/Chinese marriages on one or two specific days each week. The requisite documents are your partner's *hukou* (residence certificate) and identity card, your passport, plus proof that neither of you are currently married, e.g. a certificate of no Impediment stating that you're single, divorced or widowed. You also need two photos showing you and your partner side by side – effectively, a two-headed passport photo which any photographic studio can supply. Any documents in a foreign language must be translated and verified by your home country's embassy.

Provided the documents are in order, the marriage takes place at lightning speed. No witnesses are required; the 'registrar' simply enters your details into the marriage certificate, glues in the photo and stamps it with an official red seal. The entire process isn't very romantic, but the cost is just 31 RMB and the certificate is a beautiful, padded, red booklet which makes an excellent keepsake.

If you marry a Chinese citizen, it doesn't follow that you automatically gain Chinese citizenship, which can be very difficult to acquire (see page 245). Nor should you expect your country of origin to automatically grant your new partner citizenship – or even residency – on the grounds of marriage.

Divorce

Divorce is now far more common than it was in the '80s or '90s, although the divorce rate is still less than half that of the UK or US. If a Chinese couple want to divorce, it's a simple process conducted, like the marriage, at the Civil Affairs Department, taking just 30 minutes and costing just 9 RMB. However, if either side contests the divorce, it must be decided by a People's Court and can be a long drawn out and costly process. Any foreigner seeking a divorce in China, even if both parties agree, must take their case to court.

MILITARY SERVICE

According to law, all males between 18 and 22 are liable to serve in the armed forces for two years under selective compulsory service. However, in recent years there's been no need to conscript recruits because so many young men and women are willing to voluntarily enlist in the People's Liberation Army (PLA). The Chinese are proud of their armed forces, and a career in the army is looked upon as a wise decision.

Military service may have been shelved for the time being, but the government still requires all university students to spend their first three weeks doing military training. Both sexes take part, staying in barracks and wearing uniform for their training, which includes learning to shoot as well as the usual drills and discipline. Most enjoy the experience.

The PLA has four principal sections: the army, navy, air force and armed police, and all are under the direct control of the Communist Party of China. Recruits initially join the land forces for three years and the navy and air force for four years, which can be extended. Men can join up at age 18, irrespective of their educational achievements, but woman wishing to enlist must have graduated from high school and be aged between 18 and 19; they're only eligible for specific jobs and aren't deployed as frontline troops. The PLA is by far the largest armed force in the world. In 2011, it fielded over 4.5m troops, including reservists; almost twice as many as the US.

PETS

Many Chinese keep pets. With so many people living in apartments, small pets such as birds and tanks of exotic fish are the easiest option, while crickets are another popular pet. Owners often wear their cricket in a small porcelain pot hung from their neck, all the better to hear its 'song'. Birds are the most popular pets, particularly songbirds, which are admired for their melodic voices, and a charming sight is that of a group of elderly men, sitting and chatting in the park with their caged birds warbling around them. Don't be alarmed if you see the owners swing the cages as they walk – this is said to be beneficial to the birds as hanging on tightly to their perches improves their strength and health!

As the Chinese grow more affluent, they're turning to larger pets such as cats and dogs. There are around 75m pet dogs in China and the number is growing. This is in spite of the cost and the quite onerous regulations on dog ownership. In both Beijing and Shanghai, for example, dogs must be registered at a cost of at least 500 RMB a year and have an annual anti-rabies vaccination (although only around a fifth of dog owners comply with the latter rule). Similar restrictions

apply in other cities. Central Beijing is particularly restrictive: you cannot keep a dog any larger than 35cm (14in) high unless you live in a gated estate, therefore you're limited to one of the 'handbag' breeds, e.g. a Yorkshire terrier or Chihuahua, and you cannot walk it on the street between 8am and 8pm.

Chinese traders have been quick to meet the needs of pet owners and there are specialist breeders, pet markets selling everything from dog collars to fish tanks, and pet services such as professional dog walkers, obedience training and boarding kennels. The prices charged for some of these services put them well beyond the pockets of ordinary people. In the major cities, kennelling costs around 120 RMB a day, and if you want your dog to attend obedience classes this can involve a three-month stay at a doggy 'boarding school' at a charge of 5,000 RMB per month. Keeping a dog in modern China is a pastime for the privileged few.

Importing a Pet

A surprising number of expatriates bring their pets to China, although it's a costly and bureaucratic process. To fly a dog from Europe or the US to Beijing or Shanghai costs around 10,000 RMB, plus 6,000 RMB for the services of a pet relocation company. There's no legal requirement to use such an organisation, although they're best placed to know the latest regulations and they can handle all the paperwork for you.

Import restrictions state that you can only bring in one pet per person and then only if you have a work (Z) visa or are a permanent resident or a Chinese citizen. Your pet must have a health certificate, plus a separate certificate confirming that it's been inoculated against rabies. There are restrictions on the size of dog you can keep in certain cities and you must check the current situation – a pet relocation service can help with this. Find out also whether pets are permitted in your accommodation. Some estates allow them, but there may be restrictions on larger breeds; some private landlords won't accept tenants with dogs.

Your dog may need to go into quarantine on arrival, at your expense. In Beijing, officials make a decision whether to quarantine a dog after an inspection and, in most cases, owners are permitted to quarantine their dogs at home for 30 days, but must not allow them out during this period. If the officials decide to quarantine the dog in kennels, this costs around 1,500 RMB a week, and the animal is quarantined for 30 days. Shanghai imposes an automatic seven-day stay in quarantine and then, if tests for rabies are negative, you can take your pet home but must keep it indoors for a further 23 days.

Both Beijing and Shanghai require all dogs to be vaccinated and registered with the local PSB, which issues a photo identity card for each dog, and similar rules apply in other cities. In Beijing, initial registration costs a whopping 1,000 RMB and the annual renewal is 500 RMB, although you may be able to obtain a rebate if the dog has been neutered.

If this seems extreme, bear in mind that rabies is a huge problem in China where up to 3,000 people die from the disease every year. Stray dogs are treated as a potential health hazard and routinely rounded up and destroyed. Unsecured pets can also be stolen, as pedigree dogs fetch a lot of money. However, your family pet is unlikely to end up on a restaurant menu; dogs used for food are bred for the purpose.

⚠ Caution

If you fail to register your dog and it's found on the street, it'll be taken to a dog pound and it's highly unlikely you'll see it again. You can also be fined up to 5,000 RMB.

Bringing your dog (or any other pet) to China is a huge commitment, as is taking on a pet once you're in China, and you must consider the implications when you move on. Many countries impose quarantine restrictions on dogs imported from overseas. The UK is particularly vigilant, and insists on six months' confinement at government-approved quarantine kennels on arrival from China. Quite apart from the expense – between £300 and £400 a month, not including transportation – this can be a distressing experience for both pets and their owners.

POLICE

The Chinese police are under the control of the Ministry of Public Security and are divided into four branches. The regular police force tasked with maintaining law and order is called the Public Security Bureau (*jin cha*). If you're a victim of crime, you must report it to the PSB which has offices in every town and city – or you can telephone 110. The PSB also handles visas and registration for foreigners.

The traffic police (*jao tong jin cha*) is a department of the PSB with responsibility for China's roads. Their role is to apprehend motorists who break the law, issue tickets and decide who's to blame in accidents, but their prime concern appears to be keeping the traffic flowing smoothly and they sometimes turn a blind eye to the multitude of minor infractions of road rules that happen right in front of them. Another division of police forms the Procurator's Department (*jian cha yua*) whose task is to prepare cases for the prosecution of criminals. In this case, the word 'procurator' is used in the same sense as it is in Scotland.

All regular PSB and traffic police wear dark blue, military-style uniforms with blue shirts and peaked caps. They aren't usually armed but carry electric tipped night sticks. The only police who routinely carry guns are the armed police (*wu jin*) who operate partly under the direction of the People's Liberation Army (PLA). They're the 'heavies' of the Chinese police force and are identified by their green, military style uniform or camouflage clothes, although some work undercover in 'civvies' (civilian clothes). Unless you're particularly unlucky, you won't encounter these police except on the road where they often drive fast in heavy traffic, ignoring all the normal traffic rules and employing a strange siren that sounds like a quacking duck to warn people to get out of their way.

Few Chinese police can speak English, other than those who handle visa queries, but with rare exceptions they're friendly and genuinely helpful towards foreigners, particularly those who are polite and smartly dressed.

POPULATION

China's population is an astonishing 1.35bn – 1.38bn if you include those living in Hong Kong, Macau and Taiwan. It's estimated that a further 40m Chinese live overseas. Add them all together and it's no exaggeration to say that a fifth of the world's population is Chinese. Yet China is a remarkably homogeneous country where one ethnic group, the Han, accounts for around 92 per cent of the total population. The remainder is made up from some 114m ethnic minorities, while foreign expatriates, who number some 600,000, form an insignificant group.

Of the 56 different minority peoples, the Zhuang who live in the south and are distantly related to the people of Thailand and Laos are the largest (16m) while the Lhoba tribe in Tibet are the smallest (3,000). Two important minorities are the Hui and the Uyghur, who total around 18m and are Muslim.

About 70 per cent of China's population is of working age, while roughly a fifth is aged 14 or under. It's split roughly fifty-fifty between rural and urban locations, with a slow and steady shift towards city living, as many migrants leave the countryside in search of work. The most populous

province is Guangdong which is home to just over 104m people or almost 8 per cent of the population, while Tibet has the fewest at just 3m residents. Some of China's cities are vast. Almost 20m people live in Beijing, but even this is dwarfed by the largest of the four municipalities, Chongqing, which is home to 28.8m – more than the combined total number of inhabitants of Australia and New Zealand.

China's population may be huge, but it's growing much more slowly than in many countries. The United Nations estimates its growth rate at 0.48 per cent, the same as the UK, helped in no small part by its one-child policy. This controversial rule, which was introduced in 1978 amid concerns that the rapid growth in population was draining inadequate resources, limits the majority of people to having just one child. Two side effects of the policy are the unbalanced male/female ratio – there are roughly six men to every five women – and the strain placed on an only child who has no one to share the burden of caring for elderly parents. However, the government claims it has prevented some 400m births between 1979 and 2011. Nevertheless, a two-child policy has been suggested and could be introduced as early as 2015.

Surprisingly, research has shown that around three-quarters of Chinese support the policy, although it doesn't apply to everyone. The most affected are the city dwellers and Han Chinese. Couples who live in the countryside whose first child is a girl have the option of trying for a second child, as do couples who are both only children. The majority of ethnic minorities are also exempt from the one-child policy, which has enabled them not just to survive but grow in size. Meanwhile, many wealthy Chinese simply ignore the rule and have two or three children, shrugging off the heavy fines.

RELIGION

Modern China isn't a particularly religious country. The practice of religion was forbidden at the dawn of the People's Republic in 1949, and even today the state tolerates rather than supports it. Only some 250m Chinese claim to follow a religion. The main faiths are Taoism, Confucianism and Buddhism, but there are also some 26m Muslims and as many as 14m Christians. As religion isn't openly discussed in China, all these figures are purely speculative.

However, faith has a long history in China, dating back to the earliest recorded days when many people had animist beliefs, similar to the Shamanism practiced by the Native Americans, believing in and praying to geographical features such as mountains and rivers, and regarding the sun and the moon as gods. In rural Tibet and Sichuan province these beliefs still exist today, and farmers erect heaps of stones with scraps of cloth above them fluttering in the breeze to venerate their gods.

China's first formal religion was Taoism (sometimes called Daoism), founded by a government official named Lao Tse who was born around 600BC. It was followed a century later by Confucianism, based on the words of the philosopher Confucius. Buddhism found its way to China in the 1st century AD and its influence spread rapidly. There are Taoist, Confucian and Buddhist temples throughout the country, and the three religions are so fully integrated into the Chinese psyche that many people who claim not to be religious still follow the teachings of Confucius or Lao Tse.

Other religions followed. Christianity came to China in the 7th century, brought by Nestorians from Syria who arrived via the Silk Road. Islam took a similar route from the west and was also brought in by sea traders. Today, there are believed to be almost 6m Catholics and 8m Protestants in China, while there are Muslim communities in all the major cities and especially in the west – in Xinjiang province, once known as East Turkestan, the large Uyghur population comprises Muslims of Turkic descent.

The CPC proscribed all religions in 1949, believing that they promoted feudalism and held back progress. Temples and churches were closed, and religious leaders declared enemies of the state. However, Taoism, Confucianism and Buddhism were so close to the hearts of the Chinese that the state found it impossible to wipe them out, and religion is now permitted, albeit under state control. People are free to worship at temples and churches; old religious buildings are being restored and new ones built. Christianity, especially, is attracting younger people, and there are large congregations at Catholic Mass, which is often conducted in Latin, and for white weddings in the churches behind Tian'anmen Square.

However, the state still retains a degree of suspicion regarding religion, and religious leaders must often contend with harassment. In particular, the CPC has an on-going dispute with the Vatican, which is the only state in Europe to recognise Taiwan as a separate country from China and which wants the right to appoint its own bishops in China, a request which has been firmly denied. Religious tolerance only goes so far in China and as such, it's never advisable to discuss your religious beliefs, and positively foolish to try to convert others to your faith. Many employment contracts contain clauses forbidding this, and you can be deported if discovered.

Falun Gong

One of the newer religious movements to take hold in China, Falun Gong is the only one to be specifically banned. The ban followed some vocal demonstrations by its followers in Beijing during the '90s, egged on by its US-based founder, which the Chinese government took to be an attempt to usurp its powers. It retaliated by imprisoning hundreds of people and Falun Gong went underground. People still practise this religion, sometimes described as a moral code rather than a faith, but they do so privately and the police still keep a close eye on them. Some foreigners have been attracted by Falun Gong but it's still a very touchy subject, and any hint that you may be a supporter could result in a one-way ticket home.

SOCIAL CUSTOMS

The Chinese are very tolerant, although it's still easy to cause offence by saying or doing the wrong thing. The matter of 'face' is very important, and causing someone to lose face, particularly in front of family or colleagues, is a cardinal sin and will lose you respect as well. The teachings of Confucius – whereby everybody has a place in society and respect for one's elders or betters is paramount – still apply, and you must remember this at all times. These are the overriding principals of the Chinese social code, and provided you follow it, you won't go far wrong.

However, there are many social customs peculiar to China, some of which are described below.

◆ First names follow surnames, and forms of address are quite formal, so if you're introduced to Mr Wang Jintao you should respond to him as Mr (*Xiansheng*) Wang and never call him by his first name (Jintao). Most Chinese women retain their maiden name, so his wife may be introduced as Miss Zhang Zuyin, and you should call her Miss (*Nushi*) Zhang. The correct protocol is a handshake with Mr Wang and a nod (in effect, a miniature bow) to Miss Zhang. Some Chinese people have an English name, to facilitate dealing with foreigners, so you may be introduced to Mr Wang Jintao 'whose English name is Cole' and you should ask which name he prefers you to use. Polite respect is the key to communication – not dissimilar to the UK or US in the '50s – and you should always let the Chinese party set the level on which you interact.

◆ The Chinese ask very frank questions and expect equally frank answers. At the end of a restaurant meal, it's quite normal to ask the host how much it cost (he's paying after all!) and for him to state the amount with no embarrassment. If someone asks you your age or income, they expect you to answer truthfully and then ask how old they are or how much they earn. As a general rule, giving an honest answer to a question and then turning the question back on its author is the best policy.

◆ The Chinese are private people and don't throw their doors open to everyone. When you move into an apartment block, don't expect your new neighbours to greet you with enthusiasm and cups of tea, or even to answer the door. Their welcome is confined to a polite nod and '*ni hao*' (hallo), to which you should reply the same, and this may be as close as you ever get to them in all the time you live there.

- The universal dress code is smart casual. Although senior managers and officials wear suits and ties, most Chinese men and women dress casual all the time. But casual doesn't equal scruffy. Nothing loses you respect quicker than an unkempt appearance.

- The Chinese rarely arrive late for appointments unless they're delayed by the frequently terrible traffic jams. Try to plan ahead and arrive on time or at least phone to say if you're delayed.

- There are a number of taboo subjects in conversation. These include religion, Chinese politics and sex. All Chinese are aware of the great amount of corruption undermining their country and most are disgusted by it, but they're also ashamed about it and don't want to be reminded of it, particularly by a foreigner. How much nicer to talk about your trip on a bus where a couple of youngsters almost came to blows because both wanted to offer their seat to a young mother and baby.

- Don't sip at your drink (unless it's tea) during a banquet. The Chinese save their alcohol for the toasts, of which there are many, so if you sip and respond to the toasting (which you must) you risk ending up under the table.

- Shouting is normal in China, and doesn't indicate an impending argument or fight. It's a noisy country and the Chinese tolerate noise levels far higher than most Westerners, so many people raise their voices even when it isn't necessary. It's quite usual to see two people conversing at the tops of their voices, irrespective of any ambient noise.

- The Chinese concept of privacy is different from the West. To the Chinese, home is private, and few people other than close relatives are invited across the threshold, while an astonishing number of cars have their windows darkened (tinted) to preserve the privacy of those inside. Yet the same people happily use a public toilet with no doors on the cubicles. To the Chinese, going to the lavatory is simply a bodily function, like blowing your nose, and isn't something that needs to be hidden away.

- The Chinese are curious. Travel outside the principal tourist areas and you'll be being stared at. Many rural people have never seen a 'big nose' (as they call Westerners) before, and are genuinely fascinated. They mean no harm, and the best response is to smile and say *ni hao*.

- Attitudes to sex are still old fashioned, and China is a country where anything other than 100 per cent 'normal' sex between a man and a woman is regarded as unusual, unnatural and probably illegal. There's a specific law prohibiting sexual activity involving three or more persons and in 2010, a university professor was sentenced to three years' imprisonment for organising 'swingers' parties among consulting adults in private houses. Homosexuality, although officially legal, is also still very much frowned upon. If your sexual preferences are outside the Chinese 'norm', it's best to keep them carefully concealed.

TIME DIFFERENCE

China crosses five time zones, although officially the entire country abides by Beijing time. This creates problems for people in the far west who, in theory, need to get up two hours earlier than everyone else. Thus Xinjiang province has its own local time, which is two hours behind Beijing. If you're in Urumqi and have a meeting scheduled for 9am, always check if they mean 9am Beijing time or 9am local time, or you could find yourself turning up two hours early (or late).

China doesn't change its clocks in spring or autumn, and is always eight hours ahead of Greenwich Mean Time.

TIPPING

There's no confusion over tipping in China, where it's neither expected nor required. Officially, it's forbidden to accept a tip. The only occasion when

International Time Difference

BEIJING	LONDON	CAPE TOWN	MUMBAI	TOKYO	LOS ANGELES	NEW YORK
Noon	4am	6am	8.30am	1pm	2pm*	11pm*

* previous day

Note that this table doesn't allow for local differences due to Summer Time variations.

a small tip may be acceptable (and accepted) is when a hotel porter carries a mountain of luggage up to your room. However, there's no need to tip in restaurants, bars, hairdressers, taxis or anywhere else, and doing so is more likely to cause confusion and discomfort than pleasure.

TOILETS

It's an unwritten rule that public lavatories in China are almost unfailingly unpleasant. Most are of the squat variety, and they frequently have either low partitions between cubicles or none at all, while many have no doors either. This applies everywhere, from department stores, restaurants and office blocks to schools, government buildings and railway stations, and there's never any toilet paper. In the countryside, you're better off nipping behind a tree. The only Western style toilets to be found are in private homes and hotel en suite bathrooms, provided they were built in the '80s or later.

This can be acutely embarrassing for Westerners who are accustomed to relieving themselves in private, but the Chinese have no discomfort when it comes to their bowel habits and Chinese doctors invariably begin their examination with a blunt question about your bowels. You either have to develop a thick skin or seek out toilets in the reception area of upmarket hotels or American style fast food restaurants – McDonalds' golden arches can be a very welcome sign on a Chinese street – and make sure that you always carry toilet paper with you.

Great Wall of China

19.
THE CHINESE

Who are the Chinese? What are they really like? Let's take a candid (and slightly prejudiced) look at the Chinese people from a foreigner's viewpoint, tongue firmly in cheek, and hope that they forgive my flippancy or that they don't read this bit (which is why it's tucked away at the back of the book).

The typical Chinese man (or woman) – and they **never** use the term Chinaman – is atheist, ambitious, amusing, anonymous, arrogant, beautiful (the women, that is), black haired (into old age), a born trader, brave (with money), bureaucratic, business like, casually dressed, cheerful, commercial, complaining, corrupt, deaf, diligent, discontented, dishonest, a dreadful driver, an excellent negotiator, enterprising, family oriented, a food lover, frank, friendly, funny, a gambler, generous, a good citizen, a gossip (men and women), greedy, a Han, a home lover, honest, hospitable, humorous, impatient, an intrepid cyclist, law abiding, loud, a loyal friend, materialistic, modest, money obsessed, morally superior, naive, outspoken, parochial, a skilled plagiarist, politically correct, practical, pragmatic, private, proud, punctual, religious, republican, respectful towards their elders, rude, short-sighted, small boned, sober, sociable, stoic, thrifty, tough, unadventurous, unassuming and a worrier.

The above list of characteristics contains many contradictions (as does life in China) because there's really no such thing as an 'average' Chinese. Like the people of every nation, they don't conform to rigid stereotypes and cannot be easily pigeon-holed. However, unlike other nations, such as the UK and US, China is far from being a melting pot of different races and cultures and the majority of people share certain characteristics and attitudes.

One which binds them together is their ethnic sameness. More than 90 per cent of China's population claim they can trace their ancestry back to the Han Dynasty, the second imperial dynasty which held power some 2,000 years ago in a time which many historians claim was China's

'golden age'. As a result there's a remarkable similarity of appearance. Although it's quite untrue to say that all Chinese look alike (they often say that all foreigners all look alike to them!), they are, for the most part, small boned, short in stature, with black hair and dark brown eyes. They may share certain features with their Asian neighbours but their appearance is peculiarly Chinese and distinct from, say, Japanese, Korean or Vietnamese people.

Not only do they look typically Chinese but most think along the same lines. Although the Chinese aren't nearly as obsessive as the Japanese about conformity, they don't like to be different. Most people desire to be part of the majority, to remain anonymous and not stand out from the crowd.

It's only in some of the major cities that the Chinese display a local attitude. For example, the people of Beijing, home to China's leaders for many centuries, often give the impression of being China's elite – not unlike Londoners, New Yorkers and Parisians – and that, as such, they deserve to enjoy special privileges such as attending the top universities, the best hospitals and having the best travel facilities. A Beijing *hukou* (residency) is much more than just an address; it also confers an air of prestige on its citizens.

Shanghai folk are confident and self-assured. They **know** they're the cleverest people in China. They're also sure in their hearts that their women are the most beautiful in the country and that they wear the latest fashions with their own sense of style. Good at business, they believe it's only a matter of time before Shanghai overtakes Hong Kong as the largest financial centre in Asia. However, they aren't as well organised as Beijingers and this sometimes lets them down

The Cantonese who live in Guangdong province are more comfortable dealing with the foreign 'big noses' (as Westerners are called). Old Canton (modern Guangzhou) was the first port in China to trade with foreign lands and they have centuries of negotiating experience behind them. They're skilled wheeler dealers and excellent cooks (their cuisine is the most imaginative and varied in China).

The natives of Chengdu in Sichuan province are different again. The creators of the fieriest food in China, courtesy of the red hot Sichuan pepper, Chengdu folk enjoy a laid-back lifestyle in a city which marches to a slower beat. Many foreigners who end up there feel they're on to a good thing, and it's certainly a more relaxing place to live than in the sometimes frantic hustle and bustle of Beijing, Shanghai, Shenzhen or Guangzhou.

But all these cities give visitors a misleading impression of the Chinese; the vast majority live outside the major conurbations and have never seen a foreigner in their lives. When they do, the temptation to stare and ask questions is irresistible. Remember that China was for many centuries isolated from the rest of the world, from its imperial heyday to the years of the Cultural Revolution, when outside influence was kept at arm's length. It took the efforts of Zhou Enlai and Henry Kissinger to break this isolation in the '70s, and the pragmatism and genius of Deng Xiaoping to show the way forward in the '80s. However, for all the enormous strides that China has taken, many of its citizens are still ignorant of the goings on in the rest of the world.

It's wrong to say that the Chinese are racist but, like most nationals, they're happiest and most comfortable when surrounded by their own kind. They're fascinated by foreigners – particularly Westerners – by what they do and how they dress, but China is the centre of their universe and its people are the shrewdest in the world. They take comfort in this knowledge and this means that they never treat foreigners as superior, just different and, in some instances, rather weird, what with their strange hairy arms and their habit (i.e. the British) of ruining good tea by first putting milk into it, cold milk at that, and then killing its flavour by adding sugar as well (or even worse, drinking iced tea, as in the US).

Almost to a man, the Chinese admit to no religion. There are mosques, particularly in the western areas, and the major cities have very few churches, but the people who attend them are but a tiny minority. Having no religion isn't the same as having no moral or spiritual code, however, and like Christians and Muslims the Chinese have a strong system of beliefs. However, they're based on the teachings of philosophers such as Confucius rather than on a deity, and are ingrained in their psyche. The Chinese have places of worship but feel no obligation to attend them. Their faith is a private matter which they prefer to keep to themselves.

Just as private and important is the family. The Chinese believe utterly and implicitly in the value and importance of family; it's the keystone of their existence and all life revolves around the family. This is one of their greatest strengths. If they want something done, there's a relative who can do it and they trust him to do it well. If they need something, there's a relative who can get it. And if they're successful, there's always a relative who needs a little help, and so it goes on.

> Don't feel slighted if you're never invited to a Chinese friend's home. Many foreigners never scratch the surface of what family means to the Chinese because it's so difficult to gain entry to this exclusive inner circle. Home is a private sanctuary that's usually closed to outsiders, including other Chinese.

There's no overt class structure in modern China, although status is important. In a country where everyone is deemed to be equal by the government, your rank in society matters, whether it's inherited or earned through achievement. Status opens many doors and people are never shy of advertising it, whether by driving a new Mercedes or sporting the latest mobile phone. But there's no 'upper class' in China. The pampered offspring of wealthy parents, the so-called *nouveau riche,* may believe that they're superior, but the ordinary Chinese look down on them. As the *China Daily* reported in 2011, 'they (the *nouveau riche*) have youth, money and rotten taste'. This puts them into the same pen as footballers, models and other headline-grabbing 'celebrities' in the West, and a far cry from the imperial families of old China.

Sadly, their antics are merely one of the most visible signs of the obsession with money and materialism that's sweeping China. In the 21st century it's a sad fact that many are gripped by an unfortunate but overriding obsession with money. This is much more than extravagance – it's a desire to accumulate wealth at any cost, and is one of the major problems facing China today.

In recent years, this greed has revealed itself in a succession of shocking food safety scandals, where dangerous ingredients were added to

food products to boost profits at the expense of consumers' health. Worse still, the government body established to ensure food safety utterly failed to stop these practices, often because they were also sharing some of the illicit extra profits. Few days pass without the Chinese press reporting the downfall of yet another official for 'a severe violation of discipline and the law' – a euphemism for demanding and/or accepting bribes. Sometimes the sums involved aren't 'simply' hundreds or thousands of *renminbi* but millions or even billions! Sums so grotesque that no one could spend it all – just money for money's sake.

Money mania is strongest among the young. Witness the immortal line spoken by a young girl contestant on a television programme: 'I would sooner cry in the seat of a BMW than be happy sitting on the back of a bicycle.' Many girls are unwilling to marry unless their suitor owns both an apartment and a top-of-the range car.

Many Chinese copy their elders and betters so that the next generation risks inheriting this materialistic attitude. They may also inherit their parents' abysmal driving habits. Today's Chinese are the first to drive motorised vehicles but have no idea of the rules of the road and base their driving style on riding a bicycle, without taking into consideration the vehicle's speed, weight and size. The Chinese display some of their worst attitudes on the road: selfish, pushy, inconsiderate and determined to be first, whatever the cost.

Although friendly and polite most of the time, the Chinese can sometimes come across as incredibly rude. Just wait at any bus stop and try joining the mad scrum as everyone pushes and heaves to get on board. This isn't intentional insolence but a display of the sense of 'self'

that they have developed living in a country where there are so many people and so much competition. However, their rudeness shows itself in actions rather than words. To be verbally insulting or to lose one's temper is tantamount to losing face, something which people go to extremes to avoid.

▲ Caution

Try to avoid saying an outright 'no', as this can be offensive. If you don't agree with a Chinese colleague's idea, it's better to avoid mentioning it and hope they lose interest, rather than challenge them. Similarly, never refuse to eat something unmentionable at a restaurant meal, but take a nibble then push it to the side of your plate.

The Chinese are friendly, sociable and great entertainers who enjoy going out, particularly to restaurants. However, even restaurant meals involve a lot of rigid protocol. The head of the table is reserved for the host, with the principal guest seated next to him. He settles the bill and tells the guests when to go home. During the meal he does his best to ensure everyone has enough to eat, and guests must ensure they leave some leftovers otherwise the host may feel he has been insufficiently generous and lose face.

Food is one of the great Chinese passions, although the menu can be bizarre. There's a famous saying along the lines of, 'If it has four legs and is not a chair, if it has two wings and flies but is not an aeroplane, and if it swims and is not a submarine, the Cantonese will eat it' and it's not far wrong. Crocodile, snake, frog, donkey and dog are among the many creatures which people tuck into with gusto. Fortunately they cook this cornucopia of wildlife with great aplomb, and there are also a great many vegetable dishes, so there's no need for vegetarians or animal lovers to starve in China.

Eating out is the main form of socialising. People don't gather for barbeques, cocktail parties or sporting events. Australians and football-loving Brits will be dismayed to learn that sport is low on most Chinese people's priorities. They can wallop you at table tennis and badminton, but contact sports (other than martial arts) are shunned by nearly everyone. In ancient times, the Chinese were gatherers rather than hunters, and aggressiveness isn't a common trait.

Conversation can be a minefield. The Chinese will blithely ask you how old you are or how much you earn, but you must never bring up the subject of politics – few people are willing to discuss anything which might be considered politically sensitive. Older people have grown up in a society where it was safer to keep your political views to yourself, whereas younger people just find politics dull.

Sex can also be a taboo subject. It isn't that the Chinese don't like sex – there wouldn't be so many of them if that were true – but it's something they prefer to keep between two people. Many have an old-fashioned view of courtship and relationships, and older Chinese don't approve of Chinese girls who hang out with foreign men – or the men who attract them. Younger people have boyfriends and girlfriends but rarely display their affections in public. Yet the country has a plague of prostitutes and officials caught 'violating discipline' often say they did it to placate their 'girlfriends', so there's lots of sexual intrigue going on but it's well hidden.

Friendship also has its limits. Just because the Chinese are both polite and friendly, it doesn't follow that they want to be your friend. Most have few close friends, mainly because they're diligent at work and their social life revolves around their family.

Tea and China are inextricably linked and the humble brew remains the national drink. True, there are coffee bars springing up and Coca-Cola signs everywhere and the days of long, languorous tea ceremonies are largely over, but if you're offered a drink then it will probably be tea (don't ask for milk!).

The Chinese don't have a reputation as drinkers, and alcohol tends to be drunk only on special occasions, generally with food and usually by men. Chinese men love the strong local made liquor called *baijiu*. Often as high as 60 or 70 per cent proof, it tastes to most Westerners like a by-product of one of the major oil companies – lethal and unpalatable. The Chinese love to toast each other with *baijiu,* which is knocked back from thimble-sized glasses every few minutes at seemingly endless 'banquets'. Try to match them and you'll end up very much the worse for wear. Beer is the second most popular drink in China but it also usually accompanies a meal. Sitting in a bar sipping beer all evening isn't a Chinese pastime, although many a lonely expatriate tries to make up for this.

For heavy smokers, China is paradise. Cigarettes are available everywhere from as little as 2 or 3 *renminbi* (about 30p) for a packet of 20, and the majority of adult males smoke. Officially, smoking is banned on public transport and the authorities periodically try to ban it in other public places, but it's one of those laws which the Chinese choose to ignore and non-smokers have a hard time of it.

> Tell a smoker at the next restaurant table to you that his smoke is bothering you and you'll be met by a look of total incomprehension and quite possibly the offer of a cigarette!

Chinese men can be unusually vain, and not just young men. Well into their twilight years, most men insist on dyeing their hair black. Cosmetic surgery, too, isn't uncommon among men and those who've had it often proudly boast of the fact. Yet the womenfolk, who are some of the most beautiful in the world, are quite the opposite. Most have no idea just how lovely they are; beauty salons are rare, and they have to share their hairdressers with vain men who hog the seats at weekends. Foreign women are often envious of their Chinese counterparts because they're so effortlessly slim and good looking, while foreign men look around them in awe, thinking that all their birthdays have come at once.

Being surrounded by beautiful people isn't the only benefit of living in China. They may have their foibles, but the Chinese are among the most fascinating, intelligent and industrious people on earth. Living among them in the powerhouse that is modern China is a breath-taking rollercoaster ride of opportunity and adventure, and one which makes other countries appear flat and boring in comparison. China may not have the greatest standard of living, but few countries are experiencing such a rapid pace of progress or offer such incredible prospects for someone with daring and optimism. The Chinese may be very different from other nationalities but they wear their differences proudly, and you can learn a great deal from them. China is a country with few barriers to success, and its people are looking to the future as never before. Join them, keep an open mind, respect their culture and traditions and you won't go far wrong.

Wang sui zhong guo ren! (Long live the Chinese people!)

Li-river, Yangshuo

20.
MOVING HOUSE OR LEAVING CHINA

When you're moving house or leaving China, even just for a period of time, there are a number of things to consider and people to inform. The checklists are provided to make your task a bit easier and reduce the stress involved (which is said to be second only to divorce or bereavement). Remember that things can take time in China, so don't leave everything until the last minute. For more help, see Moving House on page 71.

MOVING HOUSE

Employees who move within China may find that their employer handles some of the legwork, particularly if they provide the accommodation, but you may need to consider the following:

◆ If you live in a rented property, you must give your landlord notice that you're leaving. Some contracts contain a clause whereby you can give a period of notice, e.g. a month or two months, but these are rare. More usually, you're legally liable to pay rent right up to the end of the fixed contract period, e.g. six months or a year. This may be negotiable if there's a lot of demand for rental property and the landlord can easily re-let.

   If you're on a fixed-period contract and you plan to move at the end of that contract, check how much notice you need to give to cancel the renewal, and make sure you inform the landlord or agent at least two weeks in advance of the required notice date. If you don't, the landlord may assume that you're staying on and try to impose penalties for breaking a new contract.

◆ If you own your property, you may want to sell. Foreigners are only allowed to own one property in China so you cannot buy a second home in your new destination. Alternatively, you can rent it out and rent your next home. Either way you must contact an agent to handle the sale or lease. Note that sales can proceed quickly in China, so that you may need to move out early to accommodate your buyer and spend time in a hotel.

◆ Car owners moving to a new city must advise the PSB's traffic department so the car can be re-registered at your new address. The PSB may insist on issuing new number plates. This is advisable, as there's a much greater chance of being stopped or having your car towed for a traffic violation if it has out-of-town (i.e. from another province) plates.

◆ Pet owners should check whether pets are permitted in the new accommodation. Birds aren't usually a problem, but you may have to re-home a dog or cat. Check out the arrangements necessary to transport your pet to a new city, particularly if it's a long way and you plan to fly.

◆ Also inform the following, if applicable:

   - your employer;

   - the local office of the Public Security Bureau (PSB). Whenever you change your address in China, you're obliged to let the PSB know within a month of moving and obtain a new registration document from the local office.

   - your electricity, gas, telephone and water suppliers, unless these bills are paid by your employer;

   - your Chinese bank, as well your overseas bank(s) if they use your Chinese address;

   - your accountant, any businesses where you have accounts, e.g. Sinopec fuel card, credit card companies, insurance companies (e.g. car, health) and any other financial institutions;

- the local post office. Your postman can arrange for your mail to be redirected (see page 89).

- your children's school(s). If you need to arrange schooling in a new area, you must give at least one semester's notice and obtain copies or any records or reports from their current school. Some schools hold a deposit for the duration of the time that a child attends, and provided all fees are paid up to the date of departure, you're entitled to ask for a refund.

- any doctor or dentist where you've recently received treatment. Retain your health records as you'll need to produce them when seeing another doctor in China.

- the embassy or embassies with whom you're registered in China;

- all regular correspondents, friends and relatives, professional and trade journals or overseas magazines to which you subscribe, and social and sports clubs you belong to. Give or send them your new address, telephone number and email address.

♦ Inform your lettings agent of your planned move as soon as possible. They or the landlord will want to inspect the property before returning your deposit or bond.

☑ SURVIVAL TIP

It's worth asking the agent whether any major redecorating is necessary; some landlords are unwilling to part with deposits, preferring to keep them and redecorate (or not) themselves. It may be cheaper and less hassle to let them do this.

♦ Arrange for your furniture to be moved to your new address using a local remover. Your agent can provide some names. Book well in advance and reconfirm the booking a few days before you move.

♦ If necessary, arrange for a cleaning company and decorators for your rented home. You may also want someone to clean your new apartment before you move in.

♦ If you're lucky enough to belong to a library, return any books you have on loan – and anything else you've borrowed from friends or colleagues

GOING ON LEAVE FROM CHINA

Even if you're only leaving China for a few months, there are still some points to consider:

♦ Check that your family's passports and Chinese visas are valid. Renewing a passport through a foreign mission takes some time, so don't be caught out. If Chinese immigration police discover that a passport or visa is out of date, you're in serious trouble; you may be held in a cell while they check your situation, and you must pay a fine of 500 RMB for each day that you've overstayed your visa. Furthermore, you'll also almost certainly miss your flight!

♦ Give your boss plenty of notice, and provide contact details for while you're away.

♦ Inform your child's school of your plans as early as possible. It's best to avoid taking leave during term time or in the run up to important examinations.

♦ Find a temporary home for pets.

♦ Check that there are sufficient funds in your bank account to cover payments for rent and utilities. Let your lettings agent know how long you'll be away. You may need to inform insurers, e.g. home insurance, if your property will be empty for more than 30 days (check the policy).

♦ Obtain some foreign currency for when you arrive for taxis, cups of coffee, etc., as it's unlikely they'll accept *renminbi*!

♦ Check that all windows and doors are locked and that everything is switched off.

LEAVING CHINA

The Chinese government doesn't require foreigners to ask for 'permission' to leave China; you simply go. However, before you leave China permanently or for an indefinite period of time, the following points should be considered, in addition to those listed above under **Moving House**:

♦ Give notice to your employer, or request a transfer, according to your contract. It may take some time to arrange a replacement or organise your next placing.

♦ Check that your family's passports are still valid and that visas cover you until you leave. You should do this at least a month before you leave, and give yourself plenty of time to renew them if necessary. If your visas are due to expire, then you must renew them at the PSB. Just because you don't intend to return, it won't stop the authorities fining you on exit for not having a valid visa.

⚠ Caution

It's against the law to export genuine antiques from China without clearance from customs. Very few antiques are genuine, but if you've been lucky enough to unearth the real thing and you try to smuggle it out in your suitcase, you could be fined or even spend some time in jail.

◆ If you're moving to a new destination – as opposed to going home – check well in advance with the country's embassy or consulate in China whether you need visas, permits, inoculations or any other documentation for entry. Getting paperwork in order can take several months. You don't need an 'exit' visa to leave China.

◆ Docido what to do with your property. If you own an apartment you may decide to keep it and let it out, but you'll need a reliable managing agent who can take care of any issues in your absence and ensure that the rent is paid to you.

◆ Decide what to do with your belongings. If you have larger items, e.g. furniture, that you want to ship abroad, you must contact an international removals company well in advance. Find out the procedure for shipping personal effects to your country of destination from the relevant embassy in China (don't rely entirely on your shipping company). Forms may need to be completed before arrival.

◆ If you have furniture or electrical goods that you aren't taking with you, advertise them in the free expat magazines, websites or on notice boards. It's usually cheaper and easier to sell them and buy them again, rather than pay to ship them overseas.

◆ Sell your car and/or electric scooter. Shipping a Chinese-made car to a Western country isn't worth the hassle, as you'll have no access to spares or the manufacturer's assistance and may have problems getting it through a vehicle inspection. The same applies to electric scooters, which are subject to much stricter rules in the West; you're unlikely to be able to ride it without tax, insurance or helmet, as you can in China!

◆ Find out the driving regulations in your destination country. You may need an international driving permit or translation of your foreign driving licence. (Your Chinese driving licence may not be accepted in some Western countries.)

◆ Organise transport for pets or find them a new home. Some countries have strict quarantine laws, and you must arrange relocation and kennelling in line with regulations.

◆ If you pay income tax in China and are leaving part way through a tax year, check whether you're entitled to a rebate.

◆ Find out the situation regarding any pension you've paid into in China. You may be able to transfer it to a new plan. Always check these points **before** taking out a pension in a foreign country.

Rice terrace, LongJi

♦ Arrange travel insurance for your family and insurance for anything you're shipping. If you have insurance that you plan to 'take with you', e.g. international health insurance, inform the insurer of your move well in advance. If you have local insurance, e.g. car, arrange to terminate the policies and ask if you're due a rebate.

♦ Obtain any x-rays or medical records from doctors or dentists who've treated you in China, particularly if you have serious or on-going medical problems (even if they're written in Chinese they'll still be useful). Carry them with your valuables in your hand baggage.

♦ Close any bank accounts and withdraw the cash, or send it to your home bank or one in the country you're travelling to. Note that withdrawing cash in a foreign currency can be a time consuming process in China. If you end up with some *renminbi*, you'll probably be able to exchange it at a bank in your destination country. If not, try a travel agent or visit the local 'Chinatown' where you're sure to find some willing purchasers.

♦ Give friends, colleagues and business associates your new or temporary address, or your email address so that they can contact you.

♦ If you're travelling by air, allow plenty of time to check in and clear security and immigration. Most airlines require you to arrive three hours before departure for international flights.

♦ Buy a copy of the relevant *Living and Working* book for the country you're heading to. If we haven't published it yet, let us know and we'll get started on one right away!

Lu tu yu kuai! **Have a safe journey!**

dragon mask

APPENDICES

APPENDIX A: USEFUL ADDRESSES

Foreign Embassies & Consulates in China

All foreign embassies are located in Beijing, although many countries also have consulates in other Chinese cities, particularly Guangzhou and Shanghai. A selection of embassies is listed below. For a list of other foreign missions in China, see 💻 embassiesinchina.com.

Australia: 21 Dongzhimenwai Dajie, Sanlitun, Beijing, 100600 PRC (☎ 010-5140 4111, 💻 china.embassy.gov.au). Consulates in Guangzhou and Shanghai.

Austria: Jianguomenwai, Xiushui Nanjie 5, Beijing, 100600 PRC (☎ 010-6532 2061, 💻 bmeia.gv.at/botschaft/peking.html). Consulate in Shanghai.

Belgium: 6 Sanlitun Lu, Beijing, 100600 PRC (☎ 010-6532 1736, 💻 diplomatie.be/beijing/default. asp). Consulate in Shanghai.

Brazil: 27 Guanghua Lu, Chaoyang District, Beijing, 100600 PRC (☎ 010-6532 2881, 💻 pequim.itamaraty.gov.br/en-us) Consulates in Shanghai and Guangzhou.

Canada: 19 Dongzhimenwai Dajie, Chaoyang District, Beijing, 100600 PRC (☎ 010-5139 4000, 💻 canadainternational.gc.ca/china-chine). Consulates in Chongqing, Guangzhou and Shanghai.

Czech Republic: 2 Ritan Lu, Jianguomenwai, Beijing, 100600 PRC (☎ 010-8532 9500, 💻 mzv.cz/beijing/en/index.html). Consulate in Shanghai.

Denmark: 1 Dong Wu Jie, Sanlitun, Beijing, 100600 PRC (☎ 010-8532 9900, 💻 ambbeijing. um.dk/en). Consulates in Guangzhou, Chongqing and Shanghai.

Finland: Beijing Kerry Centre, Level 26, South Tower, Guanghua Lu 1, Beijing, 100020 PRC (☎ 010-8519 8300, : finland.cn). Consulates in Guangzhou and Shanghai.

France: 3 Dong San Jie, Sanlitun, Chaoyang District, Beijing, 100600 PRC (☎ 010-8532 8080, 💻 ambafrance-cn.org). Consulates in Chengdu, Guangzhou, Shanghai, Shenyang and Wuhan.

Germany: 17 Dongzhimenwai Dajie, Sanlitun, Beijing 100600 PRC (☎ 010-8532 9000, 💻 peking. diplo.de/vertretung/peking/de/startseite.html). Consulates in Chengdu, Guangzhou and Shanghai.

Greece: Press & Communication Office, 17th Floor, The Place Tower, The Place, 9 Guang Hua Lu, Chaoyang District, Beijing, 100020 PRC (☎ 010-6532 1588, 💻 grpressbeijing.com). Consulates in Guangzhou and Shanghai.

Hungary: 10 Dongzhimenwai Dajie, Sanlitun, Beijing 100600 PRC (☎ 010-6532 1431, 💻 mfa.gov. hu/kulkepviselet/cn/en/mainpage.htm). Consulate in Shanghai.

India: Tianze Road, No.5 Liang Ma Qiao Bei Jie, Chaoyang District, Beijing, 100600 PRC (☎ 010-8531 2500, 💻 indianembassy.org.cn. Consulates in Guangzhou and Shanghai.

Ireland: Liangmahe South Road, Chaoyang, Beijing, 100600 PRC (☎ 010-6532 3664, 💻 embassyofireland.cn). Consulate in Shanghai.

Israel: 17 Tianzelu, Chaoyang District, Beijing, 100600 PRC (☎ 010-8532 0500, 💻 embassies.gov. il/beijing-en/pages/default.aspx). Consulate in Shanghai.

Italy: 2 Dong Er Jie, Sanlitun, Chaoyang District, Beijing, 100600 PRC (☎ 010-8532 7600, 🖳 ambpechino.esteri.it/ambasciata_pechino). Consulates are at Guangzhou and Shanghai.

Japan: 7 Ritan Lu, Jianguomenwai, Beijing, 100600 PRC (☎ 010-6532-2361, 🖳 cn.emb-japan.go.jp/index.htm). Consulates or missions in Chongqing, Dalian, Guangzhou, Qingdao, Shanghai and Shenyang,

Malaysia: 2 Liang Ma Qiao Bei Jie, Chaoyang District, Beijing 100600 PRC (☎ 010-6532 2531, 🖳 kln.gov.my/web/chn_beijing/home). Consulates in Guangzhou, Kunming and Shanghai.

Netherlands: 4 Liangmahe Nan Lu, Chaoyang District, Beijing 100600 PRC (☎ 010-8532 0200, 🖳 hollandinchina.org). Consulates at Guangzhou and Shanghai.

New Zealand: 3 Sanlitun Dongsanjie, Chaoyang District, Beijing, 100600 PRC (☎ 010-8532-7000, 🖳 nzembassy.com/china). Consulates in Guangzhou and Shanghai.

Norway: 1 Dong Yi Jie, Sanlitun, Beijing, 100600 PRC (☎ 010-8531 9600, 🖳 norway.cn). Consulates in Guangzhou and Shanghai.

Poland: 1 Ritan Lu, Jianguomenwai, Beijing, 100600 PRC (☎ 010-6532 1235). Consulates in Guangzhou and Shanghai.

Portugal: 8 Dong Wu Jie, Sanlitun, Chaoyang District, Beijing, 100600 PRC (☎ 010-6532 3497). Consulate in Shanghai.

Russia: 4 Dongzhimen Beizhongjie, Beijing, 100600 PRC (☎ 010-6532 1381, 🖳 russia.org.cn). Consulates in Guangzhou, Shanghai and Shenyang.

Singapore: 1 Xiu Shui Bei Jie, Jianguomenwai, Chaoyang District, Beijing, 100600 PRC (☎ 010-6532-1115, 🖳 mfa.gov.sg/beijing). Consulates in Chengdu, Guangzhou, Shanghai and Xiamen.

Sweden: 3 Dongzhimenwai Dajie, Sanlitun, Chaoyang District, Beijing, 100600 PRC (☎ 010-6532 9790, 🖳 swedenabroad.com). Consulate in Shanghai.

Switzerland: 3 Dong Wu Jie, Sanlitun, Beijing, 100600 PRC (☎ 010-6532 2736, 🖳 eda.admin.ch/eda/en/home/reps/asia/vchn/embbei.html). Consulates in Guangzhou and Shanghai.

South Africa: 5 Dongzhimenwai Dajie, Beijing, 100600 PRC (☎ 010-8532 0000, 🖳 saembassy.org.cn/index.asp). Consulate in Shanghai.

Spain: 9 Sanlitun Lu, Sanlitun, Beijing, 100600 PRC (☎ 010-6532 3629). Consulates in Guangzhou and Shanghai.

Thailand: 40 Guang Hua Lu, Beijing, 100600 PRC (☎ 010-6532 1749, 🖳 beijing.thaiembassy.org/menu2.htm). Consulates in Guangzhou, Kunming and Shanghai.

United Kingdom: 11 Guang Hua Lu, Jianguomenwai, Beijing, 100600 PRC (☎ 010-5192 4000, 🖳 ukinchina.fco.gov.uk/en). Consulates in Chongqing, Guangzhou and Shanghai.

United States of America: 55 An Jia Lou Lu, Beijing, 100600 PRC (☎ 010-8531 3000, 🖳 beijing.usembassy-china.org.cn). Consulates in Chengdu, Guangzhou, Shanghai, Shenyang and Wuhan.

☑ SURVIVAL TIP

The business hours of embassies vary, and they close on their own country's national holidays as well as on Chinese national or local public holidays. Always telephone to confirm the business hours before visiting.

Chinese Embassies Abroad

L isted below are the contact details for Chinese embassies and consulates in some major countries. A full list of Chinese missions abroad can be found on the PRC's Ministry of Foreign Affairs website (💻 fmprc.gov.cn/eng/wjb/zwjg/2490). Note that visa offices may be located at a different address from the main embassy, therefore always phone to check.

Australia: 15 Coronation Drive, Yarralumla, Canberra ACT 2600 (☎ 02-6273 4780, 💻 au.chineseembassy.org). Consulates in Brisbane, Melbourne, Perth and Sydney.

Canada: 515 St Patrick Street, Ottawa, Ontario K1N 5H3 (☎ 0613-789 3434, 💻 ca.chineseembassy. org/eng). Consulates in Calgary, Toronto and Vancouver.

France: 11 Av. George V, 75008, Paris (☎ 01-4952 1950, 💻 amb-chine.fr/chn). Consulates in Marseille, Lyon, Strasbourg and St Denis.

Germany: Markisches Ufer 54, 10179, Berlin (☎ 030-2758 80, 💻 china-botschaft.de). Consulates in Frankfurt, Hamburg and Munich.

Ireland: 40 Ailesbury Road, Ballsbridge, Dublin 4 (☎ 01-269 1707, 💻 ie.china-embassy.org/eng). Residents of Northern Ireland should contact the Chinese embassy in London (see below).

Italy: 56 Via Bruxelles, 00198, Rome (☎ 06-8413458, 💻 it.chineseembassy.org/ita). Consulates in Milan and Florence.

Netherlands: Willem Lodewijklaan 10, 2517 JT, The Hague (☎ 070-3065 061, 💻 chinaembassy.nl).

New Zealand: 2–6 Glenmore Street, Kelburn, Wellington (☎ 04-472 1382, 💻 chinaembassy.org.nz/ eng).. Consulates in Auckland and Christchurch

South Africa: 972 Pretorius Street, Arcadia 0083, Pretoria (☎ 012-431 6500, 💻 chinese-embassy. org.za/eng). Consulates in Cape Town, Durban and Johannesburg.

United Kingdom: 49-51 Portland Place, London W1B 1JL (☎ 020-7299 4049, 💻 chinese-embassy. org.uk/eng). Consulates in Edinburgh and Manchester.

United States of America: 3505 International Place, N.W. Washington, D.C. 20008 (☎ 0202-495 2266, 💻 china-embassy.org/eng). Consulates in Chicago, Houston, Los Angeles, New York and San Francisco.

Chambers of Commerce & Business Council

American Chamber of Commerce: The Office Park, Tower AB, 6th Floor, 10 Jintongxi Rd, Chaoyang, Beijing 100020 (☎ 010-8519 0800, 💻 amchamchina.org). There are chapters in Dalian, Shanghai, Tianjin and Wuhan.

Australian Chamber of Commerce: Austcham, Room 910 Tower A, U-Town Office Building, 1 Sanfengbei li, Chaoyangmen area, Chaoyang District, Beijing 100020 (☎ 010-6595 9252, 💻 austcham.org). Offices in Guangzhou, Hong Kong and Shanghai.

British Chamber of Commerce: Room 1001, British Centre, China Life Tower, No 16, Chaoyangmenwai Dajie, Chaoyang, Beijing 100200 (☎ 010-8525 1111, 💻 britishchamber.cn). Offices in Chengdu, Chongqing, Guangzhou, Hong Kong and Shanghai.

Canada China Business Council: Suite 11A16, Tower A, Hanwei Plaza, No 7 Guanghua Road, Chaoyang District, Beijing 100004 (☎ 010-8526 1820, 💻 ccbc.com). Additional offices in Chengdu, Nanjing, Qingdao, Shanghai, Shenyang and Shenzhen.

European Union Chamber of Commerce: Beijing Lufthansa Centre, Office C412, 50 Liangmaqiao Road, Beijing 100125 (☎ 010-6462 2066, 💻 europeanchamber.com.cn/view/home). Offices in Chengdu, Guangzhou, Nanjing, Shanghai, Shenyang, Shenzhen and Tianjin.

French Chamber of Commerce: C712 Lufthansa Centre No.50, Liangmaqiao Road, Chaoyang District, Beijing 100125 (☎ 010-6461 0260, 💻 ccifc.org). Offices in Guangzhou, Shanghai, Shenzhen and Wuhan.

German Chamber of Commerce: 8E 3rd North Ring Road,, Chaoyang, Beijing 100004 (☎ 010-6945 7709, 🖳 china.ahk.de). Also in Guangzhou and Shanghai.

New Zealand Chamber of Commerce: Room 1160, China Hotel Office, Liuhua Road, Guangzhou (🖳 bestofguangzhou.com/business/chambers...commerce/new-zealand/, ☎ 020-8667 0253).

Swiss Chamber of Commerce: Room 1108, Kunsha Center Building No 1, 16 Xinyuanli, Chaoyang, Beijing 100027 (☎ 010-8468 3982, 🖳 swisscham.org/bei). Office in Shanghai.

Clubs

Beijing American Club: 28th floor, China Resources Building, 8 Jianguomenbei Dajie, Dongcheng, Beijing 100005 (☎ 010-8519 2888, 🖳 americanclubbeijing.com).

Beijing International Club: 21, Jianguomenwai Dajie, Chaoyang District, Beijing 100020 (☎ 010-6460 6688, 🖳 bjgjjlb.com).

The British Club of Beijing: 50/F, Capital Mansions, 6 Xinyuan Nanlu, Chaoyang, Beijing 100004 (☎ 010-8488 2225, 🖳 britclubbj.org).

French Institute of China: Guangcai International Mansion, 18, Gongti Xilu, Beijing 100020 (☎ 010-6553 2627, 🖳 ccfpekin.org).

Goethe Institute, Cyber Tower, Building B, 17th floor, Cyber (Shuma) Tower, No.2, Zhongguancun Nandajie, Haidan, Beijing 100086 (☎ 010-8251 2909, 🖳 goethe.de/ins/cn/pek).

Educational Establishments

Traditional Chinese Medicine

These four universities are probably the most popular among foreigners interested in TCM, although there are many more.

Beijing University of Chinese Medicine: 11 Bei San Huan Dong Lu, Chaoyang, Beijing 100029 (☎ 010-6421 3841, 🖳 bucm.edu.cn).

Guangzhou University of Traditional Chinese Medicine: 10 Jichang Road, Sanyunli, Guangzhou 510407 (☎ 020-8659 1233, 🖳 acupuncture.edu/guangzhou).

Nanjing University of Traditional Chinese Medicine: 282 Hanzhong Road, Nanjing 210020 (☎ 025-8679 8079, 🖳 njutcm.edu.cn).

Shanghai University of Traditional Chinese Medicine: 1200 Cailun Road, Zhangjiang Hi-Tech Park, Pudong New District, Shanghai 201203 (☎ 021-5132 2222, 🖳 shutcm.com).

Chinese Martial Arts

Shaolin Temple Wushu Institute: Tagou, Deng Feng City, Henan 452491 (☎ 0371-6274 9100, 🖳 shaolintagou.com).

Taiji Training Centre: Huanghe Lu, Wenxian, Henan 454850 (☎ 0391-3816 0007, 🖳 taiji.net.cn).

Wudang Taoist Traditional Kung Fu Academy: Wudangshan, Shiyan City, Hubei 442714 (☎ mobile, 0135-9788 6695, 🖳 wudanggongfu.com).

Chinese Language

Beijing Normal University: 19 Xinjiekouwai Street, Haidian, Beijing 100875 (☎ 010-5880 7986, 🖳 bnulxsh.com).

Beijing University (Peking University): 5 Yiheyuan Road, Haidian, Beijing 100871 (☎ 010- 6275 1230), 🖳 english.pku.edu.cn). Their shortest course lasts one semester.

Beijing University of Languages and Culture: 15 Xueyuan Road, Haidian, Beijing 100083 (☎ 010-8230 3114, 🖳 blcu.edu.cn).

Fudan University: 220 Handan Road, Shanghai 200433 (☎ 021- 6511 7628, 🖳 fudan.edu.cn). Courses range from one-month tasters to full degree courses.

Tsinghua University: Foreign Affairs Office, Haidian, Beijing 100084 (☎ 010-6278 4857, 🖳 tsinghua.edu.cn/docsn/wb/lxs/elxs/htm).

Miscellaneous

General Administration of Customs: 6 Jianguomennei Avenue, Dongcheng , Beijing 100730 (☎ 010-6519 4114, 🖳 english.customs.gov.cn).

China International Travel Service: CITS Building, 1 Dongdan Beidajie, Dongcheng, Beijing 100005 (☎ 010-6522 2991, 🖳 cits.net).

China Travel Service: Taikang Financial Tower 29F, Dongsanhuan North Road No.38, Chaoyang, Beijing 100026 (☎ 010-8440 9578). This service has offices in the US (☎ 1-800 899 8618, 🖳 chinatravelservice.com) and the UK (☎ 020-7388 8838, 🖳 chinatravel.co.uk).

APPENDIX B: FURTHER READING

Newspapers & Magazines

21st Century (⌨ 21st.cn). A weekly newspaper for teenagers and Chinese learning English.

The Beijinger (⌨ thebeijinger.com). Monthly magazine aimed at Beijing expats.

Beijing This Month (⌨ btmbeijing.com). monthly magazine focusing on business and leisure in China's capital.

Beijing Today (⌨ beijingtoday.com.cn). English weekly edition of the *Beijing Youth Daily*.

Business Beijing (⌨ btmbeijing.com). Free monthly business magazine.

China Daily (⌨ chinadaily.com.cn). English language national newspaper.

China Grooves (⌨ chinagrooves.com). Free expat magazine based in Xi'an.

City Weekend (⌨ cityweekend.com.cn). Free weekly listings and classified advertisements with editions in Beijing, Guangzhou and Shanghai.

Economic Observer (⌨ eeo.com.cn/ens). English edition of the weekly Chinese newspaper.

Expat (⌨ theexpat.net). Singapore-based monthly magazine available throughout China.

Global Times (⌨ globaltimes.cn). English-language version (launched in 2009 to compete with overseas media) of the Chinese CPC newspaper. Also publishes two local English-language sections, *Metro Beijing* and *Metro Shanghai*.

People's Daily Online (⌨ english.peopledaily.com.cn). English version of the top-selling newspaper.

Shanghai Daily (⌨ shanghaidaily.com). Shanghai's English language newspaper.

South China Morning Post (⌨ scmp.com). Hong Kong daily in English.

Time Out Beijing & Time Out Shanghai (⌨ timeoutbeijing.com/index.html and timeoutshanghai.com/index.html). Monthly what's-on guides from the publishers of the listings bible.

Wall Street Journal Asia (⌨ wsj-asia.com). Asian version of the financial 'bible'.

Books

There are a great many books about China, from travel guides to fiction, although finding translations of Chinese classics or modern novels can be surprisingly difficult. Tracking down any English-language books in China is a challenge, but it's worth trying the Foreign Language Bookstore in Wangfujingdajie, Beijing or one of the branches of The Bookworm (⌨ chinabookworm.com). Many titles are available online through websites such as Amazon UK (⌨ amazon.co.uk) or China Books in Australia (⌨ chinabooks.com.au). You could also buy an eBook reader – such as Kindle – and download books via the internet (eBook readers can store thousands of books).

A selection of books is listed below by title, followed by the author's name and the publisher.

Biographies

Deng Xiaoping and the Making of Modern China, Richard Evans (Penguin)

The Man Who Loved China, Simon Winchester (Harper)

The New Emperors, Harrison E Salisbury (Harper Perennial)

The Private Life of Chairman Mao, Zhisui Li (Random House)

The Soong Dynasty, Sterling Seagrave (Corgi Books)

Culture

An Introduction to Confucianism, Xinzhong Yao (Cambridge University Press)

The Arts of China, Michael Sullivan (University of California)

China A to Z: Everything You Need to Know to Understand Chinese Customs and Culture, May-lee Chai & Winberg Chai (Plume)

The China Book, a People, a Place, a Culture, Li-Yu Hung (Black Dog)

China: Its History and Culture, William Scott Morton (McGraw Hill)

China: People, Place, Culture, History, DK Publishing

The Chinese, Jasper Becker (Oxford University Press)

Chinese Calligraphy, Zhongshi Quyang & Wen C Fong (Yale University)

Culture Wise China, Leo Lacey (Survival Books)

How to Read Chinese Paintings, Maxwell K. Hearn (Yale University)

A Social History of the Chinese Book, Joseph P McDermott (Hong Kong University)

Sources of Chinese Tradition, William Theodore de Barry (Columbia University)

Three Thousand Years of Chinese Painting, Professor Richard Barnhart et al (Yale University)

Understanding China, John Bryan Starr (Hill & Wang)

History

The Big Book of China: A Guided Tour through 5,000 Years of History, Qicheng Wang (Long River)

A Brief History of Chinese Civilisation, Conrad Schirokaver (Wadsworth)

A Brief History of the Dynasties of China, Bamber Gascoigne (Robinson)

The Cambridge Illustrated History of China, Patricia Buckley Ebrey (CUP)

China; A Cultural, Social and Political History, Patricia Buckley Ebrey (Wadsworth)

China: A History, John Keay (HarperPress)

China: A New History, John King Fairbank & Merle Goldman (Belknap)

China's Imperial Past: an Introduction to Chinese History and Culture, Charles O. Hucker (Stanford University)

Chinese Civilisation: A Source Book, Patricia Buckley Ebrey (Free Press)

The Civilization of China, Herbery Allen Giles (Kindle)

Mao's Great Famine: The History of China's Most Devastating Catastrophe, Frank Dikotter (Bloomsbury)

On China, Henry Kissinger (Allen Lane)

The Penguin History of Modern China: The Fall and Rise of a Great Power, 1850-2009, Jonathan Fenby (Penguin)

Red Star over China, Edgar Snow (Penguin)

The Search for Modern China, Jonathan D Spence (WW Norton)

The Siege at Peking, Peter Fleming (Oxford University Press)

Voices from the Whirlwind, Feng Jicai (Pantheon)

Language

1,000 Chinese Words (Berlitz)

BBC Mandarin Chinese Phrase Book & Dictionary, Dr Qian Kan (BBC Active)

Beginner's Chinese, Yong Ho (Hippocrene)

China Phrasebook, Michael Cannings (Lonely Planet)

Chinese-English Visual Bilingual Dictionary (Dorling Kindersley)

Chinese Language for Beginners, Lee Cooper (Tuttle)

Colloquial Chinese, Kan Qian (Routledge)

Easy Peasy Chinese: Mandarin Chinese for Beginners (Dorling Kindersley)

First Thousand Words in Chinese, Heather Amery (Usborne)

Hugo's Chinese in Three Months, P C T'ung & H Baker (Hugo/DK Publishing)

Learn to Write Chinese Characters, Johan Bjorksten (Yale University)

Mandarin Phrasebook (Lonely Planet)

Pocket Oxford Chinese Dictionary (OUP China)

The Times' Essential English-Chinese Dictionary, Fu Wei Ci (Federal)

Literature

The Art of War, Sun Tzu (Penguin)

A Dream of Red Mansions, Cao Xueqin (Foreign Languages Press)

The Good Earth, Pearl S Buck (Pocket)

Life and Death in Shanghai, Nien Cheng (Penguin)

Lost Horizon, James Hilton (Pocket)

Mao's Last Dancer, Li Cunxin (Penguin)

Monkey, Wu Ch'eng-en & Arthur Waley (Penguin)

Red China Blues, Jan Wong (Anchor)

Red Sorghum, Mo Yan (Arrow)

The Real Story of Ah-Q & Other Tales of China, Lu Xun (Penguin)

Romance of the Three Kingdoms, Luo Guanzhong (Foreign Language Press)

Soul Mountain, Gao Xingjian (Harper Collins)

Wild Swans: Three Daughters of China, Jung Chang (Harper Perennial)

Living & Working

Business China, Peggy Kenna & Sondra Lacy (McGraw Hill)

China Business Handbook, Robert A Capp (ACA)

China CEO: a Case Guide for Business Leaders in China, Juan Antonio Fernandez & Lui Shengjun (Wiley)

China CEO: Voices of Experience, Juan Antonio Fernandez & Laurie Underwood (Wiley)

The China Dream: the Elusive Quest for the Greatest Untapped Market on Earth, Joe Studwell (Grove Press)

The China Ready Company, Steven H Ganster with Kent D Kedl (China Pathways)

China's Economic Challenge: Smashing the Iron Rice Bowl, Neil C Hughes (East Gate)

Chinese Business Etiquette, Scott P Seligman (Warner)

The Chinese Tao of Business: the Logic of Successful Business Strategy, George T Haley et al (John Wiley)

Doing Business in China: How to Profit in the World's Fastest Growing Market, Ted Plafker (Business Plus)

How to Live and Do Business in China, Ernie Tadla (Trafford)

How to Do Business in China: 24 Lessons to Make Working in China More Profitable, Nick Dallas (McGraw-Hill Professional)

Mr China, Tim Clissold (HarperBusiness)

One Billion Customers: Letters from the Front Lines of Doing Business in China, James McGregor (Free Press)

Miscellaneous

Atlas of Birds of China, Chian Yan Wen (Henan Science and Technology Publishers)

Blue and White: Chinese Porcelain around the World, John Carswell (Art Media)

Chinese Porcelain: Art, Elegance and Appreciation, Chen Kelun (Long River)

China Study, The: The Most Comprehensive Study of Nutrition Ever Conducted and the Startling Implications for Diet, Weight Loss and Long-term Health, Colin Campbell (Ben Bella)

Factory Girls: Voices from the Heart of Modern China, Leslie T. Chang (Picador)

A Field Guide to the Birds of China, John McKinnon and Karen Phillipps (OUP)

Pictorial Guide to Pottery and Porcelain Marks, Chad Lage (Collector)

Tourism & Travel

Behind the Wall, Colin Thubron (Vintage)

Berlitz Pocket Guide – China, Ken Bernstein (Berlitz)

China: The 50 Most Memorable Trips, J D Brown (Frommer's)

China Survival Guide: How to Avoid Travel Trouble and Mortifying Mishaps, Larry Herzberg (Stone Bridge)

DK Eyewitness Travel: China, Collectif (Dorling Kindersley)

Fodor's Exploring China, Christopher Knowles (Fodor's)

The Great Railway Bazaar: by Train through Asia and **Riding the Iron Rooster: by Train through China**, Paul Theroux (Penguin)

Lonely Planet Beijing City Guide, Damien Harper (Lonely Planet)

Lonely Planet China, Damien Harper (Lonely Planet)

Marco Polo: the Travels (Penguin)

Oracle Bones: A Journey through Time in China, Peter Hessler (Harper Perennial)

River Town: Two Years on the Yangtze, Peter Hessler (John Murray)

The River at the Centre of the World, Simon Winchester (Penguin)

The Rough Guide to China, David Leffman et al (Rough Guides)

Giant Panda

APPENDIX C: USEFUL WEBSITES

This appendix contains a selection of some of the many websites dedicated to China and the Chinese. Websites about specific aspects of living, working and doing business in China are also included in the relevant chapters. **Note that it may not be possible to access all the websites listed below in China or with all search engines.**

Accommodation

The Beijinger (🖥 thebeijinger.com). Loads of classified adverts, including accommodation to rent in Beijing.

Century 21 (🖥 century21cn.com/english). 'Estate agency' franchise with branches throughout China.

City Weekend Magazine (🖥 cityweekend.com.cn). Accommodation to let in Beijing, Guangzhou and Shanghai.

Craigslist (🖥 geo.craigslist.org/iso/cn). Classifieds in a number of Chinese cities, including accommodation to rent.

Lezone Real Estate (🖥 bj-realestate.com). Apartments and serviced apartments to rent in Beijing.

Wuwoo Real Estate Service (🖥 wuwoo.com). Beijing-based property agency website featuring English-language content and a useful map.

Business

All Roads Lead to China (🖥 allroadsleadtochina.com). Business analysis, insights and news.

American Chamber of Commerce (🖥 amchamchina.org). Website of the US Chamber of Commerce in China, including some useful forums.

Australian Business Foundation (🖥 abfoundation.com.au). Includes guidance to the business start-up procedures in China.

Australian Chamber of Commerce (🖥 austcham.org). Also represents New Zealand companies.

Australian Trade Commission (Austrade, 🖥 austrade.gov.au). A site promoting trade and investment between Australia and other countries.

Business Link (🖥 businesslink.gov.uk). UK government website, including a section on international trade with information on doing business in China.

British Chamber of Commerce (🖥 britishchamber.cn). With branches in Beijing, Guangzhou and Shanghai, the website includes a job-search function and also represents Irish companies.

Canadian Chamber of Commerce of South China (🖥 lifeofguangzhou.com). Based in Guangzhou.

Canadian-China Business Council (CCBC, 🖥 ccbc.com). A Canada-China bilateral trade and investment facilitator.

China Briefing (🖥 china-briefing.com). Monthly magazine and daily news service about doing business in China.

China-British Business Council (🖥 cbbc.org). The largest membership organisation for all UK companies doing business in China.

European Union Chamber of Commerce (🖥 europeanchamber.com.cn/view/home). Representing the countries of the European Union.

Ministry of Commerce (🖥 english.mofcom.gov.cn). Information for those wishing to do business in China.

People's Bank of China (🖥 pbc.gov.cn/publish/english/963/index.html). China's central bank.

State Administration of Foreign Experts' Affairs (🖥 safea.gov.cn/english). Useful website for those wishing to work or do business in China, including details of job fairs and information on work permits.

Culture

About Chinese Culture (🖥 chineseculture.about.com). From mahjong to music, a wealth of facts from the About team, plus links to blogs and forums.

China Culture (🖥 chinaculture.org). Information site from the Ministry of Culture, highlighting current cultural events.

China Highlights (🖥 chinahighlights.com/travelguide/culture). A range of interesting articles from the Guilin branch of the China International Travel Service (CITS). Also features guides to cities and attractions.

China Museums (🖥 chinamuseums.com). Good all-round guide to some of the country's best museums.

China Today (🖥 chinatoday.com). Broad information base, including everything from arts to travel.

Shanghai Museum (🖥 shanghaimuseum.org). Probably the best museum in China.

Travel China Guide (🖥 travelchinaguide.com). A huge range of topics with a great section on culture. The section on Chinese opera is essential reading.

Education

British Council Journal (🖥 britishcouncil.org/china). A wealth of resources for would-be English teachers.

China Study Abroad (🖥 chinastudyabroad.org). China-wide language courses including written Chinese.

My China Start (🖥 international-schools.mychinastart.com). Listing of international schools in China.

Worldwide Schools (🖥 english-schools.org/china). Directory of schools providing English-language education in China.

See also **Appendix A**, which contains contacts for educational establishments specialising in the Chinese language, martial arts and traditional Chinese medicine.

Government

Central People's Government (🖥 english.gov.cn). Gateway to China's government with links to central and local government departments.

e-Beijing (🖥 ebeijing.gov.cn). Informative online portal of the Beijing municipal government.

General Administration of Customs (🖥 english.customs.gov.cn). For all queries relating to customs and the import/export of goods.

Ministry of Commerce (🖥 english.mofcom.gov.cn). Useful if you plan on doing business in China.

Ministry of Culture (🖳 ccnt.gov.cn/English/index.html). Click the Cultural China link for an overview of Chinese arts.

Ministry of Education (🖳 moe.edu.cn/publicfiles/business/htmlfiles/moe/moe_2792/index.html). Facts, statistics and links to educational establishments.

Ministry of Foreign Affairs (🖳 mfa.gov.cn/eng). Information on foreign policy and regulations which may affect foreign residents.

☑ SURVIVAL TIP

Many of the above government departments have provincial offices and you may find it easier to deal with them on a more local level.

Language

Beijing Normal University (🖳 bnulxsh.com/english/index.htm). Offers both full university courses and short courses for language learners.

Beijing University of Language and Culture (🖳 blcu-china.org). The only university in China to specialise in teaching the Chinese language and culture.

China Study Abroad (🖳 chinastudyabroad.org). Offers a range of courses based in Beijing, Dalian, Hangzhou, Kunming, Nanjing, Qingdao, Shanghai, Tianjing and Xi'an.

Fudan University, Shanghai (🖳 fudan.edu.cn). The leading university in Shanghai, offering a range of courses from full degrees to short courses.

New Concept Mandarin Limited (🖳 newconceptmandarin.com). Immersion courses in Beijing, Guangzhou, Nanjing, Shanghai, Shenzhen and Suzhou, as well as online courses and DVDs.

Omniglot (🖳 omniglot.com/writing/mandarin.htm). An in-depth look at Mandarin Chinese with many useful links.

Peking University (🖳 pku.edu.cn). Located in Beijing – and one of China's top universities – PU also offers language courses.

Study in China (🖳 chinese-tools.com/study). Search engine for language courses and institutions.

Tsinghua University, Beijing (🖳 tsinghua.edu.cn). Four different courses available, with accommodation provided if required.

Zhongwen (🖳 zhongwen.com). Rick Harbaugh's guide to Chinese characters and how they evolved over the centuries.

Living & Working

Allo Expat (🖳 beijing.alloexpat.com). Comprehensive info for expats in Beijing, including a useful expat forum.

ANZA Beijing (🖳 anzabeijing.com). Association for Australian and New Zealanders, open to other international expats.

Asia Xpat (🖳 shanghai.asiaxpat.com). City guide for Shanghai. Click tabs for a similar service in Beijing and Guangzhou.

The Beijing Page (🖳 beijingpage.com). Online directory to life in China's capital.

China Expat (🖥 chinaexpat.com). Claims to take you around China in one website.

China Job (🖥 chinajob.com). Government backed recruitment website majoring on positions for English teachers.

China Telecom (🖥 chinatelecom-h.com). State telecoms operator.

Expat Blog (🖥 expat-blog.com/en/destination/asia/china). Facts from the folk on the frontline. There are links to different nationalities, e.g. Brits in China (🖥 expat-blog.com/en/nationalities/british/in/asia/china).

Expat Interviews (🖥 expatinterviews.com/china). First-hand experiences from foreigners living in China.

Go Chengdoo (🖥 gochengdoo.com/en). Lively e-zine aimed at Western expats, with reviews of local news, sights, restaurants and events in Chengdu.

Go Kunming (🖥 gokunming.com/en). A similar service to **Go Chengdoo** (above) for expat residents of Kunming.

Irish Network China (🖥 irishnetworkchina.com). Advice and support for Irish expats.

Job China (🖥 jobchina.net). jobs website with plenty of teaching opportunities and more.

Living in China (🖥 livinginchina.com). More useful info for expats.

Middle Kingdom Life (🖥 middlekingdomlife.com/guide). An award-winning educational website founded by a professor of psychology and a school headmaster in Jilin.

My China Career (🖥 mychinacareer.com). Job-search website including relatively high level positions in most industries.

My China Start (🖥 expats.mychinastart.com). Useful website for newcomers.

Notes from Xi'an (🖥 notesfromxian.com). An Englishman's view of one of China's most fascinating cities.

Shanghai Expat (🖥 shanghaiexpat.com). Comprehensive guide to life in China's commercial hub.

Stuck in Beijing (🖥 stuckinbeijing.com). Beijing from a foreigner's viewpoint, including a guide to city locations and prices.

Media

China Central Television (🖥 english.cctv.com). China's national broadcaster.

China Daily (🖥 chinadaily.com.cn). The only national English-language daily newspaper in China.

China Internet Information Centre (🖥 china.org.cn). Chinese news resource collated from a number of official sources.

China.org (🖥 china.org.cn). Online news website available in a number of languages.

China Radio International (🖥 english.cri.cn/index.htm). Broadcasts in many languages, including English.

China Today (🖥 chinatoday.com). Broad information base including everything from arts to travel.

People's Daily (🖥 english.peopledaily.com.cn). English-language version of China's most-read newspaper.

Shanghai Daily (🖥 shanghaidaily.com). English-language version of one of China's major newspapers.

Shenzhen Daily (🖥 www1.szdaily.com). One of China's leading English-language newspapers.

South China Morning Post (🖥 scmp.com). Hong Kong daily newspaper.

Xinhua (🖥 xinhuanet.com/english2010). News from China's national news agency.

Medical Matters

Beijing Anzhen Hospital (⌨ anzhen.org, in Chinese – for information in English, see ⌨ hospitalcn.com).

Beijing Municipal Health Bureau (⌨ english.bjhb.gov.cn). Health news from the Chinese capital, with links to hospitals.

China-Japan Friendship Hospital (⌨ zryhyy.com.cn).

Peking Union Medical College Hospital (⌨ pumch.cn).

International SOS (⌨ internationalsos.com). Provides international healthcare in Beijing, Hong Kong, Nanjing, Shekou and Tianjin.

Miscellaneous

At Your Side (⌨ atyourside.asia). Personal guide/concierge service for visitors.

Azfrieght (⌨ azfreight.com). Information about shipping by air.

China Meteorological Administration (⌨ cma.gov.cn/english/forecast_gn.php). Regional weather forecasts in English.

DEFRA (⌨ defra.gov.uk/wildlife-pets/pets/travel/quarantine). Information on UK quarantine from the Department of Environment, Food and Rural Affairs.

Eachnet (⌨ eachnet.com). China's version of eBay.

Handy Shipping Guide (⌨ handyshippingguide.com). Global freight and shipping directory.

International Centre for Veterinary Services (⌨ icvsasia.com). Advice on pet care and vet services in Beijing.

Passport for Pets (⌨ passportsforpets.co.uk). Can advise on and organise pet travel from the UK and Ireland to China; used by UK and Irish governments.

Pet Relocation (⌨ petrelocation.com/resources/international-regulations/china). US company providing information on importing pets into China.

Second Chance Animal Aid (⌨ scaashanghai.org). Shanghai-based animal welfare charity with contacts for vets and advice on importing/exporting pets.

Sinotrans (⌨ sinotrans.com). The best-known freight handling company in China, useful if you're shipping overseas.

Weather (⌨ weather.china.org.cn/english).

Wikipedia (⌨ en.wikipedia.org/wiki/people%27s_republic_of_china). Dedicated portal from the community encyclopaedia.

World Care Pet Transporters (⌨ worldcarepet.com). International pet movers.

Yellow Pages China (⌨ yellowpages-china.com). Online directory of companies, importers, exporters, manufacturers and vendors.

Teaching English

ChinaJOB (⌨ chinajob.com). Government-backed organisation primarily recruiting teachers of English.

ELS Teacher Café (⌨ china.eslteachercafe.com). Forum for English-language teachers in China.

Teach English Abroad (⌨ teachabroadchina.com/travel-in-china-forum). Includes job postings and classified adverts.

Travel

Air China (🖥 airchina.com). One of China's leading airlines, based in Beijing.

Cathay Pacific (🖥 cathaypacific.com). Hong Kong's leading airline and one of the world's best.

China International Travel Service (🖥 cits.net). State-owned travel organisation established for more than 50 years.

China National Tourist Office (🖥 cnto.org). The official government tourist website.

China Travel (🖥 chinatravel.com). Claims to be the world's largest China travel information site.

China Travel Service (🖥 chinatravelservice.com). The national organisation for travel within China.

Chinese Visa Service Application Centre (🖥 visaforchina.org.uk). Handles visa applications in the UK.

Going to China (🖥 goingtochina.com). Chinese travel and tourism resource.

Just China (🖥 justchina.org). China travel guide.

Lonely Planet (🖥 lonelyplanet.com/china). Lowdown on China from the renowned travel guide book series.

Monkey Shrine (🖥 monkeyshrine.com). Travel company specialising in travel on the Trans-Siberian railway.

Railways of China (🖥 railwaysofchina.com). An unofficial overview of China's railways.

Rough Guides (🖥 roughguides.com/travel/asia/china.aspx). Advice from another top travel guide book brand.

Seat 61 (🖥 seat61.com/China.htm). Comprehensive guide to train travel in China.

Travel China (🖥 chinatravelcenter.com). Beijing-based agency.

Travel China Guide (🖥 travelchinaguide.com/cityguides). Information about China's major cities.

Wikitravel (🖥 wikitravel.org/en/china). Wikipedia's travel guide.

APPENDIX D: WEIGHTS & MEASURES

C hina uses the metric system for measurements. Those who are more familiar with Imperial measurements will find the tables on the following pages useful. Some comparisons shown are only approximate but are close enough for most everyday use.

The trickiest area is clothing. Most Chinese clothes carry metric (continental) sizes but many manufacturers also use the international sizing codes, e.g. S, M, L, XL and XXL, particularly with regard to sports clothing. However, the Chinese are generally smaller and slimmer than Westerners, so a Chinese XL may be the equivalent of an L or even an M in the West. It can also be difficult to find clothes which are in proportion; women may find that the waist fits while the hips and bust are too narrow, while men may find a shirt with the correct collar size but the body is too tight and the sleeves too short. Even children's clothing sizes are awkward as they're usually based on age, and Chinese children are smaller than their Western cousins at the same age, therefore you may need to buy an older size.

It's essential to try on all clothes and shoes before buying them. Most retailers are unwilling to refund or exchange items simply because they don't fit.

Shoe Size Comparisons (Men's & Women's)

China	33	35	37	37	39	41	41	42	43	43	44	45	46	47	48
Europe	35	36	37	37	38	39	40	41	42	42	43	44	45	45	46
UK	2	3	3	4	4	5	6	7	7	8	9	9	10	11	12
USA	4	5	5	6	6	7	8	9	9	10	10	11	11	12	13

Chinese Measurements

Although the Chinese use the standard metric system, some old-fashioned weights and measures are still in daily use and it's handy to know about them. When shopping in a market, produce is often sold by the *jin* which used to be the same as a pound in weight but now equals 500g. A kilogram is a *gong jin*, while 250g is *ban jin*, although these are rarely used. Tea has its own specific unit of measurement which takes into account its lightness and high value: it's usually sold by the *liang*, which is one tenth of a *jin*, i.e. 50g.

When calculating distance, many people eschew kilometres (*gong li*) and refer to it in units of *li* or about 500m (if you run out of petrol/gas and someone tells you it's six *li* to the nearest petrol station, you have a 3km walk ahead of you). Area also has an archaic measurement known as the *mu*. Many farmers still measure their land in *mu* – there are six *mu* to the acre and 15 *mu* to the hectare, which is the modern way of calculating area.

Women's Clothes

Continental	34	36	38	40	42	44	46	48	50	52
UK		8	10	12	14	16	18	20	22	24	26
US		6	8	10	12	14	16	18	20	22	24

Pullover's

	Women's						Men's					
Continental	40	42	44	46	48	50	44	46	48	50	52	54
UK	34	36	38	40	42	44	34	36	38	40	42	44
US	34	36	38	40	42	44	sm	med		lg	xl	

Men's Shirts

Continental	36	37	38	39	40	41	42	43	44	46
UK/US	14	14	15	15	16	16	17	17	18	-

Men's Underwear

Continental	5	6	7	8	9	10
UK		34	36	38	40	42	44
US		sm	med		lg	xl	

sm = small, med = medium, lg = large, xl = extra large

Children's Clothes

Continental	92	104	116	128	140	152
UK	16/18	20/22	24/26	28/30	32/34	36/38
US	2	4	6	8	10	12

Children's Shoes

Continental	18 19 20 21 22 23 24 25 26 27 28 29 30 31 32
UK/US	2 3 4 4 5 6 7 7 8 9 10 11 11 12 13
Continental	33 34 35 36 37 38
UK/US	1 2 2 3 4 5

Shoes (Women's & Men's)

Continental	35	36	37	37	38	39	40	41	42	42	43	44	45	46.5	47.5
UK	2	3	3	4	4	5	6	7	7	8	9	9	10	11	12
US	2.5		3.5		4.5		5.5	6.5		7.5		8.5		9.5	10.5	11.5	12.5

Weight

Imperial	Metric	Metric	Imperial
1oz	28.35g	1g	0.035oz
1lb*	454g	100g	3.5oz
1cwt	50.8kg	250g	9oz
1 ton	1,016kg	500g	18oz
2,205lb	1 tonne	1kg	2.2lb

Area

British/US	Metric	Metric	British/US
1 sq. in	0.45 sq. cm	1 sq. cm	0.15 sq. in
1 sq. ft	0.09 sq. m	1 sq. m	10.76 sq. ft
1 sq. yd	0.84 sq. m	1 sq. m	1.2 sq. yds
1 acre	0.4 hectares	1 hectare	2.47 acres
1 sq. mile	2.56 sq. km	1 sq. km	0.39 sq. mile

Capacity			
Imperial	**Metric**	**Metric**	**Imperial**
1 UK pint	0.57 litre	1 litre	1.75 UK pints
1 US pint	0.47 litre	1 litre	2.13 US pints
1 UK gallon	4.54 litres	1 litre	0.22 UK gallon
1 US gallon	3.78 litres	1 litre	0.26 US gallon

An American 'cup' = around 250ml or 0.25 litre.

Length			
British/US	**Metric**	**Metric**	**British/US**
1in	2.54cm	1cm	0.39in
1ft	30.48cm	1m	3ft 3.25in
1yd	91.44cm	1km	0.62mi
1mi	1.6km	8km	5mi

Power			
Kilowatts	**Horsepower**	**Horsepower**	**Kilowatts**
1	1.34	1	0.75

Oven Temperature		
Gas	**Electric**	
	°F	**°C**
-	225–250	110–120
1	275	140
2	300	150
3	325	160
4	350	180
5	375	190
6	400	200
7	425	220
8	450	230
9	475	240

Air Pressure	
PSI	Bar
10	0.5
20	1.4
30	2
40	2.8

Temperature	
°Celsius	°Fahrenheit
0	32 (freezing point of water)
5	41
10	50
15	59
20	68
25	77
30	86
35	95
40	104
50	122

Temperature Conversion

Celsius to Fahrenheit: multiply by 9, divide by 5 and add 32. (For a quick and approximate conversion, double the Celsius temperature and add 30.)

Fahrenheit to Celsius: subtract 32, multiply by 5 and divide by 9. (For a quick and approximate conversion, subtract 30 from the Fahrenheit temperature and divide by 2.)

NB: The boiling point of water is 100°C / 212°F. Normal body temperature (if you're alive and well) is 37°C / 98.6°F.

APPENDIX E: MAP OF PROVINCES & ADMINISTRATIVE AREAS

PROVINCES

Province	Capital City	Population (millions)
Anhui	Hefei	59.5
Fujian	Fuzhou	36.9
Gansu	Lanzhou	25.6
Guangdong	Guangzhou	104.3
Guizhou	Guizhou	34.7
Hainan	Haikou	8.7
Hebei	Shijiazhuang	71.9
Heilongjiang	Harbin	38.3
Henan	Zhengzhou	94
Hubei	Wuhan	57.2
Hunan	Changsha	65.7
Jiangsu	Nanjing	78.7
Jiangxi	Nanchung	44.6
Jilin	Changchun	27.5
Liaoning	Shenyang	43.7
Qinghai	Xining	5.6
Shaanxi	Xi'an	37.3
Shandong	Jinan	95.8
Shanxi	Taiyuan	35.7
Sichuan	Chengdu	80.4
Taiwan	Taipei	23.1
Yunnan	Kunming	46.0
Zhejiang	Hangzhou	54.4

Special Administrative Regions (SARs)

Region	Population (millions)
Hong Kong	7
Macau	0.6

Municipalities

Municipality	Population (millions)
Beijing	19.6
Chongqing	28.8
Shanghai	23
Tianjin	12.9

Autonomous Regions

Region	Capital City	Population (millions)
Guangxi	Nanning	46
Inner Mongolia	Hohhot	24.7
Ningxia	Yinchuan	6.2
Tibet	Lhasa	3
Xinjiang	Urumqi	21.8

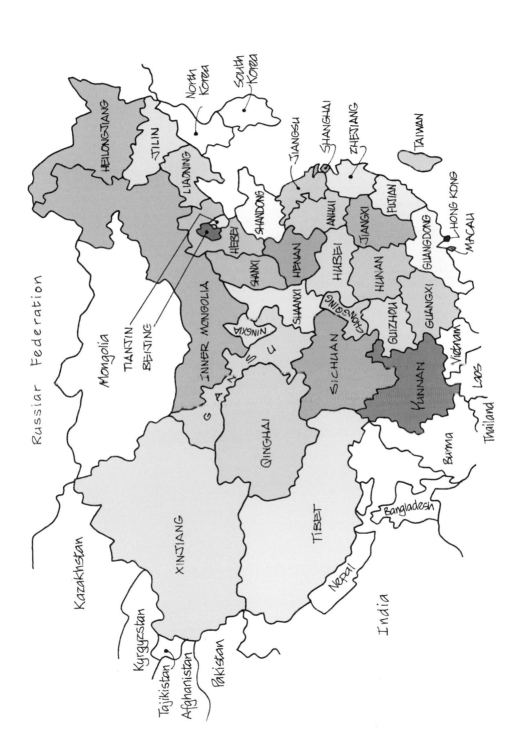

APPENDIX F: USEFUL WORDS & PHRASES

B elow is a list of words and phrases you may need during your first few days in China. They are, of course, no substitute for learning Chinese, which you should make a priority. All words are written in pinyin which is the approved way of transliterating Chinese phonetically using the Latin or Roman alphabet. A guide to pronunciation is provided on page 37.

Pronouns

I	*wo*
you (singular)	*ni*
he/she/it	*ta*
we/us	*women*
you (plural)	*nimen*
they/them	*tamen*

You can change any of the above into a possessive by adding '*de*', e.g. mine (*wo de*), his (*ta de*), theirs (*tamen de*).

Asking for Help

Do you speak English?	*Ni shuo yin yu ma?*
I don't speak Chinese	*Wo bu hui jiang zhong wen*
Please could you speak slowly?	*Qin jiang man dian?*
I don't understand	*Wo ting bu dong*
Do you understand?	*Dong ma?*
I want …	*Wo xiang yao …*
I need …	*Wo xu yao …*

Communications

Telephone & Internet

phone line	*dianhua*
mobile phone	*shou ji*
no answer	*mei ren jie*
engaged/busy	*zhan xian*
internet	*yinte wang*
computer	*diannao*
email	*dian zi you jian*
internet café	*wang ba*

Post

post office	*youdianju*
postcard/letter/parcel	*ming xin pian/xin han/bao guo*
stamps	*you piao*
How much does it cost to send a letter to Europe/USA/Australia?	*Yi fen ji dao ou zhou/mei guo/audaliyia de xin yao duo shao qian?*

Media

newspaper/magazine	*bao kan/za zhi*
Do you sell English-language newspapers?	*You ying wei bao zhi chu shou ma?*

Courtesy

yes	*shi* (this literally translates as 'is' and implies 'that's it, that's right')
no	*bu* (this means 'not so'; to explain that you don't have something, say *mei you*)
excuse me/sorry	*dui bu qi* (used when apologising or trying to pass someone)
I don't know	*wo bu zhi dao*
I don't mind	*wo bu jie yi*
please	*qing*
thank you	*xie xie*
you're welcome	*bu ke qi* or *bu yong xie*

Countries

Australia/Australian	*aodaliya/aodaliya ren*
Canada/Canadian	*jianada/jianada ren*
France/French	*faguo/faguo ren*
Germany/German	*deguo/deguo ren*
Ireland/Irish	*ai'erlan/ai'erlan ren*
Netherlands/Dutch	*helan/helan ren*
New Zealand/New Zealander	*xinxilan/xinxilan ren*
Spain/Spanish	*xibanya/xibanya ren*
UK/British	*yingguo/yingguo ren*
USA/American	*mei guo/mei guo ren*
Which country are you from?	*Ni shi nage guojia de?*
I'm British/American/Australian	*Wo shi yingguo ren/meiguo ren/audaliyia ren*

Days & Months

Monday	*xing qi yi*
Tuesday	*xing qi er*
Wednesday	*xing qi san*
Thursday	*xing qi si*
Friday	*xing qi wu*
Saturday	*xing qi liu*
Sunday	*xing qi tian* or *xing qi ri*

January	*yi yue*
February	*er yue*
March	*san yue*
April	*si yue*
May	*wu yue*
June	*liu yue*
July	*qi yue*
August	*ba yue*
September	*jiu yue*
October	*shi yue*
November	*shiyi yue*
December	*shi'er yue*

Driving

car insurance	*che xian*
driving licence	*jia shi zheng*
hire/rental car	*zu che*
How far is it to … ?	*You duo yuan … ?*
Can I park here?	*Zhe neng ting che ma?*
unleaded petrol (gas)	*qi you*
Fill up the tank please	*Jia man qi you*
I need … RMB of petrol (gas)	*Jia … renminbi qi you*
air (for tyres)	*jia man qi* or *gei tai jia qi*
water/oil	*shui/you*
car wash	*xi che*
My car has broken down	*Wo de che huai le*
I've run out of petrol (gas)	*Wo de che mei you le*
My tyre is flat	*Wo de che tai bian le*
I need a tow truck	*Wo xu yao yi ge tuo che*
bicycle/electric bicycle	*zixingche/diandong zixingche*

Emergency

Emergency!	*jin ji qing kuang*!
Fire!	*zhao huo le*!
Help!	*jiu ming*!
Police!	*jin cha*!
Stop thief!	*zhua zei*!
Watch out!	*xiao xin*!

Finding your Way

Where is … ?	*… zai nali*?
Where is the toilet?	*Cesuo zai nali*?
Where is the nearest … ?	*Zhui jin de … zai na li*?
How do I get to … ?	*Zen me zou … ?*
Can I walk there?	*Wo neng zou dao na li ma*?
How far is … ?	*You duo yuang … ?*
I'm lost	*Wo mi lu le*
left/right/straight ahead	*zuo/you/yizhi zou*
opposite/next to/near	*dui mian/pang bian/fu jin*
north/south/east/west	*bei/nan/dong/xi*
airport	*jichang*
bus/plane/taxi/train	*gonggongqiche/feiji/chuzuche/huoche*
minibus	*xiao mian bao che*
bus stop	*gong jiao che ting che dian*
Please turn on the meter	*qing da biao*
train/bus station	*huo che zhan/gong jiao che zhan*
What time does the bus arrive?	*Shen men shi hou da ba dao zhe*
What time does the train leave?	*Shen men shi hou huo che chu fa*
ticket	*piao*
bank/embassy/consulate	*yinhang/da shi guan/ling shi guan*
market/supermarket	*shichang/chaoji shichang*
police station	*jingchaju*
hotel/restaurant	*binguan/fandian*

Note that the words *binguan*, *fandian*, *jiudian* and *dajiudian* can all refer to either a hotel or a restaurant.

Greetings

Hello	*ni hao*
how are you	*ni hao ma*
good morning	*zao shang hao*
good afternoon	*xiawu hao*
good evening	*wan shang hao*
good night	*wan'an*
goodbye	*zaijian*

Health & Medical Emergencies

I feel ill	*Wo gan dao bu shu fu*
I feel dizzy	*Wo gan dao bu shu fu tou yun*
I need a doctor	*Wo xiu yao kang yi sheng*
I need an ambulance doctor/nurse/dentist	*Wo xiu yao jiu hu che* *yi sheng/hu shi/yia yi*
surgeon/specialist	*shou shu/zhuang jia*
hospital/health clinic/ A&E (emergency room)	*yiyuan/zhen shuo/ji zheng*
chemist's (pharmacy)	*yaodian*
optician's	*yang ke*
prescription	*chu fang*

In a Bar or Restaurant

waiter/waitress!	*nan fu wu sheng/nu fu wu sheng!*
menu	*cai pu*
bill	*mai dan*
well done/medium/ rare (for meat)	*ba cheng shou/wu cheng shou/* *san cheng shou*
vegetarian	*su shi zhe*
meat/fish	*rou/yu*

Numbers

zero	*ling*
one	*yi*
two	*er* (when stating a number, e.g. of an apartment it's *er*; when stating a quantity, e.g. two fish, the word used is *liang*, e.g. 'two fish' is *liang yu*)
three	*san*
four	*si*
five	*wu*
six	*liu*
seven	*qi*
eight	*ba*
nine	*jiu*
ten	*shi*
eleven	*shi yi*
twelve	*shi er*
thirteen	*shi san*
fourteen	*shi si*
fifteen	*shi wu*
sixteen	*shi liu*
seventeen	*shi qi*
eighteen	*shi ba*
nineteen	*shi jiu*
twenty	*er shi*
twenty one	*er shi yi*
thirty	*san shi*
forty	*si shi*
fifty	*wu shi*
sixty	*liu shi*
seventy	*qi shi*
eighty	*ba shi*
ninety	*jiu shi*
100	*yi bai*
200	*er bai*
500	*wu bai*
1,000	*yi qian*
5,000	*wu qian*
10,000	*yi wan*
One million	*yi bai wan*
One billion	*shi yi*

Paying

How much is this?	*Duoshao qian?*
The bill, please.	*Mai dan.*
Do you take credit cards?	*Shi yong xin yong ka ma?*

Socialising

Pleased to meet you	*Hen gao xing jian dao ni*
My name is …	*Wo de ming zi jiao …*
What's your name?	*Ni jiao shenma ming zi?*
Are you married?	*Ni jiehun le ma?*
Have you got children?	*Ni youmeiyou hai zi?*
This is my husband/wife	*Zhe shi wo de zhang fu/qi zi*
This is my son/daughter	*Zhe shi wu de er zi/nu er*
This is my friend/work colleague.	*Zhe she wo de peng you/tong shi*
What's your job?	*Ni gan shenma gongzuo?*
How old are you?	*Ni dou da le?*
How are you?	*Ni hao ma?*
Very well, thank you	*Fei chang hao, xie xie*

Shopping

What time do you open?	*Sheng ma shi jiang ying ye?*
What time do you close?	*Sheng ma shi jiang xia ban?*
I'm just looking (browsing)	*Wo kan kan*
Have you got any...	*You mei you …*
Can I try it on?	*Wo ke yi shi shi ma?*
I need size …	*Wo yao … chi cun*
larger/smaller/longer/shorter	*shao da dian/shao xiao dian/shao chang dian/shao duan dian*
May I have a bag, please?	*You dai zi ma?*
How much is this?	*Duoshao qian?*

Time

yesterday	*zuotian*
today	*jintian*
tomorrow	*mingtian*
the day after tomorrow	*houtian*
week	*xingqi*
month	*yue*
year	*nian*
minute	*fenzhong*
hour	*xiaoshi* (the hour on a clock is *dian*, e.g. 'two o' clock' is *er dian*)
What's the time?	*Jidian le?*

Culture Wise China

A guide to China for visitors, business people and immigrants. Printed in colour. Contains essential information to help newcomers avoid cultural and social gaffes. Whether you are travelling on business or pleasure, visiting for a few days or planning to stay for a lifetime, Culture Wise China will enable you to quickly feel at home. Interest in visiting and buying property in China has increased considerably in recent years, and tens of thousands of Britons visit or buy property there each year.

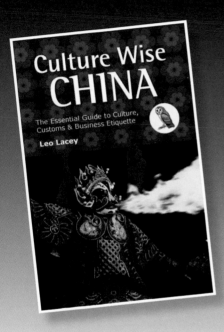

Publishing Details

ISBN:	978-1-907339-27-1
Binding:	Paperback, sewn
Price:	£10.95
Format:	200 x 130mm
Publication:	March 2011
Maps:	2
Edition:	1st
Pages:	240
Colour photos:	approx. 150

INDEX

Who Are We?

Survival Books was established in 1987 and by the mid-'90s was the leading publisher of books for people planning to live, work, buy property or retire abroad.

From the outset, our philosophy has been to provide the most comprehensive and up-to-date information available. Our titles routinely contain up to twice as much information as other books and are updated more frequently. All our books contain colour photographs and most are printed in full colour. They also contain original cartoons, illustrations and maps.

Survival Books are written by people with first-hand experience of the countries, cities and the people they describe, and therefore provide invaluable insights that cannot be obtained from official publications or websites, and information that is more reliable and objective than that provided by the majority of unofficial websites.

Survival Books are designed to be easy – and interesting – to read. They contain a comprehensive list of contents and index and many also have extensive appendices, including useful addresses, further reading and useful websites to help you obtain additional information, as well as other useful reference material.

Our primary goal is to provide you with the essential information necessary for a trouble-free life or property purchase and to save you time, trouble and money.

We believe our books are the best available – they are certainly the best-selling. But don't take our word for it – read what reviewers and readers have said about Survival Books at the front of this book.

**Most of our books are available as Paperbacks, Kindle and eBooks.
Order your copies today by visiting
www.survivalbooks.net**

WHO ARE WE?

Our Living and Working guides are essential reading for anyone planning to spend a period abroad – whether it's an extended holiday or permanent migration – and are packed with priceless information designed to help you avoid costly mistakes and save time, trouble and money.

Living and Working guides are the most comprehensive and up-to-date source of practical information available about everyday life abroad. They aren't, however, simply a catalogue of dry facts and figures, but are written in a highly readable style – entertaining, practical and occasionally humorous.

Our aim is to provide you with the comprehensive information necessary for a trouble-free life. You may have visited a country as a tourist, but living and working there is a different matter altogether; adjusting to a new environment and culture and making a home in any foreign country can be a traumatic and stressful experience. You need to adapt to new customs and traditions, discover the local way of doing things (such as finding a home, paying bills and obtaining insurance) and learn all over again how to overcome the everyday obstacles of life.

All these subjects and many, many more are covered in depth in our Living and Working guides – don't leave home without them.

The Expats' Best Friend!

London's Hidden Secrets: A mini series of three guides to the city's quirky and unusual sights that most visitors and even residents don't get to visit.

London's Secret Walks: A walking book with a difference, taking you off the beaten track to visit London's hidden and 'secret' sights.

London's Secrets: a new series including Museums & Galleries, Parks & Gardens and Pubs & Bars, with more to come.

Retiring in France: Everything a prospective retiree needs to know about one of the world's most popular retirement destinations.

Running Gîtes and B&Bs in France: An essential guide for anyone planning to invest in a gîte or bed & breakfast business.

Shooting Caterpillars in Spain: The hilarious and compelling story of two innocents abroad in the depths of Andalusia in the late '80s.

Sketchbooks series: A series of beautiful sketchbooks with walks, including Cornwall, the Cotswolds, the Lake District and London.

Where to Live in London: The only book published to help newcomers choose the best area to live to suit both their lifestyle and pocket.

For a full list of our current titles, visit our website at www.survivalbooks.net

OTHER SURVIVAL BOOKS

London's Secrets

LONDON'S HIDDEN SECRETS

ISBN: 978-1-907339-40-0, £10.95

Graeme Chesters

A guide to London's hidden and lesser-known sights not found in standard guidebooks. Step beyond the chaos, cliches and queues of London's tourist-clogged attractions to its quirkier side.

Discover its loveliest ancient buildings, secret gardens, strangest museums, most atmospheric pubs, cutting-edge art and design, and much more: some 140 destinations in all corners of the city.

LONDON'S HIDDEN SECRETS VOL 2

ISBN: 978-1-907339-79-0, £10.95

Graeme Chesters & David Hampshire

Hot on the heels of London's Hidden Secrets comes another volume of the city's largely undiscovered sights, many of which we were unable to include in the original book. In fact, the more research we did the more treasures we found, until eventually a second volume was inevitable.

Written by two experienced London writers, LHS 2 is for both those who already know the metropolis and newcomers wishing to learn more about its hidden and unusual charms.

LONDON'S SECRET WALKS

ISBN: 978-1-907339-51-6, £11.95

Graeme Chesters

London is a great city for walking – whether for pleasure, exercise or simply to get from A to B. Despite the city's extensive public transport system, walking is also often the quickest and most enjoyable way to get around – at least in the centre – and it's also free and healthy!

Many attractions are off the beaten track, away from the major thoroughfares and public transport hubs. This favours walking as the best way to explore them, as does the fact that London is a visually interesting city with a wealth of stimulating sights in every 'nook and cranny'.

320 PAGES, PRINTED IN COLOUR

LONDON'S SECRETS: PARKS & GARDENS

ISBN: 978-1-907339-93-6, £10.95

Robbi Atilgan & David Hampshire

London is one the world's greenest capital cities, with a wealth of places where you can relax and recharge your batteries. Britain is renowned for its parks and gardens, and nowhere has such beautiful and varied green spaces as London: magnificent royal parks, historic garden cemeteries, majestic ancient forests and woodlands, breathtaking formal country parks, expansive commons, charming small gardens, beautiful garden squares and enchanting 'secret' gardens. Not all are secrets, of course, but many of London's most beguiling green spaces are known only to insiders and locals.

So, whether you're a nature lover, horticulturist or keen amateur gardener, or just looking for somewhere for a bit of peace and quiet or a place to exercise or relax, you're sure to find your perfect spot in London. **Published Summer 2013.**

LONDON'S SECRET PLACES

ISBN: 978-1-907339-92-9, £10.95

Graeme Chesters & David Hampshire

London is one of the world's leading tourist destinations with a wealth of world-class attractions: amazing museums and galleries, beautiful parks and gardens, stunning palaces and grand houses, and much, much more. These are covered in numerous excellent tourist guides and online, and need no introduction here. Not so well known are London's numerous smaller attractions, most of which are neglected by the throngs who descend upon the tourist-clogged major sights. What London's Secret Places does is seek out the city's lesser-known, but no less worthy, 'hidden' attractions.

LONDON'S SECRETS: MUSEUMS & GALLERIES

ISBN: 978-1-907339-96-7, £10.95

Robbi Atilgan & David Hampshire

London is a treasure trove for museum fans and art lovers and one of the world's great art and cultural centres, with more popular museums and galleries than any other world city. The art scene is a lot like the city itself – diverse, vast, vibrant and in a constant state of flux – a cornucopia of traditional and cutting-edge, majestic and mundane, world-class and run-of-the-mill, bizarre and brilliant.

So, whether you're an art lover, culture vulture, history buff or just looking for something to entertain the family during the school holidays, you're bound to find inspiration in London. All you need is a comfortable pair of shoes, an open mind – and this book!

LONDON'S SECRETS: PUBS & BARS

ISBN: 978-1-907339-93-6, £10.95

Graeme Chesters

British pubs and bars are world famous for their bonhomie, great atmosphere, good food and fine ales. Nowhere is this more so than in London, which has a plethora of watering holes of all shapes and sizes: classic historic boozers and trendy style bars; traditional riverside inns and luxurious cocktail bars; enticing wine bars and brew pubs; mouth-watering gastro pubs and brasseries; welcoming gay bars and raucous music venues. **Published Summer 2013.**

320 PAGES, PRINTED IN COLOUR

PHOTO

CREDITS

Htjostheim, 182 © mary416, 185 © Roman Sigaev, 188 © Ecoasis, 190 © Feng Yu, 193 © Lim Yong Hian, 195 © Wikipedia, 198 © michaeljung, 200 © Pressmaster, 205 © Gary718, 206 © Wikipedia, 207 © Jack.Q, 209 © Bedo, 211 © Mailthepic, 213 © Larryye, 215 © Seesea, 216 © Wikipedia, 219 © Wikipedia, 220 © Wikipedia, 220 © Wikipedia, 222 © Ljupco , 224 © Wikipedia, 226 © Hnhanpeggy, 226 © Wikipedia, 228 © Hnhanpeggy, 231 © Pavel L Photo and Video, 233 © Christineg, 234 © @cam, 237 © Wikipedia, 241 © Graphics1976, 243 © claudio zaccherini, 244 © Jiajianzheng, 247 © Guochun, 248 © Lieska, 251 © Copestello, 253 © Nataliesusu, 254 © Graphicphoto, 256 © Eastwestimaging, 257 © Wikipedia, 259 © Andriybozhok, 260 © John Leung, 263 © Yaopengyuo, 265 © Sergeibach, 265 © Wikipedia, 265 © Jack.Q, 265 © Wikipedia, 266 © Ecophoto, 269 © Osee, 271 © Dawnbal1, 272 © Flufthecat, 277 © Aptyp_koK, 282 © Kitch, 288 © Linqong, 303 © Kostas Tsipos, 316 © Szefei, 316 © Rikki_, 316 © Stephentroell, 316 © Slovegrove, 317 © Louwkey, 317 © Joopsnijder, 317 © Picturefan1414, 317 © Curciomk.

NOTES

NOTES

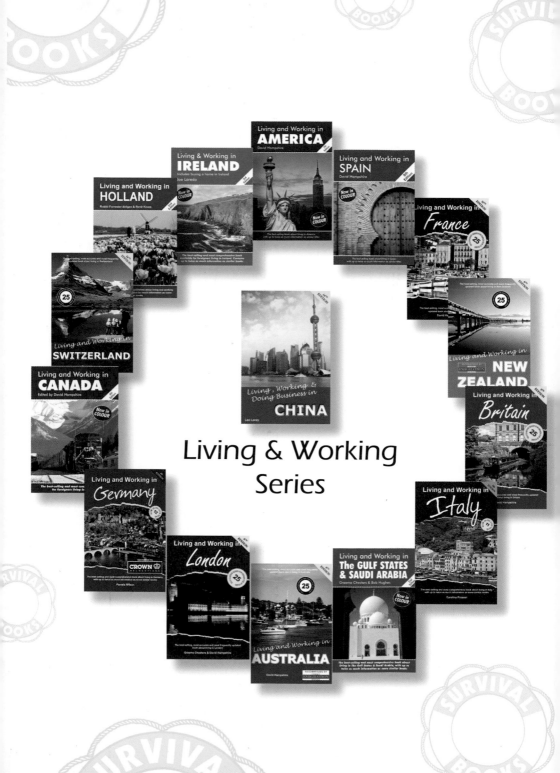

Living & Working
Series